JESUS THE MAN

JESUS THE MAN

Decoding the Real Story of Jesus and
Mary Magdalene

BARBARA THIERING

ATRIA BOOKS

New York London Toronto Sydney

ATRIA BOOKS

1230 Avenue of the Americas
New York, NY 10020

Copyright © 1992 by Dr. Barbara Thiering
Originally published in 1992 in Great Britain by Transworld Publishers Ltd

Published by arrangement with Transworld Publishers Ltd

Library of Congress Control Number: 2006051210

ISBN-13: 978-1-4165-4138-7
ISBN-10:   1-4165-4138-1

First Atria Books trade paperback edition November 2006

10 9 8 7 6 5 4 3 2 1

ATRIA BOOKS is a trademark of Simon & Schuster, Inc.

Manufactured in the United States of America

For information about special discounts for bulk purchases,
please contact Simon & Schuster Special Sales at
1-800-456-6798 or business@simonandschuster.com.

CONTENTS

MAPS

FIGURES

FOREWORD

Was Jesus married? Did he survive the crucifixion?

These are the questions that have been thrust forward in the Christian world in our own times. When they were raised in *Jesus the Man* in 1992 they were considered shocking. They have made their way slowly, and in 2003 received a sudden impetus with the extraordinary success of *The Da Vinci Code* by Dan Brown, a popular novel that claimed to be no more than fiction, but wove into its story an assumption that the answer to both of the above questions was "Yes".

Anyone familiar with the history of religion will recognize the reason for its huge circulation figures, far more than would be expected for just a simple gripping thriller: Countless readers wanted to hear that Jesus was an ordinary human being like the rest of us, that he was not supernatural. To worship a human being amounted to worshipping ourselves. The universe is far bigger than we are, and we are healthier if we are truthful about our place in it. When there are massive shifts in the cultural language, such as we are going through now with globalization, the previous icons are seen as idols and are overthrown.

The reason it was possible in *Jesus the Man* to affirm with confidence the actual facts of the life of Jesus was that hard evidence had become available. It is something new in religion to speak of real evidence, when it has been widely thought that the content of faith comes from the imaginative parts of our brain, from the power of symbols and images. Ideas about Jesus were assumed to be myths that had spontaneously arisen and could not be accounted for by historical facts. It would be deeply disturbing for such a faith if they were demonstrated to be manufactured myths.

Other accounts of Christian history that were not in accord with the New Testament, called the Apocrypha, were collected by the critical scholars of the nineteenth century. They were assumed to be productions coming from centuries later than the time of Jesus, of no historical value for his period. Then in the twentieth century two bodies of documents were found that challenged such an assumption. In 1945 some ancient codices were found in a jar in Egypt, including works that called themselves gospels and were quite different from the canonical ones. And in 1947 the first of the Dead Sea Scrolls were discovered. They have been rightly hailed as the greatest archaeological discovery of all time.

From information given in the Dead Sea Scrolls, it has become possible to develop a new technique for reading books of the New Testament. It produces provable, testable results, and its content is an actual history of Jesus and the natural origins of the Christian Church. This technique is applicable to those books that are largely made up of miracles and claims to revelation, the four gospels, Acts and the Book of Revelation.

It is called the pesher technique, from the Hebrew word *pesher* (pronounced pay-sher, plural *pesharim*), a word that means "interpretation" in the sense of "solution". It is found in the Old Testament in a context of interpretation of dreams. A Joseph or a Daniel found a factual meaning of the king's dreams in terms of actual events, events that would take place in the near future. The writers of one group of the Dead Sea Scrolls believed that scripture was intended for such treatment by men with the special knowledge of an insider. The surface form of scripture was a "mystery", seen only by outsiders, and it had a detailed "solution", concerning factual historical events that the writers were experiencing in their own time.

A hypothesis that the new Christian scripture was set up with a pesher was suggested by this information. The pesher would concern actual historical facts, rather than predictions of the future, and they would be facts that were intended to be known only by insiders, the leaders of a community that shared the gnostic assumption of an intellectual elite. Having been deliberately placed there to give an objective account, the pesher would have to be subject to rigorous tests of consistency and factuality. If it met all such tests, the hypothesis would have been proven.

After many years of work, it was found that every word of the Greek text of these New Testament books has a special or more exact meaning, going beyond the obvious and ordinary one. Each time a word appears it always has the same special meaning, and the context in which it re-appears makes full sense. The special meanings function like a code, forming what amounts to a puzzle with only one solution, able to be solved by those with an insider's knowledge.

The result is a full and detailed account of the political history of one of the most formative periods of western culture, the merging of a Hellenised west with a Jewish east. The process began with the Jewish Diaspora during the BC period. It became Christian when it attracted large numbers of Gentiles who had turned away from paganism. They eventually took it over under the influence of Jesus. But he was only one of a number of leaders who, under the pressure of Roman domination, had recognized that cultural change meant also great changes for a religious institution.

A full explanation of the pesher technique, together with significant results such as the natural explanation of the Virgin Birth and the Resurrection, and the marriage and family of Jesus, will be found in *Jesus the Man*. Its detail focuses on the chronology, which is derived from another contribution of the Dead Sea Scrolls, the solar calendar. Since writing it, continuing work has expanded the lexicon of special meanings and the consequent record of events.

I thank both the original publisher of *Jesus the Man* (Transworld Doubleday, now Random House) and Atria Books who are re-issuing it. I thank also the whole body of scholars who have done the work of study and publication of all the new sources for the history of Christianity. We have all been part of a team, and our work continues.

Barbara Thiering
Sydney, Australia, 2006

Judea, Samaria, Galilee and Syria in the First Centuries BC and AD

INTRODUCTION

There can be few people in the world who do not have some feeling of curiosity about Jesus. What kind of person must he have been, to have had such an enormous influence? Were the rise of the Church and the growth of Christianity due solely to his extraordinary personality? Were the events of his life, and his teachings, real events in history in the way we commonly understand history, or were they, as many Christians hold, something quite outside normal experience?

My own interest in such questions was as typical as anyone's could be. In Australia, Christianity arrived with the European settlers, and is still, after two hundred years, the dominant religion, most often in a Protestant form.

My family was of the middle of the middle class, where we based our manners on English and Scottish forebears. Education was valued, and going to church on Sundays. My grandmother had been devoted to the Bible, and that seemed to cause my mother to warn me against it. So I read it out of defiance, and wondered about it a great deal.

Then I was persuaded by evangelists, and became deeply involved with the Church. Remaining in it socially long after I had become restless about its doctrines, I got to know the Church very well as an institution. Eventually I could come to terms with Christianity only by seeing it as a symbolic language, pointing to something that could not be expressed in words.

Questions about the history of religion seemed more interesting than most others, and I took degrees in theology, coming eventually to the study of the Dead Sea Scrolls. I accepted that they were simply a valuable but rather remote background to Christianity, and threw myself into the study of peripheral questions. A series of articles in academic journals established my speciality in the scrolls, and university lecturing in the area gave me continual familiarity with the texts.

The more closely I studied the texts of the scrolls, the more I became dissatisfied with what other scholars were saying about certain questions. On doctrine, they did fine work: giving careful and balanced assessments of the similarities and differences between the community that wrote the Dead Sea Scrolls and what we now know as the early Christian Church. But on historical questions, they kept drawing back. Nobody ever seemed to ask "*Why* was it that these two communities were so like each other?" And, if the question was put to them, they denied that they were alike, letting the differences between them negate the very strong similarities. I got the feeling that the Christian Church was protected ground. Nothing could be like it; it was unique.

One understood, of course: it was a projection from religious experience. The object of faith must be unique, a revelation, not historically conditioned. But that made for very bad history. Historical study is, admittedly, always profoundly affected by one's own experience and values. But should that go so far that one refuses to face up to the most obvious facts, to deny facts that are there? Something like a suppression of knowledge was taking place.

Having arrived at the point where I could be quite sure there was something more to be found out, the next step was to follow it up. It proved to be a twenty-year research project.

The first stage was not a long process. It could be demonstrated, by a very close study of all the scrolls, that they are much more likely to have belonged in the Christian period, that is, the period when Jesus flourished and attracted many followers to what was later to be called Christianity, than to have been pre-Christian and having little to do with the Church.

The second stage was much longer, and its consequences went much further. There came a point where the hypothesis could seriously be posed that is set out in these pages: that the gospels of the New Testament yield a closely detailed, entirely factual history of Jesus that is not, at first sight, apparent.

Over years of testing it became clear that a technique of

interpretation suggested by the Dead Sea Scrolls fits the gospels in a way that the writers of the gospels themselves intended. They are not one dimensional: there is something else there. They act as a kind of parable, telling one story on the surface but with another story beneath. The story beneath, the actual history of Jesus, is found only by applying the technique, and it was deliberately put there. It is not subjectively found; you cannot make it what you will. Anyone working on the gospels, using the same rigorous, logical methods, must arrive at the same answer.

Many people, of course, hold that the gospels as they stand give the history of Jesus: performing miracles, walking on water, raising the dead, and so on. Others find such stories a difficulty. New Testament scholars have long taught that they are the result of the development of legends about Jesus, and that he, as a historical person, eludes us. Many scholars would resist at the outset, with some degree of incomprehension, what appears in the pages of this book, assuming that to act as if there were a discoverable history is an uncritical procedure. That no exact history can be determined is, they would claim, an item of scholarly faith.

Something deeper than scholarly caution lies behind such resistance. Both an uncritical approach that takes what is there literally, and a critical approach in the current sense, arrive at the same point, leaving Jesus as an unreal figure, a divine being on the one hand, an unknown on the other. Both approaches leave him as the object of religious awe, and Christianity as a religion that puts him at the centre of worship.

What is set out here, therefore, will run into many problems, and one of them will be the reluctance to see Jesus as a real, human, fallible figure, stripping away the mystery. The only answer is to affirm, from the evidence that is given here, that he himself, and his followers, intended that he should become known in this way, by writing the gospels as they did. They had a concept of "babes in Christ", those who need the supernatural as an element of their faith, and also of those more mature minds whose faith takes less tangible forms. They allowed for both by writing in a form that provides simple miracle stories and the like, but beneath the surface there is a rewarding exercise for more critical minds.

Perhaps, in our present generation, it will not be quite as problematic as it would once have been to assume the full humanity of Jesus. We have been living for some time with a concept of a Christianity that does not centre on the worship of a divine human being, the Christ. There are times when a religion moves away from its traditional objectifications, and yet survives, finding new forms of expression. As disturbing as it is when the old moulds of faith have become too worn and have to be discarded, the vitality of the human religious spirit is such that it will always find new words, new images, new symbols.

By 1988 my work had received sufficient attention in Australia to become the subject of a documentary film, "The Riddle of the Dead Sea Scrolls". James Mitchell was the producer, and Rowan Ayers was responsible for script and a visually beautiful and coherent presentation. It was shown by the Australian Broadcasting Corporation on Palm Sunday evening, 1990, attracting maximum attention all round the country. The intense response it evoked is recorded in a book by Dr Leonie Star, *The Dead Sea Scrolls: The Riddle Debated* (ABC Books, 1991).

The debate is still going on, as such debates will. The film, as this book also does, claims that the virgin birth, the miracles, and the resurrection can be viewed in an entirely new light. Christianity does not stand or fall by these as literal events; they never were literal events. But nor were they myths, traditional legends, as scholars have often held. Something really did happen, and what happened opens up a whole new understanding of historical Christianity.

For this book, there has been the difficult task of extracting a simplified story from the enormous amount of material that becomes available with the application of a new technique to the gospels. To simplify is also to leave out much of the reasoning that leads up to the statements being made, many of which will seem so novel and startling to those familiar with the gospels that they will be thought to be incredible. For this reason, much of the detail on which the conclusions depend is given in the Appendixes at the back of the book. The reader can find there an extensive treatment of technical matters, relying on the Greek text of the New Testament. An exact chronology is included, drawing on all chronological points that are concealed in the gospels and Acts of the Apostles.

The experiment of using this technique of interpretation is repeatable, and those who undertake to repeat and continue it will find an enjoyment and illumination that is very rare indeed. They will find nothing less than the historical Jesus, in the place where, ironically, he has been thought to be least likely to be found, in the gospels and Acts of the New Testament.

CHAPTER ONE

QUMRAN— HOME OF THE SCROLLS

To get to Qumran, where the Dead Sea Scrolls were discovered, you hire a car in Jerusalem (or, if you are hard up, get the bus; there is a surprising bus stop just outside the ruins). The road winds along the side of the Mount of Olives, on the east of Jerusalem, through Bethany, and downwards towards Jericho and the Dead Sea.

At one point you come to a plaque marking sea-level; after that you are below it. The Dead Sea is the lowest known place on the earth's surface. If you have been able to fly over it, under the clouds, you will have seen the whole expanse of it below, part of the familiar map of Israel, with the Jordan running down to it from the Sea of Galilee in the north.

Near Jericho you turn southwards; it is still a good bitumen road. If you are out of luck, you will have to drive through a herd of camels crossing the road, and face an indignant camel-driver who insists that you have upset his beasts, but will accept one hundred shekels by way of compensation. Photography rights will cost you another hundred.

The country is now very dry, with strange little hillocks and bumps just like a moonscape. There would be no vegetation at all, were it not for modern irrigation. The colours are brilliant: the sky and the sea almost always bright blue, and the cliffs on your right a golden yellow or warm brown.

After negotiating the camels, you go round a long curve, circling the north of the Dead Sea, and the plateau of Qumran begins to appear, projecting from the wall of cliffs that runs right down the coast. The plateau is like a lion *couchant*, but friendly, ready for the travelling monk to climb up the gentle slope to its back.

You can drive up now to an airconditioned restaurant, sadly out of place. It was less comfortable in the ancient world. The Roman historian Pliny wrote: "On the west coast of Lake Asphaltitis [the Dead Sea] are settled the Essenes, at some distance from the noisome odours that are experienced on the shore itself. They are a lonely people, the most extraordinary in the world, who live without women, without love, without money, with the palm trees for their only companions."[1]

The men who wound down the ancient road from Jerusalem via Jericho, or took the alternative route via the wady Kidron, which comes out at the Dead Sea a few miles south of Qumran, were leaving the world, either voluntarily or through being forced into exile. They knew that, but for the buildings on the plateau, they would find no food, and only brackish water to drink from a rare spring. The water of the Dead Sea is bitter and stinging, like unpleasant medicine. It is thick with minerals, as water runs into it but cannot get out. Objects float on it and cannot sink. The Roman general Vespasian tested this phenomenon when he came into the area looking for zealots in AD 68. He ordered some soldiers who could not swim, to be flung into the deep water with their hands tied behind them. Fortunately for them, the rumour was true: they rose to the surface and floated.[2]

It was in the caves behind the buildings on the plateau that the Dead Sea Scrolls were discovered, in February 1947.[3] Bedouin roam the area—you still see them and their settlements of black leather tents, sometimes riding their speedy little donkeys which they handle with the pride of a modern bikie. Some Bedouin boys found a number of jars containing scrolls in a cave overlooking the ruins, which had always been thought to be the remains of a Roman fortress.

Fortunately, they suspected that such things would fetch money. They took them to an antiquities dealer in Bethlehem, through whom they eventually came into the hands of Professor Sukenik, the father of Yigael Yadin, who subsequently became the leading Israeli archaeologist, a key figure in later scrolls finds, and, in 1977, Deputy Prime Minister of Israel.

Another group came into the hands of some young American

scholars spending their holidays at the School of Oriental Research in Jerusalem. They were able to recognise them as biblical and very ancient, and the discovery was announced to the world.

The first news concerned only the copies of known biblical works, especially the great scroll of the book of Isaiah, which was a thousand years older than any extant copy. The biblical scrolls, which form the majority of the hundreds subsequently found in fragmentary form, are of great interest to scholars but do not make a very great difference from the layperson's point of view. The text of the Old Testament was fixed a long time ago and has remained unaltered since. These ancient copies, all of Old Testament books, show the same text with only a few variations, which have now found their way into modern translations.

What *has* made a difference is the smaller group of scrolls that are not biblical books. Entirely new works: about a dozen complete scrolls, and the fragments of hundreds more, written about the time of the origins of Christianity.

They were found, during subsequent years, in a total of eleven caves all around the plateau, and particularly in one just across from the plateau, an artificial cave hollowed out of the marl (Cave 4). The hundreds of scrolls placed there had not been put in jars and had been reduced after two thousand years to layers of fragments.[4]

Their titles are missing, but they have been given titles suited to their contents: the Manual of Discipline (also known as the Community Rule), the War of the Sons of Light with the Sons of Darkness, the Hymns of Thanksgiving, biblical commentaries called pesharim and others.[5]

The greatest scroll of all, the Temple Scroll, had a special history.[6] It was originally located in Cave 11, alongside other scrolls handed over to archaeologists, but had been illegally kept back, and had come into the hands of an Arab dealer. A certain American clergyman whose name has not been revealed became an intermediary between the dealer and Professor Yadin. During negotiations that lasted more than seven years, huge amounts of money were demanded. Yadin was despairing of ever obtaining the scroll, when the Six Day War, in June 1967, broke out.

Yadin happened also to be a very senior military adviser, and was informed of the daily progress of the war. On the Wednesday of the war he heard that the territory that included East Jerusalem, where the Arab dealer's shop was located, was now in Israeli hands. He sent for a member of the Intelligence Corps, who went to the dealer's shop and confiscated the scroll. It was in a Bata shoebox, wrapped in a towel and cellophane, and some of the fragments that had broken off it were in a Karel cigar-box. It had been kept in a primitive cache underneath some floor tiles, and had suffered some damage. The Intelligence officer brought it to Yadin during a war council on the Thursday evening. Yadin saw to it that the dealer was paid a large amount, although he actually had no right to it, mainly to ensure that if there were any further scrolls being kept back they would be produced.

The Temple Scroll, as it came to be called, is the longest of all the Dead Sea Scrolls, about nine metres. Stretched out, it would go through two long rooms. It contains the description of the plan of a temple, and it claims that this plan was dictated by God himself, on Mount Sinai; this means that it is a pseudepigraphon, a false writing. It was written at the same time as other scrolls, but claims to have come from the time of Moses, and so to have his venerable authority. But it tells us a great deal about the mind of the writers. Had it not disappeared at the outset, it would have been available at the same time as the earlier scrolls, and would have acted as a corrective to some of the views then formed. It was not published until 1977, and in English only some years later. It is still being integrated into scrolls scholarship.[7]

The period when the buildings on the Qumran plateau were occupied, and scribal activity was going on there, is now accepted as being between about 140 BC and AD 68, a span of just over two hundred years. The evidence provided by coins found at the site, together with signs of a destruction of the buildings by the Romans in AD 68, make these bounds quite firm.[8]

It is accepted also that the scrolls were written within this general period. They belong, then, to the time of Christian origins. The question is: exactly when within that period? Jesus was teaching in about AD 30, and Paul and others were active in the fifties and sixties AD. Were the Qumran writers exact contemporaries of the Christians, or did they, as many scholars maintain, come before them? On the answer to this question depends the relevance of the scrolls to early Christianity.

CHAPTER TWO

CHRISTIAN CONNECTIONS

It soon became apparent to those studying the scrolls that the writers were similar in many ways to the early followers of Jesus Christ. This was the reason for the sensational claims made in the first few years.

For instance, the two groups, the Qumran sect and the early Christians, lived in the same small area at about the same time. Both met every day for a sacred meal of bread and wine to which only initiates were admitted.[1]

Both practised community sharing of property, a most unusual practice for Jews. Both valued celibacy, the Qumran sect very strongly, the Christians moderately. Both used baptism as a method of initiation, and both looked forward to a coming apocalyptic crisis which would usher in a new messianic age.[2]

They used the same names for themselves: both called themselves "the Way", "the New Covenant", "Sons of Light".[3] Both had a branch in Damascus, again using the name "the Way".[4] They were governed by bishops, who had similar functions in both cases.[5]

Each lived in expectation of a New Jerusalem, with an identical architectural plan: foursquare, with three gates on each side, for the twelve tribes.[6] They have numerous terms in common, with closely parallel passages in both sets of literature.[7]

There is no doubt that the members of the Qumran sect were

in some way Essene, although certain features of their life show that they went beyond the Essenes. But the sacred meal, community of property, and celibacy have been enough to identify them with the Essenes, one of the three great divisions of Jews described by Josephus, Philo, Pliny and other ancient writers (the other two being the Pharisees and the Sadducees).[8] Before the scrolls were discovered, scholars had always observed that the Essenes and early Christians were in some way related. The nineteenth century French scholar Renan wrote of Christianity as "an Essenism that had succeeded".[9] With the discovery of the scrolls, the connections became much stronger: there were parallels at every essential point.

This observation gave rise to a flood of popular literature, much of it claiming that the scrolls had virtually disproved the basis of Christianity by removing its uniqueness. In 1955, the eminent American literary critic and writer Edmund Wilson, in an influential article in the *New Yorker*, declared that the time had now come for Christianity to be "understood as simply an episode of human history rather than propagated as dogma and divine revelation . . ."[10]

The bizarre claims of Englishman John Allegro, which amounted to an assertion that the Church had stolen all its ideas from Qumran, went on over many years,[11] and made it difficult for any genuine scholar to investigate closely the question of Christian connections with the scrolls.

The main emphasis of the scholarly literature was on the differences between the scrolls and early Christian literature, which are certainly considerable. The tone is entirely different (except perhaps for the New Testament book of Revelation, which would have been very much at home at Qumran). The scrolls are legalistic, obsessive about ritual cleanliness, harshly exclusive. According to the Temple Scroll, for example, a number of categories of persons were not to be allowed into the presence of God: a man who had had a nocturnal emission; a man who had recently had sexual intercourse; lepers; menstruating women. No blind man was to be allowed into the sanctuary for the whole of his life, because this would profane the city where God dwelt.[12] By contrast, in the gospels, Jesus touched lepers, associated with the blind and the maimed, was in close contact with married men, with Gentiles, and with women.[13]

Yet the differences ought not to be used to *negate* the similarities, as has sometimes been done. An adequate scientific method must take account of both the striking similarities and the striking differences, and find a way of accounting for both.

An obvious hypothesis—which depends on knowing the date of the relevant scrolls—is that the Qumran sect represented the form of Judaism out of which Christianity came. There was a split, the Christians reacting strongly against some aspects of Qumran practice, while retaining basic organisation and some doctrines.

An explanation of this kind was apparent from the start, but was not stated in any explicit form by scrolls scholars. One of the main reasons was their dating, which, they believed, removed the relevant scrolls far from the time of the rise of Christianity.

And yet the similarities between certain persons and events alluded to in some of the scrolls, and the pattern of life of two of the principal characters in the gospels, demand careful attention in the light of other similarities.

The persons are always called by pseudonyms, and the same person can be called by a number of different pseudonyms. The account of events is influenced by the fact that the writers are seeing them through Old Testament prophecies, which, they claim, are predictions concerning their Teacher. But despite the difficulties, these scrolls are the most promising source for the history of the Qumran community.

The main figure, a hero to the writers, is known as the Teacher of Righteousness. He was given quite extraordinary importance. It was he who was the subject of Old Testament prophecy, in their belief. So all history and revelation led up to him. He was a saviour: people would be saved at the Last Judgment by faith in him. An Old Testament text was quoted in the form "the just shall live by faith", and applied to the faith of his followers in him.

. . . this concerns all those who observe the Law in the house of Judah, whom God will deliver from the house of Judgement because of their suffering and because of their faith in the Teacher of Righteousness.[14]

It seems, however, that the Teacher was at one point in deep trouble. Most of his followers had deserted him to go after another teacher. The rival had many of the same doctrines and ideas as the Teacher—he also baptised, he also looked for a New Jerusalem—but he did not share the Teacher's ideas about the ritual law. In fact, he "flouted the Law in the midst of their whole [congregation"].

. . . those who were unfaithful together with the Man of a Lie, in that they did not [listen to the word received by] the Teacher of

Righteousness from the mouth of God. And it concerns the unfaithful of the New [Covenant] in that they have not believed in the Covenant of God . . .[15]

. . . the Man of a Lie, who flouted the Law in the midst of their whole [congregation].[16]

The rival teacher was much less strict about the Law, and those who were associated with him were called "seekers-after-smooth-things", that is, they had chosen a more relaxed way of life than the stern, ascetic discipline of the Teacher.

When one of the pieces about the Teacher was being written, his life was in danger. His supporters turned to one of the psalms for comfort: they believed that it was predicted that the Teacher would be saved and his enemies would be punished.

. . . the wicked of Ephraim and Manasseh, who shall seek to lay hands on the Priest (the Teacher) and the men of his council at the time of trial which shall come upon them. But God will redeem them from out of their hand.[17]

But it seems that the Teacher did die, for some years later another writer wrote of him as being in the past, and also wrote very bitterly of the rivals. All the pieces show that the rivals had come out on top, the great majority of them falling in behind the heretic teacher, called "the Man of a Lie", "the Scoffer", and other derisive names.[18]

Another derogatory name is "the Wicked Priest". He it was who "committed abominable defilements", "defiled the temple", and was accused of drunkenness and taking the money of the community. He also underwent great physical suffering at the hands of Gentiles.

. . . the (Wicked) Priest who rebelled [and violated] the precepts [of God . . .] . . . his chastisement by means of the judgments of wickedness. And they inflicted horrors of evil sickness and took vengeance upon his body of flesh . . .[19]

. . . the Wicked Priest whom God delivered into the hands of his enemies because of the iniquity committed against the Teacher of Righteousness and the men of his council, that he might be humbled by means of a destroying scourge, in bitterness of soul, because he had done wickedly to his elect.[20]

Some scholars have taken the Wicked Priest to be a different person from the Man of a Lie. But, as will be shown, the text supports the identification of the two as one and the same person. The Wicked Priest was yet another name for the heretic teacher.

A newly discovered piece of a scroll,[21] one of the tiny fragments that had previously been overlooked, has been said by its translators to be speaking of the death of a messianic leader (the "Prince of the Congregation, the Branch of David") and to be interpreting it as an atoning suffering in terms of Isaiah 53, the passage on the Suffering Servant. The idea of a suffering Messiah has always been thought to be a Christian concept, foreign to Jewish thought. It may be that this piece also is relevant to a Christian connection.

It is around the two main figures, the Teacher of Righteousness and the Wicked Priest/Man of a Lie, that the debate about the relationship between Qumran and Christianity revolves. When did they live? What was their true identity? And what is their significance to the story of Christianity?

CHAPTER THREE

A QUESTION OF DATES

Very early in scrolls research, before all the pieces were studied and before the Temple Scroll came to light, an opinion was formed by scholars about the date when the personalities named in them lived. Some scholars still hold to it, believing it to be firmly founded; it has come to be called the "consensus case".

Maintaining that the Wicked Priest was a different person from the Man of a Lie, Professor Geza Vermes, who has translated all the main scrolls into English, put forward the suggestion that the Wicked Priest looked like a Hasmonean high priest, one of the family of high priests of the second century BC who were in power in the Jerusalem temple while the Essenes were in exile at Qumran.[1]

This theory seemed to fit with other indications that the figures in the scrolls lived before 100 BC. The Teacher was contemporary with the Wicked Priest, as the latter "persecuted" him, so he also must have lived at this time, his exact date depending on which Hasmonean was the one in question. It was therefore concluded that the Teacher was the founder of the Essenes, who appeared at about this time. He and the rival teacher, although engaged in a contest which for their followers was world shaking, were actually insignificant figures who had never been heard of before.

This dating is, I believe, open to challenge at all its essential points.

The first point that needs to be reviewed—as many of the new generation of scrolls scholars agree—is the way that palaeographical data were used.

Palaeography is the science of dating ancient manuscripts according to the stage of evolution of the actual writing, or script. For normal scripts (formal and semi-formal) this is a sound criterion, although even then it can be used only as a supporting argument, and not as absolute proof. But some scripts are just like a personal handwriting, and cannot be dated with any certainty, a fact that is known and admitted by palaeographers.[2] Yet one of the fragments, which was written in a personal handwriting, was given a firm date by one scholar as 75 to 50 BC.[3] As the text reflects the presence of the Teacher of Righteousness, the Teacher must have lived before this time. The scholar (Josef Milik) who announced the date, did not say, in his main book on the subject, what kind of script it was. This is discovered by going to the script itself, which was published in a technical journal.[4] It is then seen to be one of the more undatable types of script, and that Milik has gone beyond the evidence. But a number of scholars appear to have taken the date from his main book, without checking, and built a whole edifice of theory on it. This, they have said, was the one firm "fact" that they had to go on. It was, however, a false assumption.

Uncritical reliance on palaeography as giving precise dates has now been trenchantly criticised by the new generation of scrolls scholars.[5]

The other problems with dating can be summed up as disregarding the evidence of the texts, using some parts but not taking all relevant points fully into account.

It was the custom of the writers of the scrolls to use ordinary terms in a specialised way. For instance, the word "truth" ('emet in Hebrew) meant, for them, their own special doctrines, not truth in general. They alone had the Truth, in their view. The word appears very many times in this sense, and never in an ordinary sense.[6] This fact must be taken into account in dealing with one of the passages important for the history.

Moreover, the arrogant man seizes wealth without halting. He widens his gullet like Hell and like Death he has never enough . . . (Hab 2:5)

Interpreted, this concerns the Wicked Priest, who was called by the name of truth when he first arose . . .[7]

The consensus conclusion that the Wicked Priest was a Hasmonean high priest does not stand when the specialised meaning of "truth" is applied. The text says that he was "called by the name of truth when he first arose". If a man was "called by the name of truth" he was an initiate of the community, whose members called themselves "men of truth", "those who walked in the way of truth", and other such terms.[8] This was certainly not the case for a Hasmonean high priest, an opponent of Essenes, but it was the case for the rival teacher referred to earlier, who had been an associate of the Teacher of Righteousness before breaking away.

For this and other reasons,[9] all following from close observation of the text, it should be seen that the "Wicked Priest" was another name for the rival teacher, one of the many pseudonyms by which he was called. There is no Hasmonean high priest in the scrolls.

Taking into account the scrolls' language usage, even if it is specialised, an actual date can be established for the Teacher of Righteousness. One important text says that the Teacher was dated from a point when "Nebuchadnezzar king of Babylon" began an oppression of the Jews.

And in the Period of Wrath, 390 years for his giving them (*letitto 'otam*) into the hand of Nebuchadnezzar king of Babylon, he (God) visited them, and caused a Plant-Root to spring from Israel and Aaron to inherit his land and to prosper on the good things of his earth. And they perceived their iniquity and recognised that they were guilty men, yet for twenty years they were like blind men groping for the way. And God observed their deeds, that they sought him with a whole heart, and he raised for them a Teacher of Righteousness to guide them in the way of his heart.[10]

If this is understood literally, it means the real king of Babylon, in the sixth century BC. But the scrolls, everywhere else, say that where the word "Babylon" appears in scripture, it is a code name or disguise for "Rome". It would be one step from this for them to use "Babylon" in their own writings as a name for Rome. That step was actually taken by a group similar to themselves, in the New Testament, where "Babylon" appears twice as a code name for Rome. In one case, Peter, writing a letter from Rome added the following greetings:

She who is at Babylon, who is likewise chosen, sends you greetings; and so does my son Mark.[11]

And in the book of Revelation, anticipating the fall of Rome:

Fallen, fallen is Babylon the great! . . .

Alas! Alas! thou great city,
thou mighty cry, Babylon!
In one hour has thy judgement come.[12]

The scrolls passage is much better understood as coming from a writer who was at present groaning under a Roman oppression. He has looked up his Old Testament, in typical Qumran fashion, and has found in it a prophecy that there is to be a punishment for 390 years.[13] This, he believes, tells him how long the Roman oppression will last. So he now calls the date when the oppression began "the Period of Wrath, the 390 years for God's giving them into the hand of the ruler of Rome" (called "Nebuchadnezzar", consistently with the Babylon-Rome equation). This understanding removes a serious difficulty in the consensus case, that a Hebrew phrase meaning "for his giving them" has been translated "after his giving them", although there is not the slightest evidence that the word for "for" ever means "after".

In that case, the Teacher is to be dated from the time of a Roman oppression of the Jews. There is reason for identifying that oppression as taking place in AD 6, when the native kings were removed, the direct rule of Roman procurators was imposed, and the census of property they required led to an armed uprising and continual zealot activity.[14] Since the text in question states that the Teacher came twenty years after the oppression, then an exact date is supplied for him: AD 26.

As Jesus Christ began his ministry in AD 29, the fifteenth year of Tiberius Caesar,[15] the Teacher would on this reading have been a contemporary. The very many parallels discussed in Chapter Two between the scrolls and the early Christian Church support such an interpretation of the Teacher's date.

There are two further objections to the consensus case, both, to my mind, of major significance.

In the consensus view, the Teacher was the founder of the Essenes, who first appear under that name in the second half of the second century BC. Is it not, then, incongruous that there is no mention whatever of the Teacher in any of the long and detailed accounts of the Essenes that stemmed from the contemporary writers Josephus and Philo? Both of them had been personally involved with the Essenes,[16] and their accounts are fully informed, yet they give no hint of the existence of such a person as the Teacher, who was the saviour, and the subject of all prophecy. The consensus case supposes something analogous to a first or second century AD writer giving a full and circumstantial account of the Christians without ever mentioning Jesus, or giving the slightest hint that he existed.

This kind of supposition is very difficult for historians to live with. The possibility surely needs to be considered that the Teacher was not the founder of the Essenes, but was connected with a group that Josephus did not regard as Essene. The revised interpretation of the dating that has been suggested (AD 26) would fit the hypothesis that he came much later than the foundation, and was with a group contemporary with the Christians, a group that had Essene elements but was no longer strictly Essene.

The other objection concerns the character of the biblical commentaries, or pesharim, which will be described further below; they are the main key to the research. They were a kind of literature with which we are still familiar: when a devout person turns to the Old Testament and finds in it a whole series of predictions concerning events in his own time. Some people can still argue that the Bible is talking about Russia, or current events in the Middle East. But such a person would not argue that the Bible was talking about events that happened a century ago. For him, his own time is the time of fulfilment of prophecy. Yet, for the consensus case, that is what the Qumran writers were doing. They themselves were clearly in the Roman period: one writer says that the Romans were marching across the land at the time of writing.[17] So, if the Teacher is to be dated in the second century BC, he could have been more than a century before the time of the writer. Yet he seems to be very fresh in the writer's memory, and the conflicts around him seem to be unresolved. Further, one of the commentaries says that in a current crisis, the Teacher "will be saved", indicating that he was still alive at the time of writing.[18] Biblical scholars have avoided this point by referring to the variable nature of Hebrew tenses. But this is true of classical Hebrew only; another scholar has shown that in Qumran Hebrew the tense in question always refers to the future.[19]

There is, then, enough ambiguity and imprecision to encourage a fresh look at the dating of the figures in the scrolls.

The next step from this point is indicated by the parallels with Christianity that were mentioned earlier, showing that the Teacher and his associates did not simply share a date with the early Christians, but also some form of identity. When it is seen that in every respect (message, place of working, practice and doctrine, even in a meaning of his name) the Teacher of Righteousness was an exact counterpart of John the Baptist,[20] and the heretic teacher—the Wicked Priest— did almost everything that Jesus was accused of by his enemies, then a strong *prima facie* case arises. It looks as if the Teacher was John, and the rival leader, who was with the Teacher at first but then separated, adopting a less strict view of the law, was Jesus.

This, however, would be just another plausible idea, if there were not stronger evidence from the New Testament. Although all the gospels begin with the Baptist, it does not seem that he was part of a tightly structured hierarchical organisation like that of Qumran. Nor does there seem to be polemic between the followers of John and Jesus of the same intensity that is found in the scrolls. There are hints of a rejection of John, and of some party tension,[21] but they hardly seem to fit the scrolls.[22]

The case would rest here, were it not for the fact that there is further evidence, when the scrolls are drawn upon in a different way, that brings additional weight to the argument, and begins to put the New Testament in a different perspective.

CHAPTER FOUR

THE PESHER TECHNIQUE

In a certain group of scrolls the Hebrew word "pesher" (plural "pesharim") is to be found, introducing a procedure that gives us a vital clue; the possibility of a new approach to works that were regarded in the first century as sacred scripture.

The system works like this. The scroll writer takes an Old Testament book such as the minor prophet Habakkuk, which deals with events in 600 BC, when the armies of the Babylonians were marching towards Judea, inspiring fear and terror. He goes through it verse by verse, and after quoting each passage adds "Its pesher is . . .", then explains that it is really about events in his own time. The Babylonians stand for the "Kittim", by which he means the Romans. Some Romans were currently marching across the land, inspiring fear and terror. Other verses, he says, refer to the Teacher of Righteousness and his troubles with the Wicked Priest/Man of a Lie.

They are fearsome and terrible; their justice and grandeur proceed from themselves (Hab 1:7).
The pesher concerns the Kittim (Romans) who inspire all the nations with fear [and dread]. All their evil plotting is done with intention and they deal with all the nations in cunning and guile.

Woe to him who causes his neighbours to drink; who pours out his venom to make them drunk that he may gaze on their feasts! (Hab 2:15)

Its pesher concerns the Wicked Priest who pursued the Teacher of Righteousness to the house of his exile that he might confuse him with his venomous fury.

And at the time appointed for rest, for the Day of Atonement, he appeared before them to confuse them, and to cause them to stumble on the Day of Fasting, their sabbath of repose.[1]

The word "pesher" is used in the Old Testament to mean "interpretation of dreams".[2] A specially gifted person, a Joseph or a Daniel, could discover the hidden meaning of a dream, that was not apparent to others. The meaning had been put into the dream by God; the interpreter only had to see it, drawing on his special knowledge.

In simpler terms, the pesher is like a solution to a puzzle. A rough analogy might be the solution to a cryptic crossword. The clues do not look as if they make sense, but anyone who knows the technique and has the necessary knowledge can solve the puzzle.

Some aspects of the technique rely on giving words special meanings. For example, where the scripture says "the righteous", or "the wicked" appearing to mean all righteous or wicked men and making ethical statements, the pesharist turns the universals into particulars, and finds statements about historical events involving the Teacher of Righteousness and the Wicked Priest.[3] Thus he implies two levels of scripture: the surface containing general religious matter, suitable for ordinary readers, and beneath it specific historical matter, available only to those with special knowledge, knowledge of the events which "fitted" the text handled in this way. The surface remains valid; it is not negated by the other meaning, and it meets people's general religious needs. But it does set up a "mystery", capable of solution by skilled experts.

The meanings "found" in the Old Testament were quite obviously forced on to it. It was not set up for this kind of treatment, but grew naturally over hundreds and possibly thousands of years of tradition. But the Qumran pesharists nevertheless offer us something of the greatest importance: their definition of scripture. Scripture as a mystery, a puzzle, something that meets the needs of a whole range of readers, from the simple believer to the intellectually sophisticated.

It is well known that this kind of view was widely held in

the Greek world. In the Diaspora, where Jews away from their homeland were in contact with Greek thought and culture, they were finding allegorical meanings in the Old Testament.[4] But the scrolls give us, for the first time, hidden *historical* meanings.

The gospels quote Jesus as saying "To you [his inner circle] is given the mystery of the kingdom of God, but for those outside everything is in parables". The insiders, those who "have ears to hear", will understand the mystery.[5]

Parables are clearly on two levels: a simple story with something more complex underneath. The parable of the Vineyard plainly contains a historical meaning under the story of disloyal workers in a vineyard.[6]

All of this gives rise to a hypothesis. If a group holding such a view of scripture had set out to write a new scripture, they would have set it up as being capable of a pesher. It would be a "mystery", a kind of puzzle, capable of a solution by those with special knowledge. This time, there would be no need to force arbitrary meanings on it; it would yield the same result to all experts. It would have been designed for that purpose.

There would have been an extra incentive for writing in this way if an actual history needed to be concealed, for political or other reasons.

A hypothesis like this is capable of being tested. It is subject to a number of tests: for example, if special meanings are assigned to terms, there must be a reason for them; and then the same meanings must be found in every occurrence of the term. Each episode which is made up of a whole cluster of special meanings must make sense in itself, and be consistent with all other episodes. And the whole history found there must be generally consistent with the known character of the institution whose history is given.

In thinking about this possibility, another one arises. Dreams, which gave the model for the theory, are usually incredible. Things happen in them which do not happen in real life. In the gospels, there are a great many miracles, which the modern mind finds incredible, and which a great many people in the hellenistic world, to whom the gospels came, would also have found incredible. Were they intended for the kind of treatment that has been described?

From many points of view, the miracles are the most difficult parts of the gospels and Acts of the Apostles. There are numerous raisings from the dead, some of them quite casually presented: Lazarus was brought out of the tomb, Jairus' daughter was raised, the son of the widow of Nain was raised as he was being carried out to be buried; the widow Dorcas was revived by Peter; Eutychus, who fell down from a third-storey window, was revived by Paul.[7]

There are nature miracles which are not only difficult to believe but introduce new problems. Jesus was said to have come to a figtree in spring, when it was not the season for figs, which would not appear till September. He demanded fruit from it to satisfy his hunger, then when it did not have any he cursed it, and it withered up and died.[8]

On another occasion he sent demons into two thousand pigs, which rushed down a cliff into the sea and were drowned.[9] In the story of the feeding of the five thousand, the multitude had come out after him into the wilderness without taking food, except for a small boy who had five loaves and two fish. The disciples offered to go to nearby villages and buy food, but he turned down their offer and performed a miracle instead, distributing the loaves and fishes so that everyone was filled and there were twelve baskets of crumbs left over.[10] He then did the same thing again on another occasion, with four thousand men and seven loaves, and asked a riddle about the meaning of the numbers involved.[11] He also walked on water and stilled storms with a word.[12]

The thaumaturge (miracle-worker) of these stories is not the Jesus of the rest of the New Testament, who "emptied himself" of his glory[13] and went to the cross as a suffering human being without using miraculous powers.

Theologians and biblical scholars have long held that these stories are the result of growth of tradition, the kinds of legend that grow up about a charismatic figure. But that does not really explain why so much trouble was taken to preserve and record them, thus setting up an apparent conflict with the rest of the New Testament. They also cannot account for their appearance over such a short time, in circles that were literate. There is nothing similar to this in the scrolls, where the Teacher is given a status like that of Jesus.

The pesher technique, however, offers an entirely new approach to the miracles. They can be seen as part of the surface story, but also conceal something else, actual historical events. When the hypothesis is fully tested, it is found that they are indeed one of the most valuable sources of the history of Jesus.

Good examples of the technique are the story of turning water into wine, and the feeding of the five thousand.

According to a story in John's gospel,[14] Jesus was at a wedding, and the wine gave out. His mother was there, and said to him: "They have no wine". He replied to her, rather irrelevantly, "O woman, what have you to do with me? My hour has not yet come". She then said to the servants "Do whatever he tells you". Six stone jars were standing there, for the Jewish rites of purification, and Jesus gave instructions to fill them with water. When, however, a drink was drawn from them and taken to the steward of the feast, it had miraculously turned into wine. The steward's reaction was strange: he did not comment on the miracle at all, but merely complained that Jesus had saved the good wine until last, whereas it was more usual to serve the good wine first and the poor wine later. The gospel notes carefully that this was the first of seven "signs" that Jesus performed, and the series continues through six more of a similar nature.[15]

Using both the pesher hypothesis and some information provided by the scrolls, the meaning of this and the rest of the seven signs becomes apparent. They are indeed carefully constructed, as a record, to those who have ears to hear, of a series of changes made by Jesus in the rules of the community that had preceded him.

At Qumran, the scrolls tell us, there were two steps of initiation into the community, marked by water and by wine.[16] All members, of whatever class of life, could be given a form of preliminary membership, through a baptism by water. But only those who intended to enter the full monastic life went on two further years to receive the "Drink of the Community", that is the wine. Only celibates could receive communion. Those who were left at the level of the water, being given baptism only, were "unclean" persons: married men, Gentiles, women, and the physically handicapped.[17]

When Jesus "turned water into wine", it meant that he was breaking with tradition and allowing lower-grade persons to receive communion. From that time on, all adult members of Jesus' following, whether married, Gentiles, women, physically handicapped, racially different, slaves or free, could come to the communion rails and receive the bread and wine. In allowing that to happen, a most important statement was being made: that all were equal in the sight of God. The God whom the Christians worshipped was not the God of the Temple Scroll, who would not allow into the holy precincts of the temple anyone who had recently had sexual intercourse, any blind man, any leper.[18] A social revolution was implied in what Jesus did.

The story of the feeding of the five thousand, found in all four gospels,[19] records a later step: the ordination of ordinary men to be ministers. Another revolution was taking place: whereas in Jewish practice priests had to be born into the tribe of Levi, Jesus was conferring, by ordination, the power to exercise ministry. The "loaves" stood for levites, who distributed the twelve loaves of the Presence from the holy table.[20] Ordinary men, given levitical powers by "eating" the loaves, were now permitted to distribute the communion bread.

The results of the application of the pesher technique to the gospels and Acts, drawing upon a number of contemporary sources for the information needed, give a whole history of Jesus, and also of the community that preceded him and from which he and his followers broke away. The reason why it was necessary to conceal the history becomes apparent as the story proceeds.

It begins in the century before Jesus, in the reign of the powerful king of the Jews, Herod the Great.

CHAPTER FIVE

THE EMPIRE
OF THE JEWS

Forty years before the Christian era began, there came to the Jewish people an ambitious and immensely talented new king, Herod. He was not even Jewish: he came from Idumea in the south, of mixed Semitic race.[1] But he converted to a version of Judaism that suited him,[2] and proceeded to impose it on the world.

Judea was a poor, small country, its only true product religion. But outside it, living far more comfortably than in the homeland, were the hundreds and thousands of Jews who had settled in the great cities of Babylon, Ephesus, Alexandria, and as far away as Rome. This Jewish world outside Judea was known as the Diaspora. Jews in these cities were fully involved in commercial and intellectual life, and were often wealthy, with no desire to live in Judea, but with nostalgic memories of a land that was still for them holy. It had once been the place where God dwelt, in his temple in Jerusalem, and where the kings of the dynasty of David had presided over a golden age. The great truth of monotheism was enshrined in its religion, and Diaspora Jews were finding that pagan Gentiles were showing a growing interest in their pure form of worship.

Herod found himself far bigger than the country he had come to rule. He soon gained the trust of the Romans, supplying them with troops and money. He stood up to Cleopatra, who attempted to seduce him during a trip to Jericho,[3] and when she and Mark Antony were defeated at the battle of Actium, Herod turned to the side of the emperor Augustus.[4] The Romans looked to him to protect their interests in the east. His reign lasted from 37 BC to 4 BC.

Jews throughout the Diaspora began to feel a sense of unity and purpose under their new monarch. He in his turn began to build, determined to make Jerusalem and Judea the glory of the east. He restored Jerusalem, entirely rebuilt the temple, fortified the harbour at Caesarea, constructed a summer palace down the side of the barren cliff of Masada, and built up an army and fleet.[5]

But for these projects he needed money. There was none in the country, but plenty outside it. Moreover, among those living away from the homeland, there was a very great spiritual need. Jews needed something to bind them together, a way of expressing a commitment to Judaism that went beyond an accident of birth. And many Gentiles also wanted to convert to Judaism, with an act of public dedication.

About this time another man of considerable stature appeared on the scene: Hillel the Great. Coming from Babylonian Judaism, he taught a personal and ethical renewal which was expressed through baptism in water.[6] Those who had been so purified had become truly Jews. The idea of a New Covenant, or "religious contract", began to be formed: not the Old Covenant to which all sons of Abraham belonged by birth, but a covenant of personal choice and initiation. There would be a New Israel, a new Abraham, Isáac and Jacob.

Hillel's ideas and practices could be used to bring many Jews into the New Covenant, by baptism. Renewing their obedience to the Law, they would promise to "return to the law of Moses with all their heart".[7] Many of them had begun to use Greek names, but they would now be given Jewish names to use at the religious meetings of the New Israel.

Hillel himself contributed the ideas, and ethical teachings such as the Golden Rule. But another man played a more active part: Menahem the Diaspora Essene.[8]

Diaspora Essenes shared the divergent calendar and many traditions of Palestinian Essenes, but did not espouse their unworldliness and strict views on morality. For the Palestinians, the Diaspora kind were "seekers-after-smooth-things", taking the easy way.

Menahem was a man of talent, who founded the Magians, whose name reflected their Babylonian culture. In 44 BC they had adopted the Julian calendar, introduced the previous year. It was compatible with their own solar calendar, long regarded by Essenes as heaven's own calendar and the one on which all their prophecies were based. They began their year twice; on January 1 and at the March equinox, living like both Roman citizens and Jews.[9]

Menahem and his order moved into the position of advisers to Herod. Josephus, the Jewish historian whose record is indispensable for the full history, relates that when Herod was a boy going to his tutor, Menahem greeted him, slapped him on the backside, and prophesied that he would be king. From that time Herod held all Essenes in honour.[10]

Menahem and his successors became the "Isaac" of the New Israel. Where "Abraham" (Hillel) was the Father (a term that eventually became "Pope"), "Isaac" was the patriarch, of Babylon and the east. He acted as the real force in what soon became a mission, with Herod as its nominal head. Jewish missionaries went out to the Diaspora under his direction, looking for potential recruits for baptism, both Jewish and Gentile. If they were Gentile, they must, of course, be circumcised and take up all the practices that characterised Jews.

It was probably Menahem, with his Essene interest in calendar and prophecy, who conceived the idea of a thousand year empire of the Jews. Since the time when the prophecies of Enoch were written in the third century BC, the Essenes had been calculating world affairs, believing that heaven sent the great events at significant dates of the calendar. After a recent revision, they had arrived at the conclusion that the year 41 BC,[11] the time when Herod began his rise to power, was the year 3900 from creation. The Enoch prophecy had taught that the world was to last, in all, for 4900 years, so they were now at the beginning of the last millennium of world history. Herod, the leader who had appeared at the propitious beginning, would usher in the last period of history, when the New Israel would spread over the world to become a Kingdom of the Jews, the greatest empire yet known.

Herod's association with the Essenes meant that he had to take into account their longstanding support of the David family. The former royal family had lost the throne in the fifth century BC, but at once a party of loyalists formed around them, dreaming of their restoration, and of the return of Israelite society of old. This was the historical reason for the formation of the Essenes. They intended to restore not only the Davids, but the high priests of the family of Zadok who had held sway with them. There were still many elements in the country who believed that only a David could be the true king.

Herod agreed that a David could have power in the empire

but only as a subordinate to himself. The centre of power would be in Jerusalem and the east, but the David could be patriarch in the less important west, including Rome. There would be a triarchy, modelled on the Roman triumvirate, with its heads in the centre, east, and west; an "Abraham" in the centre under Herod, an "Isaac" in the east, and Rome and the west would be the patriarchate of "Jacob" and his descendants.

The descendant of David who was willing to co-operate with Herod's plans at this time was a man called Heli. Two generations later, he would have a grandson: Jesus.

Heli was descended from Nathan, a younger son of King David. The true genealogy of Jesus is that set out in Luke's gospel. In Matthew's gospel, Heli's line is grafted into the royal line running down through Solomon, Heli now being called "Jacob", his title as a patriarch. This explains why Joseph, the father of Jesus, has a father called Heli in one list and Jacob in the other.[12]

Jacob–Heli agreed to be the third in the triarchy, and the government of the potential kingdom was thus set up. They met at a council table, in the fashion of initiates meeting for the sacred meal of the Essenes. Thus the words of Jesus "Many will come from east and west and sit at table with Abraham, Isaac and Jacob in the kingdom of heaven" referred not to a supernatural future, but to a political future, when the Kingdom of the Jews would have come, replacing the Roman power. The daily prayer of members was "Thy Kingdom come". But at this stage, the emperor would be Herod, his throne in Jerusalem, and Rome would be under his sway as a subordinate territory.

For purposes of government and taxation, they divided the whole known world into ten provinces. Two of them were in the homeland, eight outside. Of these, five were in Asia Minor, where the greatest numbers of Jews clustered. The other three were in Babylon, Alexandria and Rome.[13]

Each province would, from the start, contain six thousand members, making sixty thousand in all. When these numbers had multiplied tenfold, as they anticipated that they would, the total membership would be six hundred thousand men. This was the number of the original Israel, according to the Old Testament. Thus the New Israel would fulfil the pattern of the Old, but renew Judaism by adapting it to the contemporary world.

CHAPTER SIX

"THE RANSOM FOR ONE'S SOUL"

Herod's scheme of initiation into a new form of Judaism was immensely successful. Jews everywhere were willing to join the worldwide society, whose meetings were held in the evenings in private houses. Entry was for members only; they had to show at the door an admission token in the form of a white stone from the river Jordan which the missionaries gave them at baptism. On the stone was written their new Jewish name. "To him who conquers," says the book of Revelation, referring to this practice, "I will give a white stone, with a new name written on the stone which no one knows except him who receives it."[1]

Wealthy Jews of the Diaspora had no objection to paying money for membership of the great society. A half-shekel fee, about a day's income, was a small price to pay.[2] Moreover, they saw it, in a way common in the hellenistic mystery cults, as a payment for salvation.[3] In coming into the New Covenant, they would now be pleasing to God and would be saved at the Last Judgment. So it was interpreted as a "ransom for one's soul", and would be paid only once in a lifetime at the solemn ceremony of full initiation.[4]

But there was no objection to members paying further half-shekels for a different reason, as a peace offering, in the place of the animal sacrifices required in the law of Moses. Diaspora Jews had no place to carry out sacrifices and had begun to reject the idea. They would pay money instead, and it would be accompanied by a declaration of freedom from sin. The peace offerings (much later called "indulgences") would be paid once a year, at the time of the annual promotion through the successive stages of membership.[5]

The missionaries, going out to the Diaspora with their leather wallets full of white stones, would come back with the same wallets full of money, in foreign currency.[6] Once put into Jewish currency by the money-changers, it would be stored in vaults, ready to be used by Herod for his vast building projects, or any subsequent causes.

In a later phase, an inventory of deposits was made, on a sheet of copper, the words beaten out laboriously, to ensure that the record could not be lost. Each sentence described the location of a vault and the large amount of money in silver and gold stored there. It grew into two strips of copper, nailed to a wall. Much later in the history it and another copy were rolled up and hidden, the first one in a cave at Qumran, where it was found with the Dead Sea Scrolls.[7]

One of the scroll fragments sets out the calculations of income arising from this practice, and it is reflected also in parables in the New Testament.[8] The aim of gaining six hundred thousand members to form a New Israel was to be achieved by a project of evangelism lasting forty years, the first generation of the millennium.

Candidates for initiation were grouped in hundreds, according to the custom of the Essenes.[9] Each hundred would produce a *minah*, translated as "a pound", that is one hundred half-shekels, in initiation fees. Each initiation fee meant a new member, so heads were counted by this means.

Four years were to be devoted to the recruiting and instruction of each batch. The missionary, who had been given a pound for his travelling expenses, would take a year to find a hundred, then spend three years with them, bringing them to full initiation. At the end of four years he would collect a pound, their hundred half-shekels.

Their local leader would then work for another four years, producing another pound. When this went on over the forty years allowed for evangelism, there were ten periods, producing ten pounds. Thus the original missionary's pound had made ten pounds, and he had done his work well. A four-year period of recruitment and instruction was typical of the provinces of Asia Minor, where Jews lived an ordinary working life in the cities and villages.

In some districts, such as Alexandria, there was interest in a longer period of instruction, bringing members to the educational level of monastics, who had a total of seven years in their schools. With a year for recruitment, the period would be eight years. There were five such periods in forty years, so the missionary's pound had made five pounds, and he had done his work well, because well educated members were of value.

In the far flung province of Rome, local ministers undertook a form of mission, but Judea was a long way away, and there was less interest in sending money back, rather a desire to keep it in Rome. So the minister there produced no income, and was sternly rebuked for his anti-centralist views.

Luke's parable of the pounds[10] thus contains information about the original mission and its financial basis. It tells of a man who had ten servants, to each of whom he gave a pound. The story of three of them is given: the first used his pound to make ten pounds more; the second made five pounds, and each of these was commended equally. But the third hid the money, and was condemned. There is a great deal of further detail in the story that does not fit the simple moral point that gifts should be used wisely. The parable, together with Matthew's parable of the talents (giving the figures in a different way, in terms of the eight outside provinces),[11] is part of the account of the original organisation that is given in many places in the gospels.

The missionaries not only gave the initiates a stone and a new name, but also a badge with an emblem of the particular order they were joining. The original twelve thousand in Judea were divided into "tribes", called after the names of the twelve tribes of Israel (Reuben, Simeon, Levi, Judah, and so on).[12] They were actually religious orders, with varying kinds of discipline and political outlook. Their emblems reflected their image: one order used a sheep, meaning that they were village Essenes, followers of the shepherd king David; another used a dove, meaning that they stood for peace; another, who were workers, used an ox. When the missionaries handed over these badges in exchange for the half-shekel, it could be said that they were "selling oxen and sheep and doves", and turning religion into a "shop".

Seventy years later there came into the mission a descendant of one of the founders, Jesus the son of Joseph the son of Heli. He took the strongest objection to selling religious salvation for money, teaching that it should be given freely, by grace. Taking a whip, he overturned the tables of the moneychangers, and drove out those who were "selling oxen and sheep and doves".[13] From this time on, there would be no initiation fees, only freewill gifts. Religion, he taught, was not a financial racket, but a gift from God. For this, and for many other protests against the Herodian system, he was expelled from the mission.

Nevertheless, in encouraging a project to bring Jews and Gentiles into a renewed kind of Judaism, Herod had laid the foundations of a new religious system and establishment. It was to go through many stages before there evolved from it something that its founders would scarcely have recognised: the Christian Church.

CHAPTER SEVEN

EXILES IN THE WILDERNESS

Qumran, in the Wilderness of Judea, had been the place of exile of the Essenes since at least the second century BC.

They were the old aristocrats, who longed for a return to the great days of Israel, when a David was on the throne and a Zadokite high priest was in the temple.[1] While they waited and prayed for such a Restoration, their priests performed all the services in a courtyard on the barren plateau, acting as if it were a temple. The lay acolytes who had accompanied them into exile lived a monastic existence in the large building east of the aqueduct, devoting their lives to the service of the priests and to prayer.

Every day, at 11 a.m., the monks ceased their work and came to the large stepped cistern on the east side of their building. Taking off their working clothes and leaving only a loincloth, they went down into the water and had a long, refreshing bath.[2] The cisterns, of which there were five with steps, were supplied with water directed through an aqueduct leading from the wady Qumran, a winter stream that filled them up once a year.[3] Taking a bath not only washed away sweat, but washed away sin, for the men must now be in a perfectly holy state. They were about to eat the holy food of priests, acting as if they themselves were priests.

A Jewish priest had to be born into a special tribe, that of

Levi. They enjoyed many privileges, especially the tithe system, by which ordinary men supported them fully, giving them one-tenth of their income, usually in the form of produce such as corn and grapes.[4] When the old families of priests were expelled with the Davids, some devoted followers continued to bring them the tithes, believing that they were the only true priests blessed by God. It was this practice that distinguished village Essenes from other Jews.

After they were exiled to Qumran, the tithe offerings made the difference between life and death. The priests and monks had water, from the deep round well that had been on the western side of the settlement since the eighth century BC; but no food would grow in the barren wilderness, except a few vegetables near a spring three kilometres down the coast. Their supporters made the journey from the north, often from Galilee, to bring them the food. In return they were allowed to stay for a time, to receive instruction and to take part in the prayers.

Tithe offerings should be eaten only by priests on behalf of God. But the worker monks needed to be fed also. So the practice grew up of admitting them to the meal of priests and treating them as honorary priests, in a state of acquired purity through their ritual baths. The meal was called the Purity, a term often found in the scrolls,[5] and it was used as a means of exercising discipline. If a monk broke any of the strict rules of behaviour, by disobedience to superiors, by bearing malice against a companión, even by "guffawing loudly", he was excluded from the Purity for periods ranging from ten days to a year.[6]

The elements in the sacred meal consisted of bread and new wine. At the beginning they were blessed, the wine and bread together by the priest, then the bread alone by the levite.[7] This meal has always been seen to resemble the Christian communion meal, and the history of the relation between the two groups shows that this was, in fact, its original form.

The building at Qumran, and its related outposts down the coast of the Dead Sea, played a vital part in the events recorded in the pesher of the gospels.

The Qumran buildings stood on an elongated plateau, separated by a narrow neck of land from a row of brown limestone cliffs in the background. They were in two clusters, separated by a wide corridor running north-south, down which the aqueduct ran to feed the water systems. On the west side of the corridor, around the deep round well, was a group of small and larger rooms, including a long north-south courtyard. On the east side a large square building, with a tower in its north-west corner, plainly acted as the main centre for monastic life. It was enclosed within what had been an ancient wall going back hundreds of years to the earlier Israelite settlement.[8] Outside the wall on the south stood a long, well-proportioned hall running east–west, and attached to it on its south a room called the pantry, as hundreds of dishes were piled up in it.[9] This hall opened directly on to the esplanade, the long southern projection of the plateau. The esplanade terminated in steep cliffs rising directly from the bed of the wady Qumran below.

Throughout the settlement was a number of rectangular cisterns with steps leading down to them, plainly used for ritual bathing; the round well was sufficient for drinking water. One large cistern, outside the wall on the south-west side, had no steps within it.

The buildings on the Qumran plateau, built from the stones with which the whole area is plentifully littered, were the main centre, constructed when the exiles came there in the second century BC. But in the Wilderness of Judea round about was a number of outposts of the monastery.

Their location, if measured in Greek stadia, corresponds exactly to certain locations in the gospels. A stadion was 607 feet and five stadia 1012 yards, or 2024 cubits, roughly a kilometre.[10]

Five stadia down from the neck of land leading to the main plateau stood a building whose few remains have been described by archaeologists.[11] It came to be called "the queen's house", for reasons that will be seen later, and it occupied a significant place in the story of Jesus.

About two kilometres further down, or three kilometres (fifteen stadia) from Qumran lie the ruins of Ain Feshkha on the shores of the Dead Sea itself. Now a favourite swimming resort for Israelis, the bases of the walls lie, half hidden in grass and shrubs, just off the main path. They include the remains of a fine Herodian door.[12]

Another fifteen stadia down the shoreline, past the great headland of Ras Feshkha, stand the ruins of another building, now called Khirbet ("ruin of") Mazin, just a little north of the exit of the wady Kidron into the Dead Sea.[13] This building is thus thirty stadia (six kilometres) from Qumran, and twenty-five from the queen's house. It includes the remains of a great watergate, which must have stood at the end of a short channel leading up from the sea; the distance to the sea is now a little over two hundred cubits (one hundred yards).

These distances may seem unimportant at first sight, but they become very relevant when a device used in the pesher is understood. After they had been exiled to the wilderness, the Essenes came to believe that they were establishing their own "temple" and "Jerusalem" at Qumran. They began to call it "Jerusalem", in the way that expatriates name places in their new country after places in the homeland. To distinguish between the two, they drew on two forms of the name Jerusalem, and these were able to be reproduced in Greek. When the singular form of the word was used, the real Jerusalem was meant; when the plural, it was the "New Jerusalem", Qumran. The two forms of the name also served the purposes of secrecy when it became necessary.

Qumran became a centre for those loyal to the traditional priests to visit. Councils were held there, and the government of the Essenes was centred at Qumran and its outposts.

When a certain leader who was the bishop of Galilee came to Ain Feshkha for the seasonal councils held at the equinoxes and solstices, he brought "Galilee" with him, for in their understanding of the role of a bishop, he was so identified with his bishopric that it resided in his person. The Christian Church still follows the same principle. An archbishop takes as his surname the name of his city, for example, "John London", so that, in a sense, wherever he is London is. When the bishop of Galilee was at Ain Feshkha, it was called "Galilee".

Ain Feshkha, which had been established as the place to which monks went when they were temporarily expelled from the monastery, was used at the time of their visits by men who had the status of outside celibates. The story includes such a leader who came from Samaria; thus the building by the shore of the Dead Sea was "Samaria" while he was there.

Mazin, further down beyond the headland, was used by men of lower status. Some of these were Essene villagers who met in Capernaum, on Lake Galilee. When they came to Mazin for the seasonal councils, it became "Capernaum".

The boat trips taken by Jesus and the disciples were on the Dead Sea, not on Lake Galilee. To go the three kilometres between Mazin and Ain Feshkha, it was easier to go by boat, as the headland of Ras Feshkha came right to the sea, forming a natural barrier.

It was Mazin that was the Capernaum "at twenty-five or thirty stadia" according to a story in John's gospel. This gospel is strangely inconsistent about locations: it can be bafflingly vague about where things happened; yet give exact distances in stadia where they do not seem to be needed. In one place it says that the disciples, rowing in a boat to Capernaum, travelled to a spot at "twenty-five or thirty stadia".[14] Mazin is thirty stadia from Qumran and twenty-five from the queen's house, which acted as an outer boundary to Qumran.

In another episode at Capernaum in John's gospel, a net of "fish" was dragged two hundred cubits (one hundred yards) to the shore. This was the length of the channel at Mazin, leading up to the watergate.

John's gospel also says that Bethany was fifteen stadia from Jerusalem, using the plural form of the name. Ain Feshkha is exactly this distance from Qumran. It reproduced the original Bethany, at about this distance east of Jerusalem, when the locations were moved to Qumran.

The distances were related to hours of walking. The rate, in the hot dry conditions, was five stadia per hour. Thus it took one hour to go to the queen's house, three to Ain Feshkha, and six to Mazin. The neck of land was the starting point of measurements because it was at the top of the chasm down which everyone had to walk to go south.

The purity rules of the Temple Scroll, a product of Palestinian Essenes, show that when a man became unclean he had to stay away for varying lengths of time and wash himself and his clothes before coming back.[15] At Ain Feshkha, the first outpost south, archaeologists found the remains of some shallow pools, with a white deposit over the bottom. Analysis proved it to be calcium carbonate. Beside the pools were paved terraces with cylindrical stones lying lengthwise.[16] These arrangements can be accounted for as being used for the washing of clothes. Essenes rubbed their white linen garments with frankincense, a starch like substance consisting mainly of calcium carbonate.[17] When they were washed the substance would come out, remaining on the bottom of the pool. The clothes would then be spread over the cylindrical stones to dry in the sun. Ain Feshkha was obviously the place to which monks went when they were expelled for episodes of uncleanness. It became also a place for celibates of the Diaspora, who because they did not live in the holy land, were classed as equal in status to such monks.

Two further places in the wilderness were part of the monastic complex. One was the place now called Khirbet Mird or Hyrcania, nine kilometres inland, on about the same latitude as Ain Feshkha.

At the time of clearing all the ruins in the area, archaeologists found Christian remains there, including copies of some of the gospels.[18] Because of the assumption that the Qumran buildings were not Christian, it has been thought that Mird was not connected with Qumran. But a charming story shows that Mird and Ain Feshkha were certainly connected in the early centuries of the Church. Some Christian anchorites who lived at Mird had a vegetable garden on the seashore at Ain Feshkha. When they needed supplies they used to harness an ass, which would trot on its own the nine kilometres down to the gardener's house, knock on the door with its head, and return up the mountain, still on its own, loaded with the vegetables.[19]

The discovery of Christian manuscripts at Mird confirms what the pesher of the gospels shows, that this site was an integral part of the history. The party that met at Mird was westernised, and became Christian, while the men who met at Qumran were those who remained Jewish.

Mird is a dramatic site, in the very heart of the Judean wilderness. A platform and buildings were constructed on the top of a low mountain, from which there is a fine view east to the Dead Sea. At the foot of the mountain on the east some Herodian graves have been found, one of them almost certainly being that of Antipater, the luckless heir of Herod who was put to death just a few days before his father died. The building had been used by Queen Alexandra Salome (76–67 BC) as a treasury, then was later taken over by Herod the Great.[20] One of its intriguing features is the existence of underground cells beneath the main platform, suitable for hermits, who would have sought solitude in these cells. They were used for the same purpose up to quite recent times.

The northern slopes of the mountain fall steeply down into the cleft of a wady (called Sekhakha) that runs north-east until it joins the wady Qumran. Thus there is a natural route from Mird to Qumran, as well as the route taken by the ass to Ain Feshkha. The ancient name for Qumran was Sekhakha, as can be seen from the Copper Scroll.[21]

In the sides of the wady at the north of Mird a remarkable feature was found by the archaeologists. Two stepped tunnels had been cut into the opposite cliff faces at a point where the wady is very confined, its bed only about two or three metres broad. The south tunnel has been cleared to a depth of about thirty metres, showing that it sloped gradually downwards, descending through steps.

From the pesher of the gospels it appears that the site of Mird corresponds to a location usually called the Wilderness, the place where John the Baptist baptised. A property of the Herods, it had gained increased importance by the time of Jesus. The tunnels may well have been connected with a baptising ritual using the symbolism of birth. The Wilderness, *erēmos* in Greek, was the place where individual ascetics practised their discipline, being called hermits, from the Greek word. Theirs was a different kind of discipline from that of coenobitic monks (monks who lived in community).

The other place that figures in the history is the site that is now the magnificent monastery of Mar Saba, at present the home of a small group of Greek Orthodox monks. It is known to have been connected with Mird in medieval times.[22] Mar Saba is one of the most spectacular buildings in the country, a series of terraces running down the side of a cliff to the gorge of the Kidron below. Although the Christian monastery was founded in the fifth century AD, the pesher indicates that it was previously a place frequented by ascetics, being on the pilgrims' route. Villagers came from Jerusalem down the dry bed of the wady Kidron, using it as a road. They stayed here overnight, then climbed down the slope near the cliff to the bed of the Kidron, continuing on their way.

When the bishop of Nazareth was at this place, which was especially connected with his order, it was *Nazara*. The building once at this site was the *Nazara* (an alternative form of Nazareth), where events in the gospels took place. One of them tells of an attempt to throw Jesus down a cliff, on the brow of which their "city" was built;[23] the detail fits this spot well.

The technique of transposition of place names accounts for many details in the gospels and Acts which are absurd on the surface. In an episode in Acts, Paul is said to have gone from Jerusalem to Jerusalem; the former in the plural form, the latter in the singular.[24] It is not one of Luke's alleged errors; there are no errors. Paul was going from Qumran to Jerusalem.

In Mark, Jesus went by boat to Gerasa, and apparently as soon as he stepped out of the boat, he was there.[25] But Gerasa, a well-known place whose ruins have been found,[26] was approximately sixty kilometres inland from the shore of Lake Galilee. In the pesher, however, he was travelling on the Dead Sea, and arrived at Ain Feshkha on the seashore; it was the place where the head of the order meeting at Gerasa came for councils.

In another episode in Mark, Jesus and the disciples set out from a location that appears to be on the west shore of Lake Galilee, travelling by boat to a desert place that seems to be on the other side of the lake. A crowd set out at the same time, and went by land. This would mean that they had to go right around Lake Galilee, north or south. Yet they arrived at the desert place before Jesus![27] However, when it is understood that they all set out from inland Mird, and the crowd went by land due east to Ain Feshkha, while Jesus went down to Mazin and up the coast by boat, it makes perfect sense.

Vague and inaccurate as the gospel accounts of locations seem to be, they do in fact give precise places and distances, and, since the time to cover distances was also fixed, the exact times taken for the journeys are also made clear.[28]

Qumran was first used, as a monastery, by Palestinian Essenes, who had come there at the time they were expelled from Jerusalem in the second century BC. But in 31 BC, everything changed.[29] The Qumran building was struck by an earthquake that devastated the whole of the Judean valley.[30] The cistern in which the monks took their daily baths suffered the worst of the shock: one side of the steps dropped a cubit below the other.[31] God, the Essenes believed, had struck their building, declaring it unclean. They abandoned the property, and it stayed desolate for twenty years.

In many ways the earthquake was a fortunate event. The Essenes moved back to Jerusalem, to the Essene Gate where they had once practised their rites independently of the Jerusalem temple. There, by renewing their co-operation with Herod, they were accepted back in the city.

Shortly before 21 BC, Herod announced that he was going to rebuild the whole temple, the very centre of Jewish faith.[32] The Essenes, hearing the public proclamation of his intentions, offered thanks to God, and set to work on a new document. For them, the year 21 BC, 3920 from the creation of the world, was the year when the Restoration should come.[33] Surely God was guiding Herod, who would be his instrument in fulfilling the prophecy.

They wrote the Temple Scroll, purporting to be a revelation from God himself, given long ago on Mount Sinai, about how the temple should be built. The plan expressed all their ideas about priestly purity and apartness. They had no hesitation about putting in their criticisms of Herod in the guise of rules about the conduct of the king,[34] because God was in charge of events and would see that the plan was accepted.

Herod, however, had other views. The return of the Essene priests would mean the return of a culture that was alien to most of the people, and would bring out the old conservatives who were strongly opposed to him. He rejected their plan.

It was a disaster for the Essenes. Not only were their hopes of re-establishing themselves in Jerusalem dashed, but their long-standing prophecy had failed. Although they soon found a way of justifying their chronological calculations, they began to withdraw from Herod, teaching their followers in the Diaspora that it was not God's plan that King Herod should rule the Kingdom when it came. There must be a king, and emperor, but he would be of the ancient line of David, not an upstart such as the Herods were. The Davids were no longer to be subordinate rulers, but supreme, answerable only to priests.

Jacob-Heli, now using the title "David",[35] would have the position if the Kingdom came in his time. After him would be his son Joseph. And, when Joseph had a son, he would be the successor to the throne of the Jewish Caesars.

In March 7 BC, Jesus was born to Joseph and Mary. He was born into an expectation that was very far from the surface appearance, that of the family of a simple village carpenter. Joseph acted as a carpenter at times, because when he was with the village Essenes he practised a craft for a living, as they did.[36] But he was also the pretender to the throne of David, and now, when the potential kingdom had extended far beyond the boundaries of Judea, his hopes were for temporal rule of the world. His son had even more chance of fulfilling the long-held hopes of a Restoration, as the numbers of members increased and as the chronological calculations were in his favour.

But Jesus was born into an ambiguity that was to affect the whole of his life. In the story of the virgin birth, the writers of the gospels used the technique of concealment to convey to those who understood, what his extraordinary situation really was.

CHAPTER EIGHT

THE VIRGIN BIRTH

According to the surface account of the New Testament,[1] and according to deeply held and widespread belief, Mary the mother of Jesus remained a virgin, and Jesus had no father but God.

This is one of the matters to which the concept of a pesher, a real history underlying an apparent history, brings considerable illumination.

Once it is known that Jesus was connected with the Essenes, an explanation of the virgin birth comes to light; a non-supernatural explanation. To some, it is disturbing to bring his conception and birth down to an ordinary human level; to others, it can be enlightening.

The New Testament itself does not give very good authority for the virgin birth: it is dealt with in only two of the four gospels, and those same two gospels give a genealogy which says that Jesus was descended from King David through his father Joseph:[2] a complete contradiction.

Nowhere is the virgin birth mentioned in the rest of the New Testament, and, in fact, Paul says very clearly that Jesus was "of the seed of David".[3] Many Protestants do not hold to its literal truth, preferring to invest it with a spiritual meaning. But it remains, of course, an important element in Catholic tradition.

What, then, is the real background? Once the Essene

connections of Jesus and his family are seen, considerable light is thrown on this question.

For the Essenes, celibacy was the highest way of life. Marriage and sex were considered to be unholy, and the aim of the higher members was to be perfectly holy in order to be pleasing to God. We are told by the ancient writers that the Essenes disdained marriage, and in this were strikingly different from other Jews, who valued family life.[4]

In the scrolls, this attitude to celibacy is put very strongly. Anyone who had recently had sexual intercourse was excluded from the temple precincts for three days.[5] If a couple had sex within the walls of the holy city, they "defiled the city of the sanctuary with their uncleanness".[6] The highest order of Essenes lived a kind of life that can be called monastic, in that they were a community of men living away from the world within the stone walls of the Qumran buildings, having all property in common and owning nothing, dedicated to religion, and renouncing marriage.

But some of them recognised that if they did not marry and have children, the race would not continue. For the holiest order, this was not a problem. It is very likely that their members were drawn from the ranks of abandoned or illegitimate children whom the Essenes took in.[7] The ancient equivalent of abortion was to expose an unwanted child in a deserted place, and the Old Testament shows that some priests had the custom of taking in the children, both males and females, and bringing them up in the sanctuary as acolytes or prophetesses.[8] As they had no family to perpetuate, celibacy was required, and came to be associated with holiness.

For some very important people in Essene ranks, however, it was essential to continue their family line. They were members of the great dynasties, the Zadoks and the Davids, who had been the high priests and kings of Israel before the fall of the temple in the sixth century BC. One reason why the movement had come into existence was to preserve these leaders and all that they stood for.

The men from these families, potential priests and kings, wanted to live a perfectly holy life, and believed that sex was defiling. So they practised it only for the sake of having children, putting the most severe restrictions on themselves and their wives.[9] For the most part they lived apart from their wives, like monks in a monastery.[10] But when the rules required that they continue the family line, they left the monastery and prepared for marriage.

There was first of all a long betrothal period of several years, then a marriage ceremony which permitted them to have sex. It was a trial marriage, lasting up to three years. When the woman became pregnant, they waited till she had advanced to three months, when there was less danger of a miscarriage, then had a second marriage ceremony, which was permanent; divorce was forbidden.[11] Thus the woman was always three months pregnant at her final wedding. As they had a strict rule against intercourse during pregnancy, there was no sex after this wedding; the husband would separate to go back to his celibate life.

The woman in such marriages must have also been dedicated to a religious ideal. She was to live apart from her husband for most of the time, remaining faithful so that he could be sure that the children were indeed his. She must be a virgin at marriage, in accordance with the high ideal of purity.

In the hellenistic world of the time, there were religious women called Vestal Virgins, the word "Virgin" meaning a kind of nun. In the same sense, the woman in an Essene marriage would, before her first wedding, be a Virgin, meaning a member of an institution or order, and she would also be, normally, a virgin physically.

However, the betrothal period was very long, and must have put strains on both parties. The New Testament, speaking of an ideal like the Essene one, discusses the case of a man who "has a virgin", whose "passions become strong".[12] If it happened that during the betrothal period and before the first wedding, the passions became too strong, and a child was conceived, then it could be said by a play on words that "a Virgin had conceived". The woman was still a Virgin legally, but not physically. It would be just like the case of a young couple conceiving a child during their engagement.

Joseph was a descendant of King David, as the genealogies make plain. He was an Essene, living according to their rules. An Essene connection for the family of Jesus has, in fact, long been apparent: James, the brother of Jesus, was said to have worn garments of white linen, and to have never used oil on his skin; both are striking characteristics of the Essenes that are mentioned together by Josephus.[13] He was also called an Ebionite.[14] The same word, 'ebionim, meaning "the Poor", is used in the scrolls for the Qumran members.[15]

It follows from all of this that the virgin birth can be explained naturally. Mary was a "Virgin", meaning a nun, betrothed to Joseph. In their case, before the first wedding took place, Mary the Virgin conceived. Joseph was then in a difficult position: he had committed a minor breach of the rules, and one option was to "put Mary away".[16] The child would then be classed as illegitimate, and would be taken in by the highest Essenes to be brought up as an orphan without a name or descendants.

Another option was to recognise the child, for if it was a boy, he would be a descendant of King David, and thus could serve the urgent political hopes of the movement. Joseph took advice from an "angel".[17] All "angels" in the story are men, of the rank of levite. It was believed that priests and levites were the incarnations of heavenly beings, "gods" (*'elohim*) and "angels",[18] and this belief was drawn upon in the pesher in order to talk about real people and events as if they were visions and miracles.

The advice he was given was that he should recognise the child, and go ahead with the first wedding as if it were the second, when the woman was normally pregnant anyway. He did so, and in accordance with the rules, there was no intercourse after this wedding, treated as a second one. This was a straightforward fact, but it was put in such a way in Matthew's gospel[19] as to give the impression that there never had been sex.

The story also says that Mary "conceived by the Holy Spirit".[20] Joseph *was* "the Holy Spirit". As priests and levites were "gods" and "angels", so lower priests, kings and princes were "spirits".

The virgin birth story gives a good example of the pesher form. It is written at the level of a miracle for those for whom the idea of a virginal conception had symbolic power, but at the same time it is written in such a way that those who had special knowledge of the Essene marriage rules and did not expect the supernatural would understand the real facts.

There were strong evangelistic reasons why a story of a virginal conception should be promoted in the hellenistic world. Pagan worship frequently included the cult of a virgin: Kore, Cybele, Diana—the name varied in different places, but the myth expressed the Greek dislike for the body, and the desire to separate the spiritual from the material. The new Judeo-Christian religion coming to pagans had to compete with such cults, and Christians found in the circumstances of Jesus' conception an ideal basis for a deliberately constructed myth.

As Jesus was of the line of David through Joseph, and as the Essenes intended to restore a David king—whether for full monarchy without Herod or in a more spiritual kind of kingship under Herod—the question of whether Jesus was legitimately conceived was a crucial one. From a strict point of view he was an extranuptial child of Joseph, and could not inherit. This was the view taken by the more eastern element, including Pharisees. Their name for Jesus was "the Man of a Lie", referring both to his teachings, heretical from their point of view, and to his illegitimacy.[21]

But from another point of view, a more liberal one, he was legitimate. He had been conceived following a ceremony in June, 8 BC, at which his parents were finally bound to each other in betrothal. There was a series of ceremonies, all designed to solemnify the marriage and also to postpone sex for as long as possible; the long betrothal becoming gradually more binding, with its final stage taking place in June, followed by the (first) wedding in September, the holiest season for Jews as the time when the great festivals were held. Then in December, sex was at last permitted. December was the least holy season, there being no ancient traditional festivals. The aim was to conceive a son in December so that he would be born the following September in the holy season.

As Jesus was conceived under a form of betrothal that could not be broken,[22] his supporters held that he was a true heir. But the question was to pursue him for the whole of his life, and was the issue around which hostility to him could focus. For some he was the Bastard; for others a king–Messiah who could be even more than a king.

Some further features of the marriage and family rules can be derived from the concealed chronology, although they are not stated explicitly in any extant source. They arose from the theory that the whole purpose of sex was to have children, preferably sons, to continue the patriarchal lines.

The potential king, and men following his model, had to wait till the age of thirty-six before the first wedding in September. The king had his own official and often actual birthday in September, as enough was known about fertility cycles to ensure that sexual activity around the December solstice would produce a child in September. If all went well, the next heir would be born near the king's thirty-seventh birthday. This was three years before his fortieth year, that of the generation, but it might be that the first child was a daughter. The rule was that if the child was a girl, the husband stayed away for three years, then came back again to renew his marriage; this time there was no three months' wait. If, however, the child was a boy, the man had to wait six years before coming back; a girl was half the value of a boy. A man who had a daughter at thirty-seven would come back at the age of forty, and if nature co-operated, he would have a son the following June, during his fortieth year.

When the woman was three months pregnant, theoretically in March, the second wedding took place, and the husband then went through several days of ceremonies of departure before going back to the monastic existence. For the next six months he was not fully enclosed, but remained apart, and was allowed out to visit his wife at the time of the birth. He then parted from her and the child for either three or six years. Under a lighter rule such as was followed by other ascetics at this time, the husband was allowed a home visit when his child was two years old. But for the rest of the time the woman stayed in a community house, where the children were cared for and educated.

While in the monastery, the husband was supported from the communal funds, those of the Poor; full monks had to bring all their property into the common stock, having nothing of their own. But while outside the married men had to work for a living and, having private property, were classed as Rich. Joseph worked as a carpenter while outside. All village Essenes worked at a craft and gave part of their income in the form of taxes for the support of indigent persons such as widows.[23] The welfare funds were administered by a village leader, and were used also to support the wife and children of the men who had returned to the monastery.

A boy at the age of twelve went through a ceremony equivalent to that of the orthodox Bar Mitzvah, when he was formally separated from his mother; this early initiation was symbolised as a kind of second birth, and he was given a ceremonial vestment to wear. When Luke says that Jesus was born in the year of the census of Quirinius,[24] which was AD 6, he was not making one of his alleged errors. Jesus was twelve years old in March, AD 6. When Mary "brought him forth" she was following the symbolism in which the boy was separated from his mother. When he was "wrapped in cloths" he was being clothed in the ceremonial vestment.

Mary, Joseph and Jesus were real people, members of a religious movement with high ideals and strict practices. They lived out a real human life in interaction with it and with its historical development. If they have become images of religion, unreal people, owing more to human imagination than to reality, it is not an unknown process in human affairs. For some, the images meet a need, and it would be hurtful to question them; for others, it is a stage of growth to go beyond images to the actuality.

CHAPTER NINE

BORN TO BE KING?

Jesus was born, not in Bethlehem, but in the building about a kilometre south of the Qumran plateau. He was born there because at the time of his birth he was officially classed as an illegitimate child.

Before the earthquake, while Qumran was still a monastery, there had been a place where the illegitimate children destined for monastic life were born and prepared for their future. It was at Mird (Hyrcania), some sixteen hours' walk from Jerusalem in a south-easterly direction.

To reach the spot, one goes east from Jerusalem through Bethany, then south-east to the mountain known as Jebel Muntar, the highest point in the district, 524 metres. From here one can still see Jerusalem in the distance, and, all around, low rounded hills with almost no vegetation. The track then follows a wady a few kilometres further.

A young girl in Jerusalem who found herself pregnant would follow this path, and on the arid bank of the wady give birth to the child, leaving it there to die.

The predecessors of the Essenes, however, had long had compassion on such children, bringing both males and females into their shrines as acolytes. When the monastic system developed, the males became monks, acting as servants of the priests.

After the earthquake, Qumran was no longer pure enough to be used as a monastery and sanctuary. When it was reoccupied about 11 BC, it was as a centre for celibates who had not fully renounced the world, like the Egyptian Therapeutae. They held less strict views on ritual and moral matters.

Some children born out of wedlock were still taken in by them, but—since women were also now allowed to come to the centre—the mothers were allowed to stay with the infants. The woman bore and nursed her child in the building that was used by women in a state of menstrual uncleanness. The Temple Scroll shows that there had to be such a place outside every city, and another scroll gives the distance away for unclean installations: two thousand cubits, that is nearly five stadia, or a kilometre; an hour's walking distance.[1]

There was a building at just this distance south of Qumran, as has been seen. A name for it is found in the Copper Scroll: "the queen's house". The Copper Scroll, a list of deposits of money in and around Qumran (coming from the second phase of the occupation of Qumran, when money, always unclean, could be stored in this defiled place), lists vaults at the buildings on the plateau, then goes beyond it to places around "Sekhakha", the ancient name for the wady which flows down and across to the Dead Sea just south of the end of the esplanade. The building was called "the queen's house" as the queen, the wife of the potential king David, was the superior there over the indigent women.

In the monastic phase the building was also known as the Manger, reproducing a certain building in Jerusalem located five stadia across from the city on the Mount of Olives. The exact distance is known from a passage in Josephus, in his account of an event which also comes into the book of Acts.[2] The event (a would be king attempting a triumphant arrival in Jerusalem) implies that the Manger was the place where the coronation procession of the Davids began. For their coronation they rode on King Solomon's mule, following an ancient ritual.[3] The ceremonial animal would be stabled on the Mount of Olives, making it the Manger.

When the heir to the Davids was banished to Qumran with the priests, a corresponding building was needed, and as the eastern locations, such as Bethany, were now on the south, it was placed five stadia to the south. It was from this point that Jesus later rode in triumphal procession, mounted on a colt, into "Jerusalem", in the plural form.

When the David was crowned, he was "born" as the adopted

Son of God, according to the words of the liturgy of coronation found in the second psalm.[4] In a symbolic sense, the Manger was "Bethlehem"; for his literal birth took place in the literal Bethlehem, south of Jerusalem.

After the earthquake, the Manger at Qumran, the symbolic "Bethlehem" became "Bethlehem of Judea". Qumran had remained "Judea", for "Judea" had been the name for its outer areas.[5]

Thus the building to the south of the Qumran plateau was "the queen's house", "the Manger", and "Bethlehem of Judea".

Jesus was conceived and born during the reign of the high priest Simon Boethus, who was in power from 23 to 5 BC.[6] He and his Boethusian party represented one of the two major points of view on ritual and moral questions that split Judaism at the time. The Boethusians took the stricter view on sexual morality, and for them Jesus was an extranuptial child, equivalent to an orphan. This meant that he must be born in the queen's house, "Bethlehem of Judea".

Herod, by now ageing and suspicious, and aware that the Davids had turned against him in their disappointment over the temple plan, was not in a mood to allow any heir who was not of his choosing to survive. Indeed, he was capable of destroying his own sons; he had his two sons by his favourite wife, Mariamme I the Hasmonean, put to death, out of jealousy, in the year that Jesus was born.[7]

The Magians, Diaspora Essenes with the liberal outlook of the "seekers-after-smooth-things", accepted the legitimacy of Jesus, and wanted to protect him. Arriving at Qumran, they asked what house he had been born in; the place would reflect his status as either orphan or prince. Herod heard of their arrival, and, wishing to find the child, asked his advisers "where the Christ should be born". They chose to answer the pesher meaning of his words—that is, "what is the place where the David is 'born' as the adopted Son of God?"—and answered it with a phrase requiring a pesher: "In Bethlehem of Judea".[8]

Herod had no knowledge of the pesher technique; he was the nominal head of the movement only and was not instructed in its mysteries. He thought they meant the literal Bethlehem. He sent there,[9] but Jesus was not in Bethlehem and so was spared by Herod's ignorance.

Throughout his life, the question of Jesus's legitimacy was determined according to which high priest was in power. If it was a member of the Boethus or related Caiaphas family,[10] he could not succeed, and his brother James was the true heir. But if it was one of the Annas family, Jesus was the potential king. In a setting in which the high priests were political appointees, his fate was necessarily determined by political changes. The question of the high priests is, then, an essential thread running through the history.

CHAPTER TEN

JOSEPH IN "EGYPT"

King Herod died in March, 4 BC, five days after executing his eldest son, Antipater. Antipater, the son of Herod's first wife, the commoner Doris, had helped to bring about the deaths of the sons of Mariamme I, his second wife, and had confidently expected to gain the throne. But his hopes, and his life, were cut short in Herod's agonised last days. He was buried at Mird, which had become Herodian property.[1]

Archelaus, who did gain the throne, had only a few days' notice of his new state. He and his brother Antipas, sons of Herod by a Samaritan mother, Malthace, were both possible candidates, and Antipas had been designated heir in an earlier will.[2] But at the last minute Herod changed his mind, and Archelaus was named king.

Nine years of hostility followed, while the weak Archelaus struggled to retain his position against the indignation of Antipas and the hostility of most of his fellow countrymen. During these years, the country was in turmoil. The Romans, who had trusted Herod to keep order, became increasingly impatient and ruthlessly put down the many candidates to kingship who now came forward, all convinced that they were divinely appointed to rule the Jews.[3]

Joseph, the father of Jesus, was in his prime at this time, and torn by conflicting loyalties. As an Essene, he was for peace, the choice his father Jacob–Heli made. His type of Essene followed a quiet and sober way of life, devoted to personal discipline, prayer and charity.

But as a David he could not stand by and let the land of his ancestors disintegrate. There was a real danger of the loss of a national identity at the hands of Rome. In 5 BC the whole Jewish people had been required to take an oath of loyalty to Caesar and to the government of Herod, and six thousand Pharisees, self-respecting religious leaders who had great influence with the ordinary people, refused to take it.[4] This was the real beginning of zealotry, in the sense of affirmation of national independence.

Joseph, returning to visit his family in March, 5 BC, joined in the protest. In this mood he allied not with the Palestinian Essenes who followed his father, but with the Therapeutae, the Egyptian ascetics who now controlled Qumran. While they occupied the settlement, Qumran was "Egypt", and Joseph with them was "Joseph in Egypt", evoking the Old Testament story.[5]

The Therapeutae were a community of both men and women living by themselves for most of the time in simple huts, then meeting together every seven weeks for a religious meal which usually went on all night, becoming an occasion of spiritual ecstasy. They partook of a plain meal of bread and water, using no wine, and in their religious fervour were said to become "drunk with the drunkenness in which there is no shame".[6]

The head of Therapeutae at this time was a man called Theudas. As Diaspora Essenes of his kind and village Essenes were similar in discipline, Joseph formed an alliance with him. The two, in warrior mode, gave themselves titles drawn from an Old Testament verse: the Star (Joseph, Star of David) and the Sceptre (Theudas).[7]

Joseph, supporting the Pharisee protest, came under the displeasure of Herod, who was in the last year of his life. Herod now had even more reason for pursuing Joseph and his family.

Joseph knew that both he and his child were in danger, and he again asked for direction from his priestly superior, the "angel". He was told: "Flee into Egypt".[8]

Qumran, "Egypt" while the Therapeutae were there, was a suitable place to hide. The caves were already used as places for solitary meditation, and there were so many in the limestone cliff that it was possible to stay undetected for a long time.[9]

After Herod's death Joseph was in less danger from the ruling family,[10] but he and Theudas continued their political alliance, which was increasingly directed against the Romans. Their base was Qumran, and they led there a nationalist party which was militarist, but not as extreme as the one that was to follow. Joseph became known as a hero for Judaism, and was long after remembered as a famous leader.

In September, AD 1, James the brother of Jesus was born.[11] Mary and Joseph, currently under the Boethusian high priest Joazar,[12] waited a little longer than the required six years following the birth of Jesus, in order to have a son in the royal month of September. At the time of his birth, James became the true heir.

Although Joazar himself was a moderate, he was associated with Archelaus and with the aggressive militant Judas the Galilean, who about this time began his rise to power. These three were given a colourful set of pseudonyms by their opponents: Archelaus was the Calf (one of the four living creatures of Ezekiel), Judas was the Beast, and Joazar the Dragon.[13]

A passage in the book of Revelation uses apparently obscure apocalyptic language to speak about Mary, Jesus, and the opposition of Joazar to Jesus' legitimacy:

> And a great portent appeared in heaven, a woman clothed with the sun, with the moon under her feet, and on her head a crown of twelve stars; she was with child and she cried out in her pangs of birth, in anguish for delivery. And another portent appeared in heaven; behold, a great red dragon, with seven heads and ten horns, and seven diadems upon its heads . . . And the dragon stood before the woman who was about to bear a child, that he might devour her child when she brought it forth; she brought forth a male child, one who is to rule all the nations with a rod of iron, but her child was caught up to God and to his throne.[14]

In AD 4 "a king arose over Egypt who did not know Joseph".[15] The Calf, the Beast and the Dragon took over Qumran for more extreme militancy under Judas the Galilean. Joseph left to join a peace party that was now beginning to form under Ananus, the head of a family which was aspiring to the high priesthood.[16] During the next two years priests and leaders on both sides hotly debated the issue of whether or not to take up arms against Rome.

Theudas and Joseph contributed something of permanent importance to western civilisation: the Christian era.

Joseph's aim was to abolish all memory of the Herods, beginning the mission again with only a David as king and potential emperor.

One way of expressing this was through the calendar. For Herod the Great, the year 41 BC had been 3900 from creation, and the beginning of the last millennium of world history, which was to last 4900 years, according to the prophecy of Enoch. Herod had declared that the first generation of forty years of the millennium was to be devoted to mission, with his particular scheme of evangelism and money-making.

Herod's advisers had counted the first forty years from creation as generation one. If, however, it had been called generation zero, as could well be argued, and the following generation the first, then the millennium did not begin until 1 BC. That year should be called 3900, and the following year, AD 1, should be called 3901. The final thousand years, and the Last Judgment, would therefore come in AD 1000.[17]

To cancel Herod's first generation by this means was a way of eliminating him from the history. The forty years for evangelism would now begin again, under a David.

The birth of James in year 1 of the millennium was intended so that he would be the first David in a thousand-year succession. But, after his brother, Jesus, was again declared to be the true heir, the dating was transferred to him. The Church that he founded adopted the millennium, not artificially at a much later date, as has been thought, but going back to the traditions of its own earlier, pre-Christian period.

So, in fact, the dating that the whole world now uses, and which is approaching the end of another millennium, was conceived near the shores of the Dead Sea to inaugurate a thousand-year religious kingdom under the sons of Joseph, the descendant of David.

CHAPTER ELEVEN

THE
PRODIGAL SON

"There was a man who had two sons, and the younger of them said to his father, 'Father, give me the share of property that falls to me'. And he divided his living between them. Not many days later, the younger son gathered all he had and took his journey into a far country, and there he squandered his property in loose living."[1]

Thus begins the gospel parable of the Prodigal Son. All the parables are chronicling history, in a systematic order.[2] The story of the Prodigal Son records events at the beginning of this era. Its moral lesson, on the value of reconciliation, arose from the actual events, but the detail in it far exceeds the moral point; the history of real people is given.

The Father of the story was Simon the Essene, who at that time was head of the ascetic community. He appears in both the gospels and in Josephus; in the latter as the Essene who in the reign of Archelaus was famous for his prophecies.[3] A dream of Archelaus was interpreted by Simon to mean that Archelaus would be king for only ten years. In this he was acting as a typical Essene prophet, believing that it was possible to foretell events with the aid of the solar calendar, and claiming also special powers of interpreting mysteries.

Simon, called Simeon in the gospels,[4] was the "angel Gabriel" who had instructed Mary before her final betrothal.[5] As an Essene superior, he was keeping the monastic Essenes together with the other ascetics at this stage, but by AD 6 would regretfully have taken classical Essenes into a separate organisation that was no longer part of the history of Qumran. Simeon's words in that year, "Lord, now lettest thou thy servant depart in peace", foresaw not his death, but his departure into a way of life that sought only spirituality and peace.[6]

A similar view was held by Jacob-Heli, the father of Joseph, the grandfather of Jesus, who had first brought Palestinian Essenes into alliance with Herod. As Jacob the patriarch of Ephesus he was in charge of the five provinces of Asia Minor, which brought in half the income under the taxation scheme.[7] Heli was the Elder Brother of the parable. His provinces, under the influence of his views, refused to take part in active nationalism such as many thought necessary at this time. They would not allow their taxes to be used for preparations for war. Pope Simeon was forced into schism, and the whole mission and its property, his "living", was divided in two.

The Younger Brother of the parable was Theudas, the head of the Egyptian Therapeutae. His name is given in a later passage, as the zealot leader who had preceded Judas the Galilean.[8] Supported by the other five provinces who were in favour of nationalism (the two home provinces, Babylon, Alexandria and Rome), he went to the "far country", Qumran. In the reoccupation, which took place about 11 BC, it was built up in a way suited to a zealot fortress, the tower being massively strengthened. Money was stored there, and vaults for deposits were opened up, the inventory being kept in the Copper Scroll. Taxes from the provinces supporting Theudas were used for buying arms and preparing for war.

Under the relaxed moral rules of the "seekers-after-smooth-things", Qumran became a place for "loose living". Women were allowed there, and some, attached to the related order of Manasseh, were the "harlots", women like the prophetess of Thyatira described in the book of Revelation, who allowed sexual licence as an expression of ecstatic religion.[9]

Theudas "squandered his property".[10] The money spent on arms, in this and the next stage of zealotry, did not bring victory. From this time on, all zealots were called "thieves", for misappropriating the money given for religious purposes.

At this time the Prodigal Son was "sent to feed swine". "Swine" in this and later occurrences meant Antipas, the tetrarch Herod, who represented a class of members regarded by strict celibates as unclean.[11]

His own moral habits were strongly condemned (he married his half-brother's wife). Theudas acted as pastor, or religious counsellor, to him in his contest with Archelaus, and remained personally close to him in a friendship that proved significant many years later.[12]

By AD 4 the more formidable Judas the Galilean appeared at Qumran, allied with Archelaus. In Jerusalem and at Mird, a peace party was formed in opposition, and soon the Prodigal Son "returned to the Father". There were better prospects for moderate nationalists like Theudas if they allied with the peace faction. The schism was partly healed, and Simeon, welcoming Theudas back, ordered that the "fatted Calf" be killed. Archelaus was the Calf, and a pressure group began to work for his dismissal.

At Qumran, however, Judas the Galilean and his rebel army moved into a phase of more desperate militancy. His companions, would-be martyrs for the cause of Judaism, held a doctrine similar to that of the Pharisees. They believed in survival after death and this inspired them to be prepared to lay down their lives, expecting a glorious resurrection.[13]

Judas was the (Wild) Beast, and Archelaus the Calf, because they had adopted forms of ministry to which the names of the four living creatures of the book of Ezekiel had long been applied (the Man, the Eagle, the Calf, the Lion).[14] According to Revelation 13, the Dragon (Joazar) had given all his power to the Beast, who had ten horns and seven heads, "with ten diadems upon its horns and a blasphemous name upon its heads". It "made war on the saints" and was followed by another beast, who had the famous number 666. The second Beast "causes all, both small and great, both rich and poor, both free and slave, to be marked on the right hand or the forehead, so that no one can buy or sell unless he has the mark, that is, the name of the beast or the number of its name".

Using apocalyptic language to speak in disguised form of political realities, the book of Revelation was describing the zealot faction, which was to continue harassing the Romans for most of the century. They were anti-Roman, eastern in outlook, and required Gentile converts to adopt Jewish identity by being circumcised. The later Beast, 666, also stood for the grades of promotion in the celibate system, by a play on Hebrew letters.[15]

In the gospels, the successors of the Beast and the Dragon are called "the Scribes and Pharisees". Judas the Galilean, taking over Qumran, had continued the scribal activity there in order to produce his own publications, such as the War Scroll. The previous Essene monastics had used a scriptorium on the upper floor to make copies of biblical books, and it was now used by a new kind of scribe. In the gospel period Judas Iscariot was the leader of the Scribes.

The War Scroll, begun at this time and continued in later years, set out the hopes of the zealots for a conquest of the whole world over a forty-year war that would end with a world empire of Jews. Much space was devoted to setting out the religious inscriptions to be used on the trumpets, standards, and shields.

Early in AD 6, "the fatted Calf was killed": Archelaus was dismissed by the Romans. In Josephus' words, "the leading men among the Jews and Samaritans, finding his cruelty and tyranny intolerable, brought charges against him to Caesar". He was sent into exile, to Vienne, in southern France, establishing a Herodian estate in that region.[16]

Judea had now become an occupied country, without its own government, ruled by Roman procurators. This was indeed "the Wrath", the beginning of oppression. Quirinius, the governor of Syria, was sent to oversee the change, and at once imposed a census, in which every man had to declare his property. Joazar counselled moderation, but Judas saw it as the ultimate challenge. They were now faced with a choice between bondage to the Romans and a heroic fight for liberty.[17]

Judas' uprising was promptly put down by the Romans. Immediately afterwards, the peace party swept into power with Ananus as high priest, trusted by the Romans to encourage peaceful co-operation. His sons, five of whom became high priests, all adopted the same policy: westernised views and reasonable friendship towards Rome.[18] Their emblem was the dove, their blessing, at the beginning of worship, was "Peace be with you".[19]

The change of power came just in time for Jesus' twelfth birthday, when he was to undergo the ceremony of a second "birth". As the Ananus family held that he was legitimate, he now went through it as the heir of the crown prince, amid demonstrations of joy. His parents took him to Qumran, to the queen's house, the Manger, where he had been born, to re-enact the event. Mary and Joseph, being in the married state, were not allowed into the katalyma, a word translated as "inn", but in other cases the word for the upper room, the sacred dining chamber; they were not allowed into the highest form of communion, reserved for separated celibates.[20]

Down at Ain Feshkha, the "farm", the pastors or shepherds were meeting for the equinox. The "angel of the Lord", Simeon–Gabriel, came to them and announced the new regime, and that the twelve-year-old Jesus would continue the succession. The ministers sang a hymn of praise, and declared the new policy: "Peace on earth".[21]

Joseph could now relinquish his warrior role, and return to his position as the crown prince, whose special duties included ministry to pilgrims in the Wilderness of Judea. For many years following he and his family lived in peace, with Jesus as the David to come.

CHAPTER TWELVE

JESUS THE YOUNG MAN

When, according to a story in Luke, Jesus was left behind by his parents in the temple, he was not, as the surface story seems to say, twelve years old. He was twenty-three, the age for full initiation. It was AD 17, "year 12" by a form of dating that had been introduced at the time of the zealot uprising.[1]

Under the ascetic rule, the choice of whether to marry or to enter the celibate life was made at the age of twenty. If the choice was for celibacy, or for the form of it used by the dynastic families, the young man began a three-year process towards full membership. Taking the great step of full initiation at twenty-three, he was admitted to communion, receiving the full sacred meal of bread and wine. He then began four years of education leading to graduation at the age of twenty-seven. During the next three years, he was admitted to ministry of the sanctuary, coming to the highest level at the age of thirty.[2]

Jesus had turned twenty in AD 14. The high priest was still Ananus, so he was still the successor of David, and had no choice but to enter the dynastic order. He would be able to marry only at the age of thirty-six, and then would have to spend almost all of his time segregated from his family.

In AD 14 Tiberius had become emperor in Rome, succeeding

from the start in gaining the goodwill of the Jews. Antipas the tetrarch of Galilee, the only Herod now in office, approved of him, and named the city of Tiberias in his honour.[3] With friendship to Rome came a higher status for Gentiles who had joined the mission.

Jesus may have spent most of his adolescent years in Galilee, but it is not impossible that there was some travel abroad. Joseph would increasingly have represented his elderly father as patriarch of the west, and may have taken his sons to see the extent of the future kingdom.

At Passover in AD 17, at the time of his twenty-third birthday, Jesus was due for the solemn step that meant becoming a "Man", an initiate. Until that step, he was a "Child", or novice.

Eleazar Annas, the son of Ananus, had become high priest, having occupied the office for a year.[4] All of the Annas priests used the titles "Father" and "God". To accept the address "God" meant that they were understood to act as an incarnation of God, receiving prayers from villagers addressed to God. The same platonic theory lay behind this practice as in using "angel" for a man in the status of Simeon. Eleazar was thus "my Father" to Jesus.[5]

The long period during which the Annas family had held office was passing. The mood of the country was beginning to turn in a more eastern direction, with less tolerance of western ways. The Roman governor, who like most of the governors usually acted on the advice of the leaders of the Jews, was on the verge of replacing Eleazar with another high priest, who in turn would be succeeded a year later by Caiaphas.

Joseph was once again being drawn into a moderate militarism, renewing his association with the remnants of the zealots. He wanted his son to become an initiate of the military party. This would mean going to a wilderness outpost twelve hours' walk down the wady Kidron.

But Jesus refused to go. He had formed his political views, which were also those of the Annas family which held that he was legitimate: peace with Rome, and acceptance of Gentiles. His reply to his parents, when they reproached him, was "I must be a member according to the doctrines of my Father [Eleazar Annas]".[6]

On this view, he would take his admission ceremony in Jerusalem, at the Essene Gate, where the Essenes had first set up their alternate sanctuary.[7] Those who met there were not monastics, but had the simple discipline of villagers. It was possible to become a full member there, with a less strict doctrine, taking examinations from the village priests.

At the first stage of the ceremony, the renewal of his baptism in Jerusalem, his parents were present, and he was expected to journey by the following day to the wilderness meeting-place. When the baptism was over, Joseph set out on the day's walk, but Jesus stayed behind. Joseph arrived at his destination, but his son did not come to the ceremony. Disappointed and embarrassed, he returned to Jerusalem, finding him at the last stage of his examination, impressing his teachers by his learning and answers.

In that same year his grandfather, Jacob-Heli, died, and Joseph became the David.[8] Jesus, for a very short time, enjoyed the position of crown prince. But with the accession of Caiaphas, a Pharisee in sympathy with Boethusian views, he was sent back to the shameful status of "Man of a Lie". James, his brother, became the crown prince, using the title of "Solomon".[9]

In AD 23, Joseph died. Mary his widow, the "crippled woman" (meaning that she was in the class of the aged) was "bound by Satan".[10] Now a celibate woman preparing to exercise a form of ministry, that of the order of Widows; she was under the authority of "Satan", a name for the chief Scribe. The Scribes and Pharisees were again rising, and Judas Iscariot had become successor of Judas the Galilean. As a zealot leader, he was called "Satan", the incarnation of an evil spirit rather than the incarnation of God. One of his duties was to look after the interests of celibate women, as the "angel Gabriel" had once done; Mary had to acknowledge him as superior under the present regime.

Jesus now felt the full force of his rejection. The political movement that wanted to put a David in power, in Judea and in the world, would, if the Kingdom came, appoint James and not himself. There would be an eastern, nationalist policy, and Gentile members would be kept in an inferior status. During his late twenties and early thirties he endured frustration and humiliation, but gathered around him a circle of friends who wanted a different direction for the mission.

CHAPTER THIRTEEN

JOHN THE BAPTIST

In AD 26 "a man went down from Jerusalem to Jericho".[1] The man was John the Baptist, the son of Zechariah the heir of Zadok. In the Dead Sea Scrolls, he is called the Teacher of Righteousness. He appeared, according to the Damascus Document (one of the scrolls), twenty years after the formation of the Plant-root.[2]

The Plant-root was a name for the zealots who had come together in AD 6. Now, in AD 26, with the arrival of the procurator Pontius Pilate, there was a renewed intensity of feeling against Rome, bringing nationalists into power.

Monastic Essenes had departed from the nationalist movement with Simeon, but John the Baptist had made a break with his family tradition by joining with the nationalists and adopting the way of life of a wilderness ascetic, a hermit, rather than an enclosed monk. His change of style was expressed in a new name, John, which had never been used in his line before.[3]

Although strongly sympathetic to the eastern outlook of the nationalists, John tried to reform them on the question of militarism. As the Damascus Document says, they had been "blind and groping for the way" until the Teacher appeared. John taught that the destruction of Romans should be left in the hands of heaven. At the appointed time when prophecy decreed that the end of the present order should come, heaven would send its angelic hosts to destroy the Sons of Darkness, leaving on earth only the righteous Sons of Light, those who had been initiated into the ascetic movement.[4]

John was an intense personality, with a strong sense of impending doom. His own words are found in some of the psalms which he wrote, part of the Hymns of Thanksgiving found among the Dead Sea Scrolls.[5]

> I have been a snare to those who rebel
>   but healing to those of them who repent,
> prudence to the simple,
>   and steadfastness to the fearful of heart.
> To traitors Thou hast made of me
>   a mockery and scorn,
> but a counsel of truth and understanding
>   to the upright of way.
> I have been iniquity for the wicked,
>   ill-repute on the lips of the fierce,
>   the scoffers have gnashed their teeth.
> I have been a byword to traitors,
>   the assembly of the wicked has raged against me;
> they have roared like turbulent seas
>   and their towering waves have spat out mud and slime.
> But to the elect of righteousness
>   Thou hast made me a banner,
> and a discerning interpreter of wonderful mysteries,
>   to try those who practise truth
>   and to test those who love correction.[6]

He was a powerful preacher, as attested in all of the records. When he preached at Mird, the Wilderness, he prophesied the destruction of all paganism. According to Josephus, this was the reason why he was put to death by the tetrarch Antipas, who feared that his anti-Roman influence would bring upon them reprisals. The scrolls also say of the Teacher "God gave him an eloquent tongue".[7]

John was certain of a coming crisis because he still held the prophecy of Enoch, that had predicted a Restoration of the Zadoks and Davids at the end of the eighth world-week, the year 3920 from creation. It had been due in the year 21 BC, and had given rise to the hopes of the Temple Scroll, but had not been fulfilled.[8] However, by allowing a zero jubilee from creation, in the manner that was used to set the new millennium, an extension to AD 29 could be permitted. Some further adjustments were possible, extending over the next two years, but John's reputation was invested in the prediction that heaven would intervene in a dramatic way in AD 29, 30 or 31 to establish the true king and high priest over a world kingdom of Jews.

Later in that same century would come the year 4000 from creation, and many held that there would be an even greater catastrophe, when the present physical order would be destroyed, leaving the righteous in a new kind of physical existence.

> The torrents of Satan shall reach
> to all sides of the world.
> In all their channels
> a consuming fire shall destroy
> every tree, green and barren, on their banks;
> unto the end of their courses
> it shall scourge with flames of fire
> and shall consume the foundations of the earth
> and the expanse of dry land.
> The bases of the mountains shall blaze
> and the roots of the rocks shall turn
> to torrents of pitch;
> it shall devour as far as the great Abyss.[9]

The rise of John coincided with two important events: the arrival in Judea of the Roman procurator Pontius Pilate, and the arrival about the same time of Agrippa Herod, who was later to become Agrippa I, king of the Jews.

Agrippa's life and personality were central to the course of the history. Josephus presents him as a reckless, charming person, with all the strength and weaknesses of the Herods.[10] Born in 11 BC,[11] he was the son of Aristobulus, one of the two heirs of Herod by Mariamme I the Hasmonean. The two brothers had followed their mother to execution, and the murdered princes had become the subject of romance, so that Agrippa was able to use popular sympathy to help him in his rise to the Herodian throne, a position for which there were better candidates than he.

Educated in Rome, like most of the young Herods, he had an entry to circles around the emperor. His closest friend was Drusus, the son of the Emperor Tiberius, and his patroness was his mother's friend Antonia, who was the most powerful Roman woman of her time. She was the sister-in-law of Tiberius, the mother of the future Emperor Claudius, and grandmother of the future emperor Gaius Caligula, whose father was her other son, Germanicus.

Antonia kept a lifelong sympathy for the young Jewish prince Agrippa, lending him money and using her influence on his behalf when he was in trouble. Through her he came to be a close friend also of her grandson Gaius. Antonia would have been one of the means through which the Jewish religion, as practised in the homes of the Herods, quickly became known in the highest circles in Rome.

Agrippa, according to Josephus, who admired him, was "naturally noble in spirit and lavish in giving".[12] He loved to give banquets for Roman high society in his house in Rome. He also gave large sums of money to the emperor's freedmen in the hope of gaining their support, thereby running through all the inheritance he had received after his mother's death. By about AD 25 he was bankrupt, owed enormous amounts to moneylenders, and finally ran away from Rome. He sailed back to Judea, withdrew to Idumea in the south, the estate from which the Herods had originally come, shut himself up in a tower and planned suicide.

But he had a faithful wife, Cypros, who was respected by those who did not trust him. He also had a sister, the famous Herodias, who was now married to the tetrarch Antipas. Cypros persuaded Herodias and the tetrarch to help him, and for a short time they gave him a living allowance and a position. But they soon withdrew their support. Herodias was later to incite her husband to challenge Agrippa when he actually gained the kingship, claiming, with good reason, that Antipas had better right, as he was a direct son of Herod the Great whereas Agrippa was only a grandson. The tetrarch was thus renewing the feud he had had with Archelaus. Two Herodian parties again formed. Agrippa, as the successor of the Calf, joined the Baptist, while the tetrarch remained with liberal Diaspora Essenes, who were not prepared to accept the strict views of the Baptist.

Two further events served to harden the party divisions: the marriage of Herodias, and a financial scandal in Rome. Herodias had been promised as a child by her grandfather Herod the Great to Herod's then heir, son of Mariamme II the daughter of Boethus. The young man, called Herod, had held the position for a short time after the execution of the Hasmonean sons, before himself losing his birthright when his mother was divorced after an assassination attempt.[13]

Herodias was married to this Herod, and had by him a daughter named Salome. But in the early twenties AD she found the tetrarch Antipas, her husband's half-brother, more attractive, and agreed to marry him.[14] He on his part wanted to marry her, but first had to divorce his Arab wife, the daughter of King Aretas, who controlled the Transjordanian territory that included Damascus. Aretas took grave exception to this, and some years later, when other issues were added, began a war with the tetrarch which again played a significant part in the history.[15]

The marriage of Herodias to the tetrarch followed the pattern of the Herodian family, to whom divorce and marriage with near relatives were customary. But it was offensive to Essene prejudices, such as the Baptist still held. For Essenes, divorce after the second wedding, when there were children, was forbidden. The Baptist sternly denounced the tetrarch and Herodias as living in sin. This was the personal reason behind the tetrarch's removal of the Baptist.[16]

The other event which outraged Palestinian sentiment and attracted the condemnation of the Baptist was a financial scandal in Rome involving the tetrarch's following. Josephus records that in AD 19 "a certain Jew, a complete scoundrel", having fled his own country for breaking religious laws, had set up in Rome as a teacher. "He played the part of an interpreter of the Mosaic law and its wisdom". With others like himself, he began to influence Roman women of high station, including a woman named Fulvia, who became a Jewish proselyte under their teaching. They also influenced her to give them money and goods, saying that they were for the temple in Jerusalem; but the money was never sent to Jerusalem and was kept for their personal expenses. Fulvia's husband, incensed, went directly to Tiberius, who ordered the Jews to be expelled from Rome.[17]

These missionaries were undoubtedly connected with the Samaritan form of the Herodian mission, the Magians. They did not revere Jerusalem and its temple, and were frequently accused, both on the surface and in the pesher of the gospels, of financial exploitation. Their later leader, Simon Magus, was said in Acts 8 to have tried to buy spiritual influence with money.[18]

In the same year as the Baptist rose to power, Pontius Pilate arrived in Judea as Roman governor. He appears to have been the most tactless and blundering of all the Roman procurators, showing complete insensitivity to Jewish religious practices. As the emperor was called the Lion, he was nicknamed the Young Lion of Wrath,[19] and the occupation under procurators, dating from AD 6, became the Period of Wrath.

Under John, two party groupings emerged: the Hebrews and the Hellenists. The Hebrews had an eastern orientation, and a strict view of morality that did not accept Jesus. Their services of worship were marked by the use of the Hebrew language, reading from the Bible in its Hebrew form. They were also opposed to the ministry of women, holding the Jewish view that they should be segregated in worship.[20]

The Hebrews included the Baptist himself, Caiaphas the high priest, James the brother of Jesus (the future David for this party), and also Gamaliel, a revered public figure who was a descendant of Hillel and head of the order of Benjamin.[21] Within that order, in a few years' time, a young man called Saul would arise, in his fervour for eastern ways calling himself a "Hebrew of the Hebrews".[22] Agrippa also was at this stage attached to the Hebrews because of the Baptist's authority over them, but he had been educated in Rome and was capable of changing sides.

The Hellenists spoke Greek in their services, used the Old Testament in its Greek translation, and allowed women into forms of ministry. For them, Jesus' conception was acceptable, and they adopted the attitude of the Magians of West Manasseh who had hailed him at his birth. With Manasseh were the order of Ephraim, the Therapeutae, still under Theudas. The scrolls from this period speak of the men of Ephraim and Manasseh as the enemies of the Teacher of Righteousness.[23]

The tetrarch Antipas, condemned by the Baptist for his morals, sided with Ephraim and Manasseh, a combination that was to prove fatal for John. Antipas with Ephraim and Manasseh formed a faction called the Figtree. When the Figtree was "cursed" by Jesus for not bearing fruit, the meaning was that he condemned it for its methods, which were compromising the mission.

There was, however, another kind of Hellenist, led by the Annas priests, who were called the Vineyard. Both names, the Figtree and the Vineyard, came from the Old Testament verse "every man under his vine and under his figtree".[24] The Vineyard stood for peace with Rome, whereas the other kind of Hellenist were for war.

When the Hebrews allied with the peace Hellenists, they outvoted the war Hellenists, and John the Baptist became leader of the movement. The event is described, in a more picturesque form, in the parable of the Good Samaritan.

John was the man who "went down from Jerusalem to Jericho

and fell among thieves". "Jericho" was the place of meeting of the servants of Agrippa.[25] John's Hebrews party was opposed in debate by the war Hellenists, and they were about to lose. John's arguments were defeated and he was subject to a partial form of excommunication, left "half dead".

But then the Good Samaritan, Jonathan Annas, came to his aid. Bringing his peace Hellenists to the support of John, he enabled John's elevation to the leadership. He literally put him on a pack animal—a form of transport used by priests—and led him to Mird, near the Wilderness, which had been developed as the substitute sanctuary after Qumran was defiled by the earthquake. The buildings included an "inn" used by pilgrims on their journeys. John was from then on established in the Wilderness, and continued there both his ascetic life and his preaching.[26]

John's reign lasted for five years only, until he met his death in AD 31. In that year he fell victim to both the failure of his prophecies and the tetrarch's personal animosity.

CHAPTER FOURTEEN

JESUS
THE MAN

What can be known about Jesus the man? The pesher of the gospels gives every detail of the events in which he was involved; but what does it say about him?

In some ways, he is still a mystery. Enigma lies at the heart of the gospel form. It conceals and reveals, yet what is revealed, concerning individuals, always has deeper layers. The personality of Jesus is seen only obliquely, in what he did or did not do, in the motifs of the carefully crafted stories. But the way the reader understands him is still a matter for interpretation. As there always has been, there will be personal projection onto and identification with the one who for so long has been the human for humankind. He may still, in Albert Schweitzer's words, "pass us by, a stranger and enigma to our times".[1] While now, at least, we can see him in his own setting, the rest of our picture of him comes from each person's perspective.

He may perhaps have been small of stature: Mary Magdalene said, to the man she thought was the gardener: "Have you carried him away? Tell me where you have laid him and I will lift him up".[2] He would normally have had the long hair and beard of a Nazirite, a Jew who had taken an ascetic vow; for Essenes it also indicated a celibate state. But during times when he fulfilled the rules of the dynastic order, he would have shaved his beard and cut his hair short.

The position he was in was his by birth, not because there was anything extraordinary about his nature. Deemed to be heir to the throne of David, he was at the centre of an evangelising movement which attributed charisma to its leaders for the sake of winning the awe and respect of followers. Priests, levites and kings were regularly thought of as incarnations of gods, angels and spirits in a hellenistic world where the idea of gods coming down in the form of men was a commonplace.[3]

But it seems that Jesus interacted with his position in an extraordinary way. In each of the decisive events of the history, he was on the side of those who suffered from the system: the poor, the handicapped, the socially excluded. His protest on their behalf was at the same time a protest for himself. Born with a stigma he did not deserve, of possible illegitimacy and inability to inherit, he fought against oppressive structures, moral and political. In doing so, he freed his own religion from its introversion, giving it to a larger society, the Greek world, which it had hated and feared. Born at a time, and in an institution, which was poised for such a change, he became the opening through which the change came.

In practice he would often have been a tool in the hands of others, who found themselves also the agents of historical processes. But when competing forces tore at him, he yielded to the side that made for liberty and human quality; the choice was surely his own.

The stories about him always reflect institutional practices; he was acting in accordance with the expectations of his community where every action was part of some kind of ritual. But sometimes personal traits are shown in the manner such rituals were performed. Several times he was expected at a communal occasion, but did not go, sometimes changing his mind and arriving later by a separate route.[4] The impression is given that he preferred to walk alone and was known to arrive mysteriously and unexpectedly.

In his personal life he followed the rules established by the dynastic Essenes, even though he also had a choice of an easier discipline. This meant very short periods of family life only, most of the time being in a state of sexual abstinence.

The writer of John's gospel shows him apparently rejecting his mother at the "wedding in Cana": "O woman, what have you to do with me? My hour has not yet come".[5] The pesher refers to differences in party: Mary was at this point on the political side of

James, holding a different doctrine and calendar.

His two problematic associations were with the Beloved Disciple, John Mark, and with Simon Magus, who shared many attitudes with John Mark, particularly their common antipathy to Agrippa I. During the gospel period they were closest of all to Jesus. Subsequently Simon Magus was derided and denounced by Peter and by Paul,[6] and John Mark lost his authority. Peter, who had not actually been close to Jesus during the gospel period, and who had not approved of many of his actions, became the leader and representative of the group that called themselves Christians. But they only adopted the name in AD 44, years after the gospel events.[7]

It will be seen, when the "resurrection" is examined according to the pesher method, that Jesus remained with his followers for many years after the crucifixion. During these years he was for the most part in seclusion, meeting with his friends from time to time to guide their movements. During those years also the four gospels and Acts were written, under the auspices of leaders of different parties. First came John's gospel, under John Mark, the actual work being done by Philip the evangelist (this gospel, contrary to scholarly opinion, is shown by the pesher to have been written by AD 37).[8] Then Mark's gospel was written under the auspices of Peter. Then Luke was written by the man who had become Jesus' physician and close companion. Then followed Matthew, under the authority of one of the Annas brothers and, finally, Acts was completed in the early sixties.[9]

Although the style of each gospel is different, reflecting the interests of different parties, it is difficult to avoid the impression, when working with them in detail, that a single mind lies behind them. Jesus was in a position to conceive the project, make suggestions, and supply the information that was needed. If that were the case, then this motive shows both a determination to give the real history, so that it would not be lost through the spread of the supernatural version of events, and also an understanding of the needs of less sophisticated members of the new religion, the "babes in Christ". Jesus could not, ultimately, act independently of the Church for which he had suffered so much.

He seems to have had high intelligence, a gift for words, a great wit; many sayings attributed to him play upon words with intricate layers of meaning. But in no sense that we now understand was he more than a gifted human being, one who saves because he first went through the suffering of being human. "God" is not found in people, nor in places, nor in words; God is that which cannot be named or defined or known. By giving us the real history of Jesus, the gospels prepare the way for understanding that beyond the forms of religion is a freedom from form. Jesus was human as we are human; he can take us only to our limit, and in taking us there, prepare us for God.

CHAPTER FIFTEEN

THE TWELVE
APOSTLES

The gospel accounts of the ministry of Jesus begin in the fifteenth year of Tiberius Caesar, AD 29.

At the March equinox of that year, Jesus underwent a renewal of his baptism at the hands of John the Baptist. But as he came up the steps out of the baptismal cistern, "he saw a schism in the 'heavens' ".[1]

By this time, both kinds of Hellenist, those for war and those for peace, had been repelled by the priestly arrogance of the Baptist. In the guise of reform, he had been attempting to restore the ritualism and exclusiveness of the old Essenes. Only true priests and levites, those born into the tribe of Levi, had rights before God; laymen were far below them. Married men, Gentiles and women were outside the ranks of the elect.

Diaspora Essenes were accustomed to letting laymen perform levitical functions, dressed in long white robes called stoles.[2] Peace Hellenists under the Annas priests were accustomed to promoting villagers, Gentiles and women. In a time when the issue of war was quiescent, these two groups were driven together against the Baptist to form an opposition, determined to get their candidate into power.

The council they formed may be called the Twelve Apostles, a name used in the surface narrative of the gospels.[3] It came into existence as a counter-government of the potential empire, each of its members representing an order or province.[4]

In the list of names given, the order is reversed, the most important members being named last. The six real leaders were Judas Iscariot, Simon the Zealot, Thaddeus, Jacob of Alphaeus, Thomas and Matthew.

The two candidates for Pope were Simon Magus, for war, and Jonathan Annas, for peace.

Simon Magus is a towering figure in the history, the major player after Jesus. His position was the head of the Magians of West Manasseh, or Samaritans; and successor to Menahem who had been the actual instigator of the mission.

In the Acts of the Apostles there is an episode presenting Simon, a magician of Samaria, using the title "the Power of God called the Great One". Peter has a vehement confrontation with him, denouncing his attempts to buy the right to give the Holy Spirit. The same Simon appears in a considerable literature outside the New Testament, chiefly in the Clementine books.[5] This literature contains historical elements as valuable as those in the New Testament. However, it has been devalued because it does not appear to accord with the New Testament.[6]

Simon was the leader of a gnostic sect, like many known figures of his time teaching that he was an incarnation of God. He had a mistress, Helena, who was said to be an incarnation of the Thought of God. She had at one time been incarnated in Helen of Troy, then in a whore in a brothel in Tyre, where Simon found her. There is good reason to suppose that Simon was the origin of the Faust legend, and Helena of the unhappy Marguerite.[7]

The pesher gives the actual history. Simon was the head of one of the missionary orders, a man of extraordinary personal gifts who could attract followers to his version of the doctrine, an amalgam of liberalised Judaism and Greek philosophy and science. As a Samaritan, he had no loyalty to Jerusalem but saw Judaism in northern terms, syncretistic and Diaspora oriented.

Following the death of the Baptist and the rise to power of the Hellenists, Simon, after a short period, became Pope. He always held zealot views, which meant that when war again became an issue he was driven together with the east, the nationalist Hebrews. In the final state of the parties about AD 50, he was the head of all eastern factions, and the bitter enemy of the Christians, who had separated out from the peace Hellenists. Simon was, for the Christians, the Antipope, the Antichrist, conducting a rival campaign for the hearts and minds of Gentiles, to bring them into what was still an essentially Jewish faith.

Simon appears in the lists of apostles as Simon the Zealot and Simon Cananaios.[8] His best known guise, however, was that of Lazarus, both Lazarus of the story of raising from the dead, and Lazarus the leper of the parable of Lazarus and the Rich Man. He was also Simon the leper.[9]

The Clementine literature presents him as a magician (the literal meaning of "Magus") who performed magical tricks and even adopted the identities of others. Simon cultivated the reputation of thaumaturge in order to gain the adherence of thousands of simple followers. From them, he and Helena gained both worship and a rich income.

Helena appears under as many pseudonyms as he. She was the Samaritan woman with whom Jesus conversed; Sapphira; Martha; the menstruous woman; the Syrophoenician woman; the "woman clothed in scarlet and purple"; "Jezebel"; Salome; Joanna; "his mother's sister".[10] The Christians objected to her both because the form of doctrine taught by Simon and herself was a serious threat to the health of their mission, and because she claimed priesthood in her own right. To be "clothed in scarlet and purple" meant that she claimed to be a cardinal and a bishop. If she was capable of this rank, she could become Pope.

John's gospel, written before the separation from Simon in AD 37, presents him sympathetically as Lazarus. But Peter then emerged as his arch opponent. The legend that the Magus in Rome attempted to fly, but was brought down from mid-air by a prayer of Peter, preserved the history in a typical Magian form.[11]

The Magus accepted Jesus as the true David, and in addition held the view that a layman could act as a levite. Jesus could, if he accepted this position, act as a levite (a subordinate priest) to him.

Jesus "loved" Simon, that is, he shared the communion meal, called the *agape*, or "love feast", with him.[12] He also seems to have had with him a personal bond that played a part in the events associated with the crucifixion. By supporting Simon at a critical time when he need not have done so, he opened himself to charges of zealot action, giving reason for his arrest. But he also demonstrated independence of Simon in relation to some of the Magus' activities. Whereas Simon was at all times hostile to Agrippa, Jesus could associate with and help Agrippa.

The rival to Simon, within the same party, was Jonathan Annas. Where Simon was called "Lightning", Jonathan was called "Thunder".[13] In the list of the apostles, he appears as Jacob of Alphaeus.

In all respects but one he agreed with Jesus. The one difference was that he held that only men born into the tribe of Levi could be priests.

It was Annas' priestliness, together with a certain pomposity that is attested by Josephus (who said that his death was brought about in the fifties AD because he irritated the Roman governor by frequently interfering)[14] that led to a division in his following. The Christians emerged from the peace Hellenists as laymen who did not need a priest as leader; Jesus could occupy all three leadership roles. Jesus, during his ministry, consistently challenged Jonathan for his position of priest.

As high priest in AD 37 Jonathan was called in Acts Stephen, meaning "crown".[15] His "martyrdom" (an excommunication) took place at the hands of zealots, and he is presented favourably as being on the side of Gentiles. But the name "crown" and "royal one", also used for him, meant that the Christians thought that he should move into the subordinate position, that of king, while Jesus was the priest.

Another name for Jonathan is Nathanael, a different form of the name Jonathan; similarly Dositheus, the name for him used in the Clementine books.[16]

Jonathan became Pope immediately following the fall of the Baptist, as both the pesher and the Clementine books show. He took from the Baptist the name and discipline of "Elijah" (that is, the life of a hermit). Thus when "Elijah" appeared on the Mount of Transfiguration, speaking with Jesus, it was Jonathan.

Judas Iscariot is the next leader of importance in the list. As the chief of the Scribes until the crucifixion, he was committed both to zealotry and eastern views. The successor of Judas the Galilean, he was called "Satan", and under this name debated with Jesus at the Temptations. On this occasion (which took place near Mird, the Wilderness), they were together working out the differences within the newly formed anti-Baptist party. Showing Jesus a map of the world as it was then known, he said: "If you will worship me, it will all be yours". The concealed meaning was: "If you will accept me as

Priest and Pope, I will make you King".[17]

Jesus replied: "You shall worship the Lord your God, and him only you shall serve". He was declaring his support for the head of the peace faction, Jonathan.

Thaddeus of the twelve apostles was in fact Theudas, in a variant of his name. The former Prodigal Son, he was now much older, remaining head of the Therapeutae, and as a moderate nationalist and leader of Alexandrian members (who could vary in their loyalties between east and west) he could join with either of the other groups. His primary association, however, was with the tetrarch Antipas, who saved him, as Barabbas, from crucifixion.

Matthew in the list of apostles was Matthew Annas, one of the Annas brothers, destined to be high priest in AD 42 and 43. He came closest in outlook of all the Annas brothers to the Christians, and during his high priesthood they were officially established under their new name. Matthew was the sponsor of the first gospel.

Thomas, next in the list, was, it appears, a member of the Herod family. He fits the history of the son of Herod the Great by Mariamme II, the daughter of the high priest Boethus. Having lost his birthright in 5 BC when his father divorced his mother, he became like Esau of the Old Testament, who also lost his birthright. For this and an organisational reason he was called the Twin, Didymus.[18] Thomas was the Herod to whom Herodias had been married before she left him for his half-brother Antipas. In the quarrel arising from this episode he was naturally on the side of the Baptist, who condemned Herodias and the tetrarch.

The first six on the list were of lower grade than the last six, and were the friends and supporters of Jesus. All were of the class of the unclean: Jewish married men (Peter and Andrew), or Gentiles (Bartholomew, that is John Mark, was a proselyte, and Philip uncircumcised; James and John of Zebedee were Gentile married men).[19]

John Mark, the Beloved Disciple, was the closest to Jesus in the early years. Details of the pesher point to him as being Eutychus, a man who appears in a story later in Acts, and as a Eutychus who appears in Josephus, a freedman of Agrippa I who was deeply hostile to his master.[20] As a proselyte, he was of the highest rank of the uncircumcised, respecting the Jewish religion in the mystical form in which it came to him, but not observing all its rituals. John Mark was the delegate of Jesus, thus enjoying active leadership of the emerging Christian group, but he lost his authority when Agrippa became ruler.

John's name "the Beloved" meant that he was a symbolic "wife" to Jesus; and Peter, who displaced him as leader after AD 37, was Jesus' "son". Fulfilling the role of a "crown prince", Peter upheld Jesus as the Christ, that is, his primary function was that of king.[21] He could not, at first, accept that Jesus could fulfil the role of high priest and Pope.

There are many details which point to Peter as being the man who appears in the pages of Josephus as a "native of Jerusalem named Simon with a reputation for religious scrupulousness". Coming forward in the reign of Agrippa, when feeling ran very high for and against him, Simon "assembled the people at a public meeting . . . and denounced Agrippa as unclean". The king, however, sent for him and exercised his charm upon him, asking him frankly what was contrary to the law in what he did. Simon, "having nothing to say, begged pardon". The king was then reconciled to him and presented him with a gift.[22]

This episode was a turning point in the history: Peter became leader of a group who still thought of themselves as Jews, but giving a new kind of Judaism to the world. When they were forced to leave the country after changing their views on Agrippa, Simon, or Cephas,[23] or Peter, remained their Jewish leader, to rise ultimately to be their chief representative in Rome. Although no doubt personally loyal to Jesus as the spiritual head, his main concern was with the form of mission. His political strengths and his personal honesty were his greatest contribution to its survival.

CHAPTER SIXTEEN

"HE HAS BEELZEBUL"

In March, AD 30, "the Sun set". John the Baptist, who was the Light, the Sun, a title of the Zadokite high priest,[1] effectively lost his power. The Restoration of the king predicted by his prophecies did not come. It was possible to give him one more year's grace, but the Twelve Apostles now came forward as the acting government, with Jonathan Annas as Pope. During his year's papacy, he acted with Jesus to give greater privileges to Gentiles, allowing them into full membership with the receiving of communion. The historic change is recorded in the miracle of "turning water into wine". (See page 24.)

At the March equinox of AD 31, after the year's grace, the Baptist was arrested as a false prophet. Held in the fortress of Machaerus by the tetrarch, he clung to a glimmer of hope: since September was the festival season favoured by the Jewish God, it might be that the Restoration was deferred until then. For six months he waited, while his supporters agonised, prayed and turned to the scriptures for comfort.

While he waited in prison, John wrote another of his psalms:

I seek Thee, and sure as the dawn
Thou appearest as perfect Light to me.
Teachers of lies have smoothed Thy people with words,

and false prophets have led them astray;
they perish without understanding
for their works are in folly.
For I am despised by them
and they have no esteem for me
that Thou mayest manifest Thy might through me.
They have banished me from my land
like a bird from its nest;
all my friends and brethren are driven far from me
and hold me for a broken vessel.[2]

His followers also turned to writing. One of them looked up Psalm 37, which was written for those in despair when the wicked seemed to be flourishing and the righteous suffering. He saw it as answering to their circumstances, and, using the pesher technique of interpreting the Old Testament which the Teacher of Righteousness himself had given them, found in its universal statements particular applications. The "righteous" meant the Teacher, and the "wicked" the Wicked Priest. Jesus' claims to be able to act as a real priest had earned him the name of Anti-Priest, which could be expressed as "Wicked Priest" in Hebrew. He was accused of acting with "the men of Ephraim and Manasseh, who shall seek to lay hands on the Priest [the Teacher] and the men of his council at the time of trial which shall come upon them".[3]

The writer, in the summer of AD 31, drew assurance from the psalm, which on this method of interpretation was a prediction that the Teacher would be saved: "But God will redeem them from out of their hand".

Behind the "men of Ephraim and Manasseh" (Simon Magus and Theudas) was the tetrarch Antipas, working out both personal animosities and political exigencies. Jesus was undoubtedly associated with these men as a member of the Twelve Apostles. He was doubtless also the best known personality, standing alone in claiming a full priesthood for laymen. His opposition to the Baptist was on the question of priestliness, and he would be seen as standing at the opposite extreme. The document was an attempt to discredit him, from a party that saw him as bringing in such an extreme form of westernisation that Jewish identity would be lost.

Mark's gospel, knowing of the charge that Jesus was associated with the faction responsible for the Baptist's death, gives a full account of the event, attributing it to the machinations of Helena, the mistress of the Magus. At the Herodian version of the village meal, where ecstatic dancing took place in the manner of the Therapeutae, "Salome danced".[4] Helena, who could use the title Salome,[5] taking advantage of the religious excitement, carried out her instructions and persuaded Antipas to execute the Baptist. She asked for his "head", possibly literally, but also metaphorically, as she wanted the headship, the papacy, to give to Simon.

One of the scrolls speaks of a period of about forty years between the death of the Teacher of Righteousness and the end of the heretics, which was expected at the time of an anticipated destruction of the city of Jerusalem. John died, according to the pesher, in September AD 31, and Jerusalem was destroyed in AD 70.[6]

Simon Magus then became Pope in succession to Jonathan Annas. As he was now the official Pope, the Baptist being dead, he used some of the Baptist's titles, including John (II) and "the Voice". But to his enemies he was another like "Satan", and was called "Beelzebul", a further name for a demonic power.[7]

The political and religious situation was again changing. Pilate was causing increasing anxiety, showing a complete lack of Roman sympathy for the Jewish religion. Even those who were normally in favour of co-operation with Rome were driven by Pilate's excesses into action against him.[8]

It was at this season that Jesus was accused of "having Beelzebul". "By the archon (ruler) of demons he casts out demons". He was purporting to attack zealotry with the peace Hellenists, but in fact was co-operating with a zealot. While Simon was Pope, Jesus had no alternative but to act with him as his king, being the David whom Simon would bring in when he gained power as both Pope and Pontifex Maximus. But he also agreed with some of Simon's views against Jonathan Annas, especially on the question of the priesthood of laymen. For the Hebrews, including the family of Jesus, this was a betrayal, and they condemned him as a renegade to the faith.

The evangelists do not attempt to deny that Jesus was at this time associated with the Magus. He was a man of great gifts, who left his mark on his age. As a leader of opposition to Agrippa, he was supported by many Jews of standing, and when Pilate presented the Romans in the worst possible light, he would be seen as a defender of the national religious identity.

The association did not endear Jesus to Peter, who had no time for the sophistications of Simon the magician. Peter was almost entirely in accord with Jonathan Annas, and had brought his sober

Essene villagers to the side of Jesus during the previous few years. But with a new openness to military action, and also a new sympathy with a kind of celibate discipline that disallowed marriage, Peter trusted the regime less and less.

The movements of parties and factions, allying and separating, supporting then denouncing each other, reflected the situation of the country as it had been since the death of Herod and the Roman occupation. During the next two years Jesus was to fall out with all factions, becoming the victim of his own independence. But for now he was in a formal relationship with Simon the chief zealot, a fact that could not be denied when he was brought to trial.

CHAPTER SEVENTEEN

MARY MAGDALENE

The account of the marriage of Jesus with Mary Magdalene lies very close to the surface of the gospel narratives. It is easy to sense an erotic element in the story of the woman with the alabaster flask of pure nard, who poured it over Jesus, so that "the house was filled with the fragrance of the ointment".[1] Those with biblical knowledge would recognise the Song of Solomon: "while the king was on his couch, my nard gave forth its fragrance".[2] The Song of Solomon was the wedding liturgy of the David kings, a beautiful verbal accompaniment to the ceremonies.

In John's gospel, it is made plain that the woman with the ointment was Mary of Bethany, that is, Mary Magdalene.[3]

The gospel of Philip, which has signs of being written at an early date, gives more. "There were three who always walked with the Lord: Mary his mother and her sister and Magdalene, the one who was called his companion. His sister and his mother and his companion were each a Mary." In a later passage it says:

And the companion of the [Saviour was] Mary Magdalene. He loved her more than all the disciples [and used to] kiss her often on her [mouth]. The rest of the disciples [were offended and] said to him: "Why do you love her more than all of us?" The Saviour answered

and said to them, "Why do I not love you like her? When a blind
man and one who sees are both together in darkness, they are no
different from one another. When the light comes, then he who sees
will see the light, and he who is blind will remain in darkness".[4]

When the Essene marriage rules are brought together with
the passage on the woman with ointment, the actual history becomes
clear. This was not a purely spiritual relationship, but a real marriage,
following the rules of the dynastic order. Jesus had to marry in order
to continue his family line, and in his case it was all the more necessary
in order to affirm his legitimacy. The marriage took place while
Jonathan was Pope, when Jesus had arrived at the due age. Although
Caiaphas was high priest, Jesus, accepted by Jonathan, was affirming
his right to continue the dynasty.

There were two occasions when the ointment was poured
out: one early in his ministry, described by Luke, and another just
before the crucifixion, given by both Mark and John.[5] They are not
duplicate narratives, as biblical critics would say, but two different
events.

The first is placed by Luke at a date that other indications
show was September, AD 30. Jesus was thirty-six and a half years
old, but if he had been born at the proper time he would have been
exactly thirty-six, the age when a man in the dynastic order must
marry. The time for the king's first wedding was September, and Jesus
was in this matter observing the accepted rules. The date of his second
ceremony was March AD 33, just before the crucifixion. There had
been a trial marriage, according to the rule that allowed a three-year
trial, then Mary had conceived in December AD 32, at the least holy
season when sexual activity was especially permitted, and was now
three months pregnant. The second wedding was the permanent one.
It was hoped that a son would be born in September AD 33, the
appropriate season for a future king. However, certain details in Acts
for that season show that Mary gave birth to a daughter.[6]

Mary Magdalene was called the woman "from whom seven
demons had gone out". This means that she also had been under
the authority of "Satan", like the "crippled woman", the Widow. Judas
Iscariot was both "Satan" and "Demon 7", a name for him as a member
of the zealot party (the "great red dragon with seven heads and ten
horns").[7] As the chief Scribe, he had the position once held by Gabriel,
which included authority over celibate women before and after
marriage.

Judas was the superior of both Mary the mother of Jesus and Mary Magdalene because they both belonged to the eastern, nationalist party. Later in the history, when a formal split between the Christians and the eastern parties took place, Mary Magdalene remained with the east and the "demons", leading to a considerable crisis.

She was called Mary as a title, not a name. The word was a form of "Miriam", the name of the sister of Moses. Marys named, including the mother of Jesus and the Magdalene, had the title Miriam[8] because they had been given a form of ministry, that of prophetess, taking part in the liturgies of orders like the Therapeutae. These ascetics celebrated the Exodus as a drama of salvation, with two choirs, one of men led by a man representing Moses, the other of women led by a Miriam.

Mary Magdalene was older than usual at the time of her marriage, being twenty-seven. This is known from the date of her "birth" (first initiation), given in the story of "Jairus' daughter", that is, Mary.[9] She had been "born", according to the pesher of the story, in "year 12", AD 17. As there is an indication that females received their first initiation at fourteen, she had been born in AD 3.[10] Normally, a woman at her first marriage was between sixteen and twenty.

The difference from normal practice could have been due to several reasons, one possibility being that she had been married previously. It will be seen that when the crisis concerning Mary arose later on, the issues included the question of whether the marriage was valid according to Essene law. Judas Iscariot, who raised an objection at the second wedding in March 33, was of the opinion that it was not.[11] The most likely reason for this was that there had been a previous wedding and a separation.

Jesus' marriage was in order to fulfil the rules of the dynastic order. It is difficult to know what the personal emotions were, without venturing too far into speculation. Very little is said to convey personal detail, except for the fact that Mary is several times presented as slightly confused, and the subject of criticism by others.[12] More than that, the pesharist is not permitted to know, being given only political and institutional facts.

CHAPTER EIGHTEEN

MIRACULOUS FEEDINGS AND WALKING ON WATER

In the year AD 32, Jesus intensified his program of promotion of Gentiles, to the point of putting them in the place of Jewish ministers. It was the year of his greatest outrages, from a Jewish point of view.

The two "miracles" of the feeding of five thousand and the feeding of four thousand are not intended, for the critical reader, to show Jesus as an extravagant wonderworker who would rather perform miracles than go and buy bread. They are records of the first ordinations to the Christian ministry, in a highly memorable form. The feeding of the five thousand, the more important of them, is included in all four gospels,[1] because it records the beginning of an apostolic succession that goes on to the present day.

From the start, the mission had attracted Gentiles, who joined it as an acceptable new religion coming from the east which had adherents among the highest members of the Roman nobility, especially women. In its original Herodian form, it was a liberalised kind of Judaism, retaining some of the best elements of Jewish thought, especially its monotheism and rejection of images.

But in the actual organisation Gentiles had been only tolerated, unless they chose to become full Jews, undergoing circumcision and adopting the dietary and ritual laws. If they did not, they were denied communion, being allowed only as far as baptism.[2]

During the seventy years since the foundation, the Gentile members had increased to the point where they were giving a whole new character to the movement. It was becoming a religion, far superior to paganism, but which also did not need Jewish identity. When Jesus appeared, he showed marked sympathy for the aspirations of Gentiles to practise the religion while retaining their own nationality and customs.

Two years previously Jesus with Annas had "changed water into wine", by allowing uncircumcised Gentiles to receive communion at an occasion when they had only come for baptism.[3]

But there was something higher than admission to communion: admission to the ministry. In the Jewish form of the religion, priests and levites had officiated in the sanctuary, where there was a table holding twelve loaves of bread. Twelve levites served the loaves to the holy persons present, either priests or celibate laymen. The association between levites and loaves was such that the levites could be called "loaves".

Seven of the loaves were reserved for priests, while five, of lower status, were served to the celibate laymen. The seven higher levites served the seven loaves, and the five lower "loaves" were ministers to the holy laymen.[4]

The step had already been taken by the Magian orders of allowing some higher Jewish laymen to act as levites. But it was a far cry from this to allowing Gentiles into the same position. Priesthood, for Jews, was a privilege of birth. True priests and levites had to be born into the tribe of Levi, and Jewish birth was a necessity for any minister of the Jewish religion.

But in March, AD 32, at Ain Feshkha, Jesus "miraculously" transformed Gentile laymen of the lowest kind into "loaves", ministers who could serve the bread at communion. By "eating the loaves," they became "loaves" themselves. They would officiate at Gentile services, where the congregation were ordinary Gentiles who thought of themselves as Christians, not Jews.

In order to receive the holiness associated with ministry, the new class also "ate two fish". The "fish" were celibate Gentiles, still regarded as higher than the married. The ceremony of initiating these Gentiles included baptising them in sea water, since, for Jews, the various kinds of water were also graded, sea water being the lowest. The emblem of the fish, later associated with Christians in Rome, came from this practice.[5]

After the ceremony, in the evening, the disciples went in the boat back to Mazin. Jesus did not go with them, but stayed at Ain Feshkha.

At the building at Mazin, a place for village members, an elaborate rite was practised for baptising both Jewish villagers and Gentiles. In a drama based on the story of Noah's Ark, a ship was used to enact the "saving" of Jewish village members, who, as they were married, were thought of as "beasts". They were being saved, by initiation, from the destruction soon to come upon the world, symbolised by the flood. When the "beasts" were aboard the ship, it sailed up the channel to the watergate, to let its cargo out on to the dry land of "salvation".[6]

In addition to Jews, Gentiles were added, having been made to pass through the sea water as "fish", and "caught" by Peter in his role of fisherman.

The boat was moored in the channel, and the "fish" were made to wade from the shore through the water, to be pulled up on to the deck of the boat by the "fisherman". On the deck also was the priest, who could pronounce a blessing over the Gentiles but not touch them.

The priest had to have a means of coming to the boat from the land without going through the water, as he wore heavy vestments and must preserve his priestly dignity. For his use a jetty was built from the shore to the boat over the water. To those who liked to joke about priestly superiority, he "walked on water".

On this occasion, the disciples arrived at Mazin, or "Capernaum", and were in the boat at 3 a.m., the "fourth watch of the night", ready to begin the ceremony. Jesus had not come. But there was a land route from Ain Feshkha to Mazin, skirting the base of the great headland of Ras Feshkha, protruding to the sea. The ascetics were accustomed to walking on their familiar paths at night, as several stories show.

The disciples needed a priest for their ceremony. Looking towards the jetty, they saw Jesus coming towards them, "walking on water". He had taken the land route, and arrived in time to take part in the service.

The "miracle" was not that he walked on water, but that he was acting like a full priest, displacing Annas. He was claiming that there was no difference between himself and a man born into the tribe of Levi. According to this view, he could rise as far as being high priest and Pope, and the Jewish priesthood would have become unnecessary. Such an action was enough to earn him the title "the Wicked [Anti-] Priest". Not only was he of doubtful legitimacy as an heir of David and so the "Man of a Lie", but he was now claiming a status that no heir of David could ever hold.[7]

Only one more offence was possible: to claim the very highest privilege of the high priest, that of entering into the Holy of Holies. Jesus was to make that claim the following September.

CHAPTER NINETEEN

THE DAY OF ATONEMENT

September, AD 32 was a season of climax. Every year the atonement had to be performed on the tenth day of the seventh Jewish month (of the year beginning in March). Only the high priest could make the atonement, entering into the Holy of Holies.[1] For members of the separated community, who had their own high priests for their own alternate sanctuary, the question of who would officiate was always a question of which party was in power.

Since the earthquake, the buildings at Mird had been developed as the community's highest sanctuary, its "holy ground". It was here that Simon Magus, as the current Pope, performed the atonement in AD 32.

The high priest always had to have a Second, who would complete the atonement if his superior failed.[2] Simon's Second in the wilderness sanctuary that day was Judas Iscariot, his subordinate in the order.

But the Herodian mission had developed an additional rite. It signified to Diaspora Jews that they also were receiving forgiveness of sins at the same time as Palestinian Jews. Three further ministers acted in a different location, representing the Diaspora. At the moment the atonement was completed, 3 p.m., they declared themselves as witnesses, bringing the good news of forgiveness to all members. From them, the news was understood as spreading to the whole world. In the actual cities of the Diaspora, their counterparts were performing the same rite.

The three bore the titles "Moses", "Elijah" and "Christ" which were names for a triarchy of Prophet, Priest and King. In AD 32 "Moses" was Theudas, the head of Ephraim, "Elijah" was a title now borne by Jonathan Annas, and "Christ" was the David king in his highest role. The function of Jesus on this day was to stand with the other two, on their west, symbolically declaring to western members that their sins were forgiven.

Before the earthquake this Diaspora rite had taken place at Mird, which was then thought of as subordinate to Qumran. But after the earthquake the roles of the two places were reversed, and Qumran, now less clean, stood for all lower areas including the Diaspora.

During the day, a Friday, Jesus was present at Qumran, taking part in a reproduction of the ceremony. The room used for it was what had been the vestry, on the western side of the complex. Part of it was covered by a half-roof reached by a flight of steps. On this raised platform, seen by a congregation sitting below, the three men were to appear, Annas in the centre.[3]

At 3 p.m. the atonement was completed. The three men, as subordinates of the high priest were to make their pronouncements. At this point Jesus acted in a way for which he could never be forgiven. In the words of one of the scrolls, "at the time appointed for rest, for the Day of Atonement, [the Wicked Priest] appeared before them to confuse them, and to cause them to stumble on the Day of Fasting, their Sabbath of repose".[4]

Jesus came onto the platform in the vestments of the high priest, the holiest garments of all. In the words of the gospels he "underwent a metamorphosis". His garments (vestments) "became dazzling white, such as no fuller on earth could whiten them".[5] The high priest's multiple robes were "whiter than white". The fuller was the man who rubbed them with frankincense to whiten the linen.

Jesus moved to the centre of the platform, displacing Annas, and there acted not simply as a priest of a lower rank, but as the high priest himself, performing the ceremony of completion of atonement.

His actions said that not only could the Christ become the Pope and Pontifex Maximus, but that the place where he stood was the sanctuary. The Diaspora was as holy as the holy land. Neither the Jewish priesthood nor the Jewish homeland were necessary.

Jesus even used the words of the Zadokite Baptist, who had said in one of his psalms that his teaching was the water of life, fertilising those baptised by him. "On the Last Day, the Great Day of the feast, Jesus stood and cried: 'If anyone thirst, let him come to me and drink. He who believes in me, as the writing said, out of his inner parts will flow rivers of living water'."[6]

John's gospel records something of the outcry that followed his appearance. In the words of the scrolls, he had "caused them to stumble" on a sabbath and the Day of Atonement. There probably was a physical fracas, in which he was attacked and the regalia removed. The event was long after remembered, coming to the mind of the writer of one of the scrolls when he read the words in one of the prophets about an arrogant man who caused an upheaval "that he may gaze on their feasts".

Later that evening, Simon Magus himself arrived, acting as a Pope who also visited his outlying territories. He could make the three-hour journey on Friday evening as, for him, the sabbath did not start till midnight. Simon appeared in person on the platform, using the Baptist title the Voice, announcing "This is my Beloved Son: hear him".[7] The words meant that Jesus had again been reduced to the position of king; he had been firmly put back in his place.

Jesus was subsequently accepted by the Christians as "the high priest of our confession". In the New Testament epistle to Hebrews (the eastern party) they argued that although he had not been born into the tribe of Levi, but the tribe of Judah (incidentally implying that his father was Joseph), he could be a priest "after the order of Melchizedek".[8] In this they were drawing on one of the titles of the Baptist, a descendant of the Melchizedek priests of Jerusalem.[9] One of the psalms shows that the David kings also had adopted this title when they took over Jerusalem.

These arguments were only of interest to Jews. For westerners, Jesus was a supreme priest and the head of their ministry because of his spiritual qualities. They preferred not to emphasise the Day of Atonement episode, disguising its date, because they no longer kept the September festivals, and also because they taught a single sacrifice for the removal of sins rather than an annual atonement. For them, what happened at the following Passover feast was the proof of Jesus' supremacy.

CHAPTER TWENTY

RAISING
LAZARUS

In December AD 32, Jesus had a personal appointment. The marriage contracted in September AD 30 was still in the trial stage, no conception having yet taken place. A child should be conceived in December, in order to be born the following September, the desirable season for the birth of a future king.

The marriage was to be renewed in Jerusalem, the literal place, still considered unclean by the separated ascetics. It would take place after the December solstice, when the religious observances for the season had been completed.

Before this, however, Jesus went from Qumran to Mird, staying there for some days, visiting Mary Magdalene and Martha-Helena, her chaperone, at the women's house. Martha was acting as a levitical deacon, "busy about much serving", while Mary "sat at the Lord's feet".[1]

This season was a less happy one for some of his associates. It was at this time that Pilate "mingled the blood of the Galileans with their sacrifices". It was one of the several occasions when the Young Lion of Wrath behaved with complete insensitivity to Jewish religious feelings,[2] possibly the time when there was a protest about his spending money from the sacred treasury for building works. He ordered his soldiers, carrying clubs, to dress in Jewish garments and mix with the protesting Jews. The soldiers bludgeoned them indiscriminately, killing many.

The three zealot leaders, Simon Magus (Pope), Judas Iscariot (his Second), and Theudas (Barabbas), led the uprising of nationalists. They were structured as a triarchy of Priest, Prophet and King, and in their minds they formed a reproduction of the triumvirate that had formerly ruled Rome. When their protest failed and their followers were routed, they themselves escaped, but had to go into hiding. Theudas-Barabbas had blood on his hands; he had killed a Roman soldier, "committed murder in the uprising".[3]

From this time, Pilate's orders were to find and round up the zealot triarchy; if he succeeded in this, he would gain credit for having put down a constant source of harassment of the Romans.

One of Simon's many pseudonyms was Lightning, used to contrast him with the other Hellenist, Annas, who was called Thunder. Simon and Judas ("Satan") were both now deposed from the leadership, as they had failed. Jesus' comment; "I beheld Satan fall like Lightning from heaven" was made in reaction to their defeat. He also commented with sympathy on the Galileans whose blood had been shed.[4]

At once the Pope of peace, Jonathan Annas, returned to power. Jesus at this time "rejoiced in the Holy Spirit" (*to pneuma to hagion*, one of Jonathan's titles), addressing him as "the Father" in a prayer.[5]

Simon had gone into hiding in the caves at Qumran, but for his enemies within the movement, this was not enough. A deposed Pope must be excommunicated to prevent him returning to power.

A contest had now broken out between Agrippa and the tetrarch, the two Herods on opposite sides. Agrippa was for the moment enjoying the patronage of his friend Flaccus, the Roman governor of Syria.[6] He had the authority to bring together the factions opposed to the Magus, and to put him under an edict of excommunication.

The method of excommunication, one retained by the Church up to the Middle Ages, was to act as if the man were literally dead, dress him in graveclothes, and put him in his own grave for several days, after which he would be sent away outside the community, spiritually "dead".[7]

Simon, also called Lazarus, was to be put in the burial cave that had been allotted to the Popes at Qumran. As the first Pope had been "Abraham", it was called "Abraham's bosom".

The cave was the one now known as Cave 4, at the end of a narrow projection jutting out west of the Qumran plateau. Its location is indicated in Luke's parable of the Rich Man and Lazarus,[8] referring to a later occasion when Simon suffered the same fate.

In that parable, the Rich Man was in his "burial place", called "Hades", and was able to speak across a chasm ("between you and us there is a great chasm fixed") to "Abraham" and to Lazarus who was in "Abraham's bosom". The chasm was a literal one, the fissure between the main esplanade and the Cave 4 projection, up which a path ran to reach the neck of land.

The commanding position of Cave 4, across from the main plateau, made it ideal for the papal tomb. The cave itself was artificial, hollowed out of the rock, with window-like openings on three sides.[9] A man placed there for a symbolic burial could still breathe, but could not escape from the windows as they overlooked a sheer drop. Entry was from the north side, via a sloping shaft that led down from an opening at the top; the opening could be sealed by a heavy stone.

Jesus, still at Mird, had no need to hide as he had not been one of the leaders of the riot. He was told about Simon's excommunication by Mary and Martha–Helena: "Lord, your friend is 'sick' (in the early stages of excommunication)".[10] But at first he could do nothing.

Then something occurred to make him change his mind. The tetrarch Antipas gained the upper hand over Agrippa, possibly because at this time Agrippa lost the friendship of Flaccus, having been betrayed to him after accepting a bribe.[11] The tetrarch ordered that Simon Magus should be released.

The action of release had to be performed through the levite of the disgraced priest. Jesus, if he chose to support Simon, could act in this role. But he did not support him politically, holding that zealot methods were contrary to his teaching of "Love your enemies".

Yet he had a personal loyalty to Simon which, apparently, outweighed other considerations. He chose to go to Qumran to carry out the release, knowing that, from the point of view of Rome, he was associating with a criminal. His friends protested, urging that he could not trust the tetrarch to support him to the extent he supported Simon.

Jesus made the journey from Mird to Qumran, the two women travelling there also. He came to the cave where Simon was, and Helena met him near it. As she pointed out, standing near her lover's place of incarceration, he would "stink", through not having the means of ritual washing.[12]

Jesus went down the narrow back of the projection. The stone was resting on the top of the shaft, sealing the exit. He ordered those standing near: "Lift up the stone!" They lifted it, and he shouted: "Lazarus, come forth!" Simon, down in the cave, understood that he had been given a reprieve. Still wearing his graveclothes, he came up the sloping shaft and climbed up through the opening. On his head was his turban, made of a cloth called a *soudarion*, the headcloth of a priest.

Jesus had now shown open support for a man wanted by Rome. He was a member of their rebel party in name and in sympathy. If Simon was betrayed to the Romans, Jesus' involvement would be examined.

For the meantime, Jesus must follow the rule of his order. He was free to go to Jerusalem, as there was no direct evidence against him of involvement in the riot. Leaving Qumran and the ascetic life behind him, he travelled to Mar Saba, then up the bed of the wady Kidron until he reached the capital. There he renewed his marriage, and lived for a season in the world.

CHAPTER TWENTY-ONE

THIRTY PIECES OF SILVER

A few months later, in March AD 33, the seasonal council of the leaders of the community was to be held, to observe Passover and associated festival days.

This would be the first gathering of leaders since December. Those wanted by Pilate had been hiding in the caves, but were prepared to risk coming out to meet at the nearby buildings at Qumran. Their fellow members, including Caiaphas and Annas, would not give them away. All were united in the society, whose essential purpose was to defend Judaism. Only if one of them broke ranks to inform Pilate of the whereabouts of the wanted zealots, would they be in danger. There could be someone with a motive to destroy a rival; but he would have to act at a moment when the rival was unprotected by the other members.

Such a moment could come. John the Baptist's prophecies had been unfulfilled a few years before, at the time when he predicted the restoration of the king. But he had also predicted the restoration of the high priest, drawing on variations in the calendar which would give the prophecy credence.[1] His preferred date for that event had been the Day of Atonement in September AD 32, and the non-fulfilment of prophecy had been one of the factors behind the uproar on that day. The prophecy, inherited by his successor in the papacy, Simon

Magus, could, however, be deferred until the following March. The most likely date for a heavenly intervention would be at the equinox, Friday, March 20. If westernised members were right, it should come on Thursday at midnight, as this was the beginning of Friday in the Julian calendar.

Simon would become vulnerable at that hour, and so also would Jesus, for he had claimed to be a high priest. An enemy within could trap both of them, together with anyone who supported them, at that time. Simon, however, had sufficient faith in the prophecy to come to the council meeting, expecting a dramatic vindication. Jesus, on the other hand, had, by his sayings, clearly recognised the possibility of his death.[2]

Judas Iscariot, as the chief Scribe, was in charge of the main Qumran property, the "Purse". Acting with the Herods, who were owners of the money stored there, he could draw on the money of the Poor (celibates) in defence of religion. Pilate, like all the Roman governors, expected considerations in return for his co-operation on political matters; it was well known that all provincial governors enriched themselves by these means.[3]

The contest between the two Herods, Agrippa and Antipas, was also a struggle over who had the right to the Qumran money, as neither had yet been appointed king. Agrippa, at this season, had reinstated himself in Pilate's favour, and had reason for acting against Simon Magus. Simon may possibly have been involved in the betrayal of Agrippa to Flaccus. The enmity between them was brought to a head years later, when Simon was responsible for the assassination of Agrippa.

Although in the same order, Judas was a rival to Simon, upholding eastern values against the western ways of the Magians. He was also bitterly antagonistic to Jesus for his claim to the high priesthood and his opposition to ritual law. With Agrippa's support, he could take his chance, alert Pilate as to the whereabouts of the zealots, and buy his own freedom with the money he was offering.

His opportunity was still some weeks away, as the seasonal gathering began early in March. At this early point, the prophecy, if it were to favour Jesus, had to have a preliminary form of fulfilment. He had claimed to be both king and high priest, and at a certain date near the beginning of March he should be brought into power as the king, a step towards his exaltation as priest. If he was to become king, he should have a coronation, riding from the Manger on "King Solomon's mule", as the David kings had done since the time of Solomon.

Jesus came to Qumran also for another reason: his second wedding was to be celebrated, as Mary Magdalene was three months pregnant. The ceremony would be held just before the significant days at the equinox, and on the evening following it he would be formally restored to the celibate state.

He and his party arrived at Qumran early in March, and his supporters went to the queen's house five stadia south of the plateau, a reproduction of the Jerusalem Manger. The ceremonial animal was brought, and Jesus was given an anticipatory coronation, his supporters shouting "Hosanna!" and proclaiming "the coming kingdom of our father David".[4]

They led him up to the place where the wady Qumran runs west-east to the Dead Sea, then turned west until they reached the foot of the chasm. The animal went up the sloping path, between the towering heights on both sides, till it reached the neck of land, then turned east again towards the buildings. There Jesus "came into Jerusalem [plural form] into the temple".

The "temple" was the name used for the lower third of the former sanctuary. Its upper and middle thirds, the "Holy of Holies" and "Holy House", associated with priests and levites, had been transferred to Mird, but the lower part, associated with the king (as the word for "temple" was the same as the word for "palace" in Hebrew) was retained, being the level where money was stored. Just outside its eastern door was the first of the vaults described in the Copper Scroll. The "temple" was the same as the "treasury", as shown in several places in the gospels. Here were to be found "the tables of the moneychangers". Qumran had been turned into a bank, where the vast income from the mission was stored, the foreign currency being changed into local currency.

The procession around King Jesus arrived at the top, and, if that day were the one for his restoration as king, a sign should have come. But there was no dramatic event.

A non-fulfilment of prophecy always gave the opportunity for reform, as it could be said that heaven would send no reward while there was heresy or wrongdoing. Jesus took his chance, as he had done on a previous occasion, to declare that the impediment was the exploitative money-making system. He overthrew the tables of the moneychangers, accusing them of turning the mission into a "den of thieves".[5]

During the next fortnight the council members met for daily discussions, during which Jesus debated with them a number of points of doctrine.

On Wednesday, March 18, the second wedding of Jesus and Mary Magdalene was held, at Ain Feshkha, "the house of Simon the leper". The liturgy set out in the Song of Solomon was drawn on; "the house was filled with the fragrance of the nard". Judas offered an objection to the marriage, for reasons that are not stated.[6]

As soon as this ceremony had taken place, Judas had increased reason to put his plan against Jesus into action. The following evening, at the sacred part of the regular evening meal, when Jesus again took communion as having returned to the celibate life, he would have the status enabling him to claim priesthood. Jonathan Annas as Pope would be presiding at the meal, but Jesus might again try to move into his position, as he had done several times previously. If he did so, Annas could easily be persuaded to support Judas against him.

So Judas went to Annas and offered to betray Jesus for thirty pieces of silver.[7] This meant that Annas would form an alliance with Judas, making him his levite, the two kinds of Hellenists thus uniting. As a levite in this position, Judas would receive for himself the tithes of villagers, represented by "thirty pieces of silver" (the number reflecting the village form of organisation).

Knowing well that all his opponents were now united against him, and that as a known supporter of Simon Magus he would be caught in any trap laid for Simon, Jesus went ahead and made his preparations for the Last Supper.

CHAPTER TWENTY-TWO

THE LAST SUPPER

The Last Supper and the trial of Jesus took place in the vestry, a long room running down from the south-east corner of the courtyard that had been the substitute sanctuary. The remains of the fireplace at which Peter stood during the trial are still to be seen there.[1]

All gospels say that the crucifixion and events preceding it took place in "Jerusalem", using the plural form of the word. As has been seen, the distances of places given in the gospels, measured in stadia, fit exactly the outposts of Qumran, but remain vague when related to Jerusalem.

The book of Revelation speaks of "the great city which is spiritually called Sodom and Egypt, where their Lord was crucified".[2] Qumran was near the ancient site of Sodom, and the name also reflected a criticism brought by the opponents of the male celibate order meeting there, headed by Judas. Qumran could also be called "Egypt" when the Therapeutae met there, as has been seen.

John's gospel makes a point of saying that the notices over the crosses could be read from the "city".[3] This would have been unlikely if they were set up outside the heights of Jerusalem; but easy if the crosses were set up, as other indications show, on the southern esplanade at Qumran, only a matter of yards south of the back entrance and on the same level.

When Qumran had been set up as a New Jerusalem, its various areas had been called after those in the capital, making it a small-scale reproduction. The aqueduct running down the centre became the "Kidron"; on its west were the "city" and the "temple"; on its east, the large monastery building was the "Mount of Olives". The large hall for villagers on the south side outside the walls was a "garden", as this was a name for a place for villagers.[4]

While the long courtyard to the west of the round well had originally been the sanctuary, the vestry south of the well was thought of as the "city", as it was the place where the priests ate their meals and changed out of their vestments into ordinary garments. Here they were "in the body", a stage below their holier state in the sanctuary.[5] The room, ten cubits or five yards wide and some thirty cubits long, had two sections, the northern one raised a cubit above the southern, so that it acted as a dais to the southern one. The northern part, where the table stood, was the "upper room" (katalyma). The table was placed east-west across it, not far from the edge of the dais. It was this arrangement that set the basic pattern for a Christian church: the holy table on a raised platform, with the communion rail at the edge of the dais.[6]

At 6 p.m., thirteen men came to this table and took their places. The pattern of seating had been long established. Jesus and Jonathan Annas sat in the centre, Jesus as the King on the west and Jonathan as the Priest on the east. They were on elevated couches a little back from the table itself, and in front of them, nearer the table, were their respective Seconds, Peter in front of Jesus and Judas in front of Annas. Peter acted as a "son" to Jesus in his position of king, and Judas had just formed the alliance with Annas that placed him there.[7]

On the south side of the table, opposite the double place in the centre, was John Mark, the Beloved Disciple. The other members were distributed on either side of the centre, both the north and south of the table.

The meal, a regular evening meal such as was held every night by the sectarians, was to last four hours, the first two being for taking common food to satisfy hunger, the next two for the sacred part. In each part, the first hour was for solid food, the second for drink.

It was based on a meal of villagers, where the owner of a house acted as host to guests, including a visiting priest and levite. The host took the seat of the king, and Jesus, in this position for the first two hours, did the work of host. One of his duties was to wash the feet of his guests, including recipients of welfare who may have been invited to the table. Jesus performed this task at the beginning of the meal, then resumed his place, to preside over the serving of the common food. At 7 p.m. he blessed and distributed a cup of fermented wine, the common drink, taken by some but not all of those present (as some had the practice of orders like the Therapeutae, abstaining from all wine).

At 8 p.m. came the time for the sacred food, the communion. Jesus could partake of it, as he was now restored to the celibate state. At this point, as John's gospel records, he "was troubled in the Spirit". A play on words conveys that he turned to Jonathan Annas beside him (called the Spirit in one of his many titles) and contested his position.[8]

While the issue was in doubt, it was also doubtful which of the two, Peter or Judas, would be his Second during the communion. If he moved to the priestly side, it would be Judas. When he said "One of you will give beside me" (paradidōmi in Greek), there was another play on words: it could mean either "betray" or "act as assistant minister". He pointed to Judas, but Peter, sitting in front of him, could not see where he was pointing. Peter beckoned to John Mark, sitting on the opposite side of the table, who was able to show him that Jesus was claiming the priestly side. At the same time John Mark changed from one side of his double seat, "the bosom", to the other, to be opposite Jesus. Jonathan Annas yielded, and moved to the position of king.[9]

Judas now knew that in Jonathan Annas he had the extra ally he needed. He stayed for another hour, acting as assistant to Jesus in the distribution of the communion bread. But shortly after 9 p.m., when the sacred wine was served, he had reason to make his excuses and leave, for he was one of those who did not drink wine.

Until 10 p.m. Jesus presided in the position of priest, receiving and answering questions according to the rules of order. Then it was time to close proceedings; at 10 p.m. they sang a hymn, and Jesus said "Arise, let us go hence".[10]

CHAPTER TWENTY-THREE

ARREST AND TRIAL

In the reproduction "Jerusalem", the "Mount of Olives" was the monastery building east of the aqueduct. After the Last Supper Jesus with his companions went across to the building, then turned down to the area of the divided cistern south of the monastery wall.

There were two hours to wait until midnight, when the test for Simon Magus and his associates would come. Jesus had given evidence of support for Simon, and was known to endorse western ways and the Julian calendar; Theudas–Barabbas also was in the same party, as a close associate of the tetrarch Antipas.

If heaven favoured Jesus at this time, the sign would come in the place with which he was most identified, the meeting hall of villagers. Both married men and Gentiles were of this rank, and the hall had been built as the place where they assembled when they came to Qumran as pilgrims.[1]

Jesus, coming to the doorway, said to John Mark, "Sit here",[2] then took Peter, James and John inside the hall. During the next two hours he wrestled with the question of his loyalties. He was not really on the side of the Magus; he had merely given him personal friendship. It would be a betrayal of his own political position if he was arrested and tried as a zealot. His political sympathies actually lay with Annas, who had come also into the village hall for the midnight vigil. For a time, Jesus turned to him for support, submitting to him, and praying to him as the Father.[3]

During one of his prayers, Annas spoke to him of a certain cup. Jesus replied: "Father, remove this cup from me; nevertheless, not my will but thine be done". The meaning of the cup would become apparent later in the day.

When Judas had left the meeting shortly after 9 p.m., he had sent a messenger on horseback to Jerusalem, to offer Pilate the bribe and to inform him of the whereabouts of the wanted men, asking for a pardon for himself at the same time.

The winding road between Jerusalem and Qumran is about forty kilometres long. Roman roads were well made, and Judas' messenger could have reached Jerusalem by midnight, come to Pilate, persuaded him that there was advantage to him if he came down to the zealot outpost that night, and brought him back by morning.

At midnight in the outer hall, Jesus said "The hour is come". After a two-hour struggle, he had decided to throw in his lot with Simon and face the punishment that would come to both of them. If there was no intervention now, he must accept that he had been branded by heaven as a false prophet.

No intervention came. The westernised version of the prophecy had been shown to be wrong. Judas, waiting in the grounds outside with his companions, was ready to act. He and those with him burst into the hall, and approached Jesus.

Having decided to stand with Simon, Jesus could act as a levite. He went to the rock podium—still visible in the hall—and took his stand on it in the position of the levite or priest. When he asked Judas and his men whom they wanted, and they replied with one of his lay titles, he said "I am [he]" using a play on words meaning that he was a priest, able to use the divine name "I Am".[4]

He was seized and arrested by Jonathan Annas and Judas. His brother James then automatically became the David. He and Caiaphas were present in the buildings, as all parties had gathered for the equinox meeting of the society. As king, James could now be called Malchus, a form of the Hebrew word for "king". Peter attacked James, "cutting off his right ear", a way of saying, using the body imagery, that he rejected him as a levitical king.[5]

Simon Magus was also arrested. He was the "young man" who was seized and "fled away naked".[6] Brought before Caiaphas, he was condemned, expelled from the ministry, and so defrocked. Reduced to the status of a novice, he became a "young man", (the stage before becoming a "man", a higher initiate).

Jesus, Simon's Second, was first brought before a court held by Annas. Then at 2 a.m. he was taken before Caiaphas, who condemned him also. At 3 a.m. he was made to stand in a place in the north part of the vestry, reserved for unclean persons.

Between 1 a.m. and 3 a.m., while Jesus was being tried, Peter, not far away from him, was going through the experience described as his "denials".

The previous evening, Jesus had given Peter one of his enigmatic sayings: "Before the cock crows twice, you will have denied me three times".[7]

Jesus knew that because of a special arrangement of hours that was in force that night, the signal called "cockcrowing" would occur twice, although normally there was only one, at 3 a.m. The reason (more fully explained in the Chronology section p. 181) was that the priests who measured time had reached a point where they were acting on a time that was three hours fast. They were preparing to make an adjustment during the coming afternoon, with the device of the three hours, darkness, (when they did not open the half-roof that was normally opened at noon to let the sun shine down). From midnight on Thursday, a double set of hours was in operation, so that midnight was also treated as 3 a.m., and the cockcrowing signal was sounded. Then, when it came to the true 3 a.m. (fast 6 a.m.), there was another cockcrowing. Those following the priests' directions had to act on the fast times. This included Peter, the chief villager, who normally slept until 3 a.m., then said prayers at 4, 5 and 6 a.m.

He had to say these prayers while Jesus was being tried, at hours that were really 1, 2 and 3 a.m. Moreover, he had to say them standing just near Jesus. The system of prayers, according to which every cubit in the vestry was allotted to a particular grade of minister and to a particular hour, meant that he had to stand near the great fire in the north vestry, close enough to be "warming himself", but not too close. Jesus stood west of him, facing his judges, who were on a raised platform on the west.

As Peter stood there, he had a choice whether to turn east or west to pray. If he turned east, he had adopted an eastern form of the doctrine; if west, a western form. Having just been disappointed by heaven's lack of support for Jesus, Peter turned east, and so was able to talk to the female doorkeeper, who was near the door on the far east of the room. At the same time, he was turning his back on Jesus on the west. At each of his three prayers on the successive hours, he was denying Jesus by the direction he chose. At the last prayer (at true 3 a.m., fast 6 a.m., the second cockcrowing), he and Jesus were standing on the same line. After saying his prayer, Peter turned south again, and Jesus made a full turn and looked at him. Peter, understanding the silent rebuke, went out, and "wept bitterly".

By 6 a.m., Pilate arrived, and the situation changed. Given information by Judas, he demanded to see the three zealots, who were all being held as false prophets. Jesus was brought, and Pilate interviewed him, finding it difficult to believe that he had the same degree of guilt as the others. He suspended judgment, and turned to Theudas.

But then a new factor appeared. The tetrarch Antipas, who had recently been losing the contest for Pilate's favour, found a way of regaining it. Determined to rescue at least Simon Magus and Theudas, he offered a higher bribe to Pilate than Agrippa and Judas had done.

In order to receive the bribe, taken from money that had been given for the mission, Pilate had to become a nominal member. To receive membership, he went through a token baptism by washing his hands.[8] Having received the money, he changed the verdict that he would have given on Theudas-Barabbas. Theudas was an old man, and the tetrarch knew that he would not be able to go through with the partial crucifixion that he had in mind for Simon, so he acted in time to have him released. Judas, now the loser, was tried in his place, the promised pardon withdrawn.

Judas thus lost his protected status with Annas, who found it expedient to take back "the thirty pieces of silver". During his trial Judas had to admit his guilt, and so "hanged himself", or effectively ensured his own death.[9] He was condemned to be crucified alongside Simon. Judas and Simon would hang as two "thieves", condemned for zealot action against Rome.

Pilate then turned to Jesus. He still had doubts about his guilt, and he also hoped he would be offered a further bribe for him. Pilate asked the Jewish priests again whether they really wanted Jesus to be put to death.

The decision was left with Annas. He made his choice: to get rid of this troublesome rebel who was continually trying to usurp his position. He could easily persuade the tetrarch, who had also come into personal conflict with Jesus. The tetrarch came to Pilate, and demanded that Jesus also be crucified.

Pilate made sure of the will of the Jews, ascertaining several times over that they really wanted these three executed. Then, at 9 a.m., he ordered that the crucifixions should be carried out.

CHAPTER TWENTY-FOUR

THE CRUCIFIXION

The crosses, made from wooden posts used to erect tents for the visiting villagers, were set up on a spot that can be determined exactly. The location lay outside the southern entrance gate to the Qumran complex, on a line nine yards south of the south-west corner of the lower vestry.[1]

A New Testament verse says that Jesus suffered "outside the gate" and "outside the camp".[2] The "camp" was a name used by pilgrims, who thought of themselves as nomads in the wilderness. The phrase "outside the camp" also had a further sense to those who knew their Old Testament: Deuteronomy 23:12 shows that it designated the latrine area.

The excavations at Qumran have shown an area south of the back gate in the enclosing wall, which contained a long narrow building running south.[3] It has been interpreted as "stables", and there is now a sign there to this effect, but the width of the building was too narrow for horses. Though outside the walls, it communicated with the south door of the courtyard, the substitute sanctuary. Further, it was adjacent to another cistern, different from the rest in not having ceremonial steps leading down into it.

This cistern, outside the wall, was reached from inside the wall. It would fit very well the rule of the Temple Scroll that a monk who had had a nocturnal emission had to go outside for three days, bathe himself and wash his garments.[4] This meant that it was a place for the unclean, and was suitably located near the latrines. The latrines themselves were for the use of priests in the sanctuary. Although there was a rule, stated in the War Scroll, that the latrine for a camp must be two thousand cubits away, this installation would have dated from the first phase of occupation, when priests on duty in the sanctuary had to say prayers at all the appointed times. They could reach the building by coming out of the south door and down the west side of the vestry.

The gospels say that the place of the crucifixion was known as "the place of a skull". This in itself indicates a graveyard, one of the most striking features of the land surrounding the Qumran buildings. It would also be the case that a very unclean place would be marked by a skull as a warning to those who might inadvertently wander into it. To go near the dead was the ultimate defilement, according to the rules of the scrolls. The priests using the latrines would have had to wash themselves in the nearby cistern before returning.

The brief notices attached to the crosses when they were erected could be easily read from the vestry, the "city". They were in Hebrew, Latin and Greek, the three languages used by the scholars who lived there.[5]

The indication of the exact line on which the crosses were put is in the statement that the crucifixion took place at the third hour. There was a principle in operation that time equals space. Each cubit in a north-south direction indicated an hour, the time when a prayer should be said on that spot. The whole area of the buildings and below was divided into segments of twelve cubits each, standing for twelve hours. They were graded and designated in such a way that certain details indicate the segment, and the line within the segment, on which the crosses were placed.[6]

Jesus was not on the middle cross, but on the western one of the three. This fact is given in the pesher, although it is of course contrary to what the surface seems to say, and contrary to all Christian tradition. The main subject of the executions was, in fact, Simon, and he was placed in the centre, the position of Pope and Priest. Judas, as his Second, was on his east, and Jesus, in the position of "king of the Jews", was in the western place.[7]

Some knowledge of the actual history is reflected in the gnostic tradition that Simon of Cyrene (the name used for Simon now that he was in his lowest status) had been crucified in the place of Jesus.[8] The place of Simon and Judas is also reflected in one of the scrolls, which speaks of the crucifixion of "seekers-after-smooth-things" by the Young Lion of Wrath, Pilate.[9] Its main concern was with the crucifixion of the two heads of Manasseh, Simon and Judas.

The three were strung up in the positions that made crucifixion a particularly cruel method of execution, fastened to the stakes in such a fashion that circulation slowed and the internal organs were damaged. It was a long, slow method of death, lasting over days and even weeks; deliberately chosen to give a slow agony.[10]

When Jesus was about to be put on the cross he was offered, as Matthew says, wine mixed with poison, but he refused it.[11] He was being offered a way of ending his sufferings quickly to avoid the intolerable pain. Suicide was not considered ignoble by zealots; indeed, much later their remaining supporters committed mass suicide on Masada rather than submit to Roman rule.[12]

But at 3 p.m. after six hours on the cross, Jesus cried out, in agony, "My God, my God, why have you forsaken me?" Quoting the words of a psalm, he was railing at Jonathan Annas for the betrayal that had put him there.[13]

The evening before, in speaking with Jonathan in the outer hall, he had discussed the giving of a cup. A cup stood for wine— and more.

A drink was brought, of "vinegar", wine that had been spoiled. It had been spoiled by poison, as later Christian sources admit.[14] The poison that had been offered earlier was now given to Jesus again, and this time he drank it. It was snake poison, taking a number of hours to act. But its first effect, together with that of the trauma he had suffered, was to render him unconscious. He bowed his head, and because as a sick man he was now defiled, he "gave up the spirit".[15]

CHAPTER TWENTY-FIVE

A DEATH
THAT FAILED

Jesus did not die on the cross. He recovered from the effects of the poison, was helped to escape from the tomb by friends, and stayed with them until he reached Rome, where he was present in AD 64.

This is not conjecture, but comes from a reading of the text by the pesher method. Its basic assumption is that nothing supernatural took place, no visions: these are the fictions for the "babes". When Jesus "appeared" in a "vision" to Peter or Paul in subsequent years, as recorded in Acts, it was the real flesh and blood Jesus, holding an audience with his ministers. He was accepted by them as a high priest, generally appearing in surroundings that lent him an atmosphere of awe and mystery; this was enough to suggest the concept of a "vision". But principally he remained in deep seclusion, living usually in celibate communities. He came back into the world at the regular times required by the marriage rules of the dynastic Essenes. Through the "visions" of his reappearances he guided his ministers, bringing them away from Palestine to settle ultimately in Rome.

The evidence for a real resurrection has been seen many times to be very weak. An empty tomb does not prove a resurrection; it only proves that the tomb was empty, and there could be many explanations for that. The excitement on the Day of Pentecost, sometimes cited as a psychological argument, proves nothing more than that the disciples believed in a resurrection.

Mark's gospel, in its original version, ended at Chapter 16, verse 8, with the women running away from the empty tomb. It contained no appearances of Jesus; these were added in a later appendix. The "appearances" seem to vary in each of the gospels, not, apparently, giving unanimous testimony such as would obviously be required for proof of such an event. John's gospel says that Mary Magdalene alone went to the tomb; the other three gospels say that three women went. John and Luke speak of two angels (or men, in the case of Luke); Mark and Matthew of only one, and for Mark he is a young man in the tomb while for Matthew he is an angel, apparently sitting outside. Each gospel records different appearances on subsequent days.

The rest of the New Testament does not support any assertion that the resurrection is the central event of Christianity. It certainly is there, and Paul has a long discussion about it in 1 Corinthians 15, listing appearances, which are apparently not the same as those of the gospels. His main argument is hardly a convincing one: "If Christ has not been raised, your faith is vain". This is an argument from consequences, not from evidence: such an argument usually betrays a weak position. When factual matters are in question, then the way to prove them is to give solid evidence that will stand up to testing. There is not much to be said for the argument "If these facts are not right, then I am going to be very upset".

Moreover, Paul does not put the weight of his case on the resurrection. Rather, the central event was the crucifixion. For Paul, the suffering of Christ was the means of atoning for sin, removing the burden of striving for perfection under the law, and removing the need for repeated sacrifices and the Jewish priesthood.

The minor writers of the New Testament, James and Jude, do not mention a resurrection, and in the epistles of John it is not explicit.

In the newly discovered gospel of Philip is a passage that can be seen to deny it: "Those who say that the lord died first and then rose up are in error, for he rose up first and then died".[1]

Some of the other newly discovered gnostic books reflect the well-known docetic tradition that Jesus did not really die on the cross, but another died in his place.[2] Although this belief obviously derives its strength from the idea that Jesus was not of mortal flesh, so could not suffer, it could hardly have flourished in gnostic circles if there had been solid and certain evidence that he had really died.

Throughout Christian history, the resurrection has not been treated as the very pivot of the faith. This is something that has developed in recent times. Since the Enlightenment, when human reason has been given greater authority, requiring evidence for beliefs, Christians have tried to find proofs for their beliefs, using the categories of science. Fundamentalism, which holds that there are certain fundamental, factually based beliefs, is a development of the twentieth century.

The foregoing observations have been widely made, by both theologians and critical thinkers outside the Church. What is new here is that we now have knowledge of a technique for reading the gospels which shows us that the evangelists themselves did not believe it, and which shows us what really happened.

The evangelists were faced with a difficult and delicate task. The story of the resurrection had been consciously propagated by a man who understood very well the religious need for myth. Simon Magus, who was at the centre of the event, was a brilliant manipulator who saw advantage in the story, to save his own life and to restore his lost power. It would be a means of keeping in membership the great numbers of Gentiles holding a hellenistic view of the immortality of the soul; it was a religious idea they could build on. Those Gentiles stayed with the Christian party, and by the time it separated were deeply influenced by the manufactured myth. Yet the Christians, standing for an ethical sensitivity in opposition to the Magus, needed to record the truth. There were other matters also that they wanted to conceal yet reveal: the whole previous history of the mission. Their answer was the pesher technique, the surface story retaining the myth for those who needed it, while the real events were told for those who "had ears to hear".

By 3 p.m. on the Friday of the crucifixion it was already the early beginning of the sabbath, when it was no longer permitted to make a journey of more than a thousand cubits.[3] Up to 6 p.m., however, it was permitted to lift up a burden.

The tetrarch Antipas, knowing well the rules for the sabbath, had his plans made. He went to Pilate, and asked him to change the method of execution of the men to burial alive. They had been crucified under Roman law, but, if Pilate wanted to get back to Jerusalem, he could hand them over to the Jews and to Jewish law. This would mean that they came under a rule found in the Old Testament and in the Temple Scroll, that hanged men should not stay on the stakes overnight.[4] Let the legs of the two men who were still alive be broken, he asked, and they could be buried in a nearby cave, and left there to die. Jesus, who seemed to be dead already, could be buried with them.

The cave the tetrarch showed Pilate was at the southern end of the esplanade on which the crosses stood. It had been hollowed out of the side of the cliff, some distance down from the top, and was reached by a narrow path running down from the edge of the esplanade.

Its main purpose, the tetrarch explained, was to be a sabbath latrine. Because of the rule restricting travel of more than a thousand cubits after 3 p.m. on Friday, it was not possible for ordinary men whose latrines were placed two thousand cubits away to use them on Friday afternoon. Yet it was necessary that they should have a latrine for use at 4 p.m., as the additional rules of ascetics forbade defecation on the sabbath (a restriction for which the Essenes were well known).

On Friday evening the cave was sealed, and, if the Jewish times were the only ones kept, it would stay sealed for a week. This was all Pilate was told, and he agreed that the men should be put there. During the week they would die.

But he was not told of the variation of times practised by Magians and others with western views. Following the Julian calendar, they held that Saturday did not start till Friday at midnight, or even at 1 a.m. if midnight was treated as zero. Following the regular routine of ascetics, which even prescribed times for bodily functions, they used the sabbath latrine at 4 p.m. on Friday, then abstained, as all did, at 4 a.m. Saturday. But whereas others returned to their normal installation two thousand cubits away on Saturday at 4 p.m., the westerners were still in their sabbath, and must again return to the cave, which was opened for them.

Simon would have to stay only for twenty-four hours, then, when Pilate was out of the way, he would be removed from the cave.

Pilate, agreeing to let the matter come under Jewish law, agreed also to let the Jews provide their own guard. He was told that the cave would be guarded at least "until the third day". But he did not understand the special language for times, which meant that it would be guarded only until the next day, Saturday, at 3 p.m., the guard being a normal arrangement to prevent the place being used for twenty-four hours.[5]

The cave had another purpose also, to be the burial and excommunication cave of the prince, the son of the David king. The David himself was buried in Cave 4, "Abraham's bosom", together with the Pope, but his son was given a less majestic place at the end of the esplanade. According to a sentence in the Copper Scroll, there was a "tomb of the son of the third Great One", in which there was a deposit of money.[6] The king, according to eastern views, was the third after priest and prophet. The cave thus had belonged to James, who was still the heir while Jesus had no son. James was the Rich Man, in both narrative and parables. He now appeared as Joseph of Arimathea, the "rich man" in whose cave Jesus was to be buried.[7]

It was thought that Jesus was dead already. He had to be put in the same cave as the other two, as it was within the permitted walking distance. He could be carried there before 6 p.m. James, as his nearest relative, was given the task of burying his brother. He spoke with Pilate, who expressed amazement that Jesus was already dead—he knew that crucifixion usually took much longer.[8]

Simon Magus and Judas were taken down from the crosses, and their legs were broken. They were carried down to the southern end of the esplanade, then down the winding path to the cave. Inside the cave, they were placed in its eastern section.

John Mark, the Beloved Disciple, had been standing near the cross of Jesus. Like all connected with the Therapeutae, he had medical knowledge. When the side of Jesus was pierced as a test for death, he saw that blood came out, and knew that this almost certainly meant that he was still alive.[9]

He passed on his information to James and to Theudas. The latter had many reasons to be grateful to Jesus. He helped James carry Jesus down to the cave, and left there, near the unconscious man, a container holding one hundred pounds of myrrh and aloes, a very large quantity.[10]

The juice of the aloe plant acts as a purgative, and when given in large quantities acts quickly.[11] Myrrh is a soothing ingredient, acting on mucous membrane. The medicines only had to be administered to effect the expulsion of the poison.

Once the three men were placed in the cave, a large stone was put into the opening at the top which was used for entry. To all outward appearances, they had now been left there to die. Pilate, after ensuring that the cave was sealed and the guard placed, returned to Jerusalem, believing his mission to have been achieved.

CHAPTER TWENTY-SIX

INSIDE
THE CAVE

The remains of the cave, or rather two adjoined caves, on the cliff-side below the end of the esplanade, can still be seen today. The path is still visible and partly usable. The outer wall of the main cave, the roof of which collapsed in antiquity, can be seen from below and beside the cliff, although it is obscured from the top.

Archaeologists made a brief survey there in 1955, looking for manuscripts, and have left a short description.[1] They observed that there were once two linked caves, although very little of them is left. The main one, called Cave 7, was directly below the end of the esplanade, reached by the path, and then by steps at its north-west corner. The lower steps are still there. At its south-west corner was Cave 8, the means of entry to which could no longer be seen. Pottery, lamps, and other remains of occupation were found, including part of a sandal and remains of dates, figs and olives. The oil lamp in Cave 8 certainly belonged to the second phase of the occupation of Qumran.

Cave 8 looked directly across to Cave 4 on the next projection, divided off by the chasm. Through the windows it was possible for a person in 8 to speak across to someone in 4. Luke's parable of the Rich Man and Lazarus gives such a setting for "Abraham's Bosom" and the Cave of the Rich Man, and supplies the first clue that 7 and 8 constituted the Cave of the Rich Man where Jesus was placed.[2]

The Rich Man of Luke's parable was in "Hades". In the reproduction Jerusalem, the end of the esplanade must have constituted the beginning of the "valley of Hinnom", the valley to the south of the real Jerusalem. It was called Gehenna, or "Hades", as the place where continual fires burned the rubbish.

It appears that Cave 7 and Cave 8 were joined, with a single entrance to both via the steps at the north-west corner of 7. The steps came down from the path to the roof, in which a large hole gave a means of access. It was this hole that was blocked by the stone when entry was forbidden.

In the eastern cave, Cave 7, Simon Magus and Judas were laid, unable to walk, dressed in their white vestments which were now their burial clothes. Both of them, being levitical celibates, were "angels". Jesus was placed in Cave 8, which was used as the actual latrine.

The guard who was placed outside was the normal attendant at the sabbath latrine. He was the lowest priest, with the special duty of ensuring that the uncleanness regulations were kept. His name was Ananus the Younger, and he was the youngest of the Annas brothers.[3] Later in the history he would take a significant place. On political questions, he was the enemy of Simon Magus. He was particularly suitable to be on guard, because he would prevent any attempt to remove Simon before 1 a.m., the latest extension of Friday by Simon's method of counting.[4]

An additional guard arrived, in the person of Theudas. He had the duty of night guard, between 9 p.m. and 3 a.m., patrolling the southern end of the grounds.

Theudas had a degree of sympathy with Jesus, and had left the medicines near him in the cave. Ananus also had no great hostility to him personally.[5]

The medicines needed to be administered by someone with professional skills, and the Magus had such skills. Theudas decided to take the chance to help Jesus. His own sabbath did not begin till midnight, with an extension to 1 a.m.; up to that time he could lift up a burden. Ananus also used western times. Theudas, who was superior to Ananus in rank, enlisted his aid to lift up the stone blocking the entrance.

The two men slid down a sloping shaft into the corridor below. Gaining the assent of Simon, they lifted him into the western chamber. Lying beside Jesus, he was able to administer the medicines and bring about the expulsion of the poison.

To do his work he needed light. There was an oil lamp in the cave, and his helpers lit it. Down on the plain, in the queen's house, which was in line with the end of the esplanade, Mary Magdalene was looking up to the cliff where she knew the burial cave was. She saw a light appearing in the western chamber, and realised that something was happening.

Pregnant women were exempt from sabbath rules, as they might have to give birth on the sabbath. Taking her own lamp, she came the two thousand cubits up to the plateau, then down to the cave, arriving there at midnight.[6] On the steps, she saw that the stone was removed from the hole over the cave, and was able to see also that Simon was in the western chamber.

The best thing to do was to go back to the buildings and fetch Peter and John Mark. Mary went back up the path, roused them and told them what she had seen.

Her information, that Simon was with Jesus, told John Mark what had happened. Jesus had probably recovered, and would need help. He and Peter would be permitted to enter by Theudas, to care for the sick. They came down to the cave and went in, Peter taking the lead.

Simon had by now been carried back to the eastern side, and the two guards were outside. It was 1 a.m, and they were now bound by sabbath law; they were not permitted to lift up a burden, but had to rest.

Simon had inadvertently left behind a sign of his presence in the western chamber: his headcloth (soudarion).[7] John and Peter saw it and knew that Mary had told the truth; Simon had been there.

The two men found Jesus alive, but lying in a weakened state. It was agreed that he must be removed from the cave, even though it meant breaking the sabbath rule, and one of them went to fetch a litter to carry him.

Then Mary, on the steps outside, stooped and looked down the opening into the east cave, where the two "angels" were. They knew that she was in the status of a separated wife, not permitted to be in contact with her husband, but they indicated to her that she had permission to go into the western chamber.[8]

Mary came down the shaft and turned towards the west.[9] In the dim light she saw Jesus standing, but, assuming him to be lying down, she thought it was someone else. Because of a physical similarity, she thought it might be his brother James. James was now officially the king, so an "Adam", the Gardener; (as Adam was in the Garden of Eden; the king was understood as the new Adam).

She expressed her willingness to help lift Jesus. The man standing spoke to her one word: "Mary". She then knew that it was Jesus, and went to touch him. He said "Do not touch me"; he was not yet cleansed from the effects of his illness.[10]

In the next hour he was helped by his friends out of the cave. Theudas and Ananus allowed them to go, because Jesus was not their main charge; their duty was to prevent the other two being taken out. Pilate had given no instructions about Jesus, who had seemed to be dead.

Jesus was brought past the buildings and down the chasm to the queen's house, where he was left to recover.

At 3 a.m. Mary Magdalene returned to the cave with the two other women, Helena and Mary the mother of Jesus, to give nursing attention to Simon and Judas. They knew that the stone had been put back by Peter, and looked to Theudas to help remove it. It could be moved, within the letter of the sabbath law, if it were rolled down, not lifted up. There was a way of doing this, and the stone crashed down the shaft, to come to a stop near Simon Magus, who dragged himself up to sit on it as if it were a throne.[11]

The fall of the stone was precipitated by an "Earthquake", one of the pseudonyms of Theudas. When Simon sat on it, he claimed again the position of Pope "Lightning", knowing that he would come into power again following the claim he was about to make.

When the women looked down through the opening, the "young man" in the tomb, who was Simon, gave them a message that could be taken in two ways. "He is risen"[12] could mean simply that Jesus had earned a higher status by his suffering, or it could be taken to mean that he had been raised from the dead, and heaven had indeed acted in favour of Simon and his party. It was undoubtedly the case that Jesus had been taken into the cave as if dead, and had come out of it alive.

The women knew the actual truth, as later Christian tradition records.[13] But the formula that was used by Simon was passed on to others, who could choose to believe in a resurrection if it helped their faith.

When the sabbath was over, Simon was removed from the cave. Judas, who had betrayed all his comrades by alerting Pilate to their whereabouts, was given no mercy. He was taken to the window of the cave, and hurled down the precipice.

"Falling headlong, he burst open".[14]

The timing of the occasion added to the belief in a heavenly intervention. It was at the equinox, in one version, of the year of the Last Jubilee. The miracle had happened, the Restoration had come. Heaven had proved that it was on the side of Jesus and his doctrine. From that time on his simpler followers would be confident that what they were doing on earth was approved in heaven.

CHAPTER TWENTY-SEVEN

THE APPEARANCES

Later that same day and during the next few days Jesus "appeared" to his ministers. The real facts were that he came to the services that had been set down for these days. Those who attended knew what had happened and accepted his ministry as they would have done at any time, amazed not at a resurrection, but at the strength and dedication that had enabled him to recover.

On the Saturday evening, at the time for the communion meal, he "appeared" at Ain Feshkha, having made the short journey down from the queen's house. The "doors were shut" simply because it was the hour for the more sacred part of the service, when guests were excluded. Thomas, whose place was the guest's seat at the table, was not present.[1]

After resting, Jesus recovered sufficiently to be able to undertake a number of journeys. For the next three days he travelled to the different places where the ascetics met, bidding them farewell before his return to the celibate life.

On the Sunday, he made the journey from Ain Feshkha to Mird, across the plain of the Buqeia. Thomas, who had been associated with the Baptist at Mird, came to the noon meal. Being of the outlook of the Hebrews, he had refused to accept the kingship of Jesus. But he now declared his belief that Jesus could be a priest, even calling him "God".[2]

Later that day Jesus arrived at Mar Saba, after travelling across the low hills from Mird. There he met with Theudas, and with his brother James. James was initially hostile, not "recognising" him; that is, not acknowledging Jesus as the legitimate heir. He attacked him for his actions in continuing the dynasty when he should have accepted that he ought not to have married.[3]

But as they shared the sacred bread and Jesus blessed it as a king, James changed his mind and again acknowledged him. James was to remain with the Jewish Christians, retaining many Jewish customs and not teaching the resurrection or virgin birth.

The next day, Monday, they had all reached Jerusalem, meeting secretly at the Essene Gate. Jesus came to the service at noon, again giving the blessing "Peace be with you". He insisted on his physical reality, that he was flesh and blood, and ate a meal with them.[4]

The Tuesday was the last festival day of the season. On this day the "ascension" was due; that is, Jesus would return to the celibate community to live in seclusion, following the period in which he had been in the world for his marriage.

With some of his friends he returned to Qumran, arriving on the Tuesday evening. He pronounced a blessing, then was "carried up into heaven".[5] The meaning was that he was taken up to the raised platform in the vestry, used by the priests for their prayers. It was "heaven" as the place where the priests and levites, or "gods" and "angels", continually worshipped God with their prayers.

The priest who received him was Jonathan Annas, dressed in white vestments. He escorted him inside the buildings, then came back to where Jesus' friends were waiting. He promised them that Jesus would return to them in three or six years' time, according to the rules of the dynastic order.

Jesus remained with his ministers, as he had promised. Sometimes in seclusion, sometimes in the world, he directed their movements, through successive representatives, or in person.

On the Day of Pentecost in June, AD 33 a grand council of Gentile ministers was held in Jerusalem. They had come from all over the world, from the far east to the far west. On that day Peter in his preaching laid great emphasis on the fact that "God" had raised up Jesus. Jonathan had received Jesus back at Qumran, so "raising him up" by promoting him to the higher status of a celibate. But it was necessary for Peter, in meeting world leaders, to obscure the fact that Jonathan, the friend of Gentiles, had in fact contributed to the crucifixion out of hostility to Jesus' anti-priestly views. In using the word "raised up" in two different senses, Peter was already beginning the process of conveying the real history through double meanings.

In September AD 33 Simon Magus became Pope again, following another failure of the prophecy.[6] His candidature was greatly aided by the "miracle" he was thought to have brought about in the burial cave. The following year he led a division of the parties and the property. One reason for this was the pressing demands made by Agrippa for money to help him return to Rome. Some members were prepared to give Agrippa some of the communal funds, which had initially belonged to the Herods, on condition that he would use his influence in Rome to further the spread of the mission. He was in a position to do so through his friendship with Antonia, the most powerful woman in Roman society.

But others had come to distrust Agrippa, and refused to hand over money to him. The result was a division of the funds, with a new place for deposits set up in the city of Caesarea, where there was a community building for Gentile celibates. The Hebrews at first stayed at Qumran, then a few years later moved to Damascus.

Jesus remained enclosed for the next three years. As his daughter had been born in September AD 33,[7] he was due to emerge into the world again in September AD 36. During those three years he may well have been involved in the making of the fourth gospel, which, as its pesher shows, was written before AD 37, when the breach with Simon Magus (Lazarus) took place. It was the first attempt to apply the two-level technique, a device evolved in order to give the true history, and especially the true facts about the "resurrection". Jesus himself may have found this solution to the dilemma in which he and his associates were placed, combining a desire for truth with a recognition of the value of a mystery. There would be several more attempts in order to bring the form to perfection, but this first resulted in a work whose surface meaning has given inspiration and spiritual strength to countless Christian believers.

CHAPTER TWENTY-EIGHT

KINGS AND GOVERNORS

The Roman Emperor Tiberius, the wily old politician who had been in power since the time Jesus was a young man, died on the island of Capri in March, AD 37.[1] The new emperor, Gaius Caligula, set off a series of crises which changed the face of the mission. His appointment was the first of a chain of events which drove the Christians out of their homeland and into independence.

Gaius' four-year reign has never been forgotten. Although his first two years were tolerable, the effects of an illness he suffered early in his reign drove him to megalomania. He truly believed himself to be a god, equal or even superior to Jupiter. A weak, demanding tyrant, he at one time ordered that he should be saved the trouble of a sea journey across four miles (6.5 kilometres) of bay, by having a series of pontoons floated, so that he could drive across them in his chariot. When a daughter was born to him he carried her to the temple of Jupiter and placed her on the knees of the statue, saying that the child belonged to both him and Jupiter, but it was possible that he was the greater. He built a temple to himself as Jupiter Latiaris, with priests appointed to worship him. In AD 40 he marched to Gaul, and then to the edge of the English Channel as if to invade Britain. Drawing his troops up in battle array, he gave them a signal—to collect shells, as "the spoils of conquered Ocean".[2]

His greatest act of provocation to the Jews was his order that a statue of himself should be set up in the Jerusalem temple.[3] Another Maccabean uprising was averted only by the deliberate procrastination of his governor and the intervention of Agrippa. In his madness, Gaius was so great a danger that every loyal minister of the mission had to turn against him. He was assassinated by a band of leading Romans on January 24, AD 41.[4]

One of Gaius's best friends was Agrippa, the Jewish prince. On his return to Rome in about AD 35, having scraped his way out of his debts, he came back into the circles of the Emperor Tiberius. Through Antonia, who lent him money, he came into constant contact with her grandson Gaius.

In AD 36 Gaius began to plot the downfall of Tiberius and to make plans for his own accession. Agrippa aided and abetted him. One day two of them were out riding in a chariot driven by the charioteer Eutychus, described as a freedman of Agrippa. He overheard Agrippa saying that he wished the ailing Tiberius would give up in favour of Gaius, who would be a far better emperor. Eutychus said nothing at the time, but soon afterwards, when he was accused of stealing some of Agrippa's clothes, he ran away, and managed to get to Tiberius in order to warn him of his danger. On his information Agrippa was arrested and imprisoned, being released only in March, AD 37, when Tiberius died.[5] His servant brought Agrippa the good news, saying in Hebrew "The lion is dead".[6]

It was not long before the new emperor Gaius sent for him, to appoint him ruler of part of the Palestinian territory, and gave him a golden chain to wear. He was later given the tetrarchy of Antipas, who had come to Rome to protest at Agrippa's elevation, but found himself banished to Gaul.[7]

As has been suggested, these events taking place in Rome may have been a vital part of the Christian history. The details concerning Eutychus would fit very well the man named John Mark, the Beloved Disciple, who appears under the name Eutychus in a story near the end of Acts.[8] He would be seen as originally a member of Agrippa's household, his chariot driver. Though born a Gentile, he had become a proselyte of the Herodian form of the Jewish religion. He had privately turned against his reckless employer, as many others had, and while in Judea with him during the late twenties and early thirties AD, had met Jesus. John Mark was, without doubt, the unnamed first disciple who had left the Baptist to turn to Jesus.[9] To leave the Baptist was, at that time, also to leave Agrippa.

Eutychus would then have formed a close association with Jesus, bringing to him the aspirations of the many Gentile proselytes who did not wish to adopt a fully Jewish way of life, but who revered the more mystical and intellectual aspects of the religion. For some years he was Jesus' chief representative, adopting the name John Mark, and becoming known in his circles as the Beloved Disciple. For two years after the crucifixion he was in close contact with him, overseeing the writing of the fourth gospel, which was issued under his name. Then he returned with Agrippa to Rome, where the episode leading to the humiliation and six months' imprisonment of Agrippa took place. John Mark–Eutychus was consequently branded as an enemy of Agrippa, so when Agrippa was made king, he lost his influence. He was replaced as chief proselyte by Luke.

At about the same time Peter began his ascendancy among the followers of Jesus. It has also been suggested that he was the good citizen Simon of Jerusalem who at first opposed Agrippa, but was won over by his charm.[10] He and John Mark had not been in sympathy with each other during the gospel period, one of the reasons being that John was a celibate, holding the Gentile version of an ascetic discipline, while Peter was a married man. John was personally closer to Jesus, and both of them could associate with Simon Magus, who for the less sophisticated Peter was compromising the faith. But with the rise of Agrippa both John Mark and Simon receded. Jesus himself, mostly in seclusion, remained at some distance from the struggle, but eventually came to support Agrippa.

At the first sign of the rise of Agrippa, Simon Magus was deposed as Pope. His fall is recorded in the story of Ananias and Sapphira,[11] who were both rebuked by Peter for financial wrongdoing, and immediately "fell down and died" (were excommunicated, the usual fate of a fallen Pope and his associates).

In AD 36 Pilate was dismissed, and Caiaphas the high priest was also replaced. In his stead the governor appointed Jonathan Annas.[12] One of the names Jonathan used in the community was Stephen, the Crown.

The appointment of Agrippa and the prospect of his imminent return to Judea was an alarming one for Jesus' brother James. It was thought that Agrippa might well make another attempt to get at the share of the money that was stored at Qumran. James, reacting against this prospect, now re-affirmed that the coming kingdom was to be ruled by a David only, without any Herods. When his father Joseph had taken this step at the turn of the era he had allied with Theudas, the two of them calling themselves the Star and the Sceptre. James now renewed the association with Theudas, and the use of the titles. He declared a portion of the Qumran treasure to belong to the Davids, represented by himself, and moved it to a new celibate centre in Damascus. This was the time when, in the words of one of the parables, James (the Rich Man) "built bigger barns". He had new vaults constructed in Damascus, in which to store the fees and offerings given to the mission by those members of it who wanted a David as king.[13]

Copies of a work known as the Damascus Document were found among the scrolls coming from this time. It was written by a group calling themselves "the New Covenant in the land of Damascus", and it tried to justify the position of the writers, who were actually exiles from their own land. It speaks of the Star and the Sceptre, and anticipates that the Messiah, when he came, would first appear in Damascus.[14]

Between Jerusalem and Damascus, a young man called Saul often had occasion to travel. He was a fervent nationalist who thought Gentiles should be kept in a very low status, as being far inferior to Jews. The sympathy shown to Gentiles by the high priest Jonathan Annas-Stephen was regarded by him as weakness, while Jesus, the bastard brother of James, was simply a renegade, a traitor to his nation, treating Gentiles as if they were as good as Jews. One day, Saul vowed, he would rid the mission of such compromisers, ensuring that only the purest form of Judaism was taught. Only then would come the day, promised by God through prophecy, when the Romans would be wiped off the face of the earth and the Jewish world empire would prevail.

CHAPTER TWENTY-NINE

"AT THE RIGHT HAND OF GOD"

The year AD 37 brought political changes that marked the beginning of a new phase in the mission, and the first steps in the separation of the Christians from the Jews. It also saw the birth of a son and heir to Jesus and Mary Magdalene.

In September AD 36 Jesus left the enclosed life, three years after the birth of his daughter. In the case of a second child there was no enforced delay, and a child was conceived. In June AD 37, "the Word of God increased", a phrase meaning that Jesus' family line had continued.[1] The son was also called Jesus, and given the title Justus, the Righteous One, a title that had been borne by James as crown prince. Jesus Justus as an adult was later with Paul in Rome when he wrote the letter to Colossians, which included greetings from Jesus Justus.[2]

Since Jonathan Annas, or Stephen, was now high priest, there was a change in the official status of Jesus. He was publicly declared the legitimate heir of David, which meant that he had to be associated with Agrippa, preserving the longstanding alliance between the Herod kings and Jesus' family. James had withdrawn into an anti-Herodian party, but Jesus, returning to celibate life after the birth of his son, and still in contact with his ministers, was prepared, on Peter's advice, to accept the new Herod.

Annas lost no time in announcing the change that he and

Jesus had been preparing, to allow full privileges to uncircumcised Gentiles. They could have a form of organisation of their own, with very little reference to Jewish ways.[3]

This made Annas too westernised for some of the other leading men in the country. Those with more eastern views pressed for his removal, and only six months after his appointment they succeeded. The crisis which resulted in his removal is described in Acts as "the martyrdom of Stephen". From the point of view of westerners, he had been made to suffer for his support of non-Jews, those who were soon to be called Christians. He did not die, however, but simply suffered the symbolic death of excommunication.[4]

The easterners succeeded only in having him removed, but they did not get their way politically. The next appointment was even more favourable to the west, the high priesthood being given to Jonathan's next brother, Theophilus. He took the country further towards Rome, by leading them in taking the oath of loyalty to Caesar.[5]

Theophilus had played little part in the history up to this point, but it appears that he had formed a personal bond with Jesus, and remained sympathetic to his followers. (It was to Theophilus that Luke dedicated his two-volume work, Luke–Acts.)

Theophilus acted both as public high priest and as Pope to the sectarians, officiating at their atonement ceremony in the sanctuary at Mird. Jesus officiated with him, acting as his Second, filling the roles of both king and levite. When Jonathan–Stephen, in the process of being stripped of his office, "gazed into heaven and saw Jesus standing at the right hand of God",[6] it meant that he was standing outside the Holy of Holies at the Mird sanctuary, at the window through which the witness must look to observe the atonement taking place. The windows at the equivalent sanctuary at Qumran are still to be seen there. Jonathan looked into the Holy of Holies, or "heaven", and saw Jesus in the place of the second, at the right hand of "God", Theophilus.

In the following year, AD 38, the tetrarch Antipas departed from the history. When, in that year, Agrippa at last arrived back in his country, displaying his royal state, Herodias was furious at her brother's pretension. He had less right to the throne than her husband, and had forfeited the trust of many in the country. She urged that they should go to Rome and there see what their wealth could do to gain justice. The indolent Antipas at first resisted: "he was content with his tranquillity and was wary of the Roman bustle". But he eventually yielded, and they set sail, with no expense spared.

Agrippa soon heard about it and sent a deputy to Rome with information about Antipas' arrangements with the Parthians to equip an army against Gaius. The tetrarch, to his dismay, was relieved of his territory, which was given to Agrippa. He and Herodias were exiled to Lyons in Gaul, increasing the extent of the Herod estates in the south of France.[7]

Antipas was succeeded in his position in the mission by Herod of Chalcis, a brother of Agrippa. He followed the Herodian style in his personal life, having married his brother's daughter, Berenice, who at sixteen made him her second husband. Berenice, daughter of Agrippa and sister of Agrippa II, was to play a part in the later history of Acts.[8]

The long-time ally of Antipas, Theudas the Prodigal Son, now lost his position, and in a few years was to lose his head also, as a result of taking too seriously his Exodus imagery. Josephus records that in AD 44 "a certain impostor named Theudas persuaded the majority of the masses to take up their possessions and to follow him to the Jordan river. He stated that he was a prophet and that at his command the river would be parted and would provide them an easy passage". He was acting as a latter-day Joshua (one text of the gospels calls him Jesus, that is Joshua, Barabbas). But the Roman governor intervened before heaven could part the waters. Theudas was captured, and they cut off his head and brought it to Jerusalem.[9]

A new generation was beginning, and would be led by the man who took up the insights of Jesus and brought them to their triumphant conclusion, the man who would become known as the apostle Paul.

CHAPTER THIRTY

SAUL THE
INDIGNANT
STUDENT

In late AD 37, a young member of the order of Benjamin, by the name of Saul, was spending part of his prenovitiate year at Qumran. Born in September, AD 17, he was just twenty years old.[1] Having watched the laicisation of Jonathan Annas-Stephen while he held the priests' vestments, he retained a lifelong dislike for him.

Saul, with other students, watched the march of the army of the Roman governor Vitellius only a short distance from Qumran. During September Vitellius brought two legions of heavily armed infantry and other infantry and cavalry down towards the Dead Sea, intending to cross to Petra to attack Aretas the Arab, who had been an enemy of the Herods since the tetrarch had divorced his daughter to marry Herodias. Vitellius came dangerously close to the remaining Qumran treasures, and it was known that he knew of their existence. Leading Jews went to meet him and implored him not to march through their land, for, they said, it was against their tradition to allow the military standards carrying images to come on holy soil. Vitellius gave in and changed his route, then made a point of showing respect for Jewish worship by attending a festival in Jerusalem.[2]

But it was not before Saul had taken part in the composition of a pesher on the prophet Habakkuk, a work that survived and has come to us in the Dead Sea Scrolls.[3] Having been instructed in the Baptist's technique of interpreting scripture, he turned to Habakkuk, applying to it the principle of turning universals into particulars. He found in it exact statements of historical fact, predictions of all the stirring events of recent years which were the subject of conversation at Qumran. It was easy to relate the Chaldeans, who "march across the breadth of the earth to take possession of dwellings which are not their own", and who were "fearsome and terrible", to the Romans, or Kittim, or, more precisely, the armies of Vitellius who were so frighteningly close. The prophet even referred to their military standards, in a disguised form, and gave rise to the comment that the Romans "sacrifice to their standards and worship their weapons of war".[4]

When the prophet referred to a certain "arrogant man", uttering four Woes (curses) against him, it was clearly, in Saul's mind, a prediction of the man who was teaching such heresies that he was threatening the very existence of Judaism. Jesus, the "Man of a Lie" (the bastard) and the Wicked Priest, the Anti-Priest, had "flouted the law in the midst of the whole congregation", declaring himself to be a priest in the place of the descendant of Levi. He was a hater of eastern celibates, called the Poor, and had broken the purity rules. This meant he had "defiled the temple". He had suffered grievously, as anyone who was at the centre a few years before could attest. His opponents had inflicted "horrors of evil sickness and taken vengeance upon his body of flesh". His treatment was considered to be well deserved, because he had attacked the Teacher of Righteousness, the Baptist. Through divine intention he had been "humbled by means of a destroying scourge, in bitterness of soul, because he had done wickedly to his elect".[5]

Saul's involvement can be seen in two passages in the document, in which he treated verses in Habakkuk in precisely the same idiosyncratic way as he, in his later role as Paul, treated them in his epistles. In one, he changed the meaning of "the righteous shall survive by his moral steadfastness" to "the just shall live by faith [in a redeeming figure]"—in the early document, faith in the Teacher; in his later epistle to the Romans, faith in Jesus. The other Habakkuk passage spoke of people who would not believe an event because it was so extraordinary. Saul changed its meaning to "a wilful refusal to believe what ought to be believed"; the Teacher's doctrine in the early document, and the Christian doctrine in a speech in Acts 13.[6]

For the three years of his further education, in Jerusalem and in Damascus, Saul continued to attack the Christian heretics and especially their leader Jesus. He was convinced that they posed a real threat to the great work of spreading the Jewish faith among Gentiles. Allied with the Boethus family of priests, he worked for their return to the high priesthood, and looked to James in Damascus as the one who would occupy the throne of David when the Kingdom came.

By AD 39, Gaius' madness was known throughout the empire. Feeling in the east became entirely anti-Roman, and this time not even those who at one time had been pro-Rome could protest. The high priest Theophilus, who had taken the oath of loyalty to Rome, lost power, and a son of Boethus began his rise.[7]

In September, AD 39, Petronius arrived as governor, with orders to set up a statue of the emperor in the temple, and, if there was opposition, to get his way by force of arms. The previous year there had been a pogrom against Jews in Alexandria, their Greek persecutors demanding that statues of Gaius be set up in every synagogue to be worshipped. Combined action against Rome was obviously necessary, and the mission's leaders would have been among the tens of thousands of Jews who came to Petronius declaring that they would endure martyrdom rather than let this blasphemy take place.[8]

No one was sorry when Gaius was stabbed to death in a narrow alley in Rome in January, AD 41. His reign of terror had brought the two mission parties together, and the west had turned towards the east.

Combined councils had been held in Damascus. In March, AD 40, Ananias–Simon came there with Jesus from the Caesarea community. One reason for the meeting was the date. For the original Herodian scheme beginning in 41 BC, this was the end of eighty years and should have seen the end of the holy war and the conquest of the world. It had plainly not happened, and this was a serious disappointment to the order of Benjamin, whose leader Hillel had been involved in the original scheme.

Whenever a prophecy was not fulfilled, there were recriminations. The victory, it was argued, had not been sent by heaven because of errors of doctrine. A reforming process began, conducted through the debates of councils. The ardent young Saul, who was now in his last year of studies under Gamaliel in Jerusalem, came to the council determined to prove that the stumbling block had been the easy doctrine of the western mission towards Gentiles.

But there was another point of view: that the impediment was Saul himself. Palestinian practices of circumcision were alienating

Gentiles who would otherwise embrace the spiritual aspects of the religion. Jesus had always taught that Gentiles could be admitted without adopting Jewish identity.

In March, while discussions preparing the council were being held, Saul attended the noon service in the vestry room of the Damascus buildings. It was the time when the villagers and proselytes of the "Way", who had come on pilgrimage there, sat in the congregation while their priest said prayers up on the half-roof.

Jesus was permitted by the Magians to act as Second, and on some occasions stood in for the priest. He would be on duty at this service. Saul, as he had written in the commentary on Habakkuk, had the strongest objection to him: he was neither a legitimate David nor a legitimate priest.

Saul took his place in the congregation. The noon hour came, and, as was the custom, part of the roof was removed, allowing the sun to shine down to indicate the time, and to reveal the priest at his prayers above. Saul prostrated himself with the rest of the congregation, averting his eyes to avoid looking too long up into the sun. The Voice, that of Jesus, spoke to him.

Jesus knew of Saul's hostility, and spoke directly to him: "You are persecuting me". Saul replied: "You are an illegitimate". Jesus answered with the "I Am", affirming that he was a full priest. He then invited Saul into the forward part of the congregation, where he could hear the sermon. As he listened to Jesus, his strenuous objections to all that Jesus stood for began to dissolve. He recognised his own state of bondage to the Law, and the way in which it was binding others.[9]

During the days that followed Saul received instruction in the eastern part of the monastery building, the "house of Judas". Ananias–Simon took part in the instruction, as Saul began to transfer his loyalty from the Hebrews to the Hellenists. But he was soon to make a distinction between the peace and war Hellenists, rejecting the latter. It was probably Simon who gave him the lesson about the resurrection which he later used as part of the accepted teaching for the less advanced members.

Saul had begun his instruction in a state of "blindness", that is as a novice. But when he received full initiation into the party, he "saw the light of life", an expression that is found in the scrolls.

Between AD 40 and 43 he was given a revised form of education, at the end of it becoming a bishop. The following year his name was changed to Paul,[10] and he was appointed to the mission to uncircumcised Gentiles in the west.

By the year AD 43, however, changes had occurred in Damascus. The temporary unity brought about by the campaign against Gaius was broken, and there was again division between east and west. Paul, now a western bishop, suffered hostility in Damascus, and led the way in severing all connections with its methods and teaching.[11]

One of the reasons why Paul could ally with Jesus was that Jesus was now acknowledged by Agrippa, and Paul's order of Benjamin had always been loyal to the ruling Herods and would remain so. While Peter was with Agrippa, Peter and Paul came together as the two chief ministers of Jesus to assist in the work of mission to the west.

CHAPTER THIRTY-ONE

ASSASSINATION
AND CHANGE

The emperor Claudius, successor to Gaius, proved to be sufficiently benign to restore good relations between the Jews and Rome. Soon after his accession the high priest Matthias was appointed, using the name "Peace" long associated with his family.[1] As a member of the Twelve Apostles and the sponsor of the first gospel, he was the high priest whom the Christians most favoured. In his reign they were given new opportunities, and began to take on a separate identity, using the name "Christian" and the word "church" for their meetings.[2]

James, the brother of Jesus, found the climate sufficiently congenial to break off his connection with Damascus and come back to Judea, establishing Jewish Christians at Qumran. A section of the Damascus Document, written at this time, refers angrily to the "princes of Judah" (James and the other brothers of Jesus) who had deserted the eastern party to go back to the heretics.[3]

June 43 was the time for Jesus to re-emerge into the world, six years after the birth of his son. A second son was born in March 44, when once again "the Word of God increased".[4]

In June 43, as the first stage of his return, he came to Joppa, where Widows and separated wives known as Sisters, lived.

At this same season a ceremony was to take place which would formalise Peter's acceptance of Agrippa. The king had impressed many as being "by nature generous in his gifts", making it "a point of honour to be high-minded towards Gentiles".[5] Peter had previously regarded many of his ways as unclean, but the king's charm worked on him to such an extent that they became reconciled.

Peter was at Joppa, where one of his duties had been to reinstate Mary, the mother of Jesus, to membership. As Dorcas the Widow, she had "died" in the eyes of the Christians, having gone to Damascus with James. But she now returned with James and was restored to fellowship.[6]

Joppa was a celibate centre used by the uncircumcised, Gentiles and women. Their buildings had three storeys, unlike the two storeys used by Jewish villagers in whose buildings the priest prayed on the roof and the congregation were on the ground floor. Gentile buildings allowed for the priest or his substitute to be on the third floor, while the Jewish married man who carried out the work of mission to Gentiles, such as Peter, stood on the second storey. This corresponded to the roof in Jewish buildings. In Gentile buildings it was still called the "roof" because of its position.

On the "roof" was another meal table, for the Jewish missionary; he did not eat with the uncircumcised below. Peter took his sacred meal here, after praying at the noon hour like a priest.[7]

On a certain occasion in June, Peter took his place at noon on the "roof", while Jesus, in the place of the true priest, was on the third storey, above. It was the custom of the higher priest to bless and send down the tablecloth to be used by villagers at their communion.

At midday the Voice of Jesus at prayer was heard by Peter. Then the tablecloth was sent down. But on this occasion it was the kind of cloth used in the Herodian form of service, not that which the village Essenes such as Peter used. Its embroidered emblems, of animals, stood for the practice of allowing the unclean, the "beasts" into communion.

Peter objected: he was not prepared to observe communion in the Herodian form, which included having uncircumcised Gentiles on the same level as Jews. Jesus commanded him: "What God has cleansed, do not make common". In agreement with Jesus, Matthew the high priest ("God") had authorised a Herodian form of service, continuing the tradition of the Annas brothers in advancing Gentiles.

As Peter finished the service, there arrived from Caesarea messengers from Cornelius, a Roman of high standing. Cornelius was soon to use the name Luke. The head of Roman uncircumcised Gentiles, he had already been promoted to be equal to a proselyte deacon. He was a servant of Agrippa, and had sent his messengers to invite Peter to Caesarea, acting in his own name, but actually as a cover for Agrippa. Peter went to Caesarea, and took part in a ceremony in which the king was admitted into the community.[8]

While Matthew remained high priest, all of the western mission were friendly to the king. But in late AD 43 he began to show a change not unlike that which came over Herod the Great in his last few years. A former friend of Gaius, he revealed some of the same tendencies, interpreting the priestly role claimed by the Herods in the sense of incarnation of a deity, and claiming worship from his followers. He saw that the desire of the eastern part of the empire for a god-emperor could be used to help promote his family's aspirations to the throne of the Caesars.

Simon Magus, a long-standing enemy, had no doubt that he should be put out of the way. The peace Hellenists, including Peter, at first did not act, but when Matthew was deposed as high priest and a Boethusian put in his place, they protested that Agrippa "did not give God [Matthew] the glory". The two kinds of Hellenists began to come together.

James of Zebedee agreed with Simon Magus that action must be taken, but the king got wind of his plot and "killed", that is, excommunicated him. At the same time Peter was attending the Passover council of AD 44. Agrippa did not regard him as a danger, but on the advice of his brother, Herod of Chalcis, he put him under discipline, in "prison".[9]

This was enough to bring Peter back into the movement of protest. He agreed to support Simon Magus in his action in this extreme situation. Jesus, "the Light", also associated himself with the movement when Simon, as the "angel of the Lord", released Peter.[10]

Soon afterwards Agrippa went to Caesarea, where a number of men of rank were gathered. During a public festival, he appeared on an elevated platform, clad in a garment woven entirely of silver. He came out in time for the first rays of the sun at daybreak, so that he literally shone. Then his flatterers and followers, as prearranged, shouted in acclamation: "You are a god!"[11]

At once he "felt a stab of pain in his heart", and was also gripped by severe stomach pains. Over the next five days he suffered agonising pain until death released him.

Acts 12 says that an "angel of the Lord" struck him, and he was "eaten by worms". To be "eaten by worms" was to be given snake poison. The "angel of the Lord", Simon, had arranged for him to be poisoned through the agency of one of his eunuchs. Josephus does not record that he was poisoned, but he also omits the murder of Tiberius, possibly avoiding statements for which he did not have direct evidence.

The Hebrews had not played any part in the assassination, and a high priest of their party was now in power. The conspirators were forced to flee the country.

A new centre was set up in Antioch, the capital of Syria, a major city. Gentile ascetics were transferred there from Caesarea. Luke was their leader, and their Jewish ministers were Peter and Paul.[12] On the island of Cyprus in the Mediterranean an associated community, more enclosed, had also been developed. Jesus was brought there, and with him Simon Magus. But Jesus was soon to be parted decisively from his former associate, by both personal events and the pressure of Peter and Paul.[13]

It was much safer and more effective now to have centres of mission outside Judea, in Diaspora locations where the funds could be kept and councils held. Only for the great councils would they go back to Jerusalem.

But the separation of centres and money meant also a final separation of the parties. Each now conducted its own mission independently of the rest. Under Peter, the western missionaries in Antioch adopted a new name: Christians. It meant that they did not look to a ruling Herod, that a David only was to be king, and that the David was Jesus. He was understood more in a kingly than in a priestly role, but could exercise the religious duties of a king. Peter was to be his successor, and was to be head of the places of meeting of married men and women, called churches.

The year AD 44 was, then, that of the foundation of the Christian Church as a separate institution. From Antioch, it would move west to its final goal, Rome.

CHAPTER THIRTY-TWO

A FAMILY
PROBLEM

For the rest of the history there were no further serious struggles with the Jews. The Christians, moving west, spent the next twenty years establishing their own identity.

The heir of Agrippa was his son, who was to be called Agrippa II. Born in AD 27, he was approaching seventeen at the time of his father's death, so was considered too young to succeed.[1] He was educated in Rome, and was an intimate of Claudius and the emperor's family. As the only surviving son of Agrippa he did not have to fight for the succession, and appears to have had a quiet disposition. He never married, and, having no heir, was the last of the Herodian dynasty.

Like all the Herods he was in touch with the mission, but had apparently been told that the Samaritans were responsible for his father's death. His policy was consistently against them. Although his uncle Herod of Chalcis, who was given by Claudius the right to appoint high priests, had chosen a Samaritan as high priest in AD 49, Agrippa took his opportunity to oppose the Samaritan when a few years later he was brought to Rome in chains for having stirred up insurrection. Jonathan Annas was also sent to Rome on the same charge. The hearing went against them and their subordinates were put to death.[2]

Agrippa the Younger's opposition to the Samaritans was the significant political factor in the separation and survival of the Christians. Paul had Agrippa's confidence, as his order had remained loyal to him and had played no part in the murder of his father. He interested him in the Christian version of the doctrine, to the extent that Agrippa exclaimed, when hearing Paul on his last visit to Judea, "You are making me a Christian!"[3]

On the island of Cyprus in September AD 44, Paul boldly confronted the Magus, who was there under the name of the magician Bar-Jesus. He accused him of immorality in the way that Peter had previously done, sending him finally into the opposing camp.

Also on the island was Jesus, the "Word of God", briefly reunited with John Mark. Paul, who was passing through Cyprus with Barnabas on his way to a preaching mission in south Galatia, brought both of them to travel with him. At this point the decisive separation between Jesus and Simon took place. Paul was firmly in charge, interpreting the will of Jesus and articulating the theological implications of his doctrine. He took Jesus with him through Galatia, where the congregations came "to hear the Word of God". John Mark began the journey with them, but pulled out as soon as they reached the mainland. His departure was connected with the fact that he was the male representative of the Magdalene, standing in as the Beloved in the place of the queen.[4]

A personal matter now came to be of greater concern to the Christians than their problems with the Jews. After the birth of Jesus' third child and second son in March 44, Mary Magdalene decided to leave her husband.

The story of the release of Peter in Acts 12 includes a scene where he came to the door of the vestry and knocked to ask for admission, as villagers did when they came to the meeting house. Mary Magdalene, as Rhoda, was the doorkeeper, a role given to the "apostle" or to a woman in an unclean state.[5]

Hearing Peter knock, she went to tell those inside who said to her: "You are raving" (mainē)"[6] The special meaning of the word was that she belonged to one of the ecstatic orders, with associated zealotry and the way of life of the "seekers-after-smooth-things". She therefore could no longer be counted with Christians.

That there was a divorce and second marriage is implied by a statement set in March AD 50: "the Lord opened the heart" (of Lydia, the woman who appeared in Philippi).[7] The date was six years after the birth of a son in March AD 44, but Mary Magdalene in AD

50 was too old for childbearing, as she had been older than was customary at the time of her marriage twenty years before. The phrase "opened the heart" also suggests that Lydia was a virgin.

From September AD 44 Jesus had been travelling with Paul in the world, whereas according to the rules he should have again become secluded. Paul, as a former Pharisee, allowed divorce, and in writing on the subject in 1 Corinthians 7 made it clear that in discouraging divorce he was speaking for the Lord, not himself.[8]

The prescriptions he set out there were drawn from the unhappy experience of these years. Mary Magdalene, from the Christian point of view, was an unbeliever. As a close companion of Helena, she shared the views of the Magus. The decisive rejection of the Magus on Cyprus also had had the effect of excluding her from the Church, and the marriage then came under the provisions of Corinthians concerning marriages with unbelievers.

The Lord's opinion, quoted in the passage, was that there should be no divorce between a Christian husband and wife. However, if one partner was an unbeliever, it was a matter for themselves. If a partner consented to stay, the other should not bring a divorce. The unbelieving partner was consecrated through the other, so that the children were not unclean but holy. But—and this was the relevant point—"if the unbelieving partner desires to separate, let it be so; in such a case the brother or sister is not bound". Paul goes on: "For God has called us to peace". Mary was a zealot, with opposite views to those of Jesus, and had chosen to separate from him.

In the brief dominical statement in the gospels, this situation is covered: "Whoever divorces his wife and marries another commits adultery against her". But the husband in this case had not brought the divorce. The text goes on to show that a wife could bring a divorce, and the same rule applied to her.[9]

A further issue was debated among the followers of Jesus: had it been a legal marriage in the first place, since, as it appears, Mary had been previously married? If divorce was not accepted, then it had not been a marriage, and the husband was free to marry again, but the children of the present marriage would not then be legitimate. Paul took the view that, as divorce was permissible, it had been a legal marriage, the children were legitimate, and the husband was free to marry again. He remained the protector and, possibly, tutor of Jesus Justus.

In March of AD 50, six years after the birth of Jesus' last son, Paul received a message through a "vision": "Come over to Macedonia and help us". The messenger was Luke, now the close associate and physician of Jesus in the place of John Mark. In writing Acts, Luke began at this point to use the first person plural, "we", when he meant himself standing in for Jesus.[10]

Paul crossed to Philippi, and there "we" encountered Lydia, a "seller of purple" from Thyatira. It was at Thyatira, in west Asia Minor, that "Jezebel" was found, according to the writer of Revelation. It was the centre for Hellenist women's orders, and Lydia was a female bishop, empowered to make other women bishops, giving them the "purple" in exchange for promotion fees. She now became baptised into the Christian version of the doctrine.[11]

The second marriage of Jesus, to Lydia, provoked intense criticism among the eastern opponents of the Christians. A section of the Damascus Document written about this time attacks the heretical followers of "Saw" (a Hebrew letter, probably the initial of the word for "Righteous") who were "caught in fornication" by "taking a second wife while the first is alive". The writers then had to deal with the objection that King David was a polygamist, and brought forward a legend that David had not read the sealed book of the Law.[12]

Polygamy was, in fact, usual among Jews at the time. It was under Greek ascetic influence that the Essenes introduced their strict laws of marriage. The Christians were caught between normal Jewish practices and the excessive rigour of the Essenes. In the epistle to Timothy, Paul has to advise that a bishop should be "husband of one wife", as if the alternative were still possible.[13]

Luke in his gospel and Acts makes as full a disclosure as possible of the history, sometimes allowing it to be quite close to the surface. If the reading of it is a serious difficulty now, it is because the person of Jesus has been allowed to lose all humanity, contrary to the Church's own desire to teach full humanity with divinity. It has rarely achieved such a balance, for the natural reason that it is almost impossible to hold both concepts together. It may be, following the urgings of our own time, that the divinity has to be sacrificed to the humanity. Jesus, and those close to him, were frail human beings, as we all are, caught in personal dilemmas which could be solved only in terms of the particular situation, not by conformity to ideal rules.

The background history helps to amplify what the New Testament says about Jesus: "For because he himself has suffered and been tempted, he is able to help those who are tempted".[14]

CHAPTER THIRTY-THREE

AWAY FROM THE EAST

In the few years prior to AD 50, a group of party leaders were in Rome, making the first attempt to revise the doctrine in a Christian direction. They had gone there following the great council in Jerusalem in AD 46, which had seen the legal establishment of the Christians as a separate mission, allowing also their development in two directions, the east under Jewish Christians.

The Rome group included Peter and John of Zebedee, now using the name Aquila.[1] With James of Zebedee and Andrew, these four had been appointed as the new "four pillars of the world".[2] Jesus and Luke, his physician, were also present, Luke using the word "we" in narrative to indicate the presence of both.

Paul, who worked separately from Jesus after the council of Jerusalem, remained in Asia Minor to continue the work of revision. He was to some extent out of fellowship with the Rome group, having gone well beyond them at the council in his advocacy of an abandonment of Jewish identity. Peter was still partly in sympathy with James, holding that the work of the mission was to bring Gentiles into an adapted form of Judaism.

A Roman historian records that in about AD 49 Jews were expelled from Rome for "rioting at the instigation of Chrestus".[3] Christians with an outlook like that of John of Zebedee, as illustrated in his book of Revelation, were capable of fervent action in expectation of heavenly support. But Roman authority would not tolerate further trouble from the Jews. They were driven out, going back to Greece, which in their world scheme was the eastern limit of the province of Rome.

At first, John of Zebedee came with Jesus to the island of Patmos, off the coast of Asia Minor. There he wrote the first part of the book of Revelation, with letters to the seven churches of the province of Asia, conveying the will of Jesus concerning the different problems, moral and doctrinal, that were besetting them. The letter to Thyatira, in which the teaching of "Jezebel" was condemned, may have brought about the change of doctrine by Lydia that led to her rebaptism at the time of her marriage the following year.

John wrote that he was on the island of Patmos "on account of the word of God and the testimony of Jesus". He was "in the Spirit on the Lord's day", that is, acting as a presbyter at the Sunday service, when he heard behind him a loud voice telling him to write what he saw, in a book. John was facing the congregation, and Jesus was behind him in the position of priest. He turned, and saw "in the midst of the [seven] lampstands one like the Son of Man". There were candles on the holy table, in the formation still used by the Roman church: three on either side running from the centre, with the Pope in the position of the central light.[4]

From Patmos they moved to Philippi, where Jesus' marriage to Lydia took place in March AD 50. For Paul, who crossed to Europe at this time and renewed his fellowship with Jesus, the year AD 50 was "the beginning of the gospel" from which he counted the true form of Christianity.

The leaders went down to Corinth and established themselves in a Gentile celibate building attached to a synagogue, on the model used by Gentile proselytes.

The ruins of ancient Corinth have been uncovered, and the synagogue identified; the Christian building, used by the leaders for some years until they were able to return to Rome, must be nearby. Standing in Corinth and looking up to the towering hill close to the city, it is possible to imagine the feelings of Jesus and his associates, exiled to this pleasant land, but praying to return to the capital where they felt their future lay.

Paul came to Corinth in AD 51, and found Aquila, with his wife Priscilla, "recently come from Italy . . . because Claudius had commanded all the Jews to leave Rome".[5]

In June AD 53 Jesus "appeared" to Paul, giving him directions: "Do not fear; preach and do not be silent, because I am with you". He went on to speak of Paul's problems with the Jewish Christians, and of the decision to make Jesus Justus, now sixteen, his true heir.[6]

In September AD 53, in Corinth, Paul took the next step in his life, his marriage. He turned thirty-six at that season, and was now living according to the conventions of the dynastic order that Jesus followed.

Leaving Corinth at the end of the season, he "cut his hair" in Cenchreae, or, more exactly, "his head was shorn", like a sheep.[7] The image was used by Nazirites when they married, as they were likened to sheep, and because they let their hair grow long while celibate in accordance with the Nazirite vow.

The place, Cenchreae, near Corinth, gives the clue that Paul's bride was Phoebe, whom he sent to Rome a few years later, entrusted with his epistle to the Romans. Phoebe was described as "a deacon of the church in Cenchreae", one who "was a helper of Many" (as a female deacon) and "of myself" (a wife).[8] She was sent to Rome during one of the periods of separation between the births of children. It was during this absence that Paul wrote in Corinthians that it was well for the unmarried to "remain, as I do"; but it was "better to marry than to suffer the fire", (the symbol of zealotry, which could have a professed celibacy that was not observed in practice).

A further clue to the woman's identity is that before Paul came to Corinth he joined in Athens a "woman named Damaris".[9] The name Damaris is the same as Tamar, and this was the name of the virgin daughter of King David in the Old Testament.[10] Jesus was the current David king, and his daughter had been born in September AD 33, just twenty years before September AD 53, the time of Paul's marriage. The introduction of Damaris at this point is an indication that Paul married the daughter of Jesus, called Tamar as a virgin before her marriage, but Phoebe after it.

In September AD 57 a dramatic incident occurred in Ephesus to which Luke devotes considerable space.[11] One of the characteristics of Acts is the appearance of long stories and speeches which seem to have little real relevance. They in fact reflect the high points of the history, and give vital information.

A man named Demetrius, a silversmith, who made silver shrines of Artemis (Diana), began a protest because "this Paul" with his preaching was undermining his trade. (In Ephesus, the temple of Diana was one of the wonders of the ancient world.) A public demonstration took place, and when it was settled, Paul left.

This event was not, in fact, as public as it appears, and it did not concern the worship of the real Diana. The tumult took place in a "church" (*ekklēsia*), and the man who tried to moderate was a "scribe" (*grammateus*). As one of the assumptions of the pesharist is that words always have the same meaning, this was a debate within one of the churches of the mission, presided over by one of the Scribes. It concerned missionary methods: whether it was permissible to allow pagans to believe that the Jewish priests and levites were incarnations of pagan gods. It had long been held that a priest was the incarnation of a Jewish god, but the Herodian mission had allowed this to go further, with the aim of making conversion of Gentiles as easy as possible. Ministers could be presented as an incarnation of Zeus and Hermes. This was the reason for the extraordinary scenes in Lystra, some years before, when Barnabas and Paul had been offered worship as if they were pagan gods.[12] Similarly, Helena could be presented by the Magians as an incarnation of Diana of the Ephesians.

The Christian reformers tried to stop this practice, but they met opposition in Ephesus, where the cult was not only a useful means of proselytisation, but was financially rewarding, as silver statuettes of Helena–Diana were sold to the devotees. Paul was, in fact, defeated in the argument, and was driven out of Ephesus, where he had been a bishop for some years.

Another of Luke's strange stories, that of the seven sons of Sceva, contains in a disguised form the account of the murder of Jonathan Annas by the Roman governor Felix.[13] Josephus gives the story directly. Jonathan had become a "constant nuisance" to Felix by his incessant attempts to interfere in the governing of the state. Felix arranged for "certain brigands" to go up to Jerusalem as if to worship God. They had daggers under their clothes, and they mingled with the crowds around Jonathan, got close to him, and stabbed him to death. The murder remained unpunished.[14] Behind it was undoubtedly the fact that Felix's brother-in-law was Agrippa II,[15] who retained a lifelong hatred of Samaritans, including Jonathan, after their involvement in the murder of his father.

Another assassination in Jerusalem took place several years later, showing the same intense party divisions in the homeland. James, the brother of Jesus, was killed at the orders of Ananus the Younger, who had just become high priest (in AD 62). Ananus convened the Sanhedrin and brought before them James and certain others. They were accused of having transgressed the Law, and delivered up to be stoned. Josephus records the event,[16] attributing it to the rash and daring character of the youngest Ananus, also to the fact that he was a Sadducee, "who are indeed more heartless than any of the other Jews when they sit in judgment".

The Church's records of it[17] say that it was because James was telling people that Jesus was the Saviour, and some people took this to mean that he was the Christ. They say also that the death of James fulfilled a verse from Isaiah (3:10), which they quote in the form "Let us do away with the righteous man, for he is unprofitable to us. Yet they shall eat the fruit of their works".

A cautious suggestion may be made—subject to closer study of the text—that the newly announced fragment of scroll which speaks of the death of a Messiah[18] may be referring to the death of James. The fragment clearly comes from Qumran, as it uses phrases found elsewhere in the scrolls (the Branch of David, the Prince of the Congregation as a name for the Messiah, and use of the Suffering Servant theme from Isaiah 53). It is therefore written by the opponents of Jesus and Paul. But James was the Messiah for Hebrews. If his death was about to occur, or had occurred (depending on the tense of the verb), it could be interpreted by his supporters in the way that the crucifixion had been interpreted, in terms of the Suffering Servant of Isaiah.

But the death of James was part of eastern Jewish Christian history. In Ephesus in AD 57, Paul and his party were accepting the fact that there was very little sympathy left for them in the east. Their thoughts had for some time been turning towards Rome as a new base for their mission. Rome had once been defined as the far west of the Jewish empire, with Jerusalem at the centre and Persia at the far east. But now the map was redrawn. Rome would be the centre, Jerusalem would be its eastern limit, and the western limit would be Spain, or even beyond. The Mountain, the holy city, had been moved, by faith. From now on the New Jerusalem would be established amidst the seven hills of Rome.

CHAPTER THIRTY-FOUR

THE GREAT PENTECOST

On leaving Ephesus, Paul began to make arrangements for the next few years, vital years for calendar theorists.

The year AD 60 was 4000 if no zero generation were allowed.[1] On the reckoning of some, a catastrophic event was due to take place, of the kind predicted in the scrolls and the gospels. The sun would be darkened, the moon not give its light, the stars would fall from heaven, and the powers in heaven would be shaken. Then the Son of Man, the king, would descend from the skies with "Great Power" (the cardinal) and "Glory" (the bishop).[2] When allied to ambitions for empire, the prophecy was understood also as describing the scene when the Jews would be swept into world rule. God would intervene to set up a Jewish emperor, either in the east or west.

The event was understood also as a "birth", and the "labour pains" (called the Tribulation) would begin three and a half years beforehand.

Paul had a slightly different version of the prophecy because of the method of his calendar of allowing a zero year from creation.[3] For him, the "labour pains" would begin in June AD 58, at Pentecost, and the End (the Eschaton) would come in December AD 61.

Early in AD 58 Paul announced that he intended to be in Jerusalem by Pentecost. Gaining, after some difficulty, the agreement of Jesus in Corinth,[4] he brought him and some of the ministers to Troas, from where they would begin the sea journey to the homeland.

In Troas there was a reunion between Paul and John Mark, or Eutychus. They had always had different opinions, especially on the matter of the Agrippa family. But Agrippa II was far less erratic than his father, and the personal events that had kept John Mark away from Jesus since AD 44 were now well in the past. The story of the reunion is told in the episode of the "young man", Eutychus, falling down from a third storey while Paul was preaching, being taken up "dead", and being "restored to life" by Paul. John Mark (who was now an old man) re-enacted his career: his high status as a substitute priest on the third storey of a Gentile place of worship, then his being reduced to the status of novice and excommunicated. He was then formally received back by Paul and made a member of the Roman Church.[5]

The party arrived in Judea in time for Pentecost, visiting both Qumran and the capital. Tension was high on a day at the June solstice when a vindication might be expected.

With a similar purpose in mind, Apollos the Egyptian, an associate of Paul, had also come to Jerusalem. According to his view of prophecy, built on the Exodus theme, there should be an end of the Exodus and a "fall of Jericho" in the year AD 58. But "Jericho" was now Jerusalem, which would fall to him as its "Joshua", its commander-in-chief. He came to the Mount of Olives building, five stadia across the Kidron valley from the city. From here the procession of conquest, like a coronation procession, would begin. Gesturing towards Jerusalem, he demanded that its walls fall down.

Josephus records this as one of the many regrettable incidents of the excitable period leading up to the fall of Jerusalem. Masses of the common people had followed, believing the prophecy. Felix, the governor, hearing of the rally, sent a large force of cavalry and infantry, slew four hundred, and took two hundred prisoners. "The Egyptian himself escaped from the battle and disappeared."[6]

Paul also was made to suffer in the atmosphere of eschatological excitement. When, at the Pentecost season, there was no sign of the onset of the Tribulation, he was blamed, and accused of bringing unclean people into sacred places.[7] He was obliged to explain himself in a series of hearings, in which he gave a full account of his life and doctrine.

After one of the hearings, Jesus came to visit him during the night. He supported Paul's hopes: "Be of good cheer. As you have been a minister of mine in Jerusalem, so you will be in Rome".[8] The word for "minister" was "martyr", meaning "witness", one of the witnesses of the atonement. But it had been given another sense, which was to be fulfilled in the case of Paul some years later.

He and his party spent the next two years in Judea, until June AD 60. They were in fact free, in the civil sense, but persecuted by the other ministers. Paul was protected by the king and by Felix the governor. As the year of the grand climax approached, however, he and all his associates took their opportunity to board a ship for Rome.

CHAPTER THIRTY-FIVE

THE FINAL JOURNEY

On board the ship that set out in June AD 60, was not only Paul, but Peter, and, since "we" was used in the narrative, Jesus and Luke.[1]

One way of looking at the prophecies for the year 4000 maintained that the catastrophic events might happen in September 60, on the Day of Atonement; or, alternately they could occur at the feast of Dedication near the beginning of December. Those who held such beliefs thought that it was safer to be on an island, from where, once the crisis was over, they could set out for the centre of empire, where they would find only people who had been initiated into the community. All others would have perished.

The island of Crete, on the longitude running between Europe and Asia, was appropriately placed between east and west. They came to its eastern harbour, Fair Havens, by the Day of Atonement. When nothing was seen on the east side, they moved round to Phoenix on the west, where they looked "north-west and south-west", towards both corners of the west.[2] (The translation alters the text to "north-east and south-east", as this was the case at the harbour at Phoenix. But it is one of Luke's deliberate errors intended to alert the critical reader.)

They waited here until the feast of Dedication, when there was a storm which some of them chose to interpret in eschatological terms: "neither sun nor stars appeared for many a day".[3] It might be a sign that something had happened in Rome. But at the same time it was the kind of "storm at sea" that took place whenever there was a non-fulfilment; a form of symbolism used several times in the gospels. There was a loss of confidence when they discovered that the heavenly calendar was against them.

The next possible date was January 1, AD 61, the Julian beginning of the year 4000 if a zero year was allowed from creation. If heaven favoured a Julian date, however, heaven must favour the west. The westernmost island was Malta, and they decided to sail on to there.

They reached Malta on the night of December 31, and landed, in the normal fashion, by dawn.[4] They intended to stay for the next three months in a communal celibate house on the island. There was no literal shipwreck; Luke's vivid account of an apparent disaster uses double meanings to convey the quarrels that broke out when there was again a non-fulfilment.

As they stood at the fire in the equivalent of the vestry building in the Malta celibate house, Paul was attacked by a "viper" which came out of the "fire"; it was also called a "wild beast". That meant he was again being accused by his political enemies of being the impediment to the fulfilment. This time there was an actual attempt to poison him, but he was able to evade it.

> When the barbarians (Rome members) saw the viper ("wild beast") hanging from his hand, they said to one another, "No doubt this man is a murderer . . . Justice has not allowed him to live." He, however, shook off the "wild beast" into the fire and suffered no harm. They waited, expecting him to swell up or suddenly fall down dead; but when they had waited a long time and saw no misfortune come to him, they changed their minds and said that he was a god.[5]

In March AD 61, they boarded another ship and sailed to Rome. Arriving on Easter Sunday, twenty-eight years from the crucifixion, the party went to their communal centre near the Appian Way, in the region of the catacombs.[6] They would continue to use the catacombs, a reproduction of the caves in faraway Qumran, sometimes to escape from authority, sometimes to bury their dead, the bodies lying on shelves to await the resurrection.

There was no cataclysm, no sudden empire. The date was adjusted again; it might be in the version of the great year that would fall in AD 64. Paul stayed in safe-keeping, awaiting hearings on charges arising from his association with Felix, who was being tried before the emperor for a series of misdemeanours while he was governor, especially the murder of Jonathan Annas.

Paul's last letter was written to Timothy, whom he had appointed as his successor in Ephesus. In it he sent a coded message: "The Word of God is not fettered"[7] meaning that Jesus was not implicated in the charges against Paul, and was living in freedom.

In March AD 64, the Christians and Jews who held by the prophecy rioted. Numbers of them were thrown into prison, and their associates, men like Peter and Paul, were kept under surveillance. The emperor was Nero, a fanatical tyrant. When Rome was partly destroyed by fire in July of that year, Nero was suspected of having started it, and he immediately looked for scapegoats. The Christians were an obvious choice.

Knowing the danger he was in, Peter tried to flee from Rome. He got as far as the church near the Appian Way, now called Domine Quo Vadis. Jesus met him there, and persuaded him to go back, to face a martyrdom such as had been accepted from the beginning by those who had vowed their readiness to shed their blood for their religion. The legend says that a visionary Jesus appeared to him, but it was the real Jesus.

Paul, too, was taken out to his death, a fate he had foreseen in writing the letter to Timothy. Peter was crucified in imitation of his master.[8]

Tacitus, the Roman historian, supplies the record of Nero's persecution:

> To scotch the rumour [that he started the fire], Nero substituted as culprits, and punished with the utmost refinements of cruelty, a class of men, loathed for their vices, whom the crowd styled Christians. Christus, the founder of the name, had undergone the death penalty in the reign of Tiberius, by sentence of the procurator Pontius Pilate, and the pernicious superstition was checked for a moment, only to break out once more, not merely in Judea, the home of the disease, but in the capital itself . . .
>
> First, then, the confessed members of the sect were arrested; next, on their disclosures, vast numbers were convicted, not so much on the count of arson as for hatred of the human race. And derision accompanied their end: they were covered with wild beast's skins and torn to death by dogs; or they were fastened on crosses, and,

when daylight failed, were burned to serve as lamps by night.[9]

There is no record of the final days of Jesus himself. He was seventy years old in AD 64, and it is probable that he died of old age in seclusion in Rome. It may be also that his family travelled north, fearing the persecution that came with the renewal of hopes for empire. There was a Herodian estate in the south of France, and they may have found refuge there, beginning the many legends found in France and England, such as that of the Holy Grail.

In AD 70, Jerusalem went up in flames, and in AD 74 the zealots destroyed themselves in a mass suicide on Masada. Nothing of the material hopes of the Kingdom of the Jews remained. But it had become the Kingdom of God, a spiritual empire held in the hearts and minds of men and women. In that more enduring form, it is with us still.

APPENDIX I

CHRONOLOGY

INTRODUCTION

A great deal of the detail of the history is discovered by a close study of the chronology given in the pesher.

The ascetic community which met at Qumran and in the Wilderness of Judea was united by its use of the solar calendar. Their different days for feasts and other observances distinguished them from ordinary Jews attending the Jerusalem temple and keeping a lunar calendar, the one that is still in use in Jewish religion.

The solar calendar had a year of 364 days, whereas the lunarists had a year of 354 days. In one of their works the solarists accuse the moon of corrupting the calendar, because it "comes in ten days too soon". Those who follow it are disobeying God by observing the festivals on the wrong dates (*Jub* 6:36-38).

A year of 364 days is 1¼ days or 30 hours short of the true solar year. The solar year of 365¼ days is reflected in the Julian calendar that most of the world now uses. It was introduced by Julius Caesar in 45 BC as a more accurate and less cumbersome way of measuring time than methods previously used. It has a year of 365 days, with the extra ¼ made up by an extra day, February 29, every four years.

A calendar must be kept in line with the actual movements of the sun; otherwise, after a number of years, its dates will be out of synchronisation with actual time; thus spring will have fallen back to what is actually winter. The method of bringing it into line is called an intercalation; February 29 is an intercalation. For the solar calendar of 364 days it has not so far been clear what the method of intercalation was. However, from certain detail in the book of Daniel it can be suggested, and the pesher of the gospels confirms, that the method was to insert 17½ days every 14 years. (In 14 years the calendar has fallen behind the sun by 420 hours, or 17½ days. A unit of 17½ days appears to be awkward, but is not in solar practice: it is 2½ weeks, and a half-week was a normal unit in the reckoning of those who used the solar calendar. See Dan 9:27.)

A normal year of 364 days was very easy to handle. It gave 52 weeks of 7 days each. (The week of 7 days was a special Jewish practice not observed in the Roman world. It came with the practice of observing every seventh day, Saturday, as a day of rest.)

With an exactly even number of weeks, the use of the solar calendar encouraged the idea of the perfect symmetry of the world. The 1st of the first month was (in the normative position) a Wednesday, and this was always the same every year, similarly with all days. It was always possible to say on what day of the week a certain date fell.

The habits derived from using it led to the notion that not only nature but the processes of history ran with perfect symmetry. God had set the sun in the sky (as opposed to the disobedient moon) as a heavenly clock, measuring days, weeks, years, multiples of years, and epochs. And as the seventh day was the holy one, so the greater divisions of time were governed by the number seven.

Seven times seven was very significant, and the years were believed to be divided into sets of 49 years, seven "weeks" of years. The book of Jubilees, which one of the Qumran writings recommends (CD 16:3–4) divides Old Testament history into sets of jubilees (49 years for this work, although in the Old Testament itself 50 years).

The major divisions of historical time were sets of 490 years. These are found in a work called the Apocalypse of Enoch, in Daniel, and in some of the scrolls fragments (4Q 180–181, 4Q 384–389, 4Q 247, 11QMelch).

Once the belief in such divisions was accepted, there was opportunity for would-be prophets. At the mathematically great divisions of time, God surely had, and would, send great events. The Essene solarists, who had a public reputation for being prophets, set to work to discover the intervals at which past great events had occurred, in order to construct a scheme that would enable them to predict future crises.

Their interest in a mathematically governed order of the universe was encouraged by their contact with Pythagorean thought, which was widely held in the hellenistic culture of the day. The Essenes were regarded by their contemporaries as following the way of life taught to the Greeks by Pythagoras (*Ant.* 15:371). One of their main concerns, and that of other ascetics who came to associate with them, was to predict coming events, and especially the end of the present order of human life and the coming of a final crisis that would inaugurate a new order. Many of them held that a crisis of that kind was to come at about the time Jesus lived. Their beliefs were to have a profound effect on his life.

A prophecy on which they relied, found in the Apocalypse of Enoch (given below) had made the great events (Noah's flood, Abraham, the Exodus) occur at regular intervals of 490 years. These were included in a system which interpreted the prophets' own time as the seventh world-week (490 years) from creation. As they lived in 238 BC (as may be calculated), the world must have been created in 3668 BC 7 × 490 years before their time. Soon after this system was established, however, they had reason to alter the scheme, and the date of creation was altered in consequence.

All of the systems suppose that the world had been created approximately 4000 years before. The general figure was derived from the Old Testament, but they had no hesitation in adjusting the detail.

It had become apparent to these prophets, from the second century BC onwards, that they were living in mathematically significant times. A number of schemes were evolved and corrected. Various forms of the schemes are found in works relying on the solar calendar (Enoch, Daniel, Jubilees, the Testaments of the Twelve Patriarchs, and parts of the Dead Sea Scrolls). These are well known, but it has not always been realised that they are related to one another and that their evolution can be traced.

The most interesting consequence of the study is the discovery of the basis on which the Christian era was set.

The Great Days

As excitement intensified, the question also arose, what season and what day would the great event come. The solar calendar offered a feature which narrowed the choices down.

Its 364 days were divided into four quarters of 91 days each. Each season consisted of three months of 30 days, and there was an extra day in every quarter. These four extra days in the year, because they were additional to a perfectly tidy 360 days, were treated as special days, the Great Days on which the big events would happen. They were placed at the beginning of the first, fourth, seventh and tenth months, as is shown in *Jub* 6:23. It is shown there also that these were the days when the great crises took place. But they were not called the 1st of the month; they were placed before the 1st, and called the 31st of the previous month, although treated as part of the following. They were actually a kind of zero day.

The full solar calendar, in its normative position, may be set out in Table A:

Table A
SOLAR CALENDAR (Day Position)

	I Equ. (Spring)					II					III				
Sun		5	12	19	26		3	10	17	24	1	8	[15]	22	29
Mon		6	13	20	27		4	11	18	25	2	9	16	23	30
Tue		7	[14]	21	28		5	12	19	26	3	10	17	24	[31]
Wed	1	8	15	22	29		6	13	20	27	4	11	18	25	
Thu	2	9	16	23	30		7	14	21	28	5	12	19	26	
Fri	3	10	17	24		1	8	15	22	29	6	13	20	27	
Sat	4	11	18	25		2	9	16	23	30	7	14	21	28	

	IV Sol. (Summer)					V					VI				
Sun		5	12	19	26		3	10	17	24	1	8	15	22	29
Mon		6	13	20	27		4	11	18	25	2	9	16	23	30
Tue		7	14	21	28		5	12	19	26	3	10	17	24	[31]
Wed	1	8	15	22	29		6	13	20	27	4	11	18	25	
Thu	2	9	16	23	30		7	14	21	28	5	12	19	26	
Fri	3	10	17	24		1	8	15	22	29	6	13	20	27	
Sat	4	11	18	25		2	9	16	23	30	7	14	21	28	

	VII Equ. (Autumn)					VIII					IX				
Sun		5	12	19	26		3	10	17	24	1	8	15	22	29
Mon		6	13	20	27		4	11	18	25	2	9	16	23	30
Tue		7	14	21	28		5	12	19	26	3	10	17	24	[31]
Wed	1	8	[15]	22	29		6	13	20	27	4	11	18	25	
Thu	2	9	16	23	30		7	14	21	28	5	12	19	26	
Fri	3	[10]	17	24		1	8	15	22	29	6	13	20	27	
Sat	4	11	18	25		2	9	16	23	30	7	14	21	28	

	X Sol. (Winter)					XI					XII				
Sun		5	12	19	26		3	10	17	24	1	8	15	22	29
Mon		6	13	20	27		4	11	18	25	2	9	16	23	30
Tue		7	14	21	28		5	12	19	26	3	10	17	24	[31]
Wed	1	8	15	22	29		6	13	20	27	4	11	18	25	
Thu	2	9	16	23	30		7	14	21	28	5	12	19	26	
Fri	3	10	17	24		1	8	15	22	29	6	13	20	27	
Sat	4	11	18	25		2	9	16	23	30	7	14	21	28	

I	Month beginning near March equinox. See further Table C (p. 186)	14/I	Passover
		15/III	Pentecost
IV	Month begining near June solstice	10/VII	Atonement
VII	Month beginning near September equinox	15/VII	Tabernacles
X	Month beginning near December solstice	31sts counted with the following month	

The quarters were related to the equinoxes and solstices of the sun: about March 20 and September 22, when the night and day are of equal length (equinoxes), and about June 21 and December 22, when they are at their most unequal (solstices). The 31sts were placed as near to these days as possible, although, as the symmetry of the calendar was out of accord with the actual intervals between these points, they usually formed an artificial equinox or solstice. So, in effect, heaven would send the great events at the equinoxes or solstices, but more exactly on the 31st near to these points.

The question of the season raised social and political issues. The ascetic communities were hierarchically graded, priests and levites being superior and laymen being inferior. The laity were capable of observing which was the longest day or longest night, but it needed the more exact knowledge of the priests to discern the equinoxes. March and September had consequently come to be the seasons for priests, and a crisis happening then would be a sign that heaven's calendar was a priestly one; if it occurred at the solstices, heaven was deemed to be inclined towards the laity.

In addition to the 31sts there was a chance that heaven might act on the dates of the traditional Jewish festivals: Passover, the 14th of the first month; Atonement, the 10th of the seventh month; Tabernacles, the 15th of the seventh month; or Pentecost, which, although it had no fixed date in the Old Testament, had been given a date by the solarists of the 15th of the third month. But the preferred dates were the 31sts.

The various schemes of the solarists for the great years may first be set out. It will be seen that in their evolved form they were crucial for the history of Jesus and his associates. They had begun much earlier, however, and they can only be understood when their earlier stages are seen.

Following this, a very exact chronology will be set out. It will be seen that the chronological notes in the pesher, when they are studied in the light of the calendar, provide the information that is needed. It will also be seen that the reasons for many of the events lie in the times.

The traditional terms BC and AD are used, in order to avoid confusion.

SCHEMES FOR THE YEARS
The actual events which were incorporated in the various schemes may first be set out. The dates are either known from the external histories, or are derived from the pesher; in the latter case they are marked (p).

Main Events

BC	238	(p)	Formation of the Plant of Righteousness (*1 Enoch* 93:10)
	167		The "abomination of desolation". Antiochus Epiphanes sets up a statue of Zeus in the temple (1 Macc 1:54)
	164		Temple rededicated after Maccabean wars (December) (1 Macc 4:52)
	140		Essenes expelled to Qumran (*T. Levi* 17:10)
	103		Judas the Essene acts as prophet (*Ant.* 13:311)
	63		Pompey takes Jerusalem (*Ant.* 14:71)
	45		Introduction of the Julian calendar
	44	(p)	Magians combine the Julian and solar calendars (A 19:19)
	40		Herod the Great takes over royal power (*Ant.* 14:389)
	37		Herod takes over Jerusalem (*Ant.* 14:487)
	31		The earthquake at Qumran (*Ant.* 15:121)
	20		Herod begins to restore the temple (*Ant.* 15:380)
	11	(p)	Qumran reoccupied
	8	(p)	Birth of John the Baptist (September)
	7	(p)	Birth of Jesus (March)
	4		Death of Herod (*Ant.* 17:190)
AD	6		Uprising under Judas the Galilean (*Ant.* 18:3, A 5:37)
	29		Ministry of Jesus begins (Lk 3:1)
	33	(p)	Crucifixion (March)
	40	(p)	Conversion of Paul
	44		Death of Herod Agrippa I (*Ant* 19:350)
	49		Accession of Herod Agrippa II (*Ant.* 20:104)
	50	(p)	Christians establish basis in Europe
	54		Accession of Emperor Nero
	58	(p)	Paul's final visit to Jerusalem
	60	(p)	The journey to Rome
	64		Persecution of Christians by Nero (Tac. *Ann.* 15:44)
	70		Destruction of Jerusalem

The Original Scheme of World History

A scheme of world history based on the solar calendar, and showing every sign of having been written as the first of several schemes, is found in the Apocalypse of Enoch (*1 Enoch* 93:3–10, 91:12–16).

The world is to last 4900 years, 10 x 490. Its history will be concluded by the Last Judgment and a new heaven. A great event took place at the end of each "week" (world week), the greatest so far being the seventh, the formation of the Plant of Righteousness, the writers of the prophecy. (They were probably the expelled descendants of the Zadoks and Davids forming themselves into a new community, proto-Essenes, to study Greek learning of the kind found in the books of Enoch.)

BC–AD	Anno Mundi	World week	Event
BC 3668	0	0	Creation
3178	490	1	Enoch born
2688	980	2	Noah and the flood
2198	1470	3	Abraham
1708	1960	4	Moses and the Exodus
1218	2450	5	The first temple built
728	2940	6	Fall of Jerusalem (not the correct date)
238	3430	7	Formation of the Plant of Righteousness
AD 253	3920	8	Restoration of the temple to the Davids
743	4410	9	Righteous judgment revealed to all
1233	4900	10	The Last Judgment

The last three items are, of course, prophecies. The important belief that remained from this scheme was that in the eighth world week, the year 3920 AM, there would come a restoration of the David kings and of the priests associated with them. They would regain control of the temple, restoring it to the true kind of worship that the first temple had seen.

Revision of the Prophecy During the Maccabean Wars

The early Essenes worked with the Maccabees to throw off the Seleucids (1 Macc 2:42). During the three years of the war of liberation they apparently expected to regain the temple for themselves, and they wrote the book of Daniel, containing some consequent revisions of their chronology. They now saw that the Restoration of 3920 was about to come, so they declared their current year (168 BC), which had been 3500 for them, to be, rather, 3920. The world had been created 420 years earlier than they had supposed, and all dates in the scheme had consequently to be adjusted. The known adjustments are in Daniel Chapter 9 and the book of Jubilees. The incorrect date for the fall of Jerusalem, 728 BC, was maintained.

BC	AM	World week	Event
4088	0	0	Creation
1638	2450	5	Entry to the Promised Land (Jub. 50:4)

1148	2940	6	
658	3430	7	Return from exile, 70 years after fall of Jerusalem in 728 BC (Dan 9:2,25)
168	3920	8	RESTORATION (Dan 9:24)
88	4000	-	Critical event in 4000, as a system of dating in 40s has now been incorporated

Revision Following Correction of Date of Fall of Jerusalem

When the Essenes did not regain the temple, and when no suitable event occurred in 88 BC (the year 4000), a reason was sought, and the error concerning the date of the fall of Jerusalem was discovered. A correction was made, and a nearly correct date was arrived at, 581 BC (actual date on present reckoning, 587 BC). The scheme was again revised, the result being found in the *Testament of Levi* 17 (part of the *Testaments of Twelve Patriarchs*). The AM dates now arrived at remained those held during the New Testament period.

BC–AD	AM	World Week	Jub	"Week" (7 years)	Event
BC 3941	0	0	0	0	Creation
581					Fall of Jerusalem
511	3430	7	0		Return from exile (*TLevi* 17:2)
462			1		First high priest (*TLevi* 17:2)
413			2		Second high priest (*TLevi* 17:3) etc.
168			7	0	"Pollution" in seventh jubilee of the world week (Antiochus) (*TLevi* 17:8)
161				1	
140				4	Essenes "return to the land of their desolation" (exile to Qumran) (*TLevi* 17:10)
133				5	
119			8	7	Eighth jubilee of world week
70			9		Ninth jubilee of world week
41	3900				Begin last millennium of world
21	3920	8			RESTORATION in eighth world week
1	3940				End first generation of millennium

AD	1	3941		
	29	3969	1	
	30	3970		
	40	3980		
	50	3990		
	60	4000		Critical event for the year 4000
	960	4900	10	Last Judgment

Exodus–Holy War Schemes

From the time of the exile of Essenes to Qumran, a new way of interpreting history was found. Present events were believed to be repeating the pattern of events in the Old Testament, from the Exodus onwards. The Exodus and the Holy War that followed it were each thought to have lasted forty years (Deut 1:3, 1QM 2:6–14), and the reigns of Kings David and Solomon were also said to have lasted forty years (2 Sam 5:4, 1 K 11:42). With a new interest in systems governed by 4, events in generations of forty years were now combined with the jubilees.

The original scheme is set out in typological form in A 13:17–25, where it appears to mean the actual history, but the terms for times indicate that it has a pesher. It was conceived as a plan for the five generations between 3800 and 4000 (141 BC and AD 60), partly retrospectively, as 141 BC was not known to be 3800 until after the correction.

BC–AD		AM (corrected)	Generation	Event
BC	141	3800	0	New Exodus for exiles to Qumran
	101	3840	1	New Holy War
	61	3880	2	Occupation of land. Judges, Samuel
	41	3900		Lesser kingship. Saul
	21	3920	3	RESTORATION. King David
AD	20	3960	4	Solomon
	60	4000	5	Divided kingdom

The terms "forty year time" (A 13:18) and "forty years" (A 13:21) always have a pesher sense "at year 40". In A 13:20 "450 years" means "at year 450", and it means 61 BC, forty years before 21 BC, which was year 490 of the eighth world week, 3920 AM.

The Old Testament names "Samuel", "Saul", "David" were used as pseudonyms for real figures who appeared at this time.

Herod the Great's Revision of the Exodus-Holy War Scheme

Herod the Great, taking royal power in 40 BC, and encouraging the ascetic community in its fervour for renewing Judaism, found himself at the beginning of the last millennium of world history (41 BC was 3900 AM). With the expectations associated with this fact he combined a new Exodus-Holy War, as he himself had begun a new phase and such a scheme was an expression of a new start. To set an Exodus at 3900 would have the further effect of cancelling out the restoration of the Davids expected in 3920. He or his advisers made a bold alteration in the prophecy.

They further drew on another point: that if a zero year were allowed from creation, all year dates should be one year later, so that 40 BC was 3900 AM. This set of dates continued to be used in addition to the previous ones. They are called here "lunisolar", and the previous ones "solar", as those using the zero year retained some features of the orthodox lunar calendar. Herod's plan was:

BC–AD		AM–S(olar)	AM–LS (lunisolar)	Event
BC	41	3900		
	40	3901	3900	New Exodus
	1	3940		
AD	1	3941	3940	New Holy War
	40	3980		
	41		3980	End of Holy War

The first forty years would be not only a new Exodus but, as the first generation of the new millennium, the period for gaining 600 000 members of the new Israel in the Diaspora, according to the plan described in Chapter 6. It would be concluded, not only by "entry to the Promised Land" (*hē epangelia*, "the promise", p-the Promised Land), but by a "harvest", the "reaping" of the full number of members.

Herod's scheme was put into practice by one party; it gave a chronological basis for the zealot uprising as a Holy War. The War Scroll (1QM) contains the more detailed working out of the forty years (col. 2). Its essential point was that the first twenty years would be spent in the east, and the second twenty years in the west, conquering the "sons of Ham and Japheth" (Ham, Egyptians; Japheth, Greeks and Romans).

The Anti-Herodian Revisions

The solarists associated with Herod still hoped for a form of restoration in 21 BC, if not the full return of the Davids, at least a return of the solar priests, the descendants of Zadok and Abiathar, and the Levi priests associated with them, to the temple. In this hope they offered the Temple Scroll, for if Herod adopted their plan for the rebuilding of the temple he would also give it over to them. But Herod rejected their plan.

A series of anti-Herodian parties sprang up, each with their own new Exodus. It was from these that the Christians evolved, and the pesher gives information about their schemes.

a) The first anti-Herodian revision, reflected in Jn 2:20, dated itself from 21 BC, the year of the frustrated Restoration. The new set of dates was:

BC–AD		AM–S	Event
BC	21	3920	Exodus–Mount Sinai–Tabernacle (*Jub.* 1:1)
AD	20	3960	Holy War
AD	60	4000	End of Holy War

Another kind of adjustment was made by some members of this party. The year 21 BC had been 3920, the end of a world week and the end of a jubilee. As with all units of time, it was possible to declare a zero unit from creation, thus postponing the date by another unit. A zero jubilee was declared, called the Last Jubilee. The phrase appears in a fragment of the scrolls, 11QMelch 7, in a context that associates it with the Teacher of Righteousness. The effect was to postpone the expected events to AD 29, 49 years later. This is the background of the announcement of Jesus in September AD 29, when he read in the synagogue the words of Isa 61:1–2 concerning "the acceptable year of the Lord" (*eniauton kyriou dekton*, meaning the jubilee year for the release of captives) and announced "Today this scripture has been fulfilled in your hearing" (Lk 4:16–21). The gospel period was the time when the postponed Restoration should come at the end of the Last Jubilee. See further p. 174 on Jn 2:20.

b) The order of Ephraim, Egyptian Therapeutae, had not supported the Herods as rulers, but wanted a return of David kings. Although in the Diaspora, they were on many points in sympathy with the Palestinian Essenes.

They had made a revision of doctrine in 31 BC, shortly before the earthquake; for this and other reasons their leader was called "Earthquake". By allowing a zero decade, they could treat 31 as the beginning of the millennium (solar). Consequently when they joined the anti-Herodian groups, they began their new Exodus ten years later than 21, in 11 BC. Their scheme was:

BC–AD		AM–S	Event
BC	31	3910	Millennium begins
BC	11	3930	Exodus

AD	30	3970	Holy War
AD	70	4010	End of Holy War

One of the variant forms of 3970 (see Variations on the Year, next page) fell in September AD 33; this was "year 40" of their Exodus. Consequently, its "year 38" (a significant year in Exodus theory, see Deut 2:14) fell in September AD 31. It was at this season that Jn 5:5 speaks of the man at the pool, who was "ill" in "year 38".

Since the Last Jubilee, now in 3969, was to fall in AD 29 according to the adjustment noted in (a) above, it was possible to combine it with revised Exodus scheme (b). The different prophecies came together in the gospel period, making it a time of intense expectation.

The final date for the proponents of a Holy War under this plan became, in actual fact, that of the fall of Jerusalem. They had become and remained involved with zealotry, and the date may well have been a factor in their attack on the Romans.

It was this group that reoccupied Qumran, some twenty years after the earthquake. The reoccupation gave them a definite starting point for a new order, and forty years later some still believed that the scheme of history revolved around it.

c) The final anti-Herodian revision was the one that established the Christian era.

The year 3940 (solar) (or 1 BC) had been the year of the end of Herod the Great's Exodus and the start of his Holy War. His son Archelaus, who became involved with the nationalists at about this time, could see the scheme continuing, with the zealot uprising as the Holy War. But another party was formed at this time, whose views were not reflected in this dating. All were opposed to Herodian rule, and some wanted peace, being opposed to the taking up of arms. They could express opposition to the Herodian scheme by declaring a zero generation of forty years from creation. Some of their members preferred counting in generations of forty years to counting in jubilees. By using a zero generation, they could say that 1 BC was 3900, not 3940 (solar). Their system, in its (north) solar version was:

BC–AD	Unrevised AM	Revised AM	Event
BC 1	3940	3900	Millennium and Exodus
AD 40	3980	3940	Holy War
80	4020	3980	End of Holy War
100	4040	4000	Critical event for 4000

As one of the policies of this party was the reign of the Davids rather than the Herods, their dating triumphed when a David—Jesus— did, in fact, become spiritual head of the Kingdom.

Their dating is reflected in Lk 3:23, where "about (*hōsei*) thirty years" has the pesher sense "the year before year 30". The verse concerns AD 29, so that AD 30 is being called year 30 of the millennium. There are also cases of dating from the variants of the millennial year (see below, page 176).

Variations on the Year

It has been seen that the Herods, by counting a zero year from creation, placed all dates a year later; these have been called lunisolar dates. There were further variations of this kind, arising from the fact that the calendar was subject to different theories about how counting should be done, and also to historical and cultural changes. They led to further complexities, the clues to which are given in the relevant sources.

The main one was a difference of 3½ years, in both a solar and lunisolar version. The variation was established in 165-164 BC, and is one of the subjects of the book of Daniel (9:27, 12:11-12).

An intercalation of 3½ years was introduced. Whereas the original solar significant year 3920 had begun at the March equinox of 168 BC, a "half-week" of 3½ years was now introduced, so that it fell again in September 165. This was also to be called 3920, and all year dates would follow from that.

This was the version of a more priestly kind of solarist. A related group with lay views arranged it a little differently, taking their 3½ years from September 168 to March 164.

In Dan 12:12, the mysterious reference to 1290 days concerns this change. (For the detail of the days, see notes on the method of intercalation pp. 189-190.)

The rationale given for the change was that it reflected the period of three years when the temple had been defiled. There had been no feasts, and so "no time", for the religious feasts were a way of marking time. An intercalation was a period of "no time", when the date at the end was the same as the date at the start. On a similar analogy, the 3½ years were a "famine", for, if there were no feasts, there was "no food".

There were technical calendar reasons for making the change, as shown by the fact that it was 3½ years rather than the three of the desolation, but it was popularised on this basis.

Those who used the new series of dates running from September 165 or March 164 were those who honoured the temple. However, another group, who lived in either Galilee or the Diaspora, did not honour the

Jerusalem temple, and so preserved the original series of dates running from 168. The difference in the two parties, against and for the temple, (here called "north" and "south") was preserved after the dates AM were again corrected. The dates of the two parties are here called north solar (NS) and south solar (SS).

The northern solar series of dates was the one used as a basis for the Christian era, as Christians came from those who did not revere the temple. This series had arrived at 41 BC as being 3900, and 1 BC as 3940, subsequently changed, as seen above, to 3900.

The lunisolar variation of Herod the Great was also applied to the southern series, so that their date was a year later than the southern solar one.

Thus, in the gospel period, the year AD 29 (Sep) was north solar (NS) 3969, AD 30 (Sep) was north lunisolar (NLS) 3969, AD 33 (Mar) was south solar (SS) 3969, and AD 34 (Mar) south lunisolar (SLS) 3969.

The latter date, SLS3969 in AD 34, is reflected in a saying in Jn 2:20 p : "this sanctuary was built [in] year 46" (ordinary sense: "in 46 years"). The saying was given in March AD 31 (see detailed Chronology). A new party had just been formed, its "sanctuary built". The year was year 46 of the SLS jubilee. Its year 49, 3969, would fall in AD 34. The jubilee in question was the Last Jubilee, the extension of the prophecy that has been shown above. The saying reflects the doctrine of the Last Jubilee, SLS version.

The Intermediate Year
Samaritan Magians came into this situation with the argument that they were neither north nor south. They revered the temple on Mount Gerizim in Samaria (Jn 4:20, *Ant.* 12:10), which was intermediate between the two. So they adopted an intermediate year between the two lay solar years: 166 BC between 168 and 164. At the time of the reoccupation of Qumran, north solar 3930 fell in 11 BC, and south solar 3930 in March, 7 BC, so the Samaritan intermediate solar (InterS) year fell in 9 BC.

There was also an intermediate lunisolar (InterLS) year, using the Herodian method.

All of these variations meant political, social, and religious differences between the parties, and were a means of identifying them. Much of the history centred around the political questions. When the north solar year dates triumphed in the hands of Christians it was a sign of victory for a viewpoint that respected some aspects of Judaism, but not the temple and priesthood.

The series of dates relevant to the gospel period were:

AD	NS	NLS	InterS	InterLS	SS	SLS
29	3969					
30	3970	3969				
31	3971	3970	3969			
32		3971	3970	3969		
33			3971	3970	3969	
34				3971	3970	3969
35					3971	3970
36						3971

Years could begin in either March or September, as has been seen. For the southern years, the September beginning, coming before March, was in the previous Julian year, thus SS3969 began in either September 32 or March 33, according to the point when the 3½ years had begun, either March 29 or September 29.

The Generation Year

For those counting in generations of forty years, there was a further point of dispute: did the generation begin in the zero year or the year called 1, for example 3940 or 3941? For solarists, who usually did not allow a zero from creation, it began in the 0 year, but for Herodian lunisolarists, in the 1 year. When combined with the fact that the lunisolar 3940 was one year later than the solar 3940, the Herodian generation year 3941 began two years later than the solar generation year 3940.

This fact is drawn upon in Matthew's story of the Magians at the birth of Jesus (Mt 2:7-16). The Magians deceived Herod not only about the place where Jesus was born, but also about the date, with the result that Herod waited two years before expecting to hear of the birth of Jesus. He asked them "what is the time (*chronos*, p-generation) when the heir of David should be born?" and was told "the southern generation year". For the Magians, solarists, this was SS3930, March 7 BC, the time when Jesus had actually been born. But for Herod, it meant 5 BC, as SLS3930 was in 6 BC, and SLS3931, his generation year, was in 5 BC. So he waited for two years, and when he discovered his mistake looked for children who were two years old.

This was the point that lay behind the saying in Jn 4:9: "the Jews do not keep the same time (*synchrōntai*) as the Samaritans". The "Jews" were Herodians (see Hierarchy, p. 357), so had a *chronos*, generation year, that was two years later than that of the solar Samaritans. The difference led to a further variation concerning the day dates.

For those keeping the anti-Herodian millennium, SLS3900 was in

AD 5, and SLS3901 in AD 6. The stirring events of AD 5 and 6 led to these years being treated as the beginning of the millennium. AD 5 was called year 0, and AD 6 year 1. Consequently, AD 17 was called year 12, (Lk 2:42, Mk 5:25,42) and AD 23 year 18 (Lk 13:11) (all p-sense).

Almost all ascetics adopted AD 6 as a significant generation year, calling it the beginning of the "Period of Wrath" (CD 1:5), the time when the Roman oppression began. Some looked up the book of Ezekiel to discover how long the Wrath was to last, and found there was to be a punishment for Israel of 390 years (Ezek 4:5). So AD 6 came to be called "the Period of Wrath, the 390 years for God's giving them into the hand of the ruler of Rome" (see pp. 16–17).

Incorporation of the Julian Calendar

In 44 BC, the Samaritan half of the order of Manasseh adopted the Julian calendar that had just been promulgated in the Roman world. They themselves were citizens of the Diaspora, and although not friendly to Rome had adopted many hellenistic ways. It was possible to combine the Julian calendar, with its year beginning on January 1, with their traditional solar one, by drawing on the December season, which had not been used for any of the ancient Jewish festivals. A religious start of the Julian year could be made at the December solstice, then a secular start on January 1. (This became the origin of Christmas.)

Its corresponding solstice was June. Both the solstices were attached as lesser seasons to the equinoxes, and treated as coming *after* the equinoxes, so that March and June formed a pair, and also September and December. This remained the Jewish Julian practice. But, when a need arose to link two successive years, December–January were treated as belonging to both, and so came to be used as the early start of the succeeding year. This came to be the Christian practice, which for a long time began a year both in January and the following March.

The date of the foundation of the Magians is given in the pesher of A 19:19. In an episode occurring in June, AD 57, their magical books were burnt, and their value was 50 000 pieces of silver. They were a "half-tribe" only, in accordance with the Old Testament tribe of Manasseh, so their western branch had 500 members. Each had paid a piece of silver as a promotion fee every year, so over 100 years the order had property worth 50 000 pieces of silver. Thus they had been founded 100 years before, in June 44 BC (both March and June, as they paired the seasons).

The 480 Year Method of Measuring Historical Periods

Solarists, relying on the number 7, divided history into sets of 490 years, the total period being 4900 years. Others, however, thought that the Last Judgment would come after only 4000 years, and the gospel period was therefore one of great tension for them.

Their method of dividing each 1000 years relied on 40 year generations. An initial 40 was followed by two sets of 480. The year 4000, falling in AD 60, was a year 480, so that 21 BC was a year 400 (A 7:6p).

As 490 years was a "week" in the terminology of Enoch, so 480 years was also thought of as a "week", but one with eight days, each "day" consisting of 60 years. The eighth day was a kind of extra day overlapping with the first day of the following week. The years 1 BC to AD 60 were the "eighth day" of the 480 years ending in AD 60.

As 60 years was a "day", and as a day, in the sense of daylight, was defined as lasting 12 hours (Jn 11:9), an "hour" was five years. For the "eighth day" in question, its 6 a.m. was 1 BC, its 7 a.m. was AD 5, its 9 a.m. AD 15, its noon AD 30, 3 p.m. AD 45, 5 p.m. (the eleventh hour) AD 55. Thus Matthew's parable of the workers in the Vineyard, who were sent out every three hours and who complained that those who were sent at the eleventh hour received the same wage as the rest (Mt 20:1-16), concerns events actually happening in certain years. The "Vineyard" was the organisation founded in Rome in 1 BC as a revised form of the Herodian mission. It was the earliest form of the Christian Church in Rome. Mark's parable of the Vineyard (Mk 12:1-11) covers the same period of years.

Marriage and Initiation Rules as a Means of Giving Dates

As shown in Chapter 8, the Essene view that sex was only for the purpose of procreation led to rigorous rules intended to postpone sex for as long as possible. Details of the pesher show that as a result of the forty year generation theory, the ideal age for a king or head of a dynasty to have a son was forty. But the first child might be a girl, so he married at thirty-six. The season for the wedding ceremony was September, but sex had to be postponed till the less holy season of December. The child was, ideally, born the following September when the man, who himself should have been born in September, was thirty-seven. As the rule was that after the birth of a son he must wait six years to return to his marriage, but after the birth of a daughter three years, the birth of a daughter as a first child meant that he could come back at the age of forty, and have the desired son during the following year. For subsequent children, there was no waiting period at the return; a child was, ideally, conceived at once, allowing him to go back to the celibate life nine months later.

Once such a man's birth date is known, the dates of his marriage follow. When a child was born and its gender was known, it was then known what would be the date of his return. All such events occurred at the equinoxes or solstices. The first son was given an official birthday, at the equinox or solstice, and, for those using the Julian calendar, also on the 1st of the Julian month. Subsequent children used their real birth date.

The initiation rules also supply dates. It becomes apparent that the main steps were taken at fixed ages. At twelve, a boy went through a ceremony like that of the Bar Mitzvah, which was understood as a second "birth" as he was separated from his mother. So Jesus, who was born in March 7 BC, was twelve in March AD 6, at the time of the census of Quirinius. Luke (2:1–2) draws on this fact to say that Jesus was "born" at the time of the census, one of his apparent blunders, as Jesus would have been only twenty-three when he began his ministry. But the meaning is his symbolic birth, and the date, March AD 6, gives his actual birth date in March, 7 BC.

At twenty, the process of adult initiation began. A man was considered eligible for marriage at this age, as shown directly in 1QSa 1:10. But if he belonged to one of the higher orders he postponed marriage and began a series of steps in initiation which were also steps in his education. At twenty-three, three years after starting the process, he received full initiation. There followed four years of education in a celibate community, leading to graduation at age twenty-seven. At thirty, after three years in a form of ministry, he had attained the highest possible grade.

The pesher draws on these rules to indicate dates in the history involving some of the main personalities.

The Detailed Chronology

An exact and detailed chronology is supplied in the gospels and Acts, for every important event from 9 BC to AD 63. It is hidden from the reader of the surface narrative, but available to the reader who knows the special meanings of terms and is thoroughly familiar with the solar calendar.

Terms with an apparently vague meaning are, in fact, precise indicators of time. Among the most useful are the simple phrases "in those days" or "in these days". They refer to the equinoxes and solstices. "In those days" means the equinoxes, as they were for priests and so more remote from the laity; "in these days" means the solstices. Moreover, the word order in Greek shows which one was meant. *En tais hēmerais ekeinais* "in the days those" means March, and *en ekeinais tais hēmerais* "in those the days" means September. *En tais hēmerais tautais* "in the days these" means June, and *en tautais tais hēmerais* "in these the days" means December. The rule for word order in these and all such phrases is that the noun is placed first at the earlier occurrence of the time.

Another example of a vague term giving an exact time is in phrases such as "three days" (*treis hēmerai*). Its p-sense is "day 3", and this means Tuesday, as Sunday was day 1, Monday day 2, and so on.

The term "the next day" (*tē epaurion*) is one of the most valuable indicators of all, as it means the 31st in a quartodecimal intercalation year.

These examples are sufficient to show why it is possible to derive an exact chronology.

The Notes to the Chronology, pp. 189-207, give full details of such terms.

A further unexpected point is that the gospels can be fully harmonised. They have long been regarded by scholars, looking at their surface sense, as giving different stories, and in no chronological order except for the passion narrative, which itself varies between John and the Synoptics Matthew, Mark and Luke. When the pesher of the stories is understood, it is seen that they are giving the same history, in strict chronological order, and that there are no differences between them. A doctrine of the inerrancy of scripture becomes a useful working hypothesis!

It is, further, possible to supply the Julian dates for the events. The solar calendar dates were on fixed days, and the Julian dates for the days may be calculated through the use of the Dominical Letters (see Finegan, *Handbook of Biblical Chronology*). In AD 29, January 1 was a Saturday, in AD 30 a Sunday, AD 31 a Monday, AD 32 (leap year) a Tuesday, AD 33 a Thursday. Table C (pp. 186-188) gives the Julian dates for the four seasons.

The method of intercalation of the calendar introduces complexities which are dealt with fully on pp. 189-192. An initial point of importance is that, as 17½ days or 2½ weeks were introduced every fourteen years, there was a change in the days on which dates fell. In the normative position, the 31st was always a Tuesday. But when the year for the intercalation came, it began on this day, then two weeks were inserted, up to a Tuesday a fortnight later. Then 3½ more days from Tuesday 6 a.m. to Friday 6 p.m. were further inserted. From then on, for the next fourteen years, the 31sts fell on Friday at 6 p.m., and all dates followed. The normative position is here called the Day position, and the alternative the Night. As the calendar was in the Night position in the period of Jesus' ministry, the 31st at the March equinox fell on a Friday. Good Friday was one of the Great Days of the solar calendar.

The quartodecimal intercalations fell, for the north solar years, in 14 BC (change to Day), AD 1 (to Night), AD 15 (Day), AD 29 (Night), AD 43 (Day), and AD 57 (Night). As the various calendars discussed above all had their own version of the year date, the process went on over a number of years, and this led to differences of practice between different parties in the same year. These are explained on p. 190.

Measurements in Hours and Minutes

The very close study of the chronology shows that there are terms indicating not only years, seasons, months and days, but also hours and even minutes.

That the ascetic community was conscious of time to such an extent is illustrated in the scrolls. On entering the celibate community, an initiate vowed to be "neither early nor late for any of the appointed times" (1QS 1:14). A long passage in the Manual of Discipline (1QS 10) speaks of the sectarian's determination to offer prayers to God at every division of time, not only of the year but also of the day. It appears that a central purpose of the community which so valued the solar calendar was to mark off all of the points of time with a prayer, acting in this way like a human clock. A primary proof of virtue was to keep the times exactly, and to be in error about them was to fail in the eyes of heaven. Heaven itself, made up of the sun, moon and stars, was a great clock, and those who obeyed it made time their paramount concern.

The members of the community were, in fact, astronomers, spending much of their exile in close study of accurate ways of measuring time. Qumran was an ideal spot for such a purpose, as the light is almost always very bright, and the shadows sharp and clear.

There is no doubt, from the surface record, that they were working with a day of 24 hours, divided into daylight 12 hours and night 12 hours (Jn 11:9). The hours of the day were at first numbered, in Jewish fashion, first hour (7 a.m.), second hour (8 a.m.) and so on. The sixth hour (noon), the ninth hour (3 p.m.), the tenth hour (4 p.m.) and the eleventh hour (5 p.m.) all appear in the narratives of the gospels (Jn 4:6, A 3:1, Jn 1:39, Mt 20:6). The great hours, when the important prayers had to be offered by leaders of the hierarchy, were 6 a.m., noon, and 6 p.m., the turning points of the sun. The term "angelus" for the Church's prayers goes back to their practice; an "angel" was a levite who prayed at the major times.

They also dealt in subdivisions of hours. The book of Revelation (8:1) speaks of "silence in heaven for half an hour". The subdivisions included the minutes around the hour, to allow for preparation for events on the hour, and a start for new events at 5 minutes past the hour (such as the closing of doors when the sacred meal began).

In the daytime, minutes could be measured by means of a sundial. Such devices were available; the gnomon, invented in the 6th century BC, was a stick marked with measurements throwing a shadow capable of giving the exact time between equinox and equinox.

Their main measuring device, however, was in the priests and celibates whose primary occupation was the offering of continual prayers to God.

Because of their equation of time with space (see further on this in Locations, p. 287), they divided the ground into cubits, each cubit representing an hour. A continual succession of hours was measured by a man standing on every successive cubit, both observing the progress of shadows and offering prayers of exactly the same length. One of the scrolls says: "You (God) have put words on a measuring line (*qaw*)" (1QH 1:28).

Such a procedure gave the accuracy of a clock. The priests knew exactly what hour it was, and were able to give directions for operating the device that told the laity when it was noon. At precisely noon, a segment of the roof was removed, allowing the congregation below to see the priest at his prayers on the roof above. When the half-roof was removed, "a great light shone down", the sun's rays shining down to the floor below. A man standing below who looked directly up would be temporarily blinded, but would be able to hear the voice of his priest, who could speak to him from above. It is this setting that Luke drew on to present the "visionary" appearances of Jesus to Paul and to Peter (see Chapters 30 and 31).

The human chronometer in its continual succession of cubit–hours could not allow for the fact that the exact solar year is 365 days, 5 hours, 48 minutes and 46 seconds long. The intercalation put in full hours, with the result that in 17 years, 3 hours too much had been put in. The "clocks" were, in effect, 3 hours fast. It was noticeable from the movements of the sun that whereas their "clock" said it was noon, it was really only 9 a.m. The way to deal with this was to leave the segment of roof where it was at the time the "clock" said noon, allowing 3 hours' darkness in the room below until the "clock" said 3 p.m., but the true time was noon. Thus the timing was adjusted. This is the reason for the "three hours' darkness" on Good Friday, an important day in the calendar which had been chosen for the adjustment.

The Ritual as a Means of Recovering History

The regularity with which special days were observed and hours were measured had another effect, that it was always possible to look back and fit great events into a time framework. What took place at centres like Qumran was fitted into the ritual, and was partly a result of the ritual. It was possible, years afterwards, to say precisely when events occurred, as they were related to the fixed procedure for the day and hour.

This was the reason, moreover, why the pesher could be set up for those who were familiar with the ritual. Celibates in Christian communities were being given a kind of holy game, a puzzle to be solved, the clues depending on their special knowledge of times. Those who set it up were preparing something with an exact solution. Each answer must be right, and a complete history would then come out. The history itself had been reconstructed from what had been experienced, and where necessary had been constructed, overriding the complexities of actual events so as to set up definite facts capable of discovery.

For this reason, the solution is testable. It is either right or wrong; it is falsifiable. The details of times are especially subject to tests, as they also involve mathematical questions. The modern reader is being asked to judge whether the pesher was, in fact, placed there, and the way to do it is to test the proffered solutions for consistency. It is possible to determine, by the normal procedures of scientific method, whether the "puzzle" has really been placed in the texts, or whether it has been artificially imposed.

The details of times, as given by the special terms, are set out on pp. 208–284. Statements of events usually give the pesher, and the reasons for what is said are amplified in the subsequent notes on locations and hierarchy.

•   •   •

Table B
NORTHERN AND SOUTHERN YEARS, SOLAR AND LUNISOLAR
FROM 41 BC TO AD 66

	NS	NLS	SS	SLS
BC 41	AM 3900 Mill.			
40	3901	3900		
39		3901		
38				
37			3900	
36			3901	3900
35				3901
34				
33				
32				
31	3910			
30	3911	3910		
29		3911		
28	3913*N			
27		3913*N	3910	
26			3911	3910
25				3911
24			3913*N	

23				3913*N
22				
21	3920 Rest.			
20	3921	3920		
19		3921		
18				
17			3920	
16			3921	3920
15				3921
14	3927*D			
13		3927*D		
12				
11	3930			
10	3931	3930	3927*D	
9		3931		3927*D
8				
7			3930	
6			3931	3930
5				3931
4				
3				
2				
1	3940			
AD 1	3941*N	3940		
2		3941*N		
3				
4			3940	
5			3941*N	3940
6				3941*N
7				
8				
9				
10	3950			
11	3951	3950		
12		3951		
13				
14			3950	
15	3955*D		3951	3950
16		3955*D		3951
17				
18				

19			3955*D	
20	3960			3955*D
21	3961	3960		
22		3961		
23				
24			3960	
25			3961	3960
26				3961
27				
28				
29	3969*N			
30	3970	3969*N		
31	3971	3970		
32		3971		
33			3969*N	
34			3970	3969*N
35			3971	3970
36				3971
37				
38				
39				
40	3980			
41	3981	3980		
42		3981		
43	3983*D			
44		3983*D	3980	
45			3981	3980
46				3981
47			3983*D	
48				3983*D
49				
50	3990			
51	3991	3990		
52		3991		
53				
54			3990	
55			3991	3990
56				3991
57	3997*N			
58		3997*N		
59				

60	4000			
61	4001	4000	3997*N	
62		4001		3997*N
63				
64			4000	
65			4001	4000
66				4001

NOTE: Intermediate solar and intermediate lunisolar not shown. InterS between NS and SS, e.g. AD 31 between 29 and 33. InterLS a year later.

The 3½ years were measured either from March to September (e.g. March 29 to September 32); or from September to March, (e.g. September 29 to March 33), see p. 173. The year starting in September 32 was thus the same year as that starting March 33.

The forty year generation year was the 0 year to solarists (e.g. 3940), but the 1 year to Herodian lunisolarists (e.g. 3941), see p. 175.

Abbreviations

AM	Anno Mundi (year of the world, from creation)
NS	North solar
NLS	North lunisolar
InterS	Intermediate solar
InterLS	Intermediate lunisolar
SS	South solar
SLS	South lunisolar
Mill.	Millennium (3900–4900, last millennium of world)
Rest.	Restoration (3920, 8th world week, prophesied Restoration of Davids and Zadokites)
*D	Day position following intercalation
*N	Night position following intercalation

Table C

The following table gives the Julian dates at which the 31sts before months I, IV, VII, and X fell, between 14 BC and AD 70.

Month I began near the March equinox in the year when the intercalation had taken place, then fell back over the next fourteen years, to ne: : the beginning of March. Similarly, IV began near the June solstice, VII near the September equinox, and X near the December solstice.

The north solar years are given; other calendars made the same change in their own version of the year. An example of SLS dates is given after the table.

"to" means "changes to at the quartodecimal year".
(L)—leap year (Julian).
For other abbreviations see p. 185.

Table C
JULIAN DATES OF 31st, 14 BC TO AD 70

			I	IV	VII	X
BC	14	(NS3927) to	Tue Mar 26	Tue Jun 25	Tue Sep 24	Tue Dec 24
	13	(L)	Tue Mar 24	Tue Jun 23	Tue Sep 22	Tue Dec 22
	12		Tue Mar 23	Tue Jun 22	Tue Sep 21	Tue Dec 21
	11		Tue Mar 22	Tue Jun 21	Tue Sep 20	Tue Dec 20
	10		Tue Mar 21	Tue Jun 20	Tue Sep 19	Tue Dec 19
	9	(L)	Tue Mar 19	Tue Jun 18	Tue Sep 17	Tue Dec 17
	8		Tue Mar 18	Tue Jun 17	Tue Sep 16	Tue Dec 16
	7		Tue Mar 17	Tue Jun 16	Tue Sep 15	Tue Dec 15
	6		Tue Mar 16	Tue Jun 15	Tue Sep 14	Tue Dec 14
	5	(L)	Tue Mar 14	Tue Jun 13	Tue Sep 12	Tue Dec 12
	4		Tue Mar 13	Tue Jun 12	Tue Sep 11	Tue Dec 11
	3		Tue Mar 12	Tue Jun 11	Tue Sep 10	Tue Dec 10
	2		Tue Mar 11	Tue Jun 10	Tue Sep 9	Tue Dec 9
	1	(L)	Tue Mar 9	Tue Jun 8	Tue Sep 7	Tue Dec 7
AD	1	(NS3941) to	Fri Mar 25	Fri Jun 24	Fri Sep 23	Fri Dec 23
	2		Fri Mar 24	Fri Jun 23	Fri Sep 22	Fri Dec 22
	3		Fri Mar 23	Fri Jun 22	Fri Sep 21	Fri Dec 21
	4	(L)	Fri Mar 21	Fri Jun 20	Fri Sep 19	Fri Dec 19
	5		Fri Mar 20	Fri Jun 19	Fri Sep 18	Fri Dec 18
	6		Fri Mar 19	Fri Jun 18	Fri Sep 17	Fri Dec 17
	7		Fri Mar 18	Fri Jun 17	Fri Sep 16	Fri Dec 16
	8	(L)	Fri Mar 16	Fri Jun 15	Fri Sep 14	Fri Dec 14
	9		Fri Mar 15	Fri Jun 14	Fri Sep 13	Fri Dec 13
	10		Fri Mar 14	Fri Jun 13	Fri Sep 12	Fri Dec 12
	11		Fri Mar 13	Fri Jun 12	Fri Sep 11	Fri Dec 11

12	(L)	Fri Mar 11	Fri Jun 10	Fri Sep 9	Fri Dec 9
13		Fri Mar 10	Fri Jun 9	Fri Sep 8	Fri Dec 8
14		Fri Mar 9	Fri Jun 8	Fri Sep 7	Fri Dec 7
15	(NS3955) to	Tue Mar 26	Tue Jun 25	Tue Sep 24	Tue Dec 24
16	(L)	Tue Mar 24	Tue Jun 23	Tue Sep 22	Tue Dec 22
17		Tue Mar 23	Tue Jun 22	Tue Sep 21	Tue Dec 21
18		Tue Mar 22	Tue Jun 21	Tue Sep 20	Tue Dec 20
19		Tue Mar 21	Tue Jun 20	Tue Sep 19	Tue Dec 19
20	(L)	Tue Mar 19	Tue Jun 18	Tue Sep 17	Tue Dec 17
21		Tue Mar 18	Tue Jun 17	Tue Sep 16	Tue Dec 16
22		Tue Mar 17	Tue Jun 16	Tue Sep 15	Tue Dec 15
23		Tue Mar 16	Tue Jun 15	Tue Sep 14	Tue Dec 14
24	(L)	Tue Mar 14	Tue Jun 13	Tue Sep 12	Tue Dec 12
25		Tue Mar 13	Tue Jun 12	Tue Sep 11	Tue Dec 11
26		Tue Mar 12	Tue Jun 11	Tue Sep 10	Tue Dec 10
27		Tue Mar 11	Tue Jun 10	Tue Sep 9	Tue Dec 9
28	(L)	Tue Mar 9	Tue Jun 8	Tue Sep 7	Tue Dec 7
29	(NS3969) to	Fri Mar 25	Fri Jun 24	Fri Sep 23	Fri Dec 23
30		Fri Mar 24	Fri Jun 23	Fri Sep 22	Fri Dec 22
31		Fri Mar 23	Fri Jun 22	Fri Sep 21	Fri Dec 21
32	(L)	Fri Mar 21	Fri Jun 20	Fri Sep 19	Fri Dec 19
33		Fri Mar 20	Fri Jun 19	Fri Sep 18	Fri Dec 18
34		Fri Mar 19	Fri Jun 18	Fri Sep 17	Fri Dec 17
35		Fri Mar 18	Fri Jun 17	Fri Sep 16	Fri Dec 16
36	(L)	Fri Mar 16	Fri Jun 15	Fri Sep 14	Fri Dec 14
37		Fri Mar 15	Fri Jun 14	Fri Sep 13	Fri Dec 13
38		Fri Mar 14	Fri Jun 13	Fri Sep 12	Fri Dec 12
39		Fri Mar 13	Fri Jun 12	Fri Sep 11	Fri Dec 11
40	(L)	Fri Mar 11	Fri Jun 10	Fri Sep 9	Fri Dec 9
41		Fri Mar 10	Fri Jun 9	Fri Sep 8	Fri Dec 8
42		Fri Mar 9	Fri Jun 8	Fri Sep 7	Fri Dec 7
43	(NS3983) to	Tue Mar 26	Tue Jun 25	Tue Sep 24	Tue Dec 24
44	(L)	Tue Mar 24	Tue Jun 23	Tue Sep 22	Tue Dec 22
45		Tue Mar 23	Tue Jun 22	Tue Sep 21	Tue Dec 21
46		Tue Mar 22	Tue Jun 21	Tue Sep 20	Tue Dec 20
47		Tue Mar 21	Tue Jun 20	Tue Sep 19	Tue Dec 19
48	(L)	Tue Mar 19	Tue Jun 18	Tue Sep 17	Tue Dec 17
49		Tue Mar 18	Tue Jun 17	Tue Sep 16	Tue Dec 16
50		Tue Mar 17	Tue Jun 16	Tue Sep 15	Tue Dec 15
51		Tue Mar 16	Tue Jun 15	Tue Sep 14	Tue Dec 14

52	(L)	Tue Mar 14	Tue Jun 13	Tue Sep 12	Tue Dec 12
53		Tue Mar 13	Tue Jun 12	Tue Sep 11	Tue Dec 11
54		Tue Mar 12	Tue Jun 11	Tue Sep 10	Tue Dec 10
55		Tue Mar 11	Tue Jun 10	Tue Sep 9	Tue Dec 9
56	(L)	Tue Mar 9	Tue Jun 8	Tue Sep 7	Tue Dec 7
57	(NS3997) to	Fri Mar 25	Fri Jun 24	Fri Sep 23	Fri Dec 23
58		Fri Mar 24	Fri Jun 23	Fri Sep 22	Fri Dec 22
59		Fri Mar 23	Fri Jun 22	Fri Sep 21	Fri Dec 21
60	(L)	Fri Mar 21	Fri Jun 20	Fri Sep 19	Fri Dec 19
61		Fri Mar 20	Fri Jun 19	Fri Sep 18	Fri Dec 18
62		Fri Mar 19	Fri Jun 18	Fri Sep 17	Fri Dec 17
63		Fri Mar 18	Fri Jun 17	Fri Sep 16	Fri Dec 16
64	(L)	Fri Mar 16	Fri Jun 15	Fri Sep 14	Fri Dec 14
65		Fri Mar 15	Fri Jun 14	Fri Sep 13	Fri Dec 13
66		Fri Mar 14	Fri Jun 13	Fri Sep 12	Fri Dec 12
67		Fri Mar 13	Fri Jun 12	Fri Sep 11	Fri Dec 11
68	(L)	Fri Mar 11	Fri Jun 10	Fri Sep 9	Fri Dec 9
69		Fri Mar 10	Fri Jun 9	Fri Sep 8	Fri Dec 8
70		Fri Mar 9	Fri Jun 8	Fri Sep 7	Fri Dec 7

OTHER CALENDARS

The Julian dates for NLS, InterS, InterLS, SS, SLS may be worked out from the above. For example, the dates SLS from 9 BC to AD 6 were:

BC	9	(SLS3927)(L)	Tue Mar 19	Tue Jun 18	Tue Sep 17	Tue Dec 17
	8		Tue Mar 18	Tue Jun 17	Tue Sep 16	Tue Dec 16
	7		Tue Mar 17	Tue Jun 16	Tue Sep 15	Tue Dec 15
	6		Tue Mar 16	Tue Jun 15	Tue Sep 14	Tue Dec 14
	5	(L)	Tue Mar 14	Tue Jun 13	Tue Sep 12	Tue Dec 12
	4		Tue Mar 13	Tue Jun 12	Tue Sep 11	Tue Dec 11
	3		Tue Mar 12	Tue Jun 11	Tue Sep 10	Tue Dec 10
	2		Tue Mar 11	Tue Jun 10	Tue Sep 9	Tue Dec 9
	1	(L)	Tue Mar 9	Tue Jun 8	Tue Sep 7	Tue Dec 7
AD	1		Tue Mar 8	Tue Jun 7	Tue Sep 6	Tue Dec 6
	2		Tue Mar 7	Tue Jun 6	Tue Sep 5	Tue Dec 5
	3		Tue Mar 6	Tue Jun 5	Tue Sep 4	Tue Dec 4
	4	(L)	Tue Mar 4	Tue Jun 3	Tue Sep 2	Tue Dec 2
	5		Tue Mar 3	Tue Jun 2	Tue Sep 1	Tue Dec 1
	6	(SLS3941) to	Fri Mar 19	Fri Jun 18	Fri Sep 17	Fri Dec 17

CHRONOLOGICAL NOTES
Detail of the Method of Intercalation

As noted in the Introduction to the Chronology, the method of intercalation of the solar calendar was to insert 17½ days every 14 years. In the quartodecimal year, the calendar arrived at a Tuesday 31st, then began a period of "no time", as the date would still be the same after 2½ weeks.

The new 31st would be on a Friday 2½ weeks later, starting at 6 p.m. In the normative position, when the 31sts fell on Tuesday, the day started at 6 a.m. The normative position is here called Day, and the alternative Night.

The changeover from Day to Night was effected in the first 36 hours of the intercalation. From Tuesday at 6 a.m. to Wednesday, the next day, at 6 p.m., there was an extra long day of 36 hours. The expression *tē epaurion* ("on the next day") is used to mean this 36 hour day. When it appears, it indicates a quartodecimal year. Following it, there were 16 days from Wednesday 6 p.m. to the Friday at 6 p.m. when the 31st was said to occur again. Dates continued from that day for the next fourteen years.

When this point is seen, it accounts for the mysterious 1290 days in Dan 12:11. ("And from the time that the continual burnt offering is taken away, and the abomination that makes desolate is set up, there shall be 1290 days.") A special intercalation of 3½ years was being made, as shown in the Introduction (p. 173). But 3½ years of the solar calendar of 364 days was 1274 days. The extra 16 were for the intercalation, due in 168 BC. In September, 168 BC, 17½ days had been inserted, but only 16 counted, the previous 1½ being treated as a zero. Then 1274 days from the new 31st brought the year date to near the March equinox, 164 BC, at the 31st.

In another practice derived from the method of intercalation, the 16 days were added to certain other days to make a total of 40 days, used for fasting. As Daniel 10:2-4 shows, the 21 days between the pentecontads, occurring every year, were a fasting period (see below p. 196 on the pentecontads). They started on the 3rd of the first month (the March equinox), lasting till the 24th. In an intercalation year, 16 days had been put in before the 31st, and with the 3 days (31st, 1st, 2nd) between these and the 21 days, there was a total of 40 days. This is the calendar reason behind Jesus' 40 days' fasting in Mk 1:13, and for the 40 days in A 1:3 (in the latter case, the day in question was day 20 of the 40 days, as *dia* with genitive has the p-sense "in the middle of").

Dan 12:12 adds another figure: "Blessed is he who waits and comes to the 1335 days". This verse was the contribution of a party with a slightly different version of the 3½ years. It counted years from the great feasts, not from the 31sts, and was not including an intercalation, which would follow its 1335 days. From Tabernacles, 15/VII, in 168 BC, to the end of Passover, 14/I, in 164 BC, was 1274 days, then there were 60 further days from 15/I to Pentecost, 15/III, giving a total of 1334 days. As *Jub* 1:1 shows, a new beginning was made on the 16th of the third month, bringing the total to 1335.

The two schools of thought, those beginning the year at a 1st, and those beginning at a feast, are reflected in the 1260 days of Rev 11:3 and 12:6. It was 1260 days from 15/VII to 1/I 3½ years later. A statement is being made that a change should be adopted concerning the method of reckoning New Year.

Although a change was made concerning the number of years from creation, as shown in the Introduction, no change could be made in the series of quartodecimal years, as they were essential to keeping the calendar in line with the sun. An intercalation was due in 168 BC, a year that at that time was thought to be AM 3920, a multiple of 14. When the years were renumbered, and the series retained, the numbers were no longer multiples of 14, only of 7. After the revision, the years AM 3941 (AD 1), AM 3955 (AD 15) and AM 3969 (AD 29) were intercalation years (NS).

The word *ho kairos*, apparently having a vague meaning "the time, season", also refers to the quartodecimal years (A 7:20, Lk 13:1, A 19:23, etc.).

Because of political differences on the question of quartodecimal years, outlined in the Introduction, it could happen that two different parties were observing different dates on the same day. A party that was intercalating in a certain year came to the 31st and stopped their succession of dates, while a party that would not intercalate till a later year went on. The latter group were said to be "advanced in their days" (Lk 1:7, Lk 2:36). Table D shows the conjunctions of days in such a situation, and also illustrates the days in the Night position. It applies to any of the four months (I, IV, VII, X), which were preceded by a 31st.

Table D
Conjunctions of Days, and Night position dates

	Night	**Day**
Tue	6 a.m.	31a
Wed	6 a.m.	1a (I, IV, VII, X)
Thu	6 a.m.	2a
Fri	6 a.m.	3a
Sat	6 a.m.	4a

Sun	6 a.m.		5a
Mon	6 a.m.		6a
Tue	6 a.m.		7a
Wed	6 a.m.		8a
Thu	6 a.m.		9a
Fri	6 a.m.		10a
Sat	6 a.m.		11a
Sun	6 a.m.		12a
Mon	6 a.m.		13a
Tue	6 a.m.		14a
Wed	6 a.m.		15a
Wed	6 p.m.	29a (XII, III, VI, IX)	15b
Thu	6 a.m.	29b	16a
Thu	6 p.m.	30a	16b
Fri	6 a.m.	30b	17a
Fri	6 p.m.	31a	17b
Sat	6 a.m.	31b	18a
Sat	6 p.m.	1a (I, IV, XII, X)	18b
Sun	6 a.m.	1b	19a
Sun	6 p.m.	2a	19b
Mon	6 a.m.	2b	20a

After fourteen years the 31st had fallen back to a date that, in Julian terms, was early in the month of March, June, September or December. For example, in AD 29, a year when a change from Day to Night was due, Tuesday 31st had fallen back to Tuesday March 8 at 6 a.m. When the 17½ days were put in, the new 31st began on Friday March 25 at 6 p.m. Tuesday, March 8, AD 29 is called *tē epaurion* in Jn 1:35. See Table C (p. 186) for the full list of north solar dates.

The Post-Position Intercalation

An alternate method of intercalating is illustrated, used in the Diaspora. Rather than allow the calendar to reach the equinox date 17½ days before the sun did, and then adjust to the sun, the alternative put in 17½ days at the equinox, so that the new 31st went ahead of the sun, falling back gradually to the equinox. For example, an intercalation put in on Friday March 25 brought the new 31st to Tuesday, April 12 at 6 a.m. The word *tē epaurion* appears at the equinox or solstice in Mt 27:62, A 22:30. These 31sts are here called the post position.

The word *eukairos* "good (convenient) time", in its p-sense means the beginning of an equinox intercalation, as *kairos* means an intercalation and *eu-* means Diaspora doctrine.

The expression "Day and Night" or "Night and Day" refers to the double position, the post position being always opposite to the main one. It is one of the useful indicators of an intercalation period, as the first term means the main position now in force. "Day and Night (*hēmeras . . . kai nyktos*) in A 9:24 shows that the year was AD 43, when the change to Day was made.

When several parties were involved during a quartodecimal period, there could be three positions: for example, Tuesday March 8 was the 31st for those who had not yet intercalated, Friday March 25 was the new 31st for those who had, and Tuesday April 12 was the 31st for those who had just intercalated on March 25.

The 31sts

The four 31sts in the year were significant days. Not only were they the days when great events were expected, but they also marked the turn of the seasons, as they were near to the equinoxes and solstices. Councils of ministers were held at these times, the leaders going from their villages up to Qumran for meetings on questions of policy. According to 1QSa 1:26–27 members going to such councils must be "sanctified" for three days. The three Preparation or Purification Days figure prominently in the chronology (cf. Jn 11:55, A 21:24). The 29th, 30th and 31st of the month were counted as the three days.

One of the names for the 31st was *to sabbaton* (singular form only). It appears to mean the sabbath, the seventh day of the week, but this is not its p-sense. It means a greater holy day, the 31st. When the calendar was in the Night position, the 31st beginning on Friday at 6 p.m., the 31st coincided with the sabbath, which for Jews began at that time. But in the Day position, *to sabbaton* means Tuesday 31st.

The plural form of the word, *ta sabbata*, meaning "week" in its ordinary sense, has the p-sense "week of years", that is seven years. The word appears at the beginning of a sabbatical year. In the gospel period, it indicates a year 3969, in its various occurrences.

Another name for the 31st was "Today" (*sēmeron*). As great events were expected on that day, it was the long awaited "Today" for fulfilment. Consequently, the 30th, the day before, was "Yesterday" (*echthes*), and the 1st, the next day, was "Tomorrow" (*aurion*). These words are always used absolutely, not relatively. In Jn 4:52 "Yesterday" means the 30th.

The Variant 31sts. "Tomorrow Today"

While the regular 31sts were on either Tuesday 6 a.m. or Friday 6 p.m., a variation on this matter had developed at the hands of Samaritans. Because of their views on the year—they used the intermediate year between north solar and south solar—they had a corresponding change in their day dates. Years and days were thought to correspond with one another, as the year had 12 months and the day (daytime) had 12 hours, as is plainly stated in Jn 11:11. A day of 24 hours corresponded to 2 years.

Recognising their association with south solarists, and the fact that their year 3969 (for example) fell 2 years before that of the south (Samaritans AD 31, south AD 33), they also placed their 31st 24 hours before that of the south, and all dates followed. For them, the 31st fell on either Monday at 6 a.m. (Day) or Thursday at 6 p.m. (Night).

Consequently, a Tuesday or Friday that was the regular 31st to others was for them the 1st of the month, as the day after the 31st.

The expression "Tomorrow Today" was used to signify this variant. The 31st was "Today" and the 1st "Tomorrow", as seen above. A Tuesday that was a 31st to others was the 1st for Samaritans, so their "Tomorrow", the 1st, was the same as "Today", the 31st.

Matthew's version of the Lord's Prayer draws on this point to say that Christians have views on some questions similar to those of Samaritans (opposition to the Jerusalem temple and related ritual, cf. Jn 8:48). The words usually rendered "Give us this day our daily bread" (Mt 6:11) mean literally "Give us tomorrow's bread today" (*ton arton . . . ton epiousion . . . sēmeron*). The form of communion meal ("the bread") that was meant for the 1st was used by them on the regular 31st.

Their Great Day, the 31st, was the previous day. The Monday, "Yesterday" for others, "Today" for them, is called *sēmeron* in Lk 5:26. The Thursday evening of the Last Supper was their 31st, whereas it was the 30th for others. It was for this reason that both Jesus and Simon Magus were held accountable for the fulfilment of prophecy on that night.

The Monday and Thursday 31sts are shown as Sam (aritan) in the Detailed Chronology.

A 31st was called "This Day" and a 1st was called "That Day". To Samaritans, the Monday or Thursday was "This Day" and the Tuesday or Friday "That Day". But to non-Samaritans, the Tuesday or Friday was "This Day". The point is illustrated in A 23:1–2. Paul, speaking on a Friday 31st (*tē epaurion*, A 22:30) called the day "This Day". The Samaritan high priest Ananias then ordered him to be struck on the mouth, for he was using a false calendar, from the Samaritan's point of view.

Another way of naming the days was similarly affected by the variant. As the 31st was counted with the following month, it could be called the first day, the 1st the second day, and the 2nd the third day. Lk 24:21 calls the 2nd of the month "the third day with all of these". But for Samaritans, these terms all referred to the previous day. In the Night position, the Thursday evening (reg. 30th, Sam 31st) was the first day (Mk 14:12), the Friday the second day (not found) and the Saturday the third day (Mt 27:64). It was for this reason that the day after Jesus' crucifixion could be called the third day.

The +2½ 31st

There was yet another 31st for some members of the movement. They were lunisolarists, Pharisees who had joined the ascetic movement, accepting the solar calendar, but retaining some of their own calendar practices. Whereas solar celibates, with their rigorous discipline, were prepared for long fasting periods and so could intercalate weeks at a time, the Pharisees, much closer to ordinary Jews, preferred to intercalate only a short period, so fasting for a shorter time but more frequently. The saying "the Pharisees fast often" (Lk 5:33, Mt 9:14) refers to their practice.

They must, however, make the same adjustment. There was another way of achieving the same result, by putting in 2½ days every two years. Seven such insertions would amount to 17½ days in fourteen years.

As Mk 2:18 shows, Pharisees in a quartodecimal year began fasting on a Tuesday 31st, at the same time as solarists. But soon after, another *sabbaton* appears, called "the other" (*heteron*) (Lk 6:6,7). They began their new 31st on the Thursday of the same week at 6 p.m. Alternately, they began it on Thursday at 6 a.m., since, as they had some of the habits of lunarists, they liked to begin their day the evening before, on Monday at 6 p.m. Transferred to the Night position, these times were Sunday at 6 p.m. following the Friday at 6 a.m., and also Monday at 6 a.m.

Events at a village level, such as the release for marriage of the man with the withered "hand" (Mk 3:1-6) are placed on these 31sts, as they were the Great Days for a village class.

When in communion with full solarists, Pharisees fixed their +2½ 31st, so that it did not continue to move on every two years. It remained as one of three 31sts held in succession every year, each being the Great Day of a different party, and all attended by those ministers who were accepted in all parties.

The Dates of Passover

The foregoing points are part of the explanation of the much debated question of Passover in the gospels. It has long been observed that the Synoptics make the Thursday evening of the Last Supper a Passover meal (Lk 22:15), while John's gospel makes the Friday a Passover, interpreting the crucifixion of Jesus as the sacrifice of the paschal lamb (Jn 19:14).

The Julian date of the Last Supper was, according to the concealed chronology, Thursday March 19, AD 33. The crucifixion took place on Friday March 20.

The previous Tuesday March 17, at 6 a.m., had been 14a/I, the regular Passover date for the solar calendar that had not yet intercalated (see Table D p. 190). When a +2½ version of this date was added for villagers under Pharisee influence, the date fell again on Thursday at 6 p.m. This was the Passover observance that was included in the Last Supper.

The +2½ date of Passover was useful to those wanting to unite different parties, for it was in conjunction with 30a of solarists who had intercalated. This 30a was, for Samaritans, their 31st. Thus they had contrived a double reason why it was a Great Day, one when heaven should send a fulfilment of prophecy. A grand climax on that night would prove that both Samaritans and ascetic Pharisees were acting in accordance with the will of heaven.

But there was another point of view about Passover, going right back to the Old Testament. More precisely, it was another point of view about the date when the unleavened bread should be eaten. For Ex 12:18, it was eaten at the same time as the Passover meal, on the 14th of the first month (cf. Ex 12:6). But for Lev 23:6, coming from another tradition, unleavened bread was to be eaten on the 15th of the first month, the day after Passover; there were two different feasts. In the week in question, 15a fell, for those who had not intercalated, on Wednesday March 18. Its +2½ version was on Friday evening, March 20, the time of the crucifixion.

An important distinction had been made by Essenes, who no longer practised animal sacrifices but substituted for them prayers and religious observances (*Ant.* 18:18–19). They had moved the emphasis of their Passover to the eating of unleavened bread, not the eating of a paschal lamb. For them, eating the bread had become the sacrificial offering. The word *to pascha*, on the surface "Passover", has the p-sense "the meal for eating unleavened bread". The Friday observance, drawn on in John's gospel, was a version of the 15th, for bread only, interpreted as a sacrifice. Jesus himself, in his suffering on the cross, was a spiritual sacrifice.

A further point was that the unleavened bread meal of Lev 23:6 was not required to be in the evening, whereas that of Ex 12:18 must be in the evening. For that reason, celibates who had their main meal at noon could hold the observance then, still calling it *to pascha*. John's gospel places *to pascha* on Friday at noon in Jn 6:4, 19:14. It could also be placed at the first meal of the day, 6 a.m. (Jn 18:28).

The word *ta azyma*, normally used for "unleavened bread", also appears. It is found only at 14a (Mk 14:1, 12, A 12:3, 20:6). Mk 14:1 uses *to pascha* and *ta azyma* together for the same time, regular 14a. It appears that *to pascha* was used for the meal of unleavened bread interpreted as a sacrifice, while *ta azyma* was the ordinary Jewish meal of unleavened bread, observed by members still preserving Jewish traditions.

Pentecontads

The new evidence of the Temple Scroll, taken with *Contemp. Life* 65, shows that the year was further divided by some solarists into seven sets of seven weeks, 49 days, thought of as pentecontads on the analogy of jubilees. The series was: 26/I, 15/III (Pentecost), 3/V, 22/VI, 10/VIII, 29/IX, 17/XI, 5/I, with three weeks from this to the beginning of the next series (11QT 18–22).

As the Hebrew letter *Nun* was used for 50, the Greek *To nyn, ta nyn*, "now", was used as a play on words to indicate a pentecontad (with article). *To nyn* means Pentecost, 15/III, and *ta nyn* means a lesser pentecontad, 26/I (A 20:32) or 29/IX (A 4:29, 5:38, 17:30, 27:22).

The terms for time in A 27:19–25 indicate that 29/IX was retained as a feast in Gentile districts, while the Jewish 31sts were not being observed. This winter feast (December 17, AD 60, in A 27:20–26) was associated with "good cheer". It was in the process of becoming part of a Christmas observance, being the first Preparation Day of the December solstice councils.

Generation

The word *ho chronos*, "time", has the p-sense "a generation of forty years". It began on the 31st.

The months

The months of the solar calendar were known by numbers only, not names, with the March equinox as I. In Jn 4:35, the June solstice is *tetramēnos* p: "4th month".

The Julian calendar was also used, and Luke uses its months, calling them by numbers. Month 3 (*mēnas treis*) means March, month 5 (*mēnas pente*) May, month 6 (*mēnas hex*) June. These phrases are always used at the 1st of the Julian month.

Words for "Year"

The word *etos* for "year" means the year beginning on the 1st of the Julian month, and the word *eniautos* means the year beginning at the solar 31st.

Numbered Days

The ordinary days of the week, Sunday, Monday etc, were called by numbers, "day 1, 2, 3, . . ." up to 7 (Saturday).

The rule for word order applying to all time phrases is: *The noun is placed first at the earlier beginning*. Days began at 6 p.m. the previous evening in orthodox Jewish reckoning, and this usage was also found among ascetics under Pharisee influence. So *hēmerai treis* ("day 3") means Monday 6 p.m., and *treis hēmerai* means Tuesday 6 a.m., the beginning for solarists.

Because of the link between days and members of the hierarchy (see Hierarchy, p. 335), the numbered days could continue until number 12, into the following week. Day 8 (Sunday) appears in Jn 20:26, A 25:6; Day 12 (Thursday) in A 24:11.

The words *meta* "after" (+ accusative) and *pro* "before" (+ genitive) are found with days, e.g. "after three days" (*meta treis hēmeras*). The p-sense of the latter phrase is "one full day after day 3" (Tuesday), that is, day 4 (Wednesday). Similarly, *pro* means "one full day before". Examples: *meta dyo hēmeras* (Mk 14:1) "after two days" p: Tuesday, as Tuesday is one full day, 24 hours, after Monday, day 2. *Pro hex hēmerōn* (Jn 12:1) "before six days"; p: Thursday, one full day before Friday, day 6.

Hōsei "about" is also used to mean a full day before. Lk 9:28, *hōsei hēmerai oktō*, Friday evening, as 24 hours before Saturday evening, the early (Jewish) beginning of Sunday.

On Friday, the sabbath, the evening began, more strictly, at 3 p.m., when some of the sabbath rules came into operation. This was also the case for the end of the sabbath, Saturday 3 p.m. So *hōsei hēmerai oktō* in the example above means Friday 3 p.m.

The rule for word order also applies to days with ordinal numbers. *Hē tritē hēmera* means the normal start, *hē hēmera hē tritē* the early beginning twelve hours before. Since, in Samaritan usage, the "third day" was the 1st of the month (see above, p. 194) and this date was Saturday 3 p.m. in the Night position, *hē tritē hēmera* means Saturday 1st at 3 p.m. (Mt 27:64), and *hē hēmera hē tritē* means the same Saturday at 3 a.m. (1 Cor 15:4).

The phrase *mia tōn hēmerōn* "one of the days'", means "number one day of the month". But this was both the 31st and the 1st, as the 31st was treated as part of the following month. The regular 31st is meant in Lk 8:22, the 1st in Lk 20:1, and the Samaritan 31st (the same as the regular 30th) in Lk 5:17.

Tē mia (with article) is found only with *ta sabbata*, p-sense "the sabbatical year", and it means the calendar 1st, of the first month of the year (regular or Samaritan).

Beginning of the Sabbatical Year

Because of the double start of a month, the year also had a double start. Consequently the sabbatical year began on both the 31st (Mk 2:23) and the 1st (A 20:7). In the Night position, the 1st fell on Saturday evening, at the end of the sabbath. It was natural to begin resting for the sabbatical year at the same time as resting from work on the sabbath day, that is, on Saturday morning. So a calendar beginning could be made on the Saturday morning, and it was also called *tē mia tōn sabbatōn* (p-sense "the 1st of the month in the sabbatical year"). This point was drawn upon by the evangelists in order to convey the fact that Jesus was removed from the burial cave early on the Saturday morning, while appearing to say that the resurrection took place on the Sunday morning, "the first day of the week".

Julian Start of the Day

It has been seen that the Julian calendar was incorporated by westernised members of the movement from the time it was introduced. This meant also recognising the Julian beginning of day, at midnight. In the Day position, the midnight start occurred before the solar 6 a.m. start, and in the Night position it occurred after the 6 p.m. start. So the sabbath began both on Friday at 6 p.m. (or, strictly, 3 p.m.) according to Jewish tradition, and also on Friday at midnight, the Julian start of Saturday, with a strict start on Friday at 9 p.m. In Diaspora usage, it was possible to place *tē epaurion* at these hours, rather than at 6 p.m. (Mt 27:62, A 23:32).

Further Names for Days

The apparently vague expressions "certain days", "many days", and "more days" have a very precise pesher sense.

Tines hēmerai "certain days" means Monday as a feast day, either the Samaritan 31st (regular 30th) (A 15:36) or 16/III, the day after Pentecost, beginning the year according to *Jub.* 1:1 (A 10:48). *Hēmerai tines* means its early start on Sunday at 6 p.m. (A 9:19, 10:48, 16:12, 24:24, 25:13).

Pollai hēmerai "many days", means Tuesday as a feast day, the regular 31st (A16:18). A man with the title "the Many" (*hoi polloi*) was equal to a "son of Levi", whose day was Tuesday (Hierarchy, p. 342). *Ou pollai hēmerai* "not many days" means "not Tuesday 31st (so Friday 31st) (as the Night position 31st was an alternative to Day) (Jn 2:12, Lk. 15:13, A 1:5).

Pleious hēmerai "more days", means Wednesday as a feast day, usually the regular 1st. *Ou pleious hēmerai* means "not Wednesday 1st (but Saturday

(6 p.m.) 1st)", for the same reason as above (A 24:11, A 25:6).

Pleiones hēmerai (A 27:20) means Thursday as a feast day (+2½ 31st).

The phrase *hikanai hēmerai* "many days" is an alternative way of referring to the equinoxes at the regular 31st. Where "those days" associates them with priests, *hikanos*, also meaning "worthy", associates them with laymen acting as lay priests, claiming to be "worthy" to do so.

· The word *hē paraskeuē*, "the Preparation" apparently means Friday, but has a more exact sense. It means the day for adjusting chronometers, for the reasons shown above p. 181. The day chosen was the +2½ version of the feast of unleavened bread, so there were two versions of it; 14a +2½, from Thursday evening, and 15a +2½, from Friday evening. John's gospel, treating 15a as the date for unleavened bread, does not show a three hours' darkness on the Friday, and gives the time of the crucifixion as noon, whereas the Synoptics say 9 a.m.; both mean the same time, the Synoptics using true time, John the fast time. John Mark himself was using fast time on the Friday night, a fact of some importance in the account of events at the burial cave.

The word *hē heortē*, "the feast", has the exact sense "the fast", and means the 31st, Samaritan or regular, which was observed by fasting, or the Day of Atonement.

Watches

The day and night were divided into three-hour periods. In the night, they were called watches. Six p.m. was *opsia*, "evening", 9 p.m. *opse*, midnight *mesonyktion*, 3 a.m. *alektorophōnia*, "cockcrowing" (Mk 13:35). The night watches could also be numbered; 3 a.m. was "the fourth watch" (Mk 6:48). When the Julian day was used, beginning at midnight, the "first watch" was at midnight (A 12:10).

The phrase *autē tē hōra* "that very hour" marks divisions of the day at 9 a.m. or 3 p.m., also 9 p.m. and 3 a.m. They were lay divisions; *autos* refers to lay grades.

Hours

Hours are used with ordinal numbers when they begin from 6 a.m., in Jewish fashion. Nine a.m. is the 3rd hour (*hōra tritē*), noon the 6th (*hōra hektē*), 3 p.m. the 9th (*hōra enatē*), 4 p.m. the 10th (*hōra dekatē*).

They are used with cardinal numbers for Julian reckoning. *Mia hōra* means 1 a.m., *hōras dyo* 2 p.m., and so on.

The word *euthys* "immediately" also indicates an hour. Its literal meaning is "straight", and it referred to the discipline of Essene villagers, who were "making the paths straight" (Mk 1:3). It is used for their prayer times, usually 3 and 4 p.m. (noon and 1 p.m. on Fridays), also at their meal times, 6 a.m. and 6 p.m. It is very frequent in Mark's gospel, which comes from these ranks.

The word *palin* "again", also refers to exact hours, but the hours of celibates; their noon meal, or hours for prayers. The word may come from the fact that their hours had a double beginning, on the hour and at 5 minutes past.

Parachrēma "immediately" means the end of the village service at 3 or 4 p.m. It may be a play on "beside the money" (*chrēma*, cf. A 4:37), as these were the hours when the collection of money at the end of the service was made.

As the twelve hours of the night paralleled the twelve hours of the day, and as village workers rose at 3 a.m., the words for hours of the day are found also for hours of the night.

The ten minutes around the hour were sub-divided, reflecting rules for activities at those times. The word "about", *hōs*, with an hour means 5 minutes to, and *eutheōs* ("immediately", but a play on *euthys* with *hōs*) means 5 minutes past the hour. At the latter time, the doors to the sacred dining chamber were closed to exclude outsiders (A 21:30). The hour was treated as having a double beginning.

There was an even narrower division, with *peri* "about", denoting 3 minutes past the hour. This probably reflected five minutes around the hour, from 2 minutes to, to 3 minutes past, treated as especially holy.

"Already"

It was often the case that observances were held earlier than usual, for example, the sabbath beginning at 3 p.m. on Friday. A comment "Is it beginning already?" led to the word *ēdē* ("already") being used for a time when events took place earlier than expected. It is used with hours, at the three-hour divisions of the day or night.

The verb *mellō* "to be about to", is used to refer forward to an event in three hours', three months' or three years' time.

Further minor points are explained in the detailed chronology.

LIST OF CHRONOLOGICAL TERMS

The terms for time on which the chronology depends are listed below, in their normal sense and pesher sense. For convenience, the English form is given, in RSV translation, followed by the Greek terms. (p: means pesher sense). For fuller explanations, see p. 189–200.

About
hōs
p: 5 minutes to hour, when preparation for action on the hour began.
Jn 19:14, *hōra ēn hōs hektē*, "hour was about a 6th" p: "it was 5 minutes to 12". (Pilate's decision before the crucifixions, which were performed on the hour.)

hōsei
p: one full unit before.
Lk 3:23, *hōsei etōn triakonta*, "about 30 years old", p: "it was AD 29" (one year before year 30, dating from AD 1 as year 1).
Lk 9:28, *hōsei hēmerai oktō* "about 8 days", p: "Friday 3 p.m." (one day of 24 hours before Saturday 3 p.m., early start of Sunday, day 8. Early start is normally 6 p.m., but 3 p.m. at beginning and end of sabbath).
Lk 23:44 *hōsei hōra hektē* "about a 6th hour", p: "9 a.m." (the watch, 3 hours, before the noon watch).

peri (with accusative)
p: 3 minutes past the hour.
Mk 6:48 *peri tetartēn phylakēn tēs nyktos* "about a 4th watch of the night", p: "3.03 a.m." (see Boat System, p. 329).
A 10:9 *peri hōran hektēn* "about a 6th hour", p: "12.03 p.m.".

About To
mellō, "be about to"
p: act 3 hours, 3 months, (or) 3 years before.
A 12:6 *ēmellen prosagagein auton ho Hērōdēs* "Herod was about to bring him out", p: "Agrippa would lead him forth in 3 hours' time".
Lk 9:31 *ēmellen plēroun* "he was about to fulfil" p: "he would enact in 3 months' time" (December).
A 24:25 *tou krimatos tou mellontos* "the coming judgment", p: "the Last Judgment in 3 years' time" (in AD 61, NLS4000).

After
meta (with accusative)
p: one full unit after.
Mk 14:1 *meta dyo hēmeras*, "after 2 days", p: "on Tuesday", 24 hours after Monday, day 2, starting 6 a.m.
Mk 10:34 *meta treis hēmeras* "after 3 days", p: "on Wednesday". 24 hours

after Tuesday, day 3, starting 6 a.m.

Mk 9:2 *meta hēmeras hex*, "after days 6", p: "on Friday", 24 hours after Thursday, early start of Friday, day 6. Friday afternoon 3 p.m. as start of sabbath.

Lk 1:24 *meta . . . tautas tas hēmeras* "after these days", p: "1a at the December Preparation Days", 24 hours after 31a.

Already
ēdē
p: time point reached earlier than expected.

Jn 11:17 *tessaras ēdē hēmeras* "4 already days", p: "3 a.m. Wednesday" (Wednesday, day 4, usually starts 6 a.m., but early start for workers at 3 a.m.).

Before
pro, with genitive
p: one full unit before.

Jn 12:1 *pro hex hēmeron* "before 6 days", p: "on Thursday", 24 hours before Friday, day 6. (Julian beginning of day, so midnight before, Wednesday midnight.)

Jn 13:1 *pro . . . tēs heortēs tou pascha* "before the feast of the Passover", p: "Thursday, 24 hours before 15a+2½ unleavened bread with 31a reg. on Friday."

A 5:36, 21:38 *pro . . . toutōn tōn hēmerōn* "before these days", p: "30a at the December Preparation Days, 24 hours before 31a."

Cockcrowing
alektorophōnia
p: the signal for 3 a.m.
(See further p. 110.)

Day
hēmera
p: festival day; significant day in the calendar.

hai hēmerai (plural)
p: the 31st, reg. or Sam, as the main day of the three Preparation Days (1QSa 1:26); or pentecontad 26/I. Word order shows the season:

en tais hēmerais ekeinais	"in the days those"	March equinox
en tais hēmerais tautais	"in the days these"	June solstice
en ekeinais tais hēmerais	"in those days"	September equinox
en tautais tais hēmerais	"in these days"	December solstice

hē hēmera (singular)
p: the 31st or 1st, or a great feast day.

en tautē tē hēmera "this day"	Sam 31st for Samaritans Reg. 31st for Hebrews
en ekeinē tē hēmera "that day"	Sam 1st (= reg. 31st) for Samaritans Reg. 1st for Hebrews

With numerals
e.g. *treis hēmerai* "three days"
p: day 3 of the week, Tuesday.
(rule for word order: if the noun is placed first, the earlier beginning of the day is meant, usually 6 p.m. the previous evening).

With other adjectives
tines hēmerai "certain days"
p: Monday as a feast day.

pollai hēmerai "many days"
p: Tuesday as a feast day, the regular 31st.

ou pollai hēmerai "not many days"
p: Friday the 31st, in the Night position ("not Tuesday 31st but Friday 31st").

pleious hēmerai "more days"
p: Wednesday as a feast day, the regular 1st.

ou pleious hēmerai "not more days"
p: Saturday the 1st, in the Night position("not Wednesday 1st but Saturday 1st").

hikanai hēmerai "many days"
p: the regular 31st, March or September equinox

kath' hēmeran "daily"
p: regular 31st, Herodian, as opposed to Samaritan 31st.

Evening
opsia
p: 6 p.m. meal.

opse
p: 9 p.m.
hespera
p: 9 p.m.

Famine
limos
p: the 3½ years between a north solar year and a south solar year. See
p. 173

Fast
asitia
p: 29/IX. ("not the wheat, *sitos*, pentecontad, in summer, but the opposite
pentecontad, in winter". Pentecost, 15/III, was the wheat festival). (A 27:21)

nēsteia
p: the Day of Atonement.

Feast
heortē
p: fast, for the 31st or the Day of Atonement.

Hour
hōra
p: on the hour (noon, 1 p.m., etc.).

Immediately
euthys
p: on the hour, at times of prayer for villagers.

eutheōs
p: at 5 minutes past the hour.

parachrēma
p: end of the village service, 3 or 4 p.m., 3 or 4 a.m.

Month
mēn
p: Julian month, 1st of the month.
mēnas treis March 1st.
mēnas pente May 1st.
mēnas hex June 1st.

Morning
prōi

p: 6 a.m.
lian prōi "exceedingly morning" 3 a.m.

Near
engys
p: two dates from different calendars in conjunction (for example, 31a regular of northern calendars with +2½ 15a of southern calendars, Jn 6:4). (See Table D, p. 190.)

Next Day
tē epaurion
p: The 36 hour day at the beginning of the 17½ day intercalation of the solar calendar every fourteen years. Normally the 31st and 1a (so "on the *aurion*", the 1st).

hexēs
p: the 31st as a non-sacred day, not a Great Day (in form *tē hexēs*).

epiousē
p: midnight, as the Julian start of the next day.

Now
to nyn
p: Pentecost, 15/III ("the *Nun*", play on Hebrew letter meaning 50, the number indicating Pentecost).

ta nyn
p: a lesser pentecontad, 26/I or 29/IX.

Passover
pascha
p: the meal for eating unleavened bread.
a) 14a/I or +2½ 14a/I (Ex 12:6 rule)
b) 15a/I or +2½ 15a/I (Lev 23:6 rule)
See further pp. 194–195

Preparation
paraskeuē
p: the day for adjusting the measurement of hours, which had become three hours fast. The feast of unleavened bread, +2½ version combined with the 31st. Friday for those keeping the Ex 12

rule, Saturday for those keeping the Lev 23 rule.

Sabbath
sabbaton
p: the 31st, Tuesday 6 a.m. (Day) or Friday 6 p.m. (Night), or the +2½ 31st.

sabbata (plural)
p: the sabbatical year.

Time
kairos
p: the quartodecimal year.

eukairos
p: the quartodecimal year, for the party placing the intercalation at or near the equinox, for the post position.

chronos
p: a generation of forty years, beginning or ending on the 31st.

Today
sēmeron
p: the 31st, as the day of fulfilment ("Yesterday, Today, Tomorrow", 30th, 31st, 1st). Samaritan or regular.

Tomorrow
aurion
p: the 1st (see "Today").

epiousios
p: the 1st.

Unleavened Bread
ta azyma
p: the Jewish feast of unleavened bread, by the Ex 12 rule.

Watch
phylakē
p: three-hourly division of the night. Term used by villagers (play on *phylakē* "prison/marriage").

Year
eniautos
p: year beginning on the 31st, Jewish.

etos
p: year beginning on the 1st of the Julian month.

Yesterday
echthes
p: the 30th ("Yesterday, Today, Tomorrow", 30th, 31st, 1st).

Abbreviations (Chronological Terms)

IC	Intercalation
Reg.	Regular (31st)
Sam	Samaritan (31st)
NS	North Solar
NLS	North Lunisolar
InterS	Intermediate Solar
Inter LS	Intermediate Lunisolar
SS	South Solar
SLS	South Lunisolar
equ. pos.	Equinox position of calendar
solst. pos	Solstice position of calendar
post. pos.	Post position of calendar

DETAILED CHRONOLOGY FROM 9 BC TO AD 64

JULIAN DATE	SOLAR DATE	HOUR	PLACE	EVENT AND TIME PHRASES

9 BC
InterS 3930
Intercalation of all calendars completed. Day position.

September Quarter

Tue Sep 17   31a(VII)

Zechariah, descendant of Zadok, prepares to perform Day of Atonement ceremony before leaving office for marriage with Elizabeth (Lk 1:5–7).
> en tais hēmerais Hērōdou basileōs tēs Ioudaias (Lk 1:5 "in the days of Herod king of Judea") 31st in Sep season for the king.
> probebēkotes en tais hēmerais autōn (Lk 1:7 "advanced in their days") celibate, so using 1st position of the calendar.

Fri Sep 27   10/VII   3 p.m.   Mird
              Atone-   major
              ment

At Mird substitute sanctuary, Zechariah concludes the Atonement service, then hands over to his second Simeon ("Gabriel", Abiathar priest) (Lk 1:8–20).
> tē hōra tou thymiamatos (Lk 1:10 "at the hour of incense") 3 p.m., climax of atonement (cf. Mk 9:2 p).
> hē gynē mou probebēkuia en tais hēmerais autēs (Lk 1:18 "my wife is advanced in her days") Elizabeth is still in celibate status.

Zechariah leaves sanctuary, now able to marry, so "dumb", not permitted to preach (Lk 1:21–22).

Fri Oct 4   31a(VII)   6 p.m.

Post position 31st.

              post pos.

Sat Oct 5   1a/VII   6 p.m.   Ain
                                 Feshkha

Zechariah at Ain Feshkha, used for marriages of priests (Lk 1:23).
> hai hēmerai tēs leitourgias (Lk 1:23 "the days of the liturgy") service for villagers

December Quarter

Tue Dec 17   31a(X)   6 a.m.

31st.

              1st pos.

Wed Dec 18   1a/X   6 a.m.

Conception of John the Baptist.
> meta . . . tautas tas hēmeras (Lk 1:24 "after these days") December solstice; 1a, 24 hrs after 31a.

8 BC

Thu May 1			Elizabeth, pregnant, conceals herself (Lk 1:24).

      mēnas pente (Lk 1:24 "months 5") Julian month 5, May, 1st of month.

Sun Jun 1	15/III Pentecost to solst. pos.	Mar Saba	Joseph and Mary begin betrothal-marriage process at Pentecost. Simeon-Gabriel explains marriage to Mary (Lk 1:26–38)

      en . . . tō mēni tō hektō (Lk 1:26 "in the 6th month"), June 1, using Jewish Julian names for months.

Tue Jun 17	31a(IV) solst. pos.	Ain Feshkha	Mary arrives at Ain F. for her betrothal ceremony (Lk 1:39).

      en tais hēmerais tautais (Lk 1:39 "in the days these") 31st at June solstice.

Wed Jun 18	1b& 15a/III Pentecost to post pos.	6 p.m.	Elizabeth, at 6 months, promoted to Mother. Mary replaces her as the chief woman during pregnancy, and speaks Magnificat (Lk 1:46–55) as substitute "Hannah" to Zechariah-"Samuel" (cf. 1 Sam 1–2).

      apo tou nyn (Lk 1:48 "from the now") from Pentecost, the Nun (50).

At a date after the betrothal wedding of Mary and Joseph but before the final wedding in September, Jesus is conceived.

September Quarter

Tue Sep 16	31a(VII)		Official birth date of John the Baptist (birth not recorded).

7 BC
SS3930
March Quarter

Sun Mar 1			Official birth date of Jesus (Lk 1:56).

      hōs mēnas treis (Lk 1:56 "about 3 months") Mar 1, 1st of Julian month 3. Kings have official birthdays at 1st of Julian month and at solar 31st.

		queen's house	Mary goes to queen's house as place of women's separation and for birth of orphans, for birth of Jesus (Lk 1:56b).

September Quarter

Tue Sep 15	31a(VII)		Season when Jesus should be born according to rules. Magians of W. Manasseh accept him, come to hail him as successor, and as a rival to the Herod dynasty. Herod is misled about the date of the birth (see p. 175).

en hēmerais Hērōdou tou basileōs
(Mt 2:1 "in days of Herod the king")
31st in September, season for kings.
ton chronon (Mt 2:7 "the time")
generation of 40 years.

5 BC
SLS3931
September Quarter
Fri Sep 1

Joseph, who has been in hiding from
Herod at Qumran ("Egypt") following his
participation in the Pharisee nationalist
protest (*Ant.* 17:41–42), comes out of
hiding on Herod's 70th birthday (Mt
2:15).

> *heōs tēs teleutēs Hērōdou* (Mt 2:15
> "until the death of Herod") until his
> 70th birthday, when active life ceased
> for men according to biblical law.
> (Herod acts in next episode; cf. rule
> that all events in narrative are
> consecutive.) Cf. *Ant.* 17:148, Herod
> is about 70 at this time.

Tue Sep 12   31a(VII)   Ain   Solar 31st occurrence of Herod's
          equ. pos.   Feshkha   70th birthday. Matthias, a Hellenist, has
been appointed high priest (*Ant.* 17:78,
165–166), so Jesus is declared legitimate
(Mt 2:20).

> *teleutēsantos . . . tou Hērōdou*
> (Mt 2:19) Herod 70, 31st occurrence.

4 BC
March Quarter
Death of Herod. Archelaus appointed heir, Antipas rejected.

1 BC
NS3940
(for pro-David party, 3900)

March Quarter
Mon Mar 9   31a(I)
          equ. pos.

Formal foundation of Vineyard in
Rome, supporting the Davids as superior
rulers. Conceived by the ex high priest
Matthias as a 60-year project for the "8th
day" of the 480 years to AD 60, NS4000.
As a "day" of 12 hours divided into 5
year "hours" (AD 5 hr 1, AD 10 hr 2, etc.)
(Mt 20:1–16, Mk 12:1–9, A 7:8).
Head of W. Manasseh, "Isaac" brought
into membership, "circumcised" (A 7:8).
He leads the party of the tetrarch
Antipas, that of Manasseh Diaspora
Essenes, the "Figtree". Thus "the Figtree

was planted in the Vineyard" (Lk 13:6).
Anti-Herodian parties declare a zero
generation to remove Herod, beginning
the millennium in 1 BC.

> tē hēmera tē ogdoē (A 7:8 "the 8th
> day") 1 BC, yr 420 of the 480 yrs 421
> BC to AD 60, 8th "day".

Tue Sep 7	31a(VII)	Ain Feshkha	Joseph due to renew marriage, 6 years from birth of son. Follows the rule for a first son, as there is a Boethus high priest (*Ant.* 17:164) (Mt 2:21). (James conceived December.)

AD 1

NS3941. Series of intercalations begins, changing from Day (Tue 6 a.m.) to Night (Fri 6 p.m.).

Sat Jan 1			Supporters of the Davids, keeping the Julian calendar as well as the Jewish, observe New Year.
Tue Mar 1		Qumran	The danger of loss of the native kingship and Jewish identity leads to the rise of zealotry. Theudas of Ephraim, with Joseph, leads a moderate nationalist group at Qumran.
Tue Mar 8	31a(I) 1st pos.	6 a.m.	"Famine" at March intercalation (3½ yrs) (A 7:11a).
Fri Mar 25	31a(I) equ. pos.	6 p.m.	Intercalation ends.
Sat Mar 26	1a/I	6 p.m.	Theudas goes to Qumran ("the far country"), where the "loose living" of the Diaspora Essenes ("seekers-after-smooth-things") is practised (Lk 15:13).

> met' ou pollas hēmeras (Lk 15:13 "after
> not many days") Sat 6 p.m. 1a, 24 hrs
> after Fri 6 p.m. 31a, which is "not
> Tue 31st (pollas hēmeras)" so Fri 31st.

September Quarter

Tue Sep 6	31a(I) 1st pos.	6 a.m.	September intercalation begins for villagers. Theudas observes this fast also, and allies with Judas the Galilean (Lk 15:15, A 7:11).

> limos ischyra (Lk 15:14 "strong
> famine") 3½ yrs for "flesh" ranks,
> villagers.
> thlipsis megale (A 7:11 "great
> tribulation") 3½ yrs Sep 1 to Mar AD
> 5.

Fri Sep 23	31a(VII) equ. pos. end of intercalation	6 p.m.	Official birthday of James.

> ho chronos tēs epangelias (A 7:17 "the
> time of the promise") NLS3940, end
> of 40 yrs for Herod's "Exodus", at
> 31st.

AD 4
SS3940

Tue Dec 2	31a(X)	6 a.m.		Intensified nationalism. Eastern parties take over at Qumran, the Scribes (East Manasseh) and Pharisees. Theudas and Joseph, the more moderate Sceptre and Star, are driven back to Simeon and the peace party, so the Prodigal Son returns (Lk 15:20).

Simeon in return allows a compromise with Diaspora practices, some use of the Julian calendar. The IC for SS3941, due Mar AD 5, is placed Dec AD 4, and Simeon is "born" as the Pope of the peace party, "Moses" on this day (A 7:20a, Lk 15:20–24).
> *en hō kairō* (A 7:20 "in which season") at IC season, December, as it is before Mar 1 (A 7:20b). Cf. Lk 13:1.

AD 5
SS3941, intercalation year
SLS3940, generation year
March Quarter

Sun Mar 1			Mird major	Simeon again declared Pope, (A 7:20–21). Jacob-Heli, the Elder Brother, allies with him on Jewish terms (Lk 15:25–32).

> *mēnas treis* (A 7:20) Mar 1, Julian month 3.
> *tosauta etē* (Lk 15:29 "these many years") 1st of month, Jewish Julian.

September Quarter

Tue Sep 1	31a(VII) 1st pos.	6 a.m.	Ain Feshkha	Simeon comes to Ain F. (A 7:23). *tesserakontaetēs chronos* (A 7:23 "40 years' time") 40 years SLS3900–3940, Sep 1 as both Julian 1st (*etē*) and solar 31st (used for *chronos*).
Thu Sep 17	30a/VI & Sam 31st equ. pos.	6 p.m.		Samaritans keep Thu 6 p.m. as their 31st, on "Tomorrow Today" principle. Simeon attacks them for their calendar and associated doctrine of ministry (A 7:28). *echthes* (A 7:28 "yesterday").
Fri Sept 18	31a(VII)	6 p.m.		The 12th birthday of John the Baptist. Elizabeth re-enacts the birth symbolically (Lk 1:57–58) *ho chronos* (Lk 1:57) SLS3940, 31st.
		midnight		Julian sabbath. Simeon is treated as having no priestly authority (A 7:26–28). *tē . . . epiousē hēmera* (A 7:26 "the

Qumran, looking south from the tower.
(*Photograph copyright Palphot, Israel*)

Qumran, looking west from the tower. The round well is on the upper left of the photograph.

Qumran. The western courtyard, interpreted as the substitute sanctuary. (*Photograph courtesy of T. Hobbs*)

Qumran. Detail of the circle of stones (foreground) near the fireplace, in the room interpreted as the north vestry; the place suggested to be where Jesus stood at his trial.

Qumran. The pillar bases and the bench outside the east door of the room interpreted as the south vestry. Looking towards the west.

Qumran. The southern esplanade, looking towards the north. It is the suggested place of the crucifixion. Exclusion cistern F is on the far mid right, and at the top left side of the flat area, the entrance to the "stables", now suggested to be the priests' latrine.

Qumran. The peak is part of the remains of Caves 7 and 8, suggested to be the joined burial cave where Jesus was placed. Taken from the chasm below.

Qumran. Lower left are the remains of Caves 7 and 8, taken from the pathway above. Cave 4 can be seen across to the right.

Cave 4, looking from the southern esplanade. It is on a separate projection across the chasm to the west.

Ain Feshkha. The Herodian Door

Khirbet Mazin. Remains of the enclosure and the watergate, looking towards the west.

Khirbet Mazin. The water channel, now silted up. Looking towards the east and the Dead Sea.

Khirbet Mird. The platform on the main hill.
(Photograph courtesy of D. Gawith.)

Khirbet Mird, looking towards the south-west. The smaller hill in the mid ground is topped by the "monument".
(Photograph courtesy of D. Gawith)

Mar Saba. A Christian monastery founded in the fifth century and reconstructed in the nineteenth century. It is suggested to be the site of "Jericho" and *Nazara*.

The wady Kidron, flowing from Jerusalem, near Mar Saba.

next day") midnight, next day by
Julian calendar. .

Sat Sep 19   1a/VII   6 p.m.   Re-enactment of circumcision and
naming of John Baptist, 1 day after
"birth" (Lk 1:59).

> en tē hēmera tē ogdoē (Lk 1:59 "in the
> 8th day") Sep AD 5, "hour 1" of the
> 60-year "day" of the Vineyard: both
> zero hour and hour 1 were used as a
> beginning.

December Quarter

Tue Dec 1   31a(X)   noon   Mird   Simeon and Ananus son of Seth
        1st pos.   (Ant. 18:26) ally to form a peace party
                           (A 7:30–35).

> etōn tesserakonta (A 7:30 "years 40")
> SLS3940, Dec, 1st of Julian month
> (etē).

AD 6
SLS3941
March Quarter

Mon Mar 1   30/XII   mid-   Mird   Year 1 of the dating from SLS3941
        1st pos.   night   Official 12th birthday of Jesus, Mar 1
               (Sun)   version.
Ceremony at Mird. Mary re-enacts the
birth (Rev 12:1–2). Zechariah, as the
Zadokite priest, utters a blessing over
him (Lk 1:67–79, cf. v.69).
At a council Zechariah ("Michael"),
Simeon ("Gabriel") and Ananus bring
about the overthrow of Joazar (Ant. 1:26,
Joazar "overpowered by a popular
faction"). Ananus is to be high priest in
his place. This means that Jesus is
legitimate; the Dragon is defeated (Rev
12:7–12, A 7:36–38).

> etē tesserakonta (A 7:36) Mar 1
> beginning of year 40, SLS3941
> (Herodian).

               6 p.m.   Joazar's attempt to exclude Mary from
communion is prevented by the rise of
Ananus, holding the position of Eagle
(Rev 12:13–16).

               9 p.m.   The council ends in conflict in which
Zechariah is killed (Rev 12:17, Lk 11:51,
Mt 23:35).
John the Baptist takes the place of his
father (Lk 1:80).

Tue Mar 2   31a(I)   6 a.m.   Qumran   Archelaus has now been dismissed by
        1st pos.   Rome, and the country is under
Quirinius (Lk 2:2b); thus the peace
faction under Simeon have "killed the

fatted Calf".

en tais hēmerais ekeinais (Lk 2:1 "in the days those") 31st in March.

Fri Mar 19	31a(I)			Equinox version of Jesus' 12th birthday. The birth is again re-enacted (Lk 2:6).

queen's house — Jesus is brought down to the queen's house, where he was actually born (Lk 2:7).

Ain Feshkha — The village pastors meet with Simeon and Ananus and agree to accept their peace policy (Lk 2:8-14). They also accept that Jesus is legitimate under Ananus and go to the queen's house to acknowledge him (Lk 2:15-20).

sēmeron (Lk 2:11 "today") the 31st, for great events.

Sat Mar 20 — 1a/I — 6 p.m. — Re-enactment of circumcision and naming of Jesus, 1 day after "birth".

hēmerai oktō (Lk 2:21 "days 8") day 8, Sun, early start 6 p.m. Sat.

Sun Mar 21 — +2½ 31st — Qumran — Jesus made an acolyte (Lk 2:22-24).

hai hēmerai tou katharismou (Lk 2:22 "the days of cleansing") +2½ 31st for lower baptisms.

Tue Mar 23 — Jerusalem — Last day of attendance. Joseph and Mary arrive in Jerusalem. Jesus is blessed by Simeon (Lk 2:25-35).

Tue Apr 6 — 31a(I) post pos. — 6 a.m. — Qumran — Theudas declares support for Archelaus (A 7:39-41). Judas the Galilean ("heavenly host") prepares for his uprising against the census. Ananus opposes Archelaus, and separates with the peace faction (A 7:42).

en tais hēmerais ekeinais (A 7:41 "in the days those") 31st, March quarter (post pos.).

June Quarter

Tue Jun 1 — 31a(IV) 1st pos. — 6 a.m. — The uprising occurs, led by Judas the Galilean. Theudas ("Moloch", the king, the Sceptre) and Joseph (the Star) take part (A 7:42-43).

etē tesserakonta (A 7:42 "years 40") SLS3901-3941, Julian 1st.

Jerusalem — Anna, aged 98, is the "Sarah", the Mother of orphans and Gentiles (Lk 2:36).

probebēkuia en hēmerais pollais (Lk 2:36 "advanced in many days") 1st position as celibate, Tue 31st (*pollai hēmerai*, Tuesday).

etē hepta (Lk 2:36 "years 7") AD 6 is year 7 from 2 BC when Anna turned 91, the age of Sarah when she ceased

bearing (Gen 17:17,21) so becoming
a Virgin again (cf. *Contemp. Life* 68,
"aged virgins" join the Therapeutae).
eōs etōn ogdoēkonta tessarōn (Lk 2:37
"until years 84") AD 6 is year 84 from
79 BC when Anna turned 14 (born
93 BC), the age of early initiation for
girls. 79 BC the year of founding the
order of Asher for women under
Queen Salome (gained power 79 BC,
Ant. 13:398). Cf. *War* 2:151 on the
longevity of Essenes. Anna has been
the Virgin from 2 BC until the
separation of Simeon, but is now a
Widow at his departure.

Fri Jun 18	31a(IV) solst. pos.	3 p.m.	Anna exercises ministry as a Widow (Lk 2:37–38).

nykta kai hēmeran (Lk 2:37 "night and
day") SLS3941, quartodecimal at
Night pos.
autē tē hōra (Lk 2:38 "that very hour")
3 p.m., lay hour.

AD 14
SS3950

Thu Mar 1		Jesus turns 20 (Lk 2:40).
Fri Mar 9	31a(I) equ. pos.	In year of accession of Tiberius (Aug 19, AD 14) new policy of friendship to Rome begins (cf. *Ant.* 18:36).

AD 15
NS3955. Series of intercalations begins, changing from Night (Fri 6 p.m.) to Day (Tue
6 a.m.)

Fri Mar 1			Jesus turns 21, age for baptism.
Fri Mar 8	31a(I)		Intercalation begins.
Mon Mar 25	30a/XII& Sam 31st& +2½ 14a. equ. pos.	Jerusalem	Joseph joins Jesus in Jerusalem for baptism ceremony (Lk 2:41).

tē heortē tou pascha (Lk 2:41 "the
feast of the Passover") Sam 31st, and
+2½ 14a unleavened bread (from
previous Fri 14a).

AD 17
InterS 3955
March Quarter

Mon Mar 1	Jesus turns 23, age for full initiation. Mary Magdalene 14, "born" at ceremony for girls (Mk 5:42).

hote egeneto etōn dōdeka (Lk 2:42
"when it was years 12") Mar 1, AD 17,
dating from AD 6 as year 1.
(See p. 176.)

Mon Mar 22	30a/XII & Sam 31st & +2½ 14a	midnight (Sun)	Jerusalem

Joseph arrives for repetition of Jesus' baptism prior to full initiation (Lk 2:42).
> *tēs heortēs* (Lk 2:42 "of the feast") Sam 31st, midnight start.

End of 12-hr ceremony. Joseph leaves for Mar Saba, expecting Jesus to arrive to take initiation (Lk 2:43–44).
> *teleiōsantōn tas hēmeras* (Lk 2:43 "when they had completed the days") noon, celibate hour.

Tue Mar 23	31a(I) equ. pos.	midnight (Mon)	Mar Saba

Joseph arrives at Mar Saba.
> *hēmeras hodon* (Lk 2:44 "a day's journey") 12 hrs Essene Gate to Mar Saba.

	3 a.m.	
	3 p.m.	Jerusalem

Joseph sets out for Essene Gate.

Joseph arrives at time for teaching. Jesus undergoing examinations for initiation in Jerusalem, showing preference for village life and Gentiles. "My father" (Lk 2:49) Eleazar Annas, high priest AD 16–17 (*Ant.* 18:34).
> *meta hēmeras treis* (Lk 2:46 "after days 3") Tue 3 p.m., 24 hrs after Mon 3 p.m., early start of Tue, day 3. 3 p.m., teaching time.

AD 18
Caiaphas becomes high priest (*Ant.* 18:35), and Jesus loses his position as crown prince. James "Solomon" appointed in his place (A 7:47).

AD 23
Wed Mar 1

Mary becomes a Widow on the death of Joseph (Lk 13:1).
> *etē dekaoktō* (Lk 13:1 "18 years") AD 23, year 18 of the millennium from AD 6 as 1.

AD 26
John the Baptist becomes Pope, 20 years from the "Period of Wrath", AD 6 (CD 1:9–11).

AD 29
NS3969, jubilee year
Series of intercalations for 3969 begin, changing from Day (Tue 6 a.m.) to Night (Fri 6 p.m.).
March Quarter

Tue Mar 1		Mird

John the Baptist prepares for rebaptisms to reformed doctrine (Lk 3:1–14).
> *en etei . . . pentekaidekatō . . .Tiberiou* (Lk 3:1 "in the 15th year of Tiberius") AD 29, 1st of Julian month. Reign counted from Mar AD 14 as Jewish year.

John is questioned by messengers from

Antipas (opposes marriage with .
Herodias) (Lk 3:15-17, Jn 1:19-27). Is
excluded from communion by Antipas
(Lk 3:18-20).

Jesus, on his 35th birthday, begins
period outside the community 18
months before marriage. Baptism by
village priest Jonathan Annas, who as
Hellenist permits the marriage
(Lk 3:21-22).

Jesus is now in world, as king, with royal
genealogy (Lk 3:23-37).

> *hōsei etōn triakonta* (Lk 3:23 "about
> years 30") year before Mar AD 30 as
> year 30, dating from 1 BC as David
> millennium.

Mon Mar 7	30a/XII& Sam 31st	6 a.m.	Mird	Baptist baptises others, in running water at Mird, speaks of Jesus as "Lamb of God", i.e. illegitimate. See p. 350. (Jn 1:29-31, Mk 1:4-8, Mt 3:1-12).

> *tē epaurion* (Jn 1:29 "the next day")
> Sam 31st, IC begins for NS3969.
> *en tais hēmerais ekeinais* (Mt 3:1 "in
> the days those") March equinox, Sam
> 31st.

Tue Mar 8	31a(I) 1st pos.	6 a.m. noon	Qumran	Baptist baptises Jesus in running water at Qumran. A schism breaks out. Baptist deprives Jesus of the right to give absolution. John Mark, chief proselyte, brings Gentiles to the side of Jesus (Jn 1:35-37, Mk 1:9, Mt 3:13-15).

> *tē epaurion* (Jn 1:35) reg. 31st, IC
> begins.
> *en ekeinais tais hēmerais* (Mk 1:9 "in
> those the days") March equinox, on
> the view that March was the true start
> of the year.

		3 p.m.		Jesus is rebaptised in still water by Jonathan Annas, the Spirit, who joins him in the schism. (Mk 1:10-11, Mt 3:16-17).

> *euthys* (Mk 1:10 "immediately")
> 3 p.m., hour for village Essenes.

		4 p.m.		Hour for teaching Gentiles (unclean). John Mark and Andrew, a married villager, join Jesus (Jn 1:38-40).

> *tēn hēmeran ekeinēn* (Jn 1:39 "the day
> that") reg. 31st, "that day" for
> Samaritans, "this day" for Hebrews.
> *hōra . . . hōs dekatē* (Jn 1:39 "hour . . .
> a 10th") 4 p.m., hour for Gentiles
> (*hōs*, 3.55 p.m.).

Wed Mar 9	1b/I	6 p.m.		End of 36 hr *epaurion* (reg.). 40-day fast

				begins.
Thu Mar 10	+2½ 31st		Ain Feshkha	Jesus goes to Ain F. as the first step to going into the world. He meets Philip, head of Shem, and joins Jonathan-Nathanael (Jn 1:43–51).
				tē epaurion (Jn 1:43) +2½ 31st, IC begins.
Fri Mar 25	31a(I) equ. pos.	6 p.m.		End of intercalation from reg. 31st.
Mon Apr 18	24/I	6 a.m.	Mird	Jesus reports back to Mird at the end of 40 days (see p. 189). He must be tested by "Satan" (Judas Iscariot) during period of betrothal (Mk 1:13, Lk 4:2, Mt 4:1–2).
				hēmeras tesserakonta (Lk 4:2 "days 40") day 40, 24/I.
Wed Apr 20	26/I			Beginning of pentecontad series for year (see p. 196). Judas offers alliance, with himself as chief priest and Jesus as world emperor. Jesus refuses (Lk 4:2–13).
				en tais hēmerais ekeinais (Lk 4:2 "in the days those") 26/I equiv. of March equinox feast for parties using pentecontads.
				achri kairou (Lk 4:13 "until a season") until March 30, NLS3969, IC year.

June Quarter

Fri Jun 24	31a(IV) solst. pos.		Ain Feshkha	Jesus to Ain F. Declares jubilee year. (Mk 1:14–15, Mt 4:17, Lk 4:14).
				meta . . . to paradothēnai ton Iōannēn (Mk 1:14) position after Baptist's betrothal ceremony (season before age 36).
				peplērotai ho kairos (Mk 1:15 "the season is fulfilled") IC for June NS3969 completed.
		3 p.m.	Mazin	Jesus to Mazin, village status. Mazin also used for mission to Gentiles. Peter and Andrew, Jewish missionaries, accept Jesus' policy for Gentiles: full membership (Mk 1:16–18).
				euthys (Mk 1:18) 3 p.m.
		4 p.m.		James and John, Gentile village members, turn from Simon Magus–Zebedee (*Clem. Hom.* 2:19–22) to doctrines of Jesus (Mk 1:19).
				euthys (Mk 1:20) 4 p.m., time for Gentiles.

September Quarter

Fri Sep 23	31a(VII) equ. pos.	noon	Mar Saba	Jesus to Mar Saba. He declares that the Last Jubilee, NS3969, is now fulfilled, and also expresses pro-Samaritan opinions.

(Lk 4:17-20).

> *en tē hēmera tōn sabbatōn* (Lk 4:16) on the 31st of the sabbatical year NS3969, starting 31a, noon before.
> *sēmeron* (Lk 4:21 "today") 31st as day of fulfilment of prophecy.
> *eniauton . . . dekton* (Lk 4:19, Isa 61:1-2) "acceptable year", jubilee year.
> *eniauton*, Jewish solar year starting 31st.

AD 30
NS3970, NLS3969
March Quarter

Fri Mar 24	31a(I) equ. pos.		Party of Antipas tetrarch prepare for power when Baptist prophecy for NS3970 fails. Pope will be Jonathan Annas, Second Judas, and King will be Jesus, legitimate for Hellenists.
	noon	Mazin	Jesus teaches in the Mazin synagogue as the David (Mk 1:21).
			euthys (Mk 1:21) 3 p.m. prayers 3 hrs earlier on Friday.
			tois sabbasin (Mk 1:21) sabbatical year NLS3969.
	1 p.m.		Judas, with support of tetrarch ("unclean spirit") claims to be Second. Jesus opposes him; he is the head of the circumcision party, requiring circumcision for Gentiles, (*Ant.* 20:34-47) (Mk 1:23-27).
			euthys (Mk 1:23) 1 p.m.
	2 p.m.		Tetrarch returns to Ain Feshkha (Mk 1:28).
			euthys (Mk 1:28) 2 p.m.
	3 p.m.		End of synagogue service. Jesus goes to centre for missionaries, "brothers" (Mk 1:29).
	4 p.m.		In centre for "sisters" and "widows", Mary the mother of Jesus modifies views to be more western (Mk 1:30-31).
			euthys (Mk 1:30) 4 p.m.
			parachrēma (Lk 4:39) 4 p.m.
	6 p.m.		Baptist discredited: "Sun set" at Jewish start of 31a. Tetrarch's party, Samaritans, in power. Sabbath therefore begins midnight: healing and carrying burdens permitted till then (Mk 1:32-34).
			opsias genomenēs (Mk 1:32) 6 p.m. meal.
Sat Mar 25	midnight (Fri)		Non-fulfilment. Jesus sets out in boat for Ain Feshkha,

				1 hour from Mazin, using extension of Julian sabbath to 1 a.m.
				prōi ennycha lian (Mk 1:35 "morning at night exceedingly") Julian morning at midnight.
				genomenēs . . . hēmeras (Lk 4:42) midnight, start of Julian day.
		1 a.m.	Ain Feshkha	Arrives Ain F. Leads prayers. (Mk 1:35-39).
June Quarter				
Thu Jun 1		3 a.m.	Mazin	Season for fulfilment in Julian practice, starting 1st of month. Jesus at Mazin helps Peter to "catch" Titus, servant of Agrippa (see p. 328). Agrippa begins to change views in favour of Jesus, begins 3 year process of instruction (Lk 5:1-5).
				di' holēs nyktos (Lk 5:5) midnight; Julian start of day being used.
				apo tou nyn (Lk 5:10 "from the now") from following solstice-Pentecost, new Hellenist government to be formed.
Sun Jun 4	29a/III	3 p.m.	Ain	Jesus to Ain F. on 1st Preparation Day of
		4 p.m.	Feshkha	season, allies with Simon Magus (Mk 1:40-45).
				euthys (Mk 1:42) 3 p.m.
				euthys (Mk 1:43) 4 p.m.
Mon Jun 5	30a/III& Sam 31st	noon	Mazin	At Mazin for days before betrothal. Jonathan Annas comes to say prayers at noon on roof of village meeting house. Roof opened at noon for villagers to see him (Mk 2:1-4a).
				palin . . . di' hēmeron (Mk 2:1) noon, middle of day.
				en mia tōn hēmerōn (Lk 5:17 "in one of the days"). Both the 31st and the 1st are the 1 (*mia*) of the month, and Sam 31st is also a 1.
		3 p.m.		Jon Annas is let down from the roof to ground floor to receive petitions of villagers and give absolution. Jesus on his west side acts as priest and gives *him* absolution (Mk 2:4b-11, Lk 5:19-24).
				euthys (Mk 2:8) 3 p.m.
				Jon Annas gives up use of priest's palanquin (Mk 2:12, Lk 5:25-26).
				parachrēma (Lk 5:25) end of 3 p.m. service.
				sēmeron (Lk 5:26) Today, Sam 31st.
	30b/III	6 p.m.		Village evening meal at Mazin. Jon Annas presiding. Process of giving full membership to uncircumcised Gentiles begins (Mk 2:13-17).

Tue Jun 6	31a(IV)
	1st pos.
	IC (June)
		6 a.m.	Mazin	Fasting for intercalation begins, Herodian NLS3969. Jesus says he will keep Samaritan InterS 3969 the following year (Mk 2:18–22).
				   hoson chronon (Mk 2:19) AD 30 as NLS3970.
				   en ekeinē tē hēmera (Mk 2:20) reg. 31st, Samaritan 1st.

		noon		Gentiles promoted to "ears of corn" (Mk 4:28)
				   en tois sabbasin (Mk 2:23) sabbatical year NLS3969 (*en* after start).
				   en sabbatō . . . tois sabbasin (Lk 6:1,2) 31st (reg.) sabbatical year.
				   NB. Textual variant *en sabbatō deuteroprōtō* shows knowledge of t*h*e pesher. Reg. 31st is first day to Hebrews, second day to Samaritans.

	31b(IV)	6 p.m.	Ain Feshkha	Betrothal of Jesus and Mary Magdalene at Ain Feshkha "Cana". "Wedding" under Hellenist rules. Sacred meal 6–10 p.m. precedes ceremony. Used also for admission of uncircumcised Gentile celibates (Philip), to full participation in the sacred meal (Jn 2:1–11). *tē hēmera tē tritē* (Jn 2:1 "the day the third") Tue 6 p.m., early start of Wed 6 a.m., 1a, third day for Samaritans.
Wed Jun 7	1b/IV & 15a/III Pent			Pentecost before solst. pos.

Thu Jun 8	+2½
	31st
		noon
		3 p.m.
				Nazirite permitted to marry (Mk 3:1–6; "hand" euphemism, cf. 1QM 7:7).
				   palin (Mk 3:1) noon.
				   euthys (Mk 3:6) 3 p.m.
				   tois sabbasin (Mk 3:2) sabbatical year NLS3969, +2½ 31st.
				   en heterō sabbatō (Lk 6:6) +2½, 31st.

Fri Jun 23	31a(IV)
	solst. pos.
		midnight
		(Thu)
				Formal appointment of Twelve Apostles (Mk 3:13–19, Lk 6:12–16).
				   en tais hēmerais tautais (Lk 6:12 "in the days these") 31st, June.
				   dianyktereuōn (Lk 6:12) middle of night. Julian start of day for Hellenists.
				   hote egeneto hēmera (Lk 6:13) midnight start of day.

		noon	Mazin	Jesus to Mazin for 3 months before wedding (Jn 2:12). *ou pollas hēmeras* (Jn 2:12 "not many days") not Tue, Day 31st (but Fri, Night 31st).
Sun Jun 25	1b/IV&			Pentecost to post position, observed by

	15a/III to post pos.			Hellenists to give conjunction with 1st.

September Quarter

Thu Sep 21	30/VI Sam 31st	6 p.m.	Qumran	Jesus goes to Qumran novice court ("Nain") and reinstates James, who is in the process of excommunication following the fall of the Baptist (Lk 7:11–17). *en tō hexēs* (Lk 7:11 "in the next" (masc. form). 6 p.m. begins next day in Jewish practice of James.
Fri Sep 22	31(VII)	noon		Messengers arrive from the Baptist, out of power at Mird, challenging Jesus' claim to be the David (Lk 7:18–20, Mt 11:2–3). *en ekeinē tē hōra* (Lk 7:21) noon. *mechri tēs sēmeron* (Mt 11:23) until Today, 31st.
Sat 6 p.m.	1a/VII	6 p.m.	Ain Feshkha	The wedding. Simon Magus officiates in the position of deacon. (Lk 7:36, cf. v.44). Mary Magdalene acts as the bride of Solomon (Lk 7:37–38, cf. Cant 1:12).

AD 31
NLS3970, InterS 3969
March Quarter

Thu Mar 1				No conception in the marriage of Jesus. He is with Mary Magdalene, Helena ("Joanna"), and Herodian women (Lk 8:1–3). *en tō kathexēs* (Lk 8:1 "in according to the next") Julian calendar, 1st of month not a sacred day.
Mon Mar 5	30a/XII & Sam 31st 1st pos.		Ain Feshkha	Jesus expresses support for Jonathan Annas and his pro-Gentile policy just before his deposition (Mt 11:25–30). *en ekeinō tō kairō* (Mt 11:25) InterS 3969 intercalation begins, Sam 31st, equinox.
Wed Mar 21	15a/I & 28b/XII equ. pos.	noon	Ain Feshkha	Jesus leaves Ain F. for Qumran (Jn 2:13). *engys . . . to pascha tōn Ioudaiōn* (Jn 2:13 "near . . . the Passover of the Jews"). Meal of unleavened bread by Lev 23 rule (15a); "Jews" (tetrarch) use 15a rule. In conjunction ("near") with 28b/XII.
	29a/XII	3 p.m.	Qumran	Arrives Qumran, in "temple", extension of lower third of courtyard, at 3 p.m., time for money collection. At non-fulfilment of expectation blames the

failure of prophecy on the financial practices (Jn 2:14-20).

tesserakonta kai hex etesin oikodomēthē ho naos houtos (Jn 2:20 "46 years this sanctuary was built"). (See p. 174.) New party dating from AD 31, SLS year 46. *en trisin hēmerais egero auton* (Jn 2:19 "in 3 days I will raise it"). Christians will establish their new sanctuary in Antioch in AD 43, when the calendar changes from Night to Day, making Tuesday (day 3) the 31st.

Thu Mar 22	30/XII & Sam 31st	noon	Simon Magus ("Beelzebul") becomes Pope in place of Jonathan Annas. Jesus still the David as Simon is Hellenist (Mk 3:20-22). A new millennium is declared, with AD 31 as year 1 (probably by intercalating the 70 years of the exile). Year dates from that point used, e.g. "year 14" (Gal 2:1).

me dynasthai autous mēde arton phagein (Mk 3:20 "they were not able not to eat bread") they had no authority to fast, as Sep to be used for their intercalation.
palin (Mk 3:20) noon.

		6 p.m.	Qumran	Jesus at Qumran. Agrippa accepts him as the David. But Jesus does not fully support Agrippa (Jn 2:23-25).

en tō pascha en tē heortē (Jn 2:23) +2½ 14a, Ex 12 rule; also Sam 31st ("fast").

Fri Mar 23	31a(I) equ. pos.	3 p.m.	Mazin	Jesus at Mazin gives parables (Mk 4:1-9).

palin (Mk 4:1) 6 p.m. division at 3 p.m. Fri.
en tē hēmera ekeinē (Mt 13:1) 31st, Samaritan 1st, starting 3 p.m. Fri.

		6 p.m.		Sabbath begins. Jesus and associates keeping Julian sabbath set out for Ain Feshkha by boat (Mk 4:35-36).

en ekeinē tē hēmera opsias genomenēs (Mk 4:35) reg. 31st (Samaritan 1st), 6 p.m.
en mia tōn hēmerōn (Lk 8:22 "in one of the days") reg. 31st counted as new moon, 1, of following month (1 falls twice).

		7 p.m.	Ain Feshkha	Arrive Ain F. *to peran* (offshore point 1000 cu from buildings, can be used after 9 p.m. Fri, 3 hrs before Julian sabbath). They stay on board.

		9 p.m.		Jesus sleeps, as now in village ranks, and 9 p.m. village bedtime (Mk 4:38). But 9 p.m. before midnight, Julian sabbath,

= 3 p.m. to 6 p.m., strict start of Jewish sabbath. Expectation for this hour fails, leading to political crisis symbolised by storm (Mk 4:37–41).

ēdē (Mk 4:37 "already") 9 p.m., 3 hours early.

Sat Mar 24		midnight (Fri)	End of crisis. Calendar adjustment made to postpone jubilee to southern sabbatical years.

1 a.m. — Extension of Julian sabbath. Meeting on shore with Theudas (Legion, Nicodemus), who now abandons hope for NLS3970 end of Exodus, (Mk 5:1–17, Lk 8:26–39, Jn 3:1–21).

euthys (Mk 5:2) 1 a.m. (sabbath 4 a.m. 3 hrs early).

nyktos kai hēmeras (Mk 5:5 "night and day") 31st now at Night position, followed by post position at Day.

chronō hikanō (Lk 8:27 "a long time") new Herodian generation from AD 31, for Agrippa, the Worthy One (lay levite).

Sun Mar 25	+2½ 31st	3 p.m.	Mazin	Meeting with Mary Magdalene and chaperone Helena prior to renewal of marriage (Mk 5:21–43).

euthys (Mk 5:29) *parachrēma* (Lk 8:47) 3 p.m.

euthys (Mk 5:42) *parachrēma* (Lk 8:55) 4 p.m.

en . . . etōn dōdeka (Mk 5:42) ("was . . . of years 12"). Initiated Mar AD 17.

June Quarter

Fri Jun 22	31a(IV) solst. pos.	Qumran	Jesus at Qumran SE section baptises (Jn 3:22).
		Jerusalem	At the same time the Baptist, in a low status in Jerusalem, baptises (Jn 3:23). It is reported to the Baptist that Agrippa is turning towards Jesus. (Jn 3:25–26).
	11.55 a.m.	Ain Feshkha	Jesus arrives at Ain F. Prepares to take part in Hellenist form of meal, with female deacon (Jn 4:1–6).

hōra . . . hōs hektē (Jn 4:6 "about 6th hour") 5 mins to 12.

noon — Helena acts as deacon. Discussion of doctrine (Jn 4:7–38).

eti tetramēnos (Jn 4:35 "still 4 months") June solstice, IV.

Sun Jun 24	1b/IV & 15a/III		Pentecost to post position.
Mon Jun 25	2b/IV &	6 a.m.	Day after Pentecost (significant day, cf.

16a/III

Jub. 1:1). Jesus stays extra day (Jn 4:40).
dyo hēmeras (Jn 4:40 "2 days") Mon,
day 2.

September Quarter

Tue Sep 4	31a(VII) 1st pos.	6 a.m.	Ain Feshkha	Jesus spends 70 days (Tue Jun 26 to Mon Sep 3, incl., end of previous season to 1st pos. start of new season) in ascetic state prior to renewal of marriage. On day 71 goes to Ain F. "Galilee" as first step into world (Jn 4:43). *meta . . . tas dyo hēmeras* (Jn 4:43) Tue 6 a.m., 24 hrs after Mon 6 a.m. (day 2). Following season, repeats days.
Thu Sep 6	+2½ 31st		Jerusalem	Jesus goes to Jerusalem (*hē patris*, Mk 6:1, Jn 4:44, not "Nazareth"; Essene Gate original place of papacy, Hillel's baptisms). *sabbatō* (Mk 6:2) +2½ 31st.
Fri Sep 14	10/VII Atonement		Ain Feshkha	Jesus comes to Ain F. before going to Qumran for the Day of Atonement (Jn 4:45). *en tē heortē . . . eis tēn heortēn* (Jn 4:45) Day of Atonement.
Thu Sep 20	30a/VI & Sam 31st	noon	Mird minor	John Mark sent out on mission for two seasons while marriage renewed. Revised rules of mission (Mk 6:6-13).
		6 p.m.	Mird major	The Herods meet for a communal meal at Mird, a Herodian property. John the Baptist is brought there, having just returned to the celibate state ("risen from the dead"). (Mk 6:14-20, Mt 14:1-5.) *en ekeinō tō kairō* (Mt 14:1) InterS 3969 IC, Sep version (cf. also Lk 5:35, *en ekeinais tais hēmerais*, IC VII 31). (Sam 31st, equinox IC).
Fri Sep 21		mid- night (Thu)		At the Julian beginning of the equinox, the Herods agree that the Baptist's prophecies have failed. Helena, leading the liturgical dance (*Contemp. Life* 83-87) is asked by Herodias to influence them to depose John and give the headship to Simon Magus. (Mk 6:21-24, Mt 14:6-7). *genomenēs hēmeras eukairou* (Mk 6:21 "the day of the good (*eu-*) season having come") InterS 3969 IC at equinox. Julian beginning of Friday, Thu midnight. *tois genesiois* (Mk 6:21 "the birthday" of the tetrarch) Sep equinox, season for birth of rulers.

3 a.m.		Helena makes her request (Mk 6:25).
		euthys (Mk 6:25) 3 a.m.
4 a.m.		The headdress worn by the Baptist as Zadokite high priest (Ezek 44:18) is brought in. The Baptist is imprisoned at Machaerus and subsequently put to death (*Ant.* 18:119).
		euthys (Mk 6:27) 4 a.m.
9 a.m.	Ain Feshkha	Jesus at Ain F. begins the promotion of Philip, uncircumcised head of Shem. His status is expressed by a lay ceremony at 9 a.m., a celibate one at noon, then another at 1 p.m. as a Shem Gentile. As he must not be touched, being uncircumcised, Jonathan Annas (*ho basilikos*) asks Jesus as a lay bishop to perform the noon ceremony at a distance, on a substitute, while Philip remains at Mazin. Philip has had a parallel ceremony the previous day at Mazin, concluding at 1 p.m. (Jn 4:46–48).
		ēmellen (Jn 4:47 "about to") 9 a.m., 3 hrs before he "dies" (goes through grades 10 to 7 at the ceremony). *echthes hōran hebdomēn* (Jn 4:52 "yesterday hour 7th") Thu 30th, at 1 p.m.
noon		Jon Annas asks Jesus to perform the ceremony at noon. Jesus declares Philip a member, and receives the substitute, ending the ceremony at noon rather than 1 p.m., to make Philip equal to a Jewish celibate (Jn 4:49–53).
		prin (Jn 4:49 "before") as a prior stage. *ēdē* (Jn 4:51) 3 hrs before 3 p.m. *en ekeinē tē hōra* (Jn 4:53) noon.
		Jesus leaves Ain Feshkha for Qumran. *heortē tōn Ioudaiōn* (Jn 5:1 "feast of the Jews") 31a reg., used by Herodians against Sam solar 31st.
3 p.m.		He arrives at Qumran, at the cistern where villagers wash. James, their bishop, is expecting an "Exodus" event for year 38 of the SS generation. Jesus persuades him to give up Essene baths (cf. *Eccl. Hist* 2:23, James did not use baths), also to change (sometimes) to the Julian sabbath.
		triakonta kai oktō etē (Jn 5:5 "38 years") Year 38 of SS3930–3970. (Sep start, Sep 8 BC to Sep AD 33.)
6 p.m.		Jewish start to sabbath. James lifts up the

royal palanquin after 6 p.m. (Jn 5:9–13).
sabbaton en ekeinē tē hēmera (Jn 5:9)
reg. 31a; Samaritan 1st.

AD 32
InterLS 3969, InterS 3970, SS3969 (Sep).
March Quarter

Thu Mar 20	30a/XII & noon Sam 31st	Mird minor	John Mark returns to Mird, to rejoin Jesus 6 months after being sent out (Mk 6:30).
Fri Mar 21	31a(I)	3 a.m.	Some members travel by land from Mird minor to Ain F., 8 hours (Mk 6:33). Jesus and John Mark go by land to Mazin (8 hrs).

> *oude phagein eukairoun* (Mk 6:31 "they
> did not have good time to eat") they
> had the *eukairos* (InterLS 3969 IC at
> equinox) not to eat, i.e. fast.

	11 a.m.	The other group arrive at Ain F. at time for 11 a.m. washing. Jesus and John Mark arrive at Mazin and take boat up to Ain F. (1 hr).
	noon Ain Feshkha	Jesus arrives at Ain F. to take the communal meal without previous washing (Mk 6:32–33). John of Zebedee, "the Five Thousand", is made a presbyter. Titus, "fish 2" takes part in the ceremony (Jn 6:1–15, Mk 6:34–44, Lk 9:10–17, Mt 14:13–21).

> *engys to pascha, hē heortē tōn Ioudaiōn*
> (Jn 6:4) Fri (noon) +2½ 15a
> unleavened bread (Lev 23 rule) (*to
> pascha*), in conjunction with 31st
> (*engys*). Hē *heortē* 31a reg, Fri noon
> before 6 p.m.
> *ēmellen* (Jn 6:6) 3 hrs before 3 p.m.
> end of Fri.
> *ēdē hōras pollēs* (Mk 6:35) noon, 3 hrs
> before 3 p.m.
> *hē . . . hēmera ērxato klinein* (Lk 9:12)
> noon, 3 hrs before 3 p.m. end of Fri.
> *opsias . . . genomenēs* (Mt 14:15) Fri
> noon as 6 p.m. Fri meal held at noon
> by celibates.

	6 p.m.	John Mark and others set out for Mazin (Jn 6:16, Mk 6:45).

> *opsia* (Jn 6:16) 6 p.m. meal.
> *euthys* (Mk 6:45) 6 p.m. (9 p.m.
> village time 3 hours early).

	9 p.m.	Jesus is still at Ain F., although he should now have arrived at the Mazin building, a 3-hour walk from Ain F. On the (Julian) sabbath travelling more than

1000 cu after 9 p.m. is forbidden (Jewish sabbath, after 3 p.m.) (Jn 6:17, Mt 14:23b).

skotia ēdē (Jn 6:17) 3 hrs before midnight.

opsias genomenēs (Mk 6:47, Mt 14:23) 9 p.m., Julian equivalent of 3 p.m., sabbath form of 6 p.m.

Sat Mar 22

2.55 a.m. John Mark starts rowing from the 1000 cu offshore point at Mazin (see p. 329).

3 a.m. He has rowed 500 cu (5 mins), so is at a point 200 cu from the beginning of the channel (Mt 14:24).

ēdē stadious pollous (Mt 14:24 "already many stadia") 3 a.m.

(ēdē). At 1 stadion, 400 cu, from the beginning of land (see p. 329).

At the same moment, Jesus has reached the beginning of land, coming from the west. He has walked from Ain F. after 9 p.m., breaking the Julian sabbath law. He begins to walk along the 100 cu jetty to the boat, thus "walking on water" (Mt 14:25).

tetartē . . . phylakē tēs nyktos (Mt 14:25 "the fourth watch of the night") 3 a.m.

3.02 a.m. The boat reaches the beginning of the channel, having covered the 200 cu remaining sea in 2 mins.

hōs stadious eikosi pente ē triakonta (Jn 6:19 "25 or 30 stadia") the land at Mazin, 30 stadia from Qumran, 25 stadia from the queen's house used as a 1 starting point (Qumran zero).

3.03 a.m. The forepoint of the boat arrives at 100 cu up the channel, meeting the 100 cu jetty. At the same moment Jesus arrives at the end of the jetty, having walked 100 cu in 3 mins.

peri tetartēn phylakēn tēs nyktos (Mk 6:48 "about the fourth watch of the night") 3.03.

John Mark is to moor the boat, as he is not bound by sabbath law. Peter leaves the boat, and asks to walk on the narrow jetty with Jesus. His insecurity on the jetty symbolises his doubts about accepting the doctrine of Jesus (Mt 14:27–30). (See p. 329.)

3.05 a.m. John Mark brings the boat alongside the jetty and moors it (Jn 6:21).

eutheōs (Jn 6:21, Mt 14:31). 3.05.

Sun Mar 23		noon	Ain Feshkha

The tetrarch has noon meal at Ain F. (Jn 6:22)

tē epaurion (Jn 6:22) InterLS 3969 IC, equ. pos., +2½ 31st, noon start.

2 p.m. — The tetrarch leaves by boat for Mazin.

3 p.m. Mazin — Arrives Mazin, joins in teaching session (Jn 6:25–58).

June Quarter

Fri Jun 20 — 31a (IV) solst. pos. — noon — Mazin — John Mark observes the common form of noon meal, not a communion (Mk 7:14–23).

Sun Jun 22 — +2½ 31st & 1b & 15a/III — 3 a.m. — Mird minor — Jesus goes to Mird minor to visit Mary, to prepare for another renewal of marriage in December.

Pentecost to post pos. — 11 a.m. — Arrives at Mird minor (Mk 7:24).

noon — Joins Helena, chaperone of Mary Magdalene, at noon meal, He is to "cast out the demon" from Mary, i.e. remove her from Judas, ("demon 7" Lk 8:2) bishop over celibate women. He says he will join Mary at 1 p.m., according to rule for her grade (same as Philip), but Helena argues that women should have the same change as Philip (Jn 4:49) to noon. (Mk 7:25–30.)

euthys (Mk 7:25) noon, lay for women.

prōton (Mk 7:27) 1 p.m.

September Quarter

Mon Sep 1 — 30b/VI Sam 31st 1st pos. — noon — Ain Feshkha — A higher form of ministry, using 7 "loaves" is given to James of Zebedee, the "Four Thousand" (Mk 8:1–9, Mt 15:32–38).

en ekeinais tais hēmerais (Mk 8:1) Sep as start of season, Sam 31st.

palin (Mk 8:1) noon (celibate meal).

ēdē hēmerai treis (Mk 8:2 "already days 3") Mon noon, 3 hrs before Mon 3 p.m., early start of Tue 3 a.m., day 3 (villagers' start of day, 3 a.m.).

euthys (Mk 8:10) 3 p.m.

4 p.m. Mazin — Jesus arrives at Mazin (Mk 8:10).

6 p.m. — Expectation for Sep fails (SS3969, Sep start, Julian month and Sam 31st). Jesus says there will be no fulfilment for this party and calendar (Mk 8:11–13, Mt 16:2–4).

(Textual variants of Mt 16:2–3 show knowledge of the pesher.

opsias . . . eudia . . . purrazei (Mt 16:2

"evening . . . fair weather . . . red)
days start previous evening at 6 p.m.;
VII (colour red for autumn) superior
month.
prōi, sēmeron cheimōn (Mt 16:3
"morning, today, winter"), also 6 a.m.
start of 31a with solarists, and X.
ta . . . sēmeia tōn kairōn ou dynasthe
(Mt 16:3, the signs of the seasons you
cannot"). Jesus is said to be opposing
the Jewish use of September as the
primary season, with the associated
start of day at 6 p.m.; and also their
placing Dec after Sep; Dec-Jan
should be treated as before Mar and
the beginning of the year.)
palin (Mk 8:13) 6 p.m.

| | | 7 p.m. | Ain Feshkha | Offshore at Ain F. Jesus warns against a Herodian kingship (Mk 8:14-21). |
| Tue Sep 2 | 31a(VII) | 6 a.m. | | He decides to stay at Ain F. rather than Qumran, before Atonement, i.e. not profess full celibacy (Jn 7:1-9). |

*engys hē heortē tōn Ioudaiōn hē
skēnopēgia* (Jn 7:2 "near the feast of
the Jews, Tabernacles") reg. 31a fast,
beginning of month containing
Tabernacles (15/VII).
ho kairos ho emos oupō parestin (Jn 7:6
"my season is not yet") lay SS3969
starts Mar 33; priestly start Sep 32
(see p. 173).

| Fri Sep 12 | 10/VII | 6 a.m. | Qumran | Day of Atonement begins. |

eis tēn heortēn . . . en tē heortē (Jn
7:10-11) fast for Day of Atonement.

| | | noon | | Jesus teaches. There is argument about whether he is the legitimate David. He announces his departure to resume marriage, as is done on the Day of Atonement (Jn 7:14-36, Mk 8:31-9:1). |

ēdē . . . tēs heortēs mesousēs (Jn 7:14
"already of the middle feast") noon,
3 hrs before 3 p.m., the climax and
central hour of 18-hr day.
meta treis hēmeras anastēnai (Mk 8:31
"after 3 days rise up") his day for
returning to the celibate state will be
1a, the date for a priest (Wed 6 a.m.,
24 hrs after Tue 6 a.m., day 3. Wed
1a normative).

| | | 3 p.m. | | At 3 p.m., the hour for Jonathan Annas to act as Diaspora priest, Jesus takes his position, and also puts on the robes of the supreme high priest (Jn 7:37-39, |

Mk 9:2-3, Lk 9:28-29, Mt 17:1-2).

en . . . tē eschatē hēmera tē megalē tēs heortēs (Jn 7:37 "in the last day, the great one of the feast") on Friday (10/VII), at the time for the priest on the Day of Atonement.

meta hēmeras hex (Mk 9:2 "after days 6") Fri 3 p.m., 24 hrs after Thu 3 p.m., early start of Fri, day 6, village hour 3 a.m.

hōsei hēmerai oktō (Lk 9:28 "about days 8") Fri 3 p.m. 24 hrs before Sat 3 p.m., early start of Sun 3 a.m., day 8, village hour.

	9 p.m.	Witnesses appear again, 3 hrs before Julian end of day. Jesus has now been reduced to bishop ("Glory") and Jon Annas acts as village priest (Lk 9:32).

bebaremoi hypno (Lk 9:32 "heavy with sleep") 9 p.m., village bedtime.

	midnight (Fri)	Pope Simon Magus ("the Voice") appears, at the Julian end of day. He has travelled from Mird major to Qumran by the north road in 3 hrs by donkey 6 p.m. to 9 p.m. Jesus is treated as laicised ("Beloved") and James, "the Cloud", replaces him (Mk 9:7).
Wed Sep 17	15/VII Tabernacles	At Tabernacles, Jesus claims to be the high priest, "the Light of the world" (Jn 8:12-58).

pentekonta etē oupō echeis (Jn 8:57 "you have not yet 50 yrs") Jesus would need to be 50 yrs old to have seen "Abraham" (Hillel), who died 19 BC (and then he would have been a baby, cf. variant, "has Abraham seen you?" Jn 8:57).

Fri Sep 19	31a(VII) equ. pos. noon	Gamaliel, of the order of Benjamin, is given higher status; not kept at novice level, "blind", but given full initiation and education, "seeing the light" (Jn 9:1-12).

sabbaton . . . hēmera (Jn 9:14) 31st.
ēdē (Jn 9:22) noon; (Fri).
ek deuterou (Jn 9:24 "out of second") 12.05 (cf. Mk 14:72) (double prayer at major hours).

	1 p.m.	Jon Annas acts with James as substitute king. Jesus opposes James' teaching on circumcision (Mk 9:14-29).

en ekeinais tais hēmerais (Lk 9:36) Sep equinox, 31st.
tē hexēs hēmera (Lk 9:37 "the next day") 31st as non-sacred day; great

			feasts for VII have now been observed. *euthys* (Mk 9:15) 1 p.m. (Fri).
	2 p.m.		James acts with ecstatic Therapeutae (Mk 9:20). *euthys* (Mk 9:20) 2 p.m.
	3 p.m.		James renounces zealotry. *euthys* (Mk 9:24) 3 p.m.
	6 p.m.	Ain Feshkha	Jesus arrives at Ain F. (Mk 9:30–32).
	7 p.m.	Mazin	He arrives at Mazin (Mk 9:33).
Sun Sep 21 +2½ 31st	3 a.m.		He leaves Mazin for Mird, en route for Jerusalem, where in December he will follow the marriage rule of the Davids (Lk 9:51). *tas hēmeras tēs analempseōs autou* (Lk 9:51 "the days of his being received up") he is now a lay bishop.
	11 a.m.		Arrives at Mird minor.
	noon	Mird major	He is refused communion at the Mird building, main sanctuary, as being laicised (Lk 9:52–55).
	2 p.m.		He arrives at the annexe to Mar Saba, 2 hrs from Mird major (Lk 9:56). He sends out John Mark as delegate for 70 days (John Mark is his deacon, *Ayin*, no. 70) (Lk 10:1–12).

December Quarter

Wed Nov 26	25/IX 1st pos.	Qumran	Jesus acts at the lay festival, Dedication, at Qumran (Jn 10:22–30). *ta enkainia* (Jn 10:22) feast of Dedication, 25/IX (1 Macc 4:52). *cheimōn* (Jn 10:22 "winter") winter feast.
Sun Nov 30	29/IX pente-contad 1st pos.	3 a.m.	Mird minor John Mark returns with Mary Magdalene, "Joy". Jesus tells him that Judas and Simon Magus have been excommunicated (Lk 10:17–20).
	9 a.m.		Jon Annas is now acting Pope. Jesus supports him and recounts his relation with the Baptist in the parable of the Good Samaritan (Lk 10:21–37). It is the pentecontad, a day for rejoicing. *en autē tē hōra* (Lk 10:21) 9 a.m.
	3 p.m.		Jesus visits Mary Magdalene with her chaperone Helena, who takes a high view of her ministry. Mary acts as wife, renewing the wedding symbolism (Lk 10:38–42, Jn 11:1–2). Helena asks Jesus to help Simon Magus (Jn 11:3–5).
Mon Dec 1	30a/IX	6 a.m.	He remains at Mird on Monday.

	& Sam 31st			*dyo hēmeras* (Jn 11:6 "2 days") Mon, day 2. He gives the Lord's prayer, for the use of villagers (Lk 11:1-4).
		noon		He has the noon meal at Mird major, now under a less strict rule (Lk 11:37-52). *aristēsē* (Lk 11:37) take noon meal for non-ascetic villagers.
		1 p.m.		Teaching (Lk 11:53-12:59). *prōton* (Lk 12:1) 1 p.m.
Tue Dec 2	31a (X) 1st pos.			He is told of further consequences of the uprising. (Lk 13:1-9). *en autō tō kairō* (Lk 13:1 "in that very season") at the lay (*autos*) IC, Julian start of SS3969. Tue 31a.
		3 p.m.		At the synagogue at Mird major he begins the promotion of Mary, his mother, to the status of Widow (see p. 368) (Lk 13:10-17). *en tois sabbasin* (Lk 13:10) SS3969, X start. *etē dekaoktō* (Lk 13:11 "years 18") she was widowed Mar AD 23, year 18 of dating from AD 6 as year 1. *parachrēma* (Lk 13:13) 3 p.m. *tō sabbatō* (Lk 13:14) 31a. *hex hēmerai* (Lk 13:14 "6 days") day 6, Fri 6 a.m., solst. pos. 31st. She would have a more priestly status if promoted at the solstice position. *tē hēmera tou sabbatou* (Lk 13:14, 16) Day pos. 31st. *tō sabbatō* (Lk 13:15) 31st.
		4 p.m.	Mird minor	He leaves for Qumran (Lk 13:1-21, Jn 11:7).
Wed Dec 3	1a/X	mid-night (Tue)	Ain Feshkha	He arrives at Ain F. (Lk 13:22-30).
		3 a.m.	Qumran	He arrives at Qumran, and is told that Simon Magus-Lazarus is in Cave 4 (Jn 11:17-18). Under the purity rules at Qumran he, in the married state, must not come in to the vestry service, but stay outside at the pillar base (*enteuthen*, Lk 13:31, cf. Rev 22:2). He replies that he is using a rule that means he will not be disqualified until he reaches Jerusalem, after the solstice position (Lk 13:31-35). *tessaras ēdē hēmeras* (Jn 11:17 "4 already days") 3 a.m. before 6 a.m. Wed, day 4. *en autē tē hōra* (Lk 13:31) 3 a.m.

				sēmeron kai aurion kai tē tritē teleioumai (Lk 13:32 "today and tomorrow and the third I am perfected") the 31st, 1st and 2nd in this position (early December) still celibate ("perfect") on the 2nd. Thu Dec 4 (2a/X) is the 3rd day counting from the 31st as 1st (method used by Hebrews).
				sēmeron kai aurion kai tē echomenē (Lk 13:33) 31st, 1st and 2nd at the solst. pos., Sun Dec 21, 2a/X, the "having day", marriage to be resumed.
		noon		Jesus orders the release of Simon Magus from Cave 4. Jonathan Annas permits the lifting of the excommunication ban (Jn 11:38-44).
				palin (Jn 11:38) noon.
				ēdē (Jn 11:39) noon before 3 p.m.
				tetartaios (Jn 11:39) of priestly level, using Wed 1a as promotion day.
Thu Dec 4	2a/X & +2½ 31st	6 p.m.	Ain Feshkha	Jesus and Simon Magus have evening meal, common hour, at Ain F. Simon's reinstatement continued (Lk 14:1-6).
				sabbatō (Lk 14:1,3) +2½ 31st.
				en hēmera tou sabbatou (Lk 14:5) 31st.
		7 p.m.		Teaching (Lk 14:7-17:10).
Thu Dec 18	30a/IX Sam 31st	3 a.m.		Jesus leaves Ain F. for Mird minor (Lk 17:11).
		11 a.m.	Mird minor	Arrives Mird minor. Simon Magus is there as "leper 10" (Lk 17:12-19).
		noon	Mird major	Teaching (Lk 17:20-18:14, Mk 10:1b-12).
		3 p.m.		Meeting with James, the Rich Man (Lk 18:18-30).
				en tō kairō toutō (Lk 18:30) SS3969, X before I, 31a.
Fri Dec 19	31a(X)	3 a.m.		Jesus sets out for Qumran to gain final permission from hierarchy to resume marriage. Expects a rite of rejection, to express view that sex is unclean. Will return to celibate life if a pregnancy occurs, at a 1a (normative Wed) the day for priests (Mk 10:32-34, Mt 20:17-19).
				meta treis hēmeras (Mk 10:34 "after 3 days") Wed 6 a.m., 24 hrs after Tue 6 a.m., day 3. 1a in normative position. James and John ask for promotion (Mk 10:35-45).
		3 p.m.		Arrives Qumran.
Sat Dec 20	1a/X	3 p.m.		Goes to Ain F.
Sun Dec 21	+2½ 31st	3 a.m.		Leaves Ain F. for Jerusalem, expecting a further rejection rite there (Lk 18:31).

			tē hēmera tē tritē (Lk 18:33) 1a, early start.

	3 p.m.	Mar Saba	He arrives at Mar Saba-"Jericho", 12 hrs from Ain F., the point where married villagers stay overnight on the pilgrimage to Qumran. Gamaliel, of the order of Benjamin, accepts him as a Nazirite. (Mk 10:46-52, Lk 18:35-43).
			    euthys (Mk 10:52) 3 p.m.
			    parachrēma (Lk 18:43) 3 p.m.
			Zacchaeus-Ananus, the youngest Annas, stands on the pillar base east of the vestry. He will act as host when Jesus stays overnight (Lk 19:1-10).
			    ēmellen (Lk 19:4) 3 hrs before 6 p.m.
			    sēmeron (Lk 19:5,9) +2½ 31st.

Mon Dec 22		Mt of Olives	Jesus goes to Jerusalem, to the building on the Mount of Olives, to resume married life (Jn 11:54).

AD 33
SS3969
March Quarter

Sun Mar 1	29a/XII			Jesus sets out for Qumran, for the seasonal meeting, and for his second wedding and return to celibate life.
Mon Mar 2	30a/XII & Sam 31st	11 a.m.	Ain Feshkha	Arrives at Ain F. Sends messenger to prepare ceremonial animal at the queen's house, the Manger. (Mk 11:1-2, Lk 19:29-30, Mt 21:1-2).
		noon		He leaves Ain F.
		1 p.m.	queen's house	Messenger arrives at queen's house (Mk 11:4). *euthys* (Mk 11:2) 1 p.m. (day of expectation like sabbath).
		2 p.m.		Jesus arrives at queen's house. He mounts the ceremonial animal (Mk 11:6-8). *euthys . . . palin* (Mk 11:3) 2 p.m.

		3 p.m.	Qumran	He and the procession arrive at Qumran (1 hr, walking pace) (Mk 11:9-10).
				    ēdē (Lk 19:37) 3 p.m.
				He goes to the temple-treasury at the time for money collection. No fulfilment has occurred for those expecting a Restoration at SS3969, 1st pos., Sam 31st. He says that it is because of the financial corruption, and overthrows the furniture for the banking system (Lk 19:45-46, Mt 21:12-13).
				    opsias ēdē . . . tēs hōras (Mk 11:11) 3 p.m., 3 hrs before 6 p.m. (as if sabbath).

Tue Mar 3	31a(I) 1st pos.	6 a.m.	Qumran	When there is no fulfilment at reg. 31st, Jesus attacks the Herodian form of mission, including that of the tetrarch, the Figtree. (Mk 11:12–14, Mt 21:18–22). *tē epaurion* (Mk 11:12) SS3969 IC, reg. 31a. *ho . . . kairos ouk . . . sykōn* (Mk 11:13 "not the season of figs") a solar IC year, not lunisolar, used by Herods. *prōi* (Mt 21:18) 6 a.m.
		9 p.m.		He leaves Qumran for Ain F. for his last night spent outside (Mk 11:19). *opse* (Mk 11:19) 9 p.m.
Wed Mar 4	1a/I	6 a.m.	Qumran	At 1a of the 1st pos., Jesus begins the resumption of celibate life, staying at Qumran. The expulsion of the Figtree is completed (Mk 11:20–25). *proi* (Mk 11:20) 6 a.m.
		noon		Jesus is attacked for his views (Mk 11:27–33, Lk 20:1–8, Mt 21:23–27). *palin* (Mk 11:27) noon. *en mia tōn hēmerōn* (Lk 20:1 "in one of the days") 1a as a beginning of the month (both 31a and 1a are a 1). Further teaching (Mk 12:1–40, Lk 20:9–47). *en ekeinē tē hēmera* (Mt 22:23), *ap' ekeinēs tēs hēmeras* (Mt 22:46) 1a "that day" by values of Hebrews (31st "this day").
		4 p.m.		Time for lower grade money offerings (Mk 12:41–44). Jesus gives teaching on the fulfilment of prophecy (Mk 13:3–37, added later).
Tue Mar 17	14a/1 to 1st pos. & 27b/XII	6 a.m.		Equinox position festival days begin. Tension is now high, as the equinox should bring a fulfilment of prophecy for SS3969 (Mk 14:1–2, Mt 26:1–5). *to pascha kai ta azyma meta dyo hēmeras* (Mk 14:1 "the Passover and unleavened bread after 2 days") 14a as unleavened bread by Ex 12 rule (see p. 195). Tue 6 a.m., 24 hrs after Mon 6 a.m., day 2.
Wed Mar 18	15/I & 29a/XII	noon		Herodian date for unleavened bread. 1st Preparation Day (Jn 11:55). *engys to pascha tōn Ioudaiōn* (Jn 11:55 "near the Passover of the Jews") 15a–b, unleavened bread for Herods by Lev 23 rule, in conjunction with

29a/XII, 1st Prep. Day. Noon for unleavened bread as first meal of day for celibates.
pro tou pascha (Jn 11:55) Wed noon, 24 hrs before Thu noon, +2½ 14a (noon start).

Thu Mar 19	30/XII & Sam 31st	midnight (Wed)	Ain Feshkha

Second wedding of Jesus and Mary Magdalene (Jn 12:1-8, Mk 14:3-9).
pro hex hēmerōn tou pascha (Jn 12:1 "before 6 days of the Passover") Wed midnight, 24 hrs before Thu midnight, Julian start of Fri day 6.

noon — Ceremonial procession repeated at equinox position (Jn 12:12-13).
tē epaurion (Jn 12:12) SS3969 IC, equ. pos. Sam 31st, noon start.
eis tēn heortēn (Jn 12:12) Sam 31st.

3 p.m. — Jesus begins the process of full entry into the celibate life. He sends deacons to go and prepare the table (Mk 14:12-16, Lk 22:7-13, Mt 26:17-19).
tē prōtē hēmera tōn azymōn (Mk 14:12, "the first day; of the unleavened bread") Sam 31st as first day; 14a +2½ unleavened bread Ex 12 rule.
hē heortē tōn azymōn hē legomenē pascha (Lk 22:1 "the feast of unleavened bread called Passover") Sam 31st and 14a +2½.
hē hēmera tōn azymōn (Lk 22:7) 14a +2½.
tē . . . prōte tōn azymōn (Mt 26:17) Sam 31st as first day, and 14a +2½.

30a/XII & Sam 31st — 6 p.m. — The evening communal meal begins, in the vestry (Mk 14:17, Mt 26:20, Jn 13:2-11).
pro . . . tēs heortēs tou pascha (Jn 13:1) Thu 6 p.m., 24 hrs before Fri 6 p.m., reg. 31st, 15a +2½ unleavened bread.
deipnou ginomenou (Jn 13:2 "supper having come") 6 p.m. common meal.
opsias genomenēs (Mk 14:17) 6 p.m.

7 p.m. — Jesus blesses the fermented wine, the common drink (Lk 22:17).

8 p.m. — At 8 p.m. Jesus is permitted to officiate at the communion, as he has returned to the celibate state (see p. 104). As he blesses and breaks the bread, he gives it symbolic meaning (Mk 14:22, Lk 22:19, Mt 26:26).

9 p.m. — The cup of sacred wine is blessed (Lk 22:20). Judas leaves, to send a message to Pilate in Jerusalem that

the wanted men are at Qumran
(Jn 13:30).
  euthys (Jn 13:30) 9 p.m., lay hour.
  nyx (Jn 13:30) 9 p.m.

9.05 p.m.   Peter moves down from the prince's seat
to the eastern deacon's seat, so he can
now converse with Jesus (Jn 13:36,
Lk 22:24-29). For the remainder of the
hour Jesus conducts discussion by
question and answer (Jn 13:36-14:31,
Lk 22:31-38).

10 p.m.   At the close of the session, they sing a
hymn and go out to the east side of the
monastery building (Jn 14:31, Mk 14:26,
Mt 26-30).

From this point, a double set of hours is used, to reflect the fact that the time arrived
at by the priests' succession of prayers was 3 hours fast (see Introduction to Chronology,
pp. 181, 199). From now until Friday at the true noon, the fast times were used, pending
the adjustment.

True hour	Fast hour	
10 p.m.	1 a.m.	For the next two hours, Jesus spends time with both John Mark within the monastery grounds, and with Peter in the outer hall for villagers. On the hour, he offers prayers to Jonathan Annas. He accepts Jonathan's direction concerning the cup of poison (Mk 14:32-38, Mt 26:36-41, Lk 22:41-42).

  mian horan (Mk 14:37 "1 hour") hour
  1 Julian, fast 1 a.m.
He rejoins John Mark and gives the
teaching in Jn 15:1-27.

11 p.m.	2 a.m.	He says another prayer (Mk 14:39, Mt 26:42).

  palin (Mk 14.39) 2 a.m.
He rejoins John Mark and gives the
teaching in Jn 16:1-33.

| Fri Mar 20 | midnight 3 a.m. (Thu) | He says the midnight-3 a.m. prayer, saying "the hour is come". It is the Julian beginning (true time) of Sam 31st equ. pos., SS3969 (see p. 193). If a Restoration is to come for Jesus and Simon Magus it should come now. There is no fulfilment, and both Simon as the Pope and Jesus as the king are left without political support (Jn 17:1-26, Mt 26:44). |

  to triton (Mk 14:41) 3 a.m.
An alternative triarchy arrives in the
outer hall to take over (Jn 18:1-11,
Mk 14:43-50, Lk 22:47-53,

Mt 26:47-56).

Simon Magus is arrested as a false
prophet, condemned, defrocked, and
confined in the monastery building, "the
[potter's] field" (Mk 14:1-52, 15:21).

1 a.m.   4 a.m.   Jesus, as a second leader under Hellenist
rules, is tried next. He is brought into
the vestry, to the judgment section in the
north near the fire (see Locations p.
322). He turns west to face Annas on the
raised western platform. Caiaphas is just
south of Annas, in line with cubit 2
(Jn 18:12-14, Mk 14:53, Lk 22:54,
Mt 26:57).

>   *prōton* (Jn 18:13) 1 a.m./4 a.m.
>   *tou eniautou ekeinou* (Jn 18:13 "of that
>   year") year starting at equinox, Jewish
>   method.

Peter is admitted to the vestry
(Jn 18:1-16, Mk 14:54, Lk 22:54,
Mt 26:58).

Jesus is questioned, and insists that the
David king can act as a priest, causing
Caiaphas to condemn him
(Mk 14:55-65, Mt 26:59-68).

Peter is standing on the same E-W line,
but below the fire on the east of centre.
He is acting on the fast times, and
stands to pray at the position for a 4
a.m. prayer. The female doorkeeper in
the passageway between the north and
south doors is on his east. Peter has a
choice whether to turn east or west for
his prayer. He turns east (*emprosthen*,
Mt 26:70) so that he can talk with the
woman, but turns his back to Jesus, thus
denying Jesus' westernised doctrine
(Jn 18:17-18, Mk 14:66-68a,
Lk 22:56-7, Mt 26:69-70).

Further hearing before Annas
(Jn 18:19-23).

2 a.m.   5 a.m.   Jesus, Peter, and the next doorkeeper
move down to the next cubit. Jesus is
now in line with Caiaphas, who tries
him as a third leader (Jn 18:24).

Peter again denies by praying towards
the east (Jn 18:25, Mk 14:68,
Mt 26:71-72).

>   *palin* (Mk 14:70) 2 a.m.

3 a.m.   6 a.m.   End of the trial of Jesus before Caiaphas.
He moves down to the next cubit, as do
Peter and the next doorkeeper. At the
end of the prayer Jesus turns and looks

at Peter (Lk 22:61). Peter has fulfilled Jesus' prediction of the evening before, "before the cock crows twice, you will deny me three times" (Mk 14:30). There had been a cockcrowing (the 3 a.m. prayer, Mk 13:35) at the fast 3 a.m., when it was true midnight; now there is a second one for the true 3 a.m. Peter has used the eastern form of prayer three times, on the hour.

> *hōsei hōras mias* (Lk 22:59 "about hour 1") 6 a.m. as the hour before 7 a.m., the 1st hour, Jewish Julian.
> *parachrēma* (Lk 22:60) 3 a.m.

3.05 a.m. 6.05 a.m. There is a repeated "cockcrowing" at 5 mins past the hour. This gives an alternative fulfilment of the prediction for those like John Mark who are not observing the fast times on this day.

> *eutheōs* (Jn 18:27, Mt 26:74) 3.05.
> *ek deuterou* (Mk 14:72 "a second time") repeated at 3.05.

4 a.m.   7 a.m. Further mocking and beating (Lk 22:63-64).

5 a.m.   8 a.m. Pilate arrives from Jerusalem (40 km, 200 stadia, 2½ hrs by horse; horse rate 80 st per hour). He tries and condemns Simon Magus.

6 a.m.   9 a.m. The tetrarch Antipas offers a bribe for Theudas. Judas ("this man") is tried in his place. Jesus is heard also, defined as the third man, the King, and made to wait (Jn 18:31-38, Mk 15:1-5, Lk 23:1-10, Mt 27:1-2, 11-14).

> *prōi* (Jn 18:28) 6 a.m.
> *phagōsin to pascha* (Jn 18:28) 6 a.m. unleavened bread for Herods, using 15a +2½. Morning meal.
> *euthys prōi* (Mk 15:1) 6 a.m.
> *en tautais tais hēmerais* (Lk 23:7 "in these days") the tetrarch uses Qumran (= parts of Diaspora) at X, (time phrase in narrative can refer to past time if it gives a grade, cf. *onta* "initiated").
> *ex hikanōn chronōn* (Lk 23:8 "long times") generation of Agrippa (*ho Hērōdēs*), the Worthy One, lay levite. Two years from Mar AD 31.

7 a.m.   10 a.m. Pilate becomes a member by a token washing of hands, in order to receive the bribe. He announces that Theudas-Barabbas is to be released, and

Judas to hang (Jn 18:38–40, Mk 15:6–15, Mt 27:15–25, Lk 23:13–19).

en tō pascha (Jn 18:39) 7 a.m. start of day (cf. Lk 22:59).

kata heortēn (Mk 15:6) 31st, 7 a.m. start.

en autē tē hēmera (Lk 23:12 "that very day") 7 a.m., lay start of day.

Agrippa mocks Jesus' claims to be king in his place, dressing him in the purple of a king-bishop, and putting on him the ascetic crown of thorns worn by Jonathan Annas (Stephen "the crown", and the Thorn, in the flesh). (Jn 19:2–5, Mk 15:16–20, Mt 27:27–30).

8 a.m. 11 a.m. Independent trial of Jesus. No bribe is offered for him, and he is condemned. (Jn 19:8–12, Lk 23:20–21).

8.55 a.m. 11.55 a.m. Pilate gives the formal order for execution (Jn 19:13–16).

paraskeuē tou pascha, hōra . . . hōs hektē (Jn 19:14 "preparation of the Passover, hour was about 6th") the 15a +2½ unleavened bread feast for adjustment of hours. 6th hour noon, fast time. *Hōs* 5 mins to the hour.

The men are taken to the unclean SW section.

Jesus is offered poison as a way of avoiding the pain to come, but refuses it (Jn 19:14–17, Mk 15:22–23, Mt 27:33–34).

9 a.m. noon The crosses are erected in the unclean area near the unstepped cistern (see Locations, p. 324). (Jn 19:23–24, Mk 15:25–27, Lk 23:33–38, Mt 27:36–38).

hōra tritē (Mk 15:25) 9 a.m.

Jesus speaks to Simon Magus whose cross is to the east of his (Lk 23:39–43).

sēmeron (Lk 23:43) 31st.

It is time for the adjustment of hours. At true 9 a.m. but fast noon the half-roof in the vestry is left over instead of being opened, leading to a "3 hours' darkness" (Mk 15:33, Lk 23:44, Mt 27:45, see p. 181), John Mark's party do not make the adjustment, as they use 15a for unleavened bread.

genomenēs hōras hektēs skotos . . . heōs hōras enatēs (Mk 15:33) a fast noon (no art.) having come (true 9 a.m.) darkness until a fast 3 p.m.

ēdē hōsei hōra hektē . . . skotos . . .
heōs hōras enatēs (Lk 23:44) 9 a.m.
the watch before noon, 3 hrs early.
Darkness until a fast 3 p.m.

noon
3 p.m.

End of adjustment.
After 6 hours on the cross, Jesus is in
intolerable pain. He cries out, both
asking for the poison and reproaching
Jonathan for his treachery.

tē enatē hōra (Mk 15:34) 3 p.m.
peri . . . tēn enatēn hōran (Mt 27:46)
3.03.

The snake poison is brought; Jesus
drinks and loses consciousness
(Jn 19:28-30, Mk 15:34-37,
Lk 23:46-47, Mt 27:46-51).
The tetrarch, planning to save Simon,
goes to Pilate and cites Jewish law to
persuade him to change the method of
execution to burial alive. The legs of
Simon and Judas are broken. The side of
Jesus is pierced as a test for death. John
Mark confirms that blood flows, an
indication that he may be alive.
(Jn 19:31-37).

paraskeuē (Jn 19:31 "preparation")
3 p.m. before 6 p.m., 15a +2½ for
adjustment of hours, used in John's
gospel.
en tō sabbatō (Jn 19:31) reg. 31a.
megalē hē hēmera ekeinou tou sabbatou
(Jn 19:31 "the great day of that
sabbath") 31a at SS3969, jubilee,
Restoration at Jewish start of 31st,
sabbath start.
ēdē (Jn 19:33) sabbath starts 3 hrs
early.

Simon Magus and Judas are placed in
Cave 7. It adjoins Cave 8, used as a
sabbath latrine by lay celibates, (see
Locations, p. 292). The entrance is at its
north-west corner, to which steps lead
from the cliff above. Entry is through a
large hole on the roof, which can be
blocked by a large stone.

4 p.m.

James, who as the Prince and the Rich
Man is responsible for Cave 8, arrives
and opens it by removing a secondary
stone (*lithos*, no art.) blocking its inner
entrance. It is used at 4 p.m. (Mt 27:52).
James returns to the boundary of the
buildings (Mt 27:53). James asks Pilate
for permission to take Jesus down from

		the cross (Jn 19:38). John Mark tells Theudas (Nicodemus, "Earthquake") that Jesus is not dead (Mt 27:54).
	5 p.m.	Women, using the unclean area at 5 p.m., see Theudas–Nicodemus wrap Jesus in linen garments (*othonia*, worn by Therapeutae, cf. *Contemp. Life* 38), and conceal under the garments a very large quantity of aloes and myrrh (Mk 15:40–41, Lk 23:49, Mt 27:55–56, Jn 19:40).
		James asks Pilate for permission to take Jesus down to the cave. It is before 6 p.m., so James can still lift up a burden. Jesus is carried down to the cave. James removes the *othonia* and dresses Jesus in a *sindōn*, a garment worn by Palestinian Essene novices (Lk 23:50–53).
31a(1)	6 p.m.	Pilate is standing at the edge of the esplanade, supervising the burials. James asks him for permission to bury Jesus. Pilate is told by John Mark that Jesus is dead. Although he is surprised, he gives permission. James wraps Jesus in an outer *sindōn*, and leaves him in Cave 8. After 6 p.m. he can roll a stone, although not lift it; he rolls the secondary stone (*lithos*) into place, closing Cave 8. He leaves through the opening above Cave 7 (Jn 19:42, Mk 15:42–46, Lk 23:54, Mt 27:57–60).
		dia tēn paraskeuēn tōn Ioudaiōn (Jn 19:42) Fri 6 p.m. as 15a +2½ for adjusting hours.
		ēdē opsias genomenēs . . . paraskeuē . . . prosabbaton (Mk 15:42) 6 p.m. as 3 hrs before 9 p.m. (fast time).
		hēmera paraskeuēs . . . sabbaton epephōsken (Lk 23:54) 6 p.m., Jewish beginning of sabbath.
		opsias genomenēs (Mt 27:57) 6 p.m.
	7 p.m.	The women have reached the queen's house on the plain after one hour's walk (not bound by sabbath rule). They can look up to Cave 8 (Mk 15:47, Lk 23:55–56, Mt 27:61).
	9 p.m.	It is time to seal the outer opening with the main stone. The chief concern is to guard Simon Magus, the "Deceiver" to Caiaphas (Mt 27:62–63). The problem is solved by putting the chief jailer, Ananus, on guard; he as a servant of

Agrippa is the political foe of Simon
Magus (Mt 27:62–66).

tē . . . epaurion (Mt 27:62) SS3969 IC,
reg. 31st, equ. pos., true 9 p.m., fast
midnight.

meta tēn paraskeuēn (Mt 27:62 "after
the Preparation") Fri, 24 hrs after
Thur 14a +2½ unleavened bread,
day for adjustment of hours. Now the
next day for adjustment. 9 p.m. as
fast midnight, Julian start.

meta treis hēmeras (Mt 27:63, "after
3 days") Wed 6 a.m., 24 hrs after Tue
6 a.m., day 3. Wed 1a, normative 1st.
Rule also applies to,Night position,
Sat 6 p.m. Simon has made the same
claim as Jesus, to be a priest whose
promotion day is the 1st.

heōs tēs trites hēmeras (Mt 27:64 "until
the third day") until the 1st, called
the third promotion day by
Samaritans.

Theudas comes on duty as the night
guard. He has orders from the tetrarch
to ensure the safety of Simon Magus.
He knows also that Jesus is not dead.
Keeping the Julian sabbath, he orders
Ananus to help him move the main
stone aside. The two go down into the
cave, move the inner stone, and carry
Simon Magus into the western chamber,
where he applies the aloes and revives
Jesus. Mary Magdalene, in the queen's
house below, sees a light in the chamber.

Sat Mar 21   midnight   Mary arrives near the cave, sees that the
                    (Fri)   stone has been removed, and sees Simon
                                     Magus ("the Lord") in the western
                                     chamber. She goes to fetch Peter and
                                     John Mark.

tē . . . mia tōn sabbatōn (Jn 20:1 "the
first of the week"). Fri midnight as
Julian start of 31st, counted as first
day of month and year (see p. 198).
Sabbatical year SS3969.

prōi skotias eti ousēs (Jn 20:1
"morning, darkness still being")
midnight as Julian beginning of day.

1 a.m.   They arrive at the opening to the cave.
                John Mark looks down into Cave 7 and
                sees the garments (*ta othonia*). Peter goes
                down into Cave 7, sees that Cave 8 is
                open and that Simon Magus' *soudarion*
                (headcloth) has been left in there. Simon

Magus has been returned to the eastern cave. Peter goes into Cave 8 and sees Jesus first, then John Mark enters and sees him next (1 Cor 15:5). John Mark goes to fetch a litter to carry him away (Jn 20:3-10).

2 a.m.

Mary returns to the cave. She looks down into Cave 7 and sees Simon Magus and Judas there in the positions of First and Second. Simon allows her to go into the western chamber (*hopou, ta opisō*, Jn 20:12,14). She sees Jesus, now standing (Jn 20:11-17).

Peter and John Mark enter Cave 8, prepared to carry Jesus away. They find him able to walk. (Cf. *GPet*. 10:36-39, two men entered the sepulchre, and "they saw . . . three men come out from the sepulchre, and two of them sustaining the other, and a cross [the litter] following them".) They take him up the path, permitted by Ananus and Theudas, whose duty is to guard Simon Magus. He is taken down to the queen's house.

3 a.m.

The three women arrive on top of the west chamber. They know that the main stone has been put back by Peter to confine Simon Magus. But Theudas "Earthquake" wants to help Simon. He must not lift up the stone, but he can roll it down the sloping shaft into the east cave. It crashes down, and Simon Magus is able to roll it further and sit on it as if on a papal throne. He now claims to have returned to the position of Pope "Lightning", through having worked a "miracle" on Jesus. Ananus is put down in rank. The women enter the cave, and Simon tells them he has brought about a resurrection. (Mk 16:1-7, Lk 24:1-8, Mt 28:1-7).

diagenomenou tou sabbatou (Mk 16:1 "the sabbath past") Fri 3 a.m., midpoint (*dia*) of the 31st Fri 3 p.m. to Sat 3 p.m.

lian prōi (Mk 16:1 "exceedingly morning") 3 a.m., 3 hrs before 6 a.m., early morning for villagers.

tē mia tōn sabbatōn (Mk 16:2) 31b as first day of month and year (see p. 198).

Sabbatical year SS3969. 3 a.m., villagers' start of day.

			anateilantos tou hēliou (Mk 16:2 "the sun having risen") Jesus, the Light, the Sun, has been moved from the cave.
			opse . . . sabbatōn (Mt 28:1 "evening of the sabbath") 3 a.m. as "evening" (normally 9 p.m.) to a day starting 6 a.m., of the sabbatical year.
			eis mian sabbatōn (Mt 28:1) 31b as first day of the month and sabbatical year.
			orthrou batheōs (Lk 24:1 "dawn deep") 3 a.m.
	6 a.m.		The women see Jesus at the queen's house (Mk 16:8, Lk 24:9-11, Mt 28:8-10).
			tachy (Mt 28:7) 6 a.m. as the "solstice" of the day (Julian method).
	3 p.m.	Qumran	Ananus the guard is removed from duty at the cave, as the Jewish sabbath law no longer applies.
	4 p.m.		Celibates keeping Jewish rules now go to Cave 4. But for those under Julian times it is still the sabbath. They have already missed Fri 4 a.m., and now use the sabbath latrine at 4 p.m. Simon Magus is removed and Judas is thrown from the window.
			Agrippa ("the soldiers") is told of the release of Simon, and offered money to take no further action. Pilate will also be bribed if necessary (Mt 28:11-15).
1a/1 equ. pos.	6 p.m.	Ain Feshkha	The evening common meal and communion are held at Ain F. (Jn 20:19).
			opsias tē hēmera ekeinē tē mia sabbatōn (Jn 20:19) 6 p.m., 1st ("that day", for Hebrews), 1st of month of sabbatical year SS3969, Jewish start.
	9 p.m.		At the hour for the sacred wine or teaching, Jesus comes. John Mark is made bishop (see Hierarchy, p. 368) (Jn 20:19-23).
			tōn thyrōn kekleismenōn (Jn 20:19 "the doors shut") 9.05 p.m., the hour at the evening meal when guests may be excluded.
Sun Mar 22	3 a.m.		Jesus is now under the rule for the sick, who must stay outside Qumran for three days (11QT 45:7-12). He acts like an outside Nazirite during this time, walking long distances to the various outposts, as an ascetic discipline. (His

feet had not been nailed, cf. Jn 20:25.)
(Cf. *Ant.* 18:64, on the Christ, probably
a genuine passage. It was known to
Josephus that after Pilate had
condemned him to be crucified, "on the
third day he appeared to them living".
On the Monday, the literal 3rd day, he
was in Jerusalem.)

noon	Mird major	He arrives at the Mird building (9 hrs) to have the communal meal with Thomas. He shares the meal, and again shows that he is physically present (Jn 20:26–29). (The eastern Christian tradition did not teach the resurrection.)

> *meth' hēmeras oktō* (Jn 20:26 "after days 8") Sun noon, 24 hrs after Sat noon, celibate form of Sat 6 p.m., early start of Sun, day 8.
> *palin* (Jn 20:26) noon.
> *tōn thyrōn kekleismenōn* (Jn 20:26) doors shut at noon (12.05) for celibate meal, as only members present. (Cf. *War* 2:129–132.)

4 p.m.	"Emmaus"	He walks 2 hours from the Mird building to the annexe of Mar Saba, "Emmaus" (see Locations, p. 292), meeting James (Cleopas) (see p. 425) and Theudas (his unnamed companion). On the way to Mar Saba they discuss recent events (Lk 24:13–26).

> *en autē tē hēmera* (Lk 24:13 "that very day") 4 p.m., + 1 hour (cf. Lk 23:12 7 a.m.).
> *en tais hēmerais tautais* (Lk 24:18) James refers back to John the Baptist's promotion of Agrippa in Jerusalem, in June AD 30 and 31.
> *tritēn tautēn hēmeran* (Lk 24:21) 2a is third day for Hebrews.

5 p.m.	Mar Saba	They arrive at Mar Saba, and have further discussion of Essene laws (Lk 24:27).
2a/1 & +2½ 31st	6 p.m.	They have the evening communal meal by Herodian rules for villagers (Lk 24:28–29).

> *pros hesperan* (Lk 24:29 "towards evening") 6 p.m. before 9 p.m., evening but not celibate *opse*.
> *keklinen ēdē hē hēmera* (Lk 24:29 "the day has already reclined") 6 p.m., 3 hrs before 9 p.m. bedtime.

8 p.m.	At the hour for communion bread, Jesus performs the ceremony of blessing, and

			James and Theudas acknowledge him as the true David (Lk 24:30-31).
	9 p.m.		Jesus takes 3 hours' rest, "not appearing" (as a priest) (Lk 24:31).
			James and Theudas walk 12 hours to Jerusalem (Lk 24:32-33). *autē tē hōra* (Lk 24:33) 9 p.m.
Mon Mar 23	9 a.m.	Essene Gate	They arrive at the Essene Gate (Lk 24:33-35).
	noon		They begin the noon meal, where common food is taken according to Herodian rules. Jesus arrives and takes the position of bishop, proving that he is physically present by eating common food (Lk 24:36-43).
	3 p.m.		End of service. Jesus sets out for Ain F. (24 hrs).
Tue Mar 24	3 p.m.	Ain Feshkha	He arrives at Ain F. accompanied by Peter, who joins Mary Magdalene ("Great Joy") and escorts her back to Jerusalem (Lk24:50-53, Mt28:16-20). *dia pantos* (Lk24:53 "through all") Herodian calendar and doctrine. *pasas tas hēmeras* (Mt 28:20 "all the days") Herodian calendar.
	6 p.m.	Qumran	Jesus arrives back at Qumran. Cf. 11QT 45:9, return after sunset for those who have been ill. He has the evening meal with John Mark, and tells him to remain in communion with Qumran (A 1:1-5). *di hēmeron tesserakonta* (A 1:3 "through days 40") Tue Mar 24 as day 21, the middle one (*dia*) of the 40 days' fasting at the Mar solar IC, Wed Mar 4 to Sun Apr 12. *ou meta pollas tautas hēmeras* (A 1:5 "not after many these days") Sat, Jun 20, AD 33. *pollai hēmerai* Tue 31st, *ou pollai hēmerai*, not Tue but Fri 31st, Night position, *meta*, 24 hrs after, Sat 1a.
	midnight		Jesus parts from John Mark to go to celibate quarters. James, the Cloud, his Second as king, conducts him there. Jonathan Annas, as the priest over both villagers and Diaspora celibates (the Abbot) receives him (A 1:9-11).

June Quarter

| Mon Jun 1 | 30/III & Sam 31st | midnight Mazin (Sun) | Occasion for reconciliation with Agrippa, June 1 (Julian significant date) 3 years after Agrippa was first baptised |

(Lk 5:1-11). Peter begins ceremony at Mazin. Jesus comes down from Qumran. This is day 70 from the day he went in. From the next day he is to become further enclosed. (Jn 21:1-2).

palin (Jn 21:1) midnight.

en ekeinē tē nykti (Jn 21:3) midnight.

3.03 a.m.   Jesus acting as priest joins the boat at the end of the jetty. He accepts Agrippa, and in doing so accepts great numbers of western uncircumcised Gentiles who have been won by the Herodian form of mission and will now become Christian (Jn 21:4-8).

prōias . . . ēdē genomenēs (Jn 21:4) 3.03, 3 hrs before 6.03.

6 a.m.   They have the village meal in the Mazin building, a reproduction of the upper vestry where there is a fire (Jn 21:9-14).

ēdē triton (Jn 21:14) 6 a.m., 3 hrs before 9 a.m.

7 a.m.   Jesus asks Peter to take up the celibate life, with the *agape* form of communion meal. He replies that he can only accept the village form, as a "friend" (Jn 21:15).

8 a.m.   The question and answer are repeated. Peter is to act as the chief Nazirite, over the "sheep", on behalf of Agrippa (Jn 21:16).

palin deuteron (Jn 21:16) 8 a.m.

9 a.m.   Peter is left in his village state now, but will later enter the celibate life as a widower (Jn 21:17-19).

to triton (Jn 21:17) 9 a.m.

(Jn 21 was added to John's gospel after the reconciliation between John Mark-Eutychus and the ministers of Agrippa II in AD 58.)

Tue Jun 2	31a(IV)	3 a.m.	Ain Feshkha	Theudas leaves Qumran after 70 days and goes to Jerusalem, a 24 hr journey (A 1:12).

sabbatou . . . hodon (A 1:12 "a sabbath day's journey") 24 hr journey, as *sabbaton* is the 31st. On a normal day, 12 hrs travel 3 a.m. to 3 p.m., but as the *sabbaton* is 36 hrs at the IC, 24 hrs' travel.

Wed Jun 3	1b/IV & 15a/III	3 p.m.	Jerusalem	He joins the Twelve Apostles at the Essene Gate (A 1:13-14) (Pentecost to solstice position).
Fri Jun 19	31a(IV)	noon		Replacement of Judas, 3 years from the appointment of the Twelve Apostles (A 2:5-26).

en tais hēmerais tautais (A 1:15 "in the days these") June solst., 31st.
en panti chrono (A 1:21 "in all the time") the 40 year generation of Agrippa, b. 11 BC, NS3930–3970, to AD 30.

Sun Jun 21	1b/IV & 15a/III Pentecost to post pos.	midnight (Sat)	The Day of Pentecost begins. Agrippa completes his June promotion to the office of archbishop. (See Hierarchy, p. 368.) He permits services in western churches to be held in native languages (A 2:1–4).

tēn hēmeran tēs pentekostēs (A 2:1) 15a/III combined with solst. pos., also true solstice.

	9 a.m.	Hour for laity.

A council of Gentiles from all world provinces is being held. Peter preaches in the presence of Agrippa.
hōra tritē tēs hēmeras (A 2:15) 9 a.m.
en tais eschatais hēmerais (A 2:17 "in the last days") the next Fri 31st, in Sep 33, SS3970 Sep start.
en tais hēmerais ekeinais (A 2:18 "in the days those") March AD 34, SS3970 (in speech, refers forward).
achri tēs hēmeras tautēs (A 2:29) until Pentecost (a lay feast).

Mon Jun 22	Agrippa further promoted (A 2:41)

en tē hēmera ekeinē (A 2:41) day after Pentecost as significant. day (Jub 1:1).

September Quarter

Tue Sep 1	31a (VII) 1st pos.	midnight Jerusalem	Agrippa begins Sep promotion (A 2:43–45).

kath hēmeran (A 2:46). Herodian reg. 31st (Lk 11:3).

	6 a.m.	Jewish start of the day (A 2:47).

kath hēmeran (A 2:47) 6 a.m. Jewish start of reg. 31st.

	3 p.m.	Occasion for Jewish villagers to come to substitute temple at Essene Gate, acc. to Ezek 46:1–3. James is prince at the corner outside the eastern door. At the same time he is beginning his 4-year betrothal period, aged 32, so "lame" (no longer in celibates' procession by Essene rules) and also dependent on Agrippa, who "feeds" outside celibates, so a "beggar". Peter teaches him a more relaxed rule, which allows him to attend services in the lower sanctuary while betrothed (A 3:1–26).

epi tēn hōran tēs proseuchēs tēn enatēn

(A 3:1 "upon the hour of prayer the 9th") 3 p.m. as the time for petitions of villagers.

kath hēmeran (A 3:2) Herodian 31st, 3 p.m.

mellontas (A 3:3) 3 p.m. as early service before 6 p.m.

James enters the lower sanctuary for worship (A 3:7–10).

parachrēma (A 3:7) 3 p.m.

Peter preaches, including the point that Jesus will return to the world in Sep 36, as a daughter has just been born and he must come back in 3 years. AD 36 will be SLS3971, the last possible chance for a fulfilment (A 3:11–26, esp.v.21).

achri chronōn apokatastaseōs pantōn (A 3:21 "until the times of Restoration") until Sep AD 36, SLS3971, Herodian generation.

tas hēmeras tautas (A 3:24 "the days these") (in speech), June the superior season for fulfilment.

	6 p.m.	There has not been a fulfilment of the Exodus (early SS3970), and the Hebrews blame Peter's doctrine. He is confined until the following morning. Agrippa's Sep promotion is completed (A 4:1–4).

eis tēn aurion (A 4:3) Jewish start of Wed 1a.

hespera ēdē (A 4:3) 6 p.m., 3 hrs before non-celibate evening 9 p.m.

Wed Sep 2	1a/VII	6 a.m.	No fulfilment at 1a, day of expectation for non-Essenes. Jonathan Annas falls as Pope; Simon Magus again becomes Pope John (A 4:5–21).

epi tēn aurion (A 4:5) 1a as Tomorrow.

sēmeron (A 4:9) 1a treated by non-Essenes as Today, day of fulfilment (IC will be transferred to 1a).

December Quarter

Tue Dec 1	31a(X)	James has a further promotion in December (A 4:22). He is treated as the David, and associated with the generation of Jesus, 3930–3970.

etōn pleionōn tesserakonta (A 4:22 "of more 40 yrs") SS3970, Dec solstice, Julian 1st. Extension from Sep, Jewish Julian.

Wed Dec 16	29/IX pente-contad	Mt of Olives	Married members stay in the Mount of Olives annexe building. They hear the news that Jesus has been given a pardon

by Pilate through the influence of the
Herods (A 4:27).
ta nyn (A 4:29 "the now", fem.)
pentecontad (*Nun*, Heb. 50).
Agrippa's party treats pentecontads,
esp. 26/I, 15/III, and 29/IX as
significant days.

AD 34
SS3970, SLS3969
March Quarter

Fri Mar 19	31a(I) equ. pos.		Jerusalem	Non-fulfilment for March SS3970. Agrippa party blames Samaritans (A 4:32).

en tais eschatais hēmerais (A 2:17 "in
the last days") Fri, counted as last day
of week, plural for significant day (in
prophecy used by Peter Jun 33 to
refer to Mar 34).
en tais hēmerais ekeinais (A 2:18 "in
the days these") Mar equ. (in
prophecy, as above).

Sat Mar 20	1a/I	6 p.m.	Caesarea	John Mark receives promotion, 1 year from becoming bishop. Now cardinal "Great Grace" (A 4:33). He allies with Simon Magus ("Great Power") in an anti-Agrippa party. They want to withdraw their money from Qumran to keep it from Agrippa. Philip-Protos joins them, as Agrippa has defrauded him of money (*Ant.* 18:157). The failure of the 40 yr generation from the reoccupation of Qumran gives them a reason for separating from Qumran and setting up a new Magian centre in Caesarea. Barnabas, who holds some of the Qumran property as a replacement for Judas, brings his share to Caesarea. The Caesarea members with John Mark reform the financial system by abolishing fees (A 4:32-37).

AD 35
SLS3970

Fri Sep 16	31a(VII) equ. pos.	noon	Caesarea	Last chance for 3970. Simon Magus is blamed for the failure, especially his immorality concerning Helena. He is also blamed for having promised to accept the financial reform, but continuing to receive fees from the east. Moreover, Agrippa is on the rise in Rome, and once he gains the kingship Simon will decline. He is

excommunicated by Peter, now rising
with the rise of Agrippa.

3 p.m.

Helena is excommunicated also, as she
claims priesthood and is under the same
rules as Simon (A 5:1-11).

 hōs hōrōn triōn diastēma (A 5:7 "about
3 hrs' interval") 3 p.m., as the hour
for Helena, treated as the beginning
of the day. Julian hours from noon.
2.55 (*hōs*).

Helena's excommunication completed, at
the time used for women (A 5:10).

 parachrēma (A 5:10) 3 p.m.

AD 36
SLS3971
All intercalations completed. Night position.

September Quarter

| Sat Sep 15 | 1a/VII equ. pos. | 6 p.m. | Jerusalem |

Jesus comes back into the world for the
conception of a child. Simon Magus
allies with the Jerusalem members. Peter
acts as Second to Jesus. Herod of
Chalcis, brother of Agrippa but opposed
to him, begins his promotion, preparing
to replace the tetrarch (A 5:12-16).

December Quarter

| Sat Dec 8 | 25/IX Dedication | 6 p.m. | Jerusalem |

The last chance for 3971 was in
September, but some members hope for
a fulfilment at Dedication. John Mark has
now returned from Rome after betraying
Agrippa (*Ant.* 18:179). Caiaphas and
Ananus, supporters of Agrippa, blame
him for the non-fulfilment and put him
under discipline in the north vestry
(A 5:17-18).

| Sun Dec 9 | | midnight (Sat) | |

Simon Magus has regained some power
with the news of Agrippa's arrest, and
now begins a challenge to Caiaphas. His
policy allows proselytes like John Mark
to be ministers in the lower sanctuary
(A 5:19-20).

 dia nyktos (A 5:19) midnight.

3 a.m.

John Mark acts as a minister to village
workers at their 3 a.m. service (A 5:21).
hypo ton orthron (A 5:21 "under
dawn") 3 a.m.

| Wed Dec 12 | 29/IX pente-contad | 3 p.m. | |

The Hebrews call a council at the
pentecontad, attempting to retain
power. They produce proof that John
Mark is not in the north vestry but in
the lower sanctuary (A 5:21-26). John
Mark speaks, defying Caiaphas,

and anticipating the election of Jonathan
Annas as high priest (v.29). Jesus has
just returned to the celibate life as Mary
is 3 mths pregnant (v.30). Gamaliel of
the Hebrews recounts the history of the
uprising, and warns against the anti-
Agrippa party. John Mark is punished
(A 5:27-40).

> *ta nyn* (A 5:38) 29/IX pentecontad.

AD 37
March Quarter

Fri Mar 15	31a(I) equ. pos.	Jerusalem	Jonathan Annas has been appointed public high priest in place of Caiaphas (*Ant.* 18:95). Hellenists and Samaritans are in power. John Mark is released. Agrippa is appointed king by Gaius on the death of Tiberius, but remains in Rome (A 5:41-42).

> *pasan . . .hēmeran* (A 5:42) Agrippa's
> calendar.

June Quarter

Fri Jun 14	31a(IV)	midnight (Thu) Jerusalem	In preparation for the return of Agrippa, the war Hellenists (Samaritans) strengthen against him by promoting Philip-Protos and uncircumcised Gentiles like him. John Mark steps down as delegate of Jesus. Hellenists and Hebrews are divided against and for Agrippa. The issue on which they publicly differ is that of the circumcision of the convert Izates (Hebrews for, Hellenists through Simon Magus-Ananias against) and the giving of ministry to his mother queen Helena (*Ant.* 20:17-48) (A 6:1-6, Lk 18:1-8).

> *en . . . tais hēmerais tautais* (A 6:1 "in
> the days these") June, at the 31st.

noon	Jesus Justus has been born, and given official birthdays Jun 1 and at the solar 31st. Agrippa is appointed head of the ascetics (A 6:7).

September Quarter

Mon Sep 23	10/VII Atonement	6 p.m. Mird	On the night before Atonement, the high priest has to be kept awake to avoid impurity (cf. *Ant.* 17:166) and is also tested for true doctrine. An alliance of Hebrews and war Hellenists is formed against Jonathan Annas (A 6:8-10).
Tue Sep 24		midnight	Jonathan speaks for 3 hrs, giving a

		(Mon) 3 a.m.		history of the ascetic movement from early 1st century BC, in typological form (A 7:1-53).
				He is rejected as high priest. His brother Theophilus has been appointed in his place (*Ant*. 18:123-124).
		3 p.m.		Theophilus completes the sectarian atonement, with Jesus acting as his Second. Jonathan Annas, now reduced to a witness, looks through the side window into the Holy of Holies (A 7:55-58).
		4 p.m.		He is excommunicated into the equivalent of Cave 4, used by lay celibates at 4 p.m. (cf. Mt 27:52, 28:13) (A 7:60).

Sat Sep 28	15/VII
	Taber-
	nacles
		6 p.m.		Following the oath of loyalty to Gaius (*Ant*. 18:124) the Hebrews move their property from Qumran to Damascus to keep it from Agrippa. Peter and John of Zebedee ("the church", see p. 302) move into Qumran. Thus there are now 3 sets of meeting places: (a) Hellenists in Caesarea against Agrippa; (b) Hebrews in Damascus, also against him; (c) the party soon to become Christian and Jewish Christian, for Agrippa, in Jerusalem, Mird and Qumran. Saul, of the order of Benjamin, is for Agrippa and meets at Qumran, but also goes to Damascus (A 8:1-3).
				    en ekeinē tē hēmera (A 8:1)
				    Tabernacles, levitical feast.

Mon Sep 30	30a/VI &
	Sam 31st
	post pos.
			Caesarea	The anti-Agrippa party in Caesarea give independent baptisms. Philip-Protos joins them, thus dividing Gentiles for and against Agrippa. Simon Magus acts as a Pope in schism, using the title the Power of God, the Great One. Philip becomes a minister in Simon's party. Some members are re-baptised at *Mem* level (see p. 371). (A 8:4-13).
				    hikano chronō (A 8:11 "a long time")
				    the 40 year generation of Agrippa I,
				    the Worthy One (*hikanos*) begins.
				    Appointed king Sep AD 37, territory
				    extended Mar 41. 3½ years between.

AD 38 Sat Mar 1			Damascus	Formal inauguration of the Damascus centre, in year 8 of the new dating from AD 31 as year 1 (A 9:33). *ex etōn okto* (A 9:33 "out of years 8")

AD 38 year 8 from AD 31 as year 1. Julian start Jan 1. *ex*, one time unit later, Mar 1.

AD 39

Tue Sep 29   31a(VII)
post pos.

Caesarea   Those who received *Mem* baptism in AD 37 now receive full initiation, *Samekh*, two years later. Peter and John from Qumran are again in fellowship with Caesarea. They take part in the initiation ceremony (A 8:14-17). Simon Magus wants to continue the practice of simony, paying money for episcopal office, but Peter sternly rebukes him and separates on this point. He also shows that he knows of a poison plot against Agrippa (A 8:18-24).

December Quarter

Tue Dec 29   31a(X)   noon   Caesarea   Simon Magus in Caesarea sends
post pos.   Philip-Protos to Gaza, the centre for uncircumcised Gentiles of Ham, to recruit Titus for the plot against Gaius and the plot against Agrippa. (2 days Caesarea to Gaza at donkey rate, 3 times walking rate) (A 8:26).
                                    kata mesêmbrian (A 8:26) noon/south.

Thu Dec 31   +2½   noon   Gaza   Philip arrives at Gaza, where Titus, head of Ham, is holding a service according to Jerusalem Herodian rules, following synagogue hours (A 8:27-29).

2 p.m.   He comes to the reading from prophets (1 p.m. law, 2 p.m. prophets, 3 p.m. writings). Philip is invited to interpret, and suggests that the passage on the "sheep led to slaughter" refers to Agrippa, the head of Nazirite sheep and the "lost sheep". (A 8:29-34).

4 p.m.   Titus is given full immersion baptism like a Jewish novice (A 8:36-40).

AD 40

NS3980

(End of Holy War in original Herodian scheme, NS version.)

Mon Feb 29   noon   Damascus   Saul, a servant of Agrippa, is opposed to any form of Essene celibate rule. He blames the Essenes for the non-fulfilment of Herod the Great's scheme. But in Damascus he meets Jesus, present for a council of all three ascetic groups to deal with the question of Gaius. Saul changes his politics, and begins rebaptism, using both the Julian 1st and the solar 31st (A 9:1-8).

				periëstrapsen phōs (A 9:3 "a light flashed about") the half-roof was removed at noon, letting the sun shine down to the ground floor.
	6 p.m.			He is at *Nun*, "blind", and cannot take communion (A 9:9). *hēmeras treis* (A 9:9 "days 3") Mon 6 p.m., early start of Tue 6 a.m., day 3.
Tue Mar 1	noon			Ananias-Simon, present for the council, does not trust Saul, as he is an agent of Agrippa. But Jesus asks him to give Saul his *Samekh* full initiation (to be completed in Sep 40, when Saul turns 23). Saul is accepting a celibate type of rule, the Diaspora Essene Way (A 9:10–16).
	12.05 p.m.			Saul admitted to the celibate meal as an initiate, so "sees the light" (A 9:17–18). *eutheōs* (A 9:18) 12.05, when members are allowed to remain at the meal.
	6 p.m.			Saul also takes the common meal in the evening (A 9:19)
Fri Mar 11 31a(I)	noon			Process repeated at the 31st.

AD 43
NS3983
Series of intercalations for 3983 begin, changing from Night (Fri 6 p.m.) to Day (Tue 6 a.m.).

March Quarter

Fri Mar 1		Qumran	Saul to Qumran, where he becomes a deacon in the Herodian ministry, with Peter (Gal 1:18, 2 Cor 12:2). *meta etē tria* (Gal 1:18 "after years 3") Mar 1, AD 43, one year after Mar 1, AD 42, "year 3" as Paul's year for full initiation at *Samekh*. Now becomes *Ayin* deacon. Julian 1st of month. *pro etōn dekatessarōn* (2 Cor 2:12 "before years 14"), March 1, AD 43, one year before March 1, AD 44, "year 14" in the new dating from AD 31 as "year 1".
Sun Mar 24 29b/XII	6 p.m.	Damascus	Saul arrives in Damascus for equinox form of promotion (A 9:19). *hēmeras tinas* (A 9:19 "certain days") Sun 6 p.m. as early start of Mon 6 a.m., Sam 31st.
Mon Mar 25 30a/XII & Sam 31st equ. pos.	noon 6 p.m.		Saul preaches (A 9:20). *eutheōs* (A 9:20) 12.05, noon service. Herod of Chalcis (brother of Agrippa I, replacing Antipas as "the Jews") attacks

				Saul (A 9:23).
				hēmerai hikanai (A 9:23 "many days") 30b, early start of 31a, reg. 31st at equinox, used by lay levites, "worthy ones".
Tue Mar 26	31a(I)	6 a.m.		Gates watched. Saul escapes (A 9:24). *hēmeras . . . kai nyktos* (A 9:24 "day and night") reg. 31st at equinox position, the calendar having now changed to Day at the intercalation. Followed by Night at the post position.
Thu Mar 28	+2½ 31st		Jerusalem	Disputes at the council over the admission of Gentiles. Saul is sent away to Tarsus to avoid the plot against Agrippa (A 9:26-30).
Sat Mar 30	+2½ 1st		Qumran	The leaders plotting against Agrippa assemble at Ain Feshkha (A 9:31).
Thu Apr 11	30a/XII & Sam 31st post pos.	noon	Lydda	James has returned from Damascus to an Essene centre at Lydda (cf. *War* 2:567). Peter reinstates him as a member of Jewish Christians (A 9:32-35). *eutheōs* (A 9:34) 12.05, noon service. Mary the mother of Jesus and James has returned with James, and is also to be re-instated. Ceremony begins with re-enactment of her excommunication. Peter is sent for, to complete the ceremony. Joppa was one hour's ride from Lydda by horse, the mode of transport on main roads west of Jerusalem. *en tais hemerais ekeinais* (A 9:37) Mar equinox, Sam 31st, post position.
		3 p.m.	Joppa	Peter arrives at Joppa (1½ hrs Joppa to Lydda for messenger, 1½ hrs Lydda to Joppa for Peter). Re-instates Mary (A 9:39-42).
Fri Apr 12	31a(I) post pos.	6 a.m.		Peter stays at Joppa with anti-Herodian party (A 9:43). *hemeras hikanas* (A 9:43 "many days") 30b, early start of 31a, reg. 31st, used by lay levites, "worthy ones".

June Quarter

| Wed June 5 | 29/III 1st pos. | 12.03 p.m. | Caesarea | Cornelius-Luke, head of Japheth uncirc. Gentiles, presides at a noon meal. An "angel" directs Luke to send to Joppa for Peter (A 10:1-6). *hōsei peri hōran enatēn tes hēmeras* |

				(A 9:3 "about around the 9th hour of the day") noon, as the unit (watch of 3 hrs) before 3 p.m., 9th hr (Jewish). *Peri* .03.
		3 p.m.		Messengers sent from Caesarea to Joppa at end of service (A 10:7-8).
Thu June 6	30/III & Sam 31st	noon	Joppa	Peter is conducting a noon service on the platform in the Joppa vestry, the place where the Jewish lay missionary stands. Above him is another roof, where the Jewish priest stands.
				tē . . . epaurion (A 10:9 "the next day") start of IC for NS3983, Jun, Thu 30th as Sam 31st early start at noon.
		12.03 p.m.		Peter arrives on platform (A 10:9).
				peri hōran hekten (A 10:9 "about a 6th hour") 12.03.
				As the meal begins, the half-roof above Peter is opened, and a tablecloth bearing Herodian emblems is let down. Calf (tetrapod), Eagle (Bird), snake (replacing Man), but no Lion (A 10:12).
		3 p.m.		Peter refuses to join in Herodian communion (A 10:11-14). Jesus on third storey above tells Peter that Matthew, the high priest, has given membership to Agrippa (A 10:15). The cloth is removed at the end of the service (A 10:16)
				euthys (A 10:16) 3 p.m.
				epi tris (A 10:16) 3 p.m.
				The messenger arrives from Caesarea (24 hrs, 48 kms at 2 kms per hour on good coast road, twice the walking rate for wilderness roads) (A 10:17-23).
Fri Jun 7	31a(IV) pos.	1st noon		Peter leaves for Caesarea. 9 hrs travel to 9 p.m., using Julian sabbath (A 10:23).
				tē . . . epaurion (A 10:23 "the next day") NS3983 IC, reg. 31st, noon start.
Sun Jun 9	1b-2a/IV & 15a/III to solst. pos. Pentecost & +2½ 31st	noon		Peter arrives at Caesarea. 24 hrs travel, 9 hrs on Fri + 15 hrs Sat 9 p.m. to Sun noon (A 10:24).
				tē . . . epaurion (A 10:24) NS3983 IC, +2½ 31st.
		3 p.m.		He enters the service (A 10:25).
				apo tetartēs hēmeras mechri tautēs tēs hōras ēmēn tēn enatēn (A 10:30 "from a 4th day until this hour I was the 9th") from Wednesday, 4th day of week, to Sunday, 4th day (2a) in

				Samaritan usage. "This hour" 3 p.m. Luke "the 9th", minister at 3 p.m., the 9th hour.
				Peter preaches (A 10:34-43).
				Agrippa baptised (A 10:44-48).
	6 p.m.			Peter stays extra day in Caesarea (A 10:48).
				hēmeras tinas (A 10:48 "certain days") Mon as feast day, extra day after Pentecost (*Jub.* 1:1). Sun 6 p.m. early start.

September Quarter

Sun Sep 1				Agrippa II, born Sep 1, AD 27, turns 16, becomes Herod crown prince (in Herodian system equal to David king Lion in 4 "living creatures", so "wild beast".)
Sun Sep 8	+2½ 31st	3 p.m.	Caesarea	Ceremony of 3 months before repeated, but crown prince emblem, "wild beasts" added to cloth. Reported by Peter A 11:5-16.
Mon Sep 9			Jerusalem	Peter in Jerusalem. Herod of Chalcis objects to the promotion of Agrippa. Peter defends (A 11:2-4).
Tue Sep 17	10/VII Atonement			Matthew Annas deposed as high priest (*Ant.* 19:342).

December Quarter

Tue Dec 24	31a(X) solst. pos.	midnight (Mon)		Gentile centre, village level "Church" established in Antioch. Name "Christian" adopted for party of Peter (westernised village Essenes, holding Jesus to be the David) (A 11:26)
				eniauton holon (A 11:26 "a whole year") year starting solst. pos. 31st.
	6 a.m.			Matthew-Agabus, deposed high priest, arrives in Antioch (A 11:28). Calendar established: Dec-Jan Julian start as intermediate between NS and NLS year. NS3983 IC from Dec 43 to Jun 47, "famine".
				en tautais tais hēmerais (A 11:27 "in these the days") Dec solstice 31st.

AD 44
NLS3983, SS3980

March Quarter

Sun Mar 1			Qumran	Saul, Barnabas and Titus have been sent

to Qumran by Matthew, for a council preparing for the anticipated exile and new outside base for Christians (A 11:30, Gal 2:1-2).

>*dia dekatessarōn etōn* (Gal 12:1 "through 14 years") Mar 1 44, year 14 of the dating from Mar 31 as year 1, Julian 1st of month.

Fri Mar 6	31a(I) 1st pos.		Qumran

Agrippa attacks the Christians plotting against him (A 12:1). James of Zebedee, of the order of Asher ("Tyre and Sidon") expelled. Peter imprisoned on the advice of Herod of Chalcis (A 12:2-3).

>*kat' ekeinon . . . ton kairon* (A 12:1 "according to that season") NLS3983 IC, Mar, 1st pos. 31st.

Fri Mar 20	14a/I to 1st pos. Unleav. Bread	6 p.m.

Peter under guard in north vestry (A 12:3b-4).

>*hai hēmerai tōn azymōn* (A 12:3 "the days of unleavened bread") 14a, Ex 12 rule.

Sat Mar 21	15a/I	6 p.m.

Peter brought into outer hall for remainder of 3½ day sentence (A 12:5).

>*meta to pascha* (A 12:4 "after the Passover") Sat 6 p.m., 24 hrs after Fri 6 p.m., both dates unleavened bread by Ex 12 and Lev 23 rules.

Mon Mar 23	30b/XII equ. pos. Sam 31st	9 p.m.

Peter to be released at midnight, celibate start of Tue 31st. He is about to enter the celibate life as a widower. The anti-Agrippa party seize power at Qumran at the non-fulfilment of the Herodian plan for SS3980. Simon Magus and Jesus ("The Light") release Peter and give him the vestments of a celibate (A 12:6-8).

>*ēmellen* (A 12:6) 9 p.m., 3 hrs before midnight.
>*te nykti ekeinē* (A 12:6) 9 p.m., 31st.

Tue Mar 24	31a(I) equ. pos.	midnight (Mon)

Peter led by Jesus and Simon Magus out of the hall for villagers, through its iron door (opened from inside) into the grounds of the celibate community.

>*prōten phylakēn kai deuteran* (A 12:10 "1st watch and 2nd") Julian 1st watch of night, starting midnight. Guard for 2nd watch preparing. Over married villagers.

	12.05 a.m.

Simon Magus leaves him, Jesus stays. Peter makes his confession to him (A 12:10-11).

>*eutheōs* (A 12:10) 12.05.

	3 a.m.

Peter knocks at the vestry door at the

time for the workers' early service. Mary
Magdalene, 9 months pregnant, acts as
doorkeeper ("sent out") under Herodian
rules. She does not admit Peter, both
because he is now a celibate "angel", and
because she is politically opposed, on
the side of Agrippa (A 12:12-15).
He is admitted, after showing that he
retains some village rules (A 12:16-17).

| | | 6 a.m. | | Day start of 31st. Theudas holds his demonstration at the Jordan, at year 38 of the revised Exodus AD 6 to 46 (*Ant.* 20:97-99). |

genomenēs . . . hēmeras . . . tarachos
(A 12:18 "a day come . . . a stir") 31st
for demonstration.

| Thu Apr 9 | 30a/XII & Sam 31st post pos. | 6 p.m. | Caesarea | Marsus, Roman governor of Syria, opposed to Agrippa, wants pro-Roman Matthew restored as high priest (A 12:20, 23, cf. *Ant.* 19:341-342). Eunuch Blastus agrees to poison Agrippa, who has returned to Caesarea (A 12:19). |
| Fri Apr 10 | 31a(I) post pos. | 6 a.m. | | Agrippa appears as divine king at dawn of final 31st, SS3980, end of original Herodian Holy War, (A 12:21, *Ant.* 19:343-346). |

taktē . . . hēmera (A 12:21 "at
appointed day") 31st in Herodian
scheme.

| | | 3 p.m. | | Snake poison, ordered by Simon Magus, takes effect (A 12:23). |

parachrēma (A 12:23) 3 p.m.

| | | | Qumran | Birth of second son to Jesus (A 12:24). |

June Quarter

| Fri Jun 5 | 31a(IV) 1st pos. | 6 p.m. | Antioch | Antioch Gentile Church begins new mission. Peter (Simeon Niger), Barnabas and Saul are Jewish ministers, Luke deacon. (A 13:1-2). |

nēsteuontōn (A 13:2 "fasting") for
NLS3983, June, 31st, 1st pos.

| Tue Jun 23 | 31(IV) solst. pos. | 6 a.m. | | Barnabas and Saul appointed to external mission (A 13:3). |

nēsteusantes (A 13:3 "fasting") IC for
post pos.

| Wed Jun 24 | 1b/IV & 15a/III to post pos. | 6 p.m. | | Pentecost. |

September Quarter

| Fri Sep 4 | 31a(VII) 1st pos. | 6 p.m. | Seleucia | Saul and Barnabas at Seleucia (A 13:4). |

Mon Sep 21	30b/VI equ. pos.	noon	Cyprus-Salamis	They join Jesus and John Mark at Salamis on Cyprus. Saul acts as "herald" to Jesus in procession (A 13:5).
Tue Sep 22	31a(VII)	noon	Cyprus-Paphos	At Paphos they join Agrippa II (Sergius Paulus) (see p. 427). (Aged 17, born AD 27, *Ant.* 19:354) Simon Magus-Elymas present at Cyprus celibate centre, attempts to influence him on appointment of high priests. Paul denounces Simon as the murderer of Agrippa I, excludes him for 1 year (A 13:6-12).

achri kairou (A 13:11 "until a season") until Sep 45, InterS 3983 IC (Cf. Lk 13:8, parable on this event. *Tria etē* (Lk 13:7) yr 3 of Claudius, Sep 1, AD 44).

	3 p.m.		Exclusion of Simon Magus to village rank begins (A 13:11).

parachrēma (A 13:11) 3 p.m.

AD 45
InterS 3983

March Quarter

Fri Mar 5	31a(I) 1st pos.	3 p.m.	Perga	Paul's party arrive in Perga in Pamphylia (A 13:13).
Sat Mar 6	1a/I	9 p.m.		The formal separation of Mary Magdalene begins. John Mark her representative returns to Qumran. He is also joining Jewish Christians, linked with Samaritans opposed to Agrippa II (A 13:13).
Tue Mar 23	31a(I)	noon 3 p.m.	Antioch of Pisidia	Paul preaches at a council (A 13:14). He gives an address, including an outline of the community history (A 13:16-41).

tē hēmera tōn sabbatōn (A 13:14) sabbatical year InterS 3983. After reading law (1 p.m.) and prophets (2 p.m.), so 3 p.m. (A 13:15). 31b start of sabbatical year.

Fri Apr 9	31a(I) post. pos.		Further preaching at post position (A 13:42).

to metaxy sabbaton (A 13:42) 31st.

September Quarter

Fri Sep 3	31a(VII)	Jesus preaches at Antioch of Pisidia (levitical centre of Asia Minor) on day of expectation of David Messiah, 40 yrs from Sep AD 5, millennium of peace party, SLS3941-3981, Sep start.

tō . . . erchomenō sabbatō (A 13:44

			"the coming sabbath") 31st for the Messiah, the "Coming One."
Tue Sep 21	31a(VII) equ. pos.	Iconium	Council at Iconium (A 14:1–4). *hikanon chronon* (A 14:3 "a long time") Sep 45, 3½ years before accession of Agrippa II, the Worthy One, in March AD 49.
Wed Sep 22	1a/VII	Lystra	Simon (Silas, "lame man") youngest brother of Jesus, initiated at 23 (born AD 22) (A 14:8–10) (see Hierarchy, p. 371). Herodian form of doctrine, identifying missionaries as pagan gods, reformed by Paul (A 14:11–17).
Thu Sep 23	+2½ 31st noon		Paul arrives at Derbe (A 14:20b). *tē epaurion* (A 14:20 "next day") IC for InterS 3983, Sep, equ. pos. +2½ 31st.

AD 46
SLS3981

Fri Mar 4	31a(I) 1st pos. Night	Antioch	Paul arrives back in Antioch of Syria, now under John Mark ("Grace of God") and Jewish Christians (A 14:26–27). Observes 40th anniversary of David peace party (A 14:28). *chronon ouk oligon* (A 14:28 "no little time") lit. "time not few". 40 years since the dismissal of Archelaus (*oligon*–Herodian). Jewish Christians have upper hand in Antioch, teach eastern views (A 15:1). Paul and Barnabas to be sent to Jerusalem to answer for teaching (A 15:2).

June Quarter

Wed June 1		Caesarea	They bring Jesus Justus ("Great Joy") on 9th birthday, to school in Caesarea (A 15:3).
Fri Jun 3	31a(IV) 1st noon pos. Night	Jerusalem	Council of Jerusalem. Peter speaks for Herodians (A 15:6–11). *aph' hēmerōn archaiōn* (A 15:7 "in the early days") from AD 29, the *archē*, beginning of new world-week (Mk 1:1).
	3 p.m.		"Silence"–Hebrew must be spoken in Jerusalem at 3 p.m. or else silence. Barnabas argues for his teaching (A 15:12).
	3.30 p.m.		James speaks, argues for anti-Agrippa doctrine, Davids only. Gives Jewish Christian ruling (A 15:13–21). *meta . . . to sigēsai* (A 15:13 "after they were silent") 3.30 p.m., after half-hour's silence (Rev 8:1).

Sun Jun 5	lb/IV & 15a/III to solst. pos. (Pentecost)		Decision to send Jude (3rd brother of Jesus, with Jewish Christians) and Simon-Silas, (4th brother) to Antioch (A 15:22).
Tue Jun 21	31a(IV) solst. pos. Day	Antioch	They arrive in Antioch (A 15:30). Antioch celebrates 40th anniversary of uprising, June version (A 15:33). *chronon* (A 15:33) 40 yrs.
	6 a.m.		Paul announces intention to work in Galatia for Agrippa party (A 15:36). *meta . . . tinas hēmeras* (A 15:36 "after certain days") 24 hrs after Mon 6 a.m. Sam 31st. Barnabas changes to eastern views, joins John Mark (A 15:37).

AD 48

SLS3983 (intercalations completed. All at Day position.)

Sun Sep 1		Derbe- Lystra	12th birthday of Timothy (a Herod, born Sep AD 36, see p. 419). (A 16:1).
Tue Sep 17	31a(VII)		Equinox birthday of Timothy.
Wed Sep 18	1a/VII		Timothy's symbolic "circumcision" given by Paul, his tutor (A 16:3). Circumcision of prince 1a (cf. Lk 2:21, 1:59).

AD 49

SLS3984

Herod of Chalcis makes Ananias, a Samaritan, high priest (*Ant.* 20:103). Simon Magus servant of Ananias, uses his name. Herod of Chalcis dies (*Ant.* 20:104) and Agrippa II becomes king.

Mon Sep 1			Agrippa II, aged 22, receives *Nun* ("the Number") (grade, and Heb. no. 50, A 16:5).
Tue Sep 16	31a(VII)	Phrygia	Paul, aged 32, begins 4 years' betrothal. Forbidden by Matthew to preach in Ephesus (A 16:6).

In late 49 the party of Jesus, Peter, John of Zebedee-Aquila and Luke ("Christians") are forced by Samaritan influence to leave Rome. (Cf. Suetonius, *Vita Claudii* 25:4). The "Beloved Son" is "killed" by the keepers of the Vineyard (Mk 12:7-8). They come to Greece, Patmos and Troas.

AD 50

NS3990, generation year and sabbatical.

Sun Mar 1		midnight Troas (Sat)	Paul arrives at Troas, now under Luke as chief proselyte. Jesus and Luke present. Jesus seen by Paul at midnight, Luke speaks for him, asks Paul to come to Philippi for second wedding (A 16:9). *dia nyktos* (A 16:9) midnight.
		noon 12.05 p.m.	Jesus and Luke leave noon meal, as Jesus is entering married state (A 16:10). *eutheōs* (A 16:10) 12.05, doors closed, outsiders leave meal.
Sun Mar 15		midnight Neapolis	They arrive at Neapolis (A 16:11) Mar 15

(Sat)			Ides of March. Roman calendar also used on reaching Europe.

(Sat)   Ides of March. Roman calendar also used on reaching Europe.
tē . . .epiousē (A 16:11 "the next day") midnight Julian, start of next day.

Sun Mar 15   29b/XII   6 p.m.   Philippi   They arrive at Philippi (A 16:12).
hēmeras tinas (A 16:12 "certain days") early start of Mon 6 a.m., Sam 31st.

Tue Mar 17   31a/(I)   midnight (Mon)   Second wedding of Jesus, with Lydia, a female bishop from the Thyatira Virgins. (A 16:13–14). Six years from birth of last son in Mar 44.
tē . . . hēmera tōn sabbatōn (A 16:13) Mon midnight, Julian beginning of sabbatical year NS3990.

3 a.m.   Lydia baptised by Christian doctrine (A 16:15).
Jesus and Luke now in village grade, attend vestry at 3 a.m. (A 16:16).

6 a.m.   Agrippa, Bernice, Apollos and Ananus the Younger are at Philippi for council for NS3990. Bernice preaches, as she is the chief Herodian woman, sister of Agrippa II (A 16:16b–17, *Ant* 18:132).
epi pollas hēmeras (A 16:18 "upon many days") Tue, 31a reg.

9 a.m.   Paul forbids Bernice to preach (A 16:18).
autē tē hōra (A 16:18) 9 a.m.
Agrippa attacks Paul (A 16:19–21). Paul and Silas put under discipline, reduced to congregation under deacon Ananus the Younger (A 16:22–24).

Wed Mar 18   1a/I   midnight (Tue)   Non-fulfilment of prophecy for NS3990 causes crisis (80 yrs since Qumran earthquake, 31 BC, NS3910). Apollos (the new "Earthquake," head of Ephraim) brings Alexandrians to the west, leaves Damascus, allies with Ananus the Younger and Paul (A 16:25–34).
kata . . . to mesonyktion (A 16:25) midnight.
parachrēma (A 16:26) service ends at midnight.

3 a.m.   Ananus the Younger ("the Jailer") agrees to accept doctrine of Jesus, is baptised (A 16:33).
en ekeinē tē hōra tēs nyktos (A 16:33) 3 a.m.
parachrēma (A 16:33) 3 a.m.

6 a.m.   Paul insists on reinstatement to the ministry (A 16:35–37).
hēmeras . . . genomenēs (A 16:35) 1a.

September Quarter

Tue Sep 1

Tue Sep 15   31a(VII)   noon

Agrippa, aged 23, receives full initiation.
Paul brings Jesus to celibate community
in Thessalonica, as Lydia now 3 mths
pregnant (A 17:2-3). Divisions over
validity of marriage. Opponents of it are
themselves associated with sodomy
(A 17:2-9).

> *epi sabbata tria* (A 17:2 "upon 3
> weeks") 21 years, (3x7). Sep 50, 3rd
> "week" of jubilee, starting Sep 29,
> NS3969.

midnight
12.05
a.m.

Paul and Silas leave celibate house for
Beroea, a Herodian centre
(A 17:10).

> *eutheōs dia nyktos* (A 17:10) 12.05,
> midnight, outsiders excluded.

AD 51

March Quarter

Tue Mar 16   31a(I)   Beroea

Paul announces Jesus, arriving for birth.
(A 17:13). Daughter born (as there is no
statement that there is a son).

> *kath' hēmeran* (A 17:11 "daily")
> Herodian regular 31st.

December Quarter

Wed Dec 1

Paul plans to begin courtship period.
Timothy and Silas sent to Thessalonica
for permission from Jesus. To return
following June (A 17:14-15).

> *hōs tachista* (A 17:16 "quickest")
> following solstice, shortest night.

Athens

Paul in Athens. Agrippa present, has
"paroxysm" against Samaritan influence
(A 17:16). Paul introduces Agrippa
calendar and doctrine (A 17:17-21).

> *kata pasan hēmeran* (A 17:17 "every
> day") Herodian calendar, 1st of Julian
> month. *Eukairoun* (A 17:21 "spent
> their time") used post pos.

Wed Dec 29 29/IX   6 p.m.
        post pos.

Paul makes speech supporting Ananus,
anti-Samaritan candidate for high priest
(A 17:22-31).

> *ta nyn* (A 17:30) 29/IX pentecontad.
> *chronous tēs agnoias . . . hēmeran en
> hē mellei krinein* (A 17:30-31 "times of
> ignorance . . . a day in which he
> [God] is about to judge".) Ananus
> calendar not that of solar gnostics.
> He holds new millennium 4000, NLS,
> Dec 61, 3 mths before he becomes
> public high priest (Mar 62,
> *Ant.* 20:197).

Fri Dec 31	31a(X) post pos.		Paul leaves higher ministry, becomes worker deacon before marriage (A 17:33) 18 months before betrothal. Associates with Ananus (Dionysius) and Tamar (Damaris)-Phoebe (A 17:34).

AD 52
March Quarter

Tue Mar 14	31a(I)	Corinth	Paul worker in Corinth with married couple Aquila and Priscilla 18 months before wedding. (A 18:1-4). *kata pan sabbaton* (A 18:4 "every sabbath") Herodian calendar, regular 31st.

(Agrippa now in Rome, where he uses influence to have the Samaritan high priest Ananias punished. Felix is appointed governor of Judea. He is a friend of Agrippa and will marry his sister Drusilla (*Ant.* 20:134-142).

June Quarter

Thu Jun 1		Corinth	Timothy and Silas arrive, bringing Jesus from Thessalonica, transferred to Corinth celibate centre (A 18:5). Paul writes I Thessalonians (A 18:5b, I Thess 3:6).
Wed Jun 14	1b/IV & 15a/III to post pos. Pentecost	6 p.m. Corinth	Paul receives permission to court, so reduced to congregation. Titus, Gentile celibate (Ham) becomes tutor to son of Jesus aged 15 now receiving title Justus, and called Titius after his master (A 18:6-7). *apo tou nyn* (A 18:6 "from now") Pentecost to post pos.

AD 53
June Quarter

Fri Jun 1		midnight Corinth (Thu)	Jesus Justus turns 16. Paul begins 3 months period before marriage. Jesus speaks to him at midnight service, gives permission to marry and proclaims Jesus Justus crown prince (*laos*) (A 18:9-10). *en nykti* (A 18:9) midnight. *eniauton kai mēnas hex* (A 18:11 "a year and 6 months"). June 1, Julian month 6. 18 months from Jan 1, AD 52, when Paul began marriage process.

September Quarter

Sat Sep 1		midnight Corinth (Fri)	Timothy turns 17, servant of proconsul Gallio (see p. 427). Wedding of Paul, aged 36, and Tamar-Phoebe, aged 20. Objections raised by Samaritans, dismissed by anti-Samaritan Timothy (A 18:12-16).

| Tue Sep 11 | 31a(VII) | | | Further ceremony at 31st, then Paul separates for 3 months (A 18:18a). *hēmeras hikanas* (A 18:8 "days many") 31st at equinox season. |

December Quarter

Sat Dec 1				Paul begins 1 month's preparation (follows pattern of Jesus in December 32). Goes to "Syria", unclean place near Athens (A 18:18) (see p. 310).
Tue Dec 11	31a(X)			
Fri Dec 28	31a(X) post pos.			
Mon Dec 31	+2½(b)		Cenchreae	Marriage consummated, 2 years from leaving higher ministry. Paul "shorn" as Nazirite "sheep" entering married state (A 18:18b).

AD 54
March Quarter

| Wed Mar 27 | 29/XII post pos. | 6 p.m. | Ephesus | Second wedding of Paul, as Tamar-Phoebe is 3 months pregnant (A 18:19a). |
| Fri Mar 29 | 31a(I) | noon | | Paul resumes ministry. Dialogues in synagogue (A 18:19-21). |

September Quarter

| Sun Sep 1 | | | Phrygia | Paul to Phrygia, where Tamar-Phoebe awaits birth of child (A 18:23, cf. A 16:6). Daughter born. Timothy, aged 18, receives first stage of initiation (A 18:23b). |

October 13, AD 54, accession of the emperor Nero. He gives part of Galilee and further cities to Agrippa (*Ant.* 20:159).

| Tue Dec 10 | 31a(X) 1st pos. | | Ephesus | Apollos receives Christian membership in addition to Baptist membership, instructed by Aquila and Priscilla (A 18:24-28). |
| Wed Dec 25 | 29/IX pentecontad post pos. | | Ephesus | Agrippa II, who graduated as a *Qof* in Sep 54, aged 27, receives a further promotion at the December pentecontad. Accepts Christian baptism in addition to the Baptist form of baptism (A 19:1-7) |

AD 55
March Quarter

| Sat Mar 1 | | | Ephesus | Paul in Ephesus, speaks in synagogue at ordinary sabbath service (not a significant solar date). Mar 1 a Saturday in AD 55. (A 19:8). This is the 11th hour of the Vineyard, (Mt 20:9). Agrippa II is the worker received at this hour. |

epi menas treis (A 19:8 "upon months
3") March 1, Julian month 3.

Tue Mar 11   31a(I)

Paul teaches in school of Tyrannus
(A 19:9).
kath' hemeran (A 19:9 "daily") reg.
31st, Herodian.
NB. Textual variant "from the 5th
hour to the 10th"(D text) shows
knowledge of the system. In an
Essene monastery, work ceased at the
5th hour, 11 a.m., to prepare for the
noon sacred meal (*War* 2:129) and
the pesher shows that the afternoon
session of teaching proselytes ended
at 4 p.m., the 10th hour.

AD 57
NS3997, intercalation series begins, changing from Day to Night.
March Quarter
Tue Mar 1   Ephesus

Paul has been minister in Ephesus for
the first two years of Nero's reign, as
Nero favours Agrippa and Paul is the
servant of Agrippa (A 19:10).
epi etē dyo (A 19:10 "upon year 2")
year 2 of Nero, counting from Mar 1,
AD 55. Years of Roman emperors now
being used.

Fri Mar 25   31a(I)   6 p.m.

Intercalation for March 57 completed.
Triennial series in use, AD 57–60,
AD 60–63.
trietian nykta kai hemeran (A 20:31,
referring to Paul's time in Ephesus)
AD 57, triennium, and NS year for
change to Night with Day at post pos.

June Quarter
Wed Jun 1

Paul appointed archbishop in Ephesus
(A 19:11). He issues 1 Corinthians with
Ananus-Sosthenes (1 Cor 1:1). Sends
message "Maranatha (Our Lord, come!)"
to Jesus, who has gone to Corinth, to
persuade him to accompany Paul to the
east for June 58 (1 Cor 16:22). In
Ephesus, Felix, Roman governor of
Judea, receives initiation as a Jew in
Herodian form, 3 years after marrying
Drusilla, sister of Agrippa. Samaritan
magician Atomus joins in instruction,
but Felix rejects. Plans to expel high
priest Ananias and kill Jonathan Annas.
Magians, founded 44 BC, persecuted and
their library destroyed (A 19:13–19,
cf. *Ant.* 20:142, 162–167).

Fri Jun 24	31a(IV) Night	6 p.m.		Solstice birthday of Jesus Justus, aged 20. Begins 3 yrs to full initiation, "confirmed" (A 19:20).

September Quarter

Thu Sep 1				Paul makes plans for renewal of marriage, 3 years from birth of daughter. Phoebe-Tamar has returned from Rome where she was sent with Epistle to Romans (Rom 16:1-2). Paul turns 40. His 40-yr generation celebrated in Ephesus (A 19:21-22). *chronon* (A 19:22 "a time") 40 years.
Tue Sep 6	31a(VII) 1st pos.	noon-2 p.m.		Simon Magus in Ephesus attacks Agrippa and Paul. Contest between Helena (called Artemis-Diana of Ephesians) and Bernice, sister of Agrippa, as chief woman over Gentiles in Ephesus (A 19:23-40). *kata ton kairon ekeinon* (A 19:23 "at that time") NS3997 IC, 31st. *epi hōras dyo* (A 19:34 "upon hour 2") 2 p.m., end of celibate meal. *peri tēs sēmeron* (A 19:40 "about today") 31st as Today.
Fri Sep 23	31a(VII)		Troas	Paul goes to Troas to renew marriage. Expects Titus to come there from Corinth with message from Jesus in answer to letter, but he does not come. Paul fears loss of favour with Jesus (2 Cor 2:12-13).

December Quarter

Thu Dec 1				Paul leaves Troas for Thessalonica (Macedonia) as wife 3 months pregnant. Appoints Timothy to Ephesus (A 20:1, 1 Tim 1:3).
Tue Dec 6	31a(X) 1st pos.		Thess-alonica	Titus arrives with good news from Jesus, that he will come to east with Paul (2 Cor 7:5-6).

AD 58
NLS3997, NS3998

March Quarter

Wed Mar 1			Athens	Paul arrives in Athens to visit wife at 6 months in "Syria" (unclean place) (A 20:3). *mēnas treis* (A 20:3 "3 months") March 1, 3rd Julian month.
Tue Mar 7	31a(I) 1st pos. Day		Thessa-lonica	Paul returns to Thessalonica celibate house. Paul, Jesus and Luke stay at Thessalonica, Peter and others to Troas (A 20:5).
Mon Mar 20	13b/I	6 p.m.		Paul's party leave Philippi.

Tue Mar 21 14a/I &   6 a.m.   "Days of unleavened bread" 14a.,
            27b/XII   unleavened bread by Ex 12 rule (A 20:6).
Wed Mar 22 15a/I &   6 a.m.   They arrive at Samothrace (border, *apo*,
            28b/XII   "from" Philippi and sail from there
                                             (A 20:6).
                                                  meta tas hēmeras tōn azymōn (A 20:6
                                                  "after the days of unleavened bread")
                                                  Wed 6 a.m., 24 hrs after Tue 6 a.m.
                                                  days of unleavened bread.
            29a/XII   6 p.m.   Troas   They arrive at Troas (A 20:6).
                                                  achri hēmeron pente (A 20:6 "until day
                                                  5") Wed 6 p.m., early start of Thu,
                                                  day 5.
Thur Mar 23 Sam 31a(I) 6 p.m.   25th anniversary of Last Supper.
            &
            14a/I+2½
Fri Mar 24 31a(I)   6 p.m.   25th anniversary of crucifixion.
            15a/I+2½   Observed in Troas (A 20:6).
                                                  hēmeras hepta (A 20:6 "days 7") Fri
                                                  6 p.m. Jewish start of Sat, day 7.
Sat Mar 25 1a/I   6 p.m.   25th anniversary of consecration of John
                                             Mark–Eutychus as archbishop
                                             (Jn 20:19–23). He is now reconciled
                                             with Christians, "raised from dead", in
                                             Troas, Gentile building with 3rd floor.
                                             Paul takes part in ceremony of re-
                                             admission (A 20:7–12).
                                                  en . . . tē mia tōn sabbatōn (A 20:7 "on
                                                  the 1 of the week") first day of month
                                                  of sabbatical NLS3997. Cf. Jn 20:19.
            9 p.m.   Sermon replaces wine in proselyte
                                             communities (cf. Jn 13:31–14:31). Paul
                                             gives dialogue, due to end 10 p.m. (cf.
                                             Jn 14:31).
                                                  mellōn exienai tē epaurion (A 20:7
                                                  "about to depart the next day") 3 hrs
                                                  before midnight, Julian start of 1a,
                                                  now being used by proselytes to
                                                  begin the intercalation, in order to
                                                  make 1a the significant day (so
                                                  changing from Saturday to Sunday in
                                                  the Night position).
Sun Mar 26 midnight   Prolongs sermon till midnight (A 20:7).
            (Sat)   *mechri mesonyktiou* (A 20:7 "until
                                                  midnight").
            3 a.m.   Prolongs sermon till 3 a.m. (A 20:9).
                                                  epi pleion (A 20:9, "upon more")
                                                  extension by 3hrs.
            6 a.m.   Bread and water taken (A 20:11a).
                                                  eph' hikanon (A 20:11. "upon much")
                                                  6 a.m.
                                                  achri augēs (A 20:11 "until dawn")
                                                  until 6 a.m.

| | 1b/I | 6 a.m. | | Paul's party set out for the east (A 20:13). |
| Fri Mar 31 | 24/I | | Miletus | They arrive at Miletus (A 20:15). |

te . . . echomenē (A 20:15 "the following") 2 days before pentecontad, as in A 21:26.

| | | | Patmos | They sail to Patmos ("beside Ephesus" A 20:16) from border, outpost of Miletus A 20:17. Agrippa there (A 20:25), Paul asks permission for Jesus to spend Sunday Pentecost (June 25) at Qumran (A 20:16). |

tēn hēmeran tēs pentekostēs (A 20:16) 15a/III & 1b/I at solstice, June 25 (in speech, question starting ei).

| Sun Apr 2 | 26/I to 1st pos. | midnight (Sat) | | Pentecontad service for 26/I, Herodian. Paul resigns his ministry in Ephesus. Speaks to the congregation, represented by John of Zebedee ("elders of the church", A20:18–24), then to Agrippa (A 20:25–35). |

ta nyn (A 20:32) pentecontad, 26/I to 1st position, observed by Herodians. en tē sēmeron hēmera (A 20:26) pentecontad as Today, Herodian view.

| | | 3 a.m. | | End of service. Agrippa embraces Paul as he concludes his ministry in Ephesus (A 20:36–38). |

mellousin (A 20:38) term to finish in 3 hrs.

| | | 6 a.m. | | They sail for the east. |
| Tue Apr 11 | 31a(I) post pos. | | Rhodes | Arrive at Rhodes for post position. |

te . . . hexēs (A 21:1, "the next") 3rd pos. 31st.

To Patara (A 21:1), then Myra for change of ship (cf. A 27:5). Route via Cyprus to Sidon (Phoenicia) (cf. A 27:3–5).

June Quarter

| Thu Jun 1 | | | Tyre | Arrive Tyre for birth of Paul's child, as first son has official birthday 1st of month (A 21:3). |
| Fri Jun 2 | | 6 p.m. | | Child born. Paul told not to go to Qumran, as will not be in celibate state till solstice (A 21:4). Child a daughter. |

hēmeras hepta (A 21:4 "days 7") Fri 6 p.m. Jewish start of Sat day 7.

| Sat Jun 3 | | 6 a.m. | | They farewell Paul's family and sail from Tyre (A 21:5–6). |

exartisai tas hēmeras (A 21:5 "complete the days") last day of week, not treated as sabbath.

| Sat Jun 3 | | 6 p.m. | Ptolemais | They arrive at Ptolemais (A 21:7). |

hēmeran mian (A 21:7 "day 1") Sat

				6 p.m., Jewish start of Sun, day 1.
Mon Jun 5	30a/III & Sam 31st 1st pos.	6 a.m.	Caesarea	They arrive at Caesarea, to the Gentile celibate community of Philip, now reconciled following John Mark (A 21:8-9). *tē epaurion* (A 21:8) Sam 31st. IC begins for NLS3997, IV.
Tue Jun 6	31b(IV)	6 p.m.		Agabus-Matthew prepares Paul for return to celibate state in Jerusalem under Herodian rule (A 21:10-14). *hēmeras pleious* (A 21:10 "days more") Wed 1a, Jewish start Tue 6 p.m.
Wed Jun 7	1a/IV	6 a.m.		Jesus and Luke go to Qumran (A 21:15-16). *meta . . . tas hēmeras tautas* (A 21:15 "after days these") Wed 1a June. 24 hrs after Tue 31a June.
	1b/IV & 15a/III	6 p.m.		Pentecost to solstice position. Paul goes independently to Jerusalem (A 24:11, referring back). *ou pleious . . . moi hēmerai dōdeka* (A 24:11 "not more . . . to me days 12) Wed 6 p.m., Jewish start of Thu, day 12 is not a feast to Paul, so not Pentecost. (Paul observes Pentecost at solstice.)
Thu Jun 22	30/III Julian	midnight Jerusalem (Wed)		Jesus and Luke meet Paul in Jerusalem for betrothal of Simon-Silas ("man 4", born AD 22). Paul due to return to celibate life, asked by James to give his money to Silas, and prove his loyalty to the celibate doctrine (A 21:18-25). *tē epiousē* (A 21:18 "the next day") midnight, Julian next day.
Fri Jun 23	31a(IV)	6 a.m.		Paul with Silas goes to treasury ("temple") at Essene Gate, where reserve funds are kept. (A 21:26). *tē echomenē hēmera* (A 21:26 "the having day") day for Silas to begin marriage progress. *tōn hēmerōn tou hagismou* (A 21:26 "of the days of purification") final of the 3 preparation days 29th, 30th, 31st.
		noon 12.05 p.m.		Non-fulfilment of expected beginning of Tribulation, by Herodian reckoning (3½ yrs June 58 to Dec 61, NLS4000, Julian. Great events 31st. Paul is blamed because of support for Trophimus. Paul is denied readmission, prepares to defend his record in a speech from steps near the vault (= pulpit) (A 21:27-36). *ēmellon hai hepta hēmerai* (A 21:27 "the seven days about to . . . " The

great Saturday to begin in 3 hours (strict rule).

eutheōs (A 21:30) 12.05, doors of sacred meal chamber shut to exclude outsiders.

	3 p.m.	Paul makes his speech (A 21:37–22:21). *pollēs . . . sigēs* (A 21:40 "great silence") Fri 3 p.m., when Hebrew (Aramaic) must be spoken, or else silence. *sēmeron* (A 22:3 "today") 31st.
	4 p.m.	End of service. (A 22:22–23). Agrippa (*chiliarch*) orders Paul to be admitted as village celibate, without property, so beaten as "slave". Paul points out rules of Rome province: membership is "bought" by Agrippa's grade, so not "slaves", and in Paul's reformed version, membership is given free (A 22:22–29).
	4.05 p.m.	Paul treated as heretic (A 22:29). *eutheōs* (A 22:29) 4.05.
	6 p.m.	Plenary council meet to test Paul for heresy. House of priests led by Ananias, Samaritan high priest. Paul threatens him with dismissal (fulfilled in AD 59) (A 22:30–23:5). Paul unites both houses of laity against priests. (A 23: 6–9). *tē epaurion* (A 22:30) Fri 6 p.m., IC for NLS3997, at solstice 31st. *achri tautēs tēs hēmeras* (A 23:1 "until this day") 31st is "this day" to Hebrews (Paul), "that day" to Samaritans (Ananias). Ananias punishes Paul for use of the phrase (A 23:2).
	10 p.m.	End of meeting.
Sat Jun 24	midnight (Fri)	Jesus speaks with Paul, appoints him as bishop/martyr to Rome (A 23:11). *tē . . . epiousē nykti* (A 23:11 "the next night") midnight Julian, beginning next day. Jewish Christians led by Jude (*Mem*, 40) begin their sabbath abstinence from food, to end Sat midnight. Plan to ask Agrippa to reopen case against Paul on Saturday evening. Timothy advises Agrippa to rule against them (A 23:12–22) *genomenēs . . . hēmeras* (A 23:12 "the day come") midnight.
1a/IV	6 p.m.	Agrippa rules in favour of Paul, allows him to go to Caesarea to give further instruction to Felix (A 23:24). At the

			same time, Apollos the Egyptian ("soldier 200", a *Resh*, see p. 365) is to be sent to Caesarea, with fellow zealots, under arrest. He has staged a demonstration the previous December (*Ant*. 20:169-172, A 21:38 *pro toutōn tōn hemerōn*) (A 23:23).
			aurion (A 23:20) 1a.
		9 p.m.	The party sets out, the prisoners and their escort by horse, Paul on a donkey, as he is in the celibate state (A 23:24). From Jerusalem to Antipatris it is 45 kms, 225 stadia, 3 hours by horse at 75 stadia per hour.
			apo tritēs hōras tēs nyktos (A 23:23 "from 3rd hour of the night") 9 p.m., the time when travel is again permitted by those keeping the Julian sabbath.
Sun Jun 25		midnight Antipatris (Sat)	Escort and prisoners, leading the way (*ēgagon*) arrive at Antipatris. Chief escort returns to Jerusalem (A 23:31-32)
			dia nyktos (A 23:31) midnight. *tē epaurion* (A 23:32) IC for NLS3997, solstice position. 1a Julian used to make 1a the significant day (cf. Troas practice, p. 272) (31st becomes part of previous month).
		3 a.m.	Escort arrives back at Jerusalem, and horsemen arrive at Caesarea, counted as a further 225 stadia, 3 hrs, from Antipatris (A 23:33a).
	1b/IV & 15a/III Pentecost	6 a.m.	Pentecost to post position.
Mon Jun 26		3 a.m.	Paul arrives at Caesarea. He is presented to Felix (A 23:33b-35).
Fri Jun 30			Samaritans arrive in Caesarea, attack Paul's credentials as a teacher. A day that is not significant for solarists is used, but significant in Roman calendar as the end of the half year (A 24:1-9).
			meta . . . pente hēmeras (A 24:1 "after 5 days") Fri 6 a.m., 24 hrs after Thu 6 a.m., day 5.
		3 p.m.	Paul replies (A 24:10-21). (*sēmeron* A 24:21 refers back, in speech).
Mon Jul 10	30a/III post pos.	6 a.m.	Felix promoted to Pe elder (A 24:22a). Appoints Paul for 2 yrs until Felix graduates in presence of Agrippa (A 24:22b).

6 p.m.				Felix with Drusilla (his wife, sister of Agrippa) begins instruction.

Paul teaches ethics and the prophecy for AD 61 (NLS4000) (A 24:24-26).

> meta . . . hēmeras tinas (A 24:24 "after days certain") Mon 6 p.m., 24 hrs after Sun 6 p.m., early start of Mon 6 a.m., Sam 31st.
>
> tou krimatos tou mellontos (A 24:25 "the judgment about to be") Last Judgment in 3 years.
>
> to nyn (A 24:25) Pentecost in AD 59.
>
> kairon . . . metalabōn (A 24:25 "receiving a season") AD 59, InterS 3997. (Samaritan calendar adopted by Felix in 59 when he changes sides.)

AD 59
InterS 3997

Fri Jun 22	31a(IV)	Felix promoted to bishop. Hopes to receive a bribe from Paul, under guise of welfare funds, to make Ananus high priest (A 24:26).

(In 58 or 59, during a conflict between pro- and anti-Herodians in Caesarea, Felix attacks the pro-Herodians, and is only reluctantly persuaded to desist (*Ant.* 20:173-178). The pro-Herodians (called Jews by Josephus) are the party of Agrippa and Paul; the anti-Herodians (called Syrians) are the Samaritans. From this point Paul and Felix are on opposite sides.)

AD 60
NS4000

March Quarter

Sat Mar 1				Festus arrives to succeed Felix as governor (*Ant.* 20:182, A 24:27). Felix, now with the Samaritans, turns against Paul (A 24:27). Felix will sail for Rome in June to face charges of misconduct before Nero, brought by the pro-Herodians (*Ant.* 20:182).

> dietias (A 24:27 "two years") at the end of the triennium 57–60, divided 1 + 2, so at the end of the 2 years. Starts Mar 1.

Wed Mar 5	1a/1 1st pos.	6 a.m.	Qumran	Festus visits Qumran expecting a demonstration at 1a. They are planning to have Paul excommunicated, knowing that he wishes to go to Rome to act as accuser of Felix (A 25:1-5).

> meta treis hēmeras (A 25:1 "after 3 days") Wed 6 a.m., 24 hrs after Tue

				6 a.m., day 3.
Sat Mar 22	1a/I equ. pos. Night	3 p.m.	Qumran	Festus again visits Qumran at next 1a (A 25:6).

hēmeras ou pleious oktō ē deka (A 25:6 "days not more 8 or 10") Sat 6 p.m., Jewish start of Sun 6 a.m. day 8. It is also a 1a which is not a Wed, so "not a more day". Festus receives nominal membership like all Roman governors, both a number 8 (*Nun*) and a number 10 (*Lamedh*), in both parties, Hebrews and Hellenists (Hellenists 2 grades higher for Gentiles).

| Sun Mar 23 | | midnight (Sat) | Caesarea | Festus arrives at Caesarea (2½ hrs Qumran to Jerusalem, 6 hours Jerusalem to Caesarea, by fast Roman transport) (A 25:6). |

tē epaurion (A 25:6) Sat midnight, Julian 1a now used, InterLS 3997, equ. position.

Paul argues his case to become accuser of Felix, on grounds of his support for Agrippa ("Caesar") (A 25:7–12).

| Tue Apr 8 | 31a(I) post pos. | | | Festus holds further hearing. Paul asks to be sent to Nero (*Sebastos*, the emperor) (A 25:17–21, refers back, in speech). |

tē hexēs (A 25:17) 31st, non-sacred.

June Quarter

| Sun Jun 1 | 29b/III 1st pos. | 6 p.m. | Caesarea | Agrippa and Bernice arrive for 1st position (A 25:13). |

hēmerōn . . . tinōn (A 25:13 "days certain") early start of Mon 6 a.m. Sam 31st.

| Wed Jun 4 | 1a/IV | | | Festus describes his second hearing of Paul (Apr 8) and his decision to hear him in the presence of Agrippa, representative of Caesar (A 25:14–22). |

pleious hēmeras (A 25:14 "more days") Wed 1a.

| Sat Jun 21 | 1a/IV solst. pos. | 6 p.m. | | Agrippa conducts hearing for Paul. |

aurion (A 25:22 "tomorrow") next 1a.

| Sun Jun 22 | | midnight (Sat) | | Beginning of day of Pentecost, year NS4000. A fulfilment may come in favour of laity, observing pentecontads. Agrippa and Bernice attend banquet. It is also Felix's "graduation" as *Qof* (cf. A 24:22). Felix is to be sent to Rome for trial. Paul's credentials are again challenged, and he defends his record (A 25:23–26:23). |

tē . . . epaurion (A 25:23) Sat midnight, Julian 1a IC for InterLS

3997, IV.

mellōn sēmeron (A 26:2) 3 hrs before 3 a.m., "Today" of expectation.
epangelias (A 26:6 "promise") Promised Land for Apollos Egyptian, NS4000 (yr 38 was June 58).
nykta kai hēmeran (A 26:7 "night and day") IC year for change to Night, followed by Day post pos.

	3 a.m.		Paul concludes speech. He denies that he is one of the Samaritan ecstatics, and Agrippa confirms that Paul has instructed him in Christian doctrine, so is anti-Samaritan (A 26:24–29).

achri tēs hēmeras tautēs (A 26:22 "until this day") Pentecost as lay day.
sēmeron (A 26:29) 3 a.m., "Today" of expectation.

	1b/IV & 15a/III Pentecost	6 a.m.	Paul is accepted as in good standing with Agrippa, so able to represent him in Rome. Agrippa and Festus withdraw (A 26:30–32). (A dispute over the temple has broken out, with Agrippa and Festus opposed to traditional Jews, who are sending their own delegation to Nero. *Ant.* 20:189–195.) Paul is taking the opportunity to bring the whole party to Rome for AD 61, NLS4000.
Mon Jun 23			Jesus, Luke and Paul embark in the same ship as Felix, the prisoner. Ananus–Demas also comes to argue for Agrippa. Agrippa's representative is Gaius, now the chief proselyte ("centurion"), a servant of Nero, so called Julius, of Nero's order (A 27:1). The ship sails (A 27:2).
Tue Jun 24		Sidon	Arrive at Sidon. Paul, under celibate discipline, is allowed a visit to wife and child, 2 yrs from birth. Sidon a "Syria", unclean place (A 27:3).
Tue Jul 8	31a(IV) post pos.	Myra	Arrive at Myra of Lycia (A 27:5). (The Mediterranean is divided by a line from Myra to Alexandria, and a line down from Illyricum (cf. Rom 15:20). Sea journey takes 1 month from Jewish ports to Crete, with Myra line as half-way; and 1 month from Crete to Malta, with Illyricum line half-way.)

September Quarter

Mon Sep 1	30a/VI	Myra	They embark in a ship of the Alexandrian mission, limited to west of the Myra line (A 27:6).

Tue Sep 2	31a(VII) 1st pos.		They set out from Myra. *en hikanais . . . hēmerais* (A 27:7 "in many days") 31a.
Fri Sep 12	10/VII	Cnidus	No fulfilment on Day of Atonement at Cnidus (A 27:7).
Fri Sep 19	31a(VII) equ. pos.	3 p.m. Fair Havens	They arrive at Fair Havens in Crete, mid-point of Mediterranean. No fulfilment at equinox (A 27:8–9). *hikanou . . . chronou* (A 27:9 "much time"). New Herodian generation at millennium. *ēdē* (A 27:9) 3 p.m. for 6 p.m. on Friday.
Tue Sep 30	10/VII	3 p.m.	No fulfilment at Day of Atonement after equinox (A 27:9–10). *tēn nēsteian ēdē parelēlythenai* (A 27:9 "the Fast already past") Day of Atonement, 3 p.m. end. As the December season combines the solar and lunisolar 4000, the fulfilment may come then. They sail to Phoenix on the west side of Crete, to look for a fulfilment from SW to NW (A 27:12) (See p. 157).

December Quarter

Wed Nov 26	25/IX		Phoenix	No fulfilment at Feast of Dedication in favour of Alexandrians ("south wind") (A 27:13). They decide to go to Cauda a smaller island, for the pentecontad (A 27:13–17).
Sun Nov 30	29/IX		Cauda	The pentecontad, winter feast. No event (A 27:18a). *cheimazomenōn* (A 27:18 "suffering winter") winter feast 29/IX.
Tue Dec 2	31a(X) 1st pos.			Expulsions ("throwing out") at the non-fulfilment (A 27:18). *tē hexēs* (A 27:18 "the next") 31st as a non-sacred day.
Wed Dec 3	1a/X			Further expulsions. No priest (Sun) nor David prince (Star) were brought into power on the 1st. Apocalyptic symbolism, cf. Mk 13:24–25 (A 27:19–20a). *tē tritē* (A 27:19) 1a as the third day, Samaritan. *epi pleionas hēmeras* (A 27:20 "upon more days") 1a/X, December season as extension of VII; 1a as now the significant day.
Wed Dec 17	29/IX solst. pos.	6 p.m.		Next pentecontad, winter feast. They are on the Illyricum line, half way to Malta. At the non-fulfilment at the main winter

feast there is a loss of faith in the chronology that makes AD 60 the year 4000. The chronology of the Davids, making AD 100 the year 4000, is to be preferred (A 27:20b).

> cheimōnos . . . ouk oligou (A 27:20 "no little winter") 29/IX winter feast, now non-Herodian (oligon, Herodian).

Thu Dec 18	midnight (Wed)	At the Julian start of the pentecontad, Paul announces that the Herods will stay in membership, subordinate to the David. "Good cheer" is to begin, in a week starting with the solar Preparation Days (A 27:22, 25) (Christmas not yet fully established).

> pollēs . . . asitias (A 27:21 "much not wheat") winter pentecontad, the opposite of Pentecost (15/III), wheat festival.
>
> ta nyn (A 27:22) 29/IX.
>
> tautē tē nykti (A 27:23 "this night") lay feast, midnight.

AD 61
NLS4000, NS4001

Thu Jan 1	midnight Malta (Wed)	They arrive near Malta. From midnight to 3 a.m. the boat approaches land, travelling at 15 stadia per hour (boat rate, as in the gospels). At midnight the water is 20 fathoms (80 cubits, 40 yds) deep, at 1 a.m. 15, at 2 a.m. 10, at 3 a.m. 5 (A 27:29).

> tessareskaidekate nyx (A 27:27 "14th night") 14th counting from Thu 18th (30th) as first day (Samaritan method), to Wed Dec 31st 6 p.m.
>
> nyx 9 p.m.
>
> kata meson tēs nyktos (A 27:27) midnight.
>
> brachy (A 27:28 "short") 1 a.m. (cf. Lk 22:58).

	3 a.m. Malta	They arrive at port and say a prayer (A 27:29).

> hēmeran (A 27:29) 3 a.m.
>
> mellontōn (A 27:30) 3 a.m. before 6 a.m.

	6 a.m.	Paul conducts a 6 a.m. meal and service for village ranks (A 27:33-38). He opposes the full monastic regime on Malta, which allows no meal till noon (Essenes, War 2:130) (A 27:33).

> achri . . . ou hēmera ēmellen ginesthai (A 27:33 "until a day was about to come") 6 a.m., Jewish start, 3 hrs

before monastic 9 a.m. watch.
tessareskaidekatēn sēmeron hēmeran
(A 27:33 "14th today day") 14th day
by Paul's Hebrew method of counting,
from Fri Dec 19th as first day,
starting 6 a.m.
"Today" for great event, Jan 1 in west.

9 a.m.   On shore, they do not join in monastic
rites, but stay with Gentiles
(A 27:39-40).
> *hote . . . hēmera egeneto* (A 27:39
> "when it became day") 9 a.m. 3 hrs
> before noon, monastic start of day.

noon   Their celibates join in the noon
monastic meal, but village ranks
excluded (A 27:41).

3 p.m.   The question of Felix arises: some want
to strip him of membership. But Gaius
rules that even insincere converts should
be kept in membership (A 27:42-43).

4 p.m.   Gentiles taught after monastic hours at
the time the fire is lit. Apollos ("viper")
now makes a further attack on Paul,
accusing him of influencing Felix to
murder Jonathan Annas. He tries to
poison him. But Paul is saved from the
plot (A 28:3-5).

6 p.m.   Paul at the village meal presides in the
place of the priest (A 28:6).
> *epi poly* (A 28:6) 6 p.m.

Tue Jan 6   31a(X)   6 a.m.   Paul's party join in communion at the
post pos.   post-position 31st. (A 28:7-8).
> *treis hēmeras* (A 28:7 "3 days") day 3.
> Tue following, post pos. 31st.

March Quarter
(The days for dates in 61 were the same as those in 33, the year of the crucifixion.
Luke places events on the anniversary of events in the Passion season.)

Mon Mar 2   30/XII 1st   (Triumphal entry) They sail from Malta
pos.   in another mission ship from
Alexandria, under "Jacob and Esau"
(A 28:11).
> *meta . . . treis mēnas* (A 28:11 "after
> 3 months") March 2, 24 hrs after
> March 1.

Tue Mar 3   31(I)   Syracuse   (Cleansing of temple) Arrive at Syracuse
(A 28:12a).

Mon Mar 9   6 p.m.   Service at Syracuse (A 28:12).
> *hēmeras treis* (A 28:12 "days 3") Mon
> 6 p.m.
Leave Syracuse.

Rhegium   Arrive Rhegium, at the southern limit of
Italy (A 28:13).

Mon Mar 16				Leave Rhegium (A 28:13). *meta mian hēmeran* (A 28:13 "after 1 day") Mon 6 a.m., 24 hrs after Sun 6 a.m., day 1.
Fri Mar 20	31a(I)	noon	Puteoli	Arrive Puteoli. They join in noon communion as presbyters (A 28:13). *deuteraioi* (A 28:13 "second-day men.") Presbyters, promoted Fri 31st as Samaritan second day.
		3 p.m.		Observance for 3 p.m. Good Friday (A 28:14). *hēmeras hepta* (A 28:14 "day 7") Fri 3 p.m., early start of Saturday.
Sat Mar 21	31b	6 a.m.		Leave Puteoli for Rome (15 hrs by fast transport, 80 stadia per hr, 1200 stadia, 240 kms, 150 miles).
		9 p.m.	Rome	Arrive at the border of Rome, "the Rome" (A 28:14). (Probably the site of the church of Domine Quo Vadis, at the end of the Appian Way, just south of the ancient walls. Treated as reproducing the Essene Gate, on the south border of Jerusalem. The "Forum of Appius" for ministers, "Tavern 3" (A 28:15) for the congregation, the original "Vineyard", the Sadducee-Essene mission in Rome.)
Sun Mar 22		6 a.m.		Easter Sunday. Sunday is now observed as the anniversary of the resurrection, not Saturday, the Jewish holy day. Paul holds a eucharist (A 28:15).
		6 p.m.		They go further into Rome, to an equivalent of "Bethany" ("Rome" A 28:16, no art.). The pattern of distances indicates 15 stadia from "the Rome", perhaps the site of San Clemente near the Colosseum (occupied as a private house at this time) (A 28:16).
Tue Mar 24		6 p.m.		End of attendance days, when villagers return to private life. Anniversary of "ascension". Paul explains that he has been transferred to Rome province (A 28:17). *meta hēmeras treis* (A 28:17 "after days 3") Tue 6 p.m., 24 hrs after Mon 6 p.m., early start of day 3, Tue.
Tue Apr 7	31a(I) post pos.	6 a.m.		Paul acts as a village minister, finishing teaching at 9 p.m. (A 28:23-28). *taxamenoi . . . autō hēmeran* (A 28:23 "they appointed a day for him"). Post pos. *apo prōi heōs hesperas* (A 28:23 "from morning to evening") from 6 a.m. to 9 p.m., village evening.

(Shortly after this Paul was arrested and placed in custody, on charges, laid by Apollos, of complicity in the murder of Jonathan Annas. Felix was acquitted (*Ant.* 20:182) and Nero showed further opposition to Agrippa and his supporters by ruling against him in the dispute over the temple (*Ant.* 20:194). Paul in prison wrote letters: first Philemon and Colossians, written with Timothy. In Philemon he sent greetings from John Mark, Aristarchus-Peter, Ananus-Demas, and Luke. In Colossians, the same group were present, but Aristarchus-Peter had become a prisoner (Col. 4:10); probably reflecting the support of Nero for the anti-Herodians (cf. *Ant.*20:183–184). Aristarchus, Mark, and Jesus Justus were grouped together as "of the circumcision" (Col. 4:11). Timothy and John Mark were subsequently sent back to Asia (Phil 2:19).)

AD 62

(In about March, 62, Ananus-Demas was made high priest in Jerusalem. During his 3-month reign he caused James, the brother of Jesus, to be stoned to death (*Ant.* 20:197–203. In about September, 62, Paul wrote 2 Timothy to Timothy in Asia, asking him to come back to Rome before winter (2 Tim 4:21). Ananus-Demas "in love with this present world" has deserted Paul and gone to Thessalonica (2 Tim 4:10). Timothy is asked to bring Mark with him, "for he is very useful in serving me" (2 Tim 4:11). "Luke alone is with me". But "at my first defence . . . the Lord stood by me and gave me strength to proclaim the message fully" (2 Tim 4:17). Jesus was physically present, encouraging Paul. Paul was "rescued from the lion's mouth", i.e. not condemned by Nero. He expected to be acquitted at the next hearing (2 Tim 4:18). He also sent the code message that Jesus was not a prisoner: "the word of God is not fettered" (2 Tim 2:9).

AD 63

Tue Mar 1	Rome	Paul is free, and now receives a salary for ministry, like priests' tithes, making him a "hired servant", so in a "hired house" (A 28:30).
		dietian holēn (A 28:30 "two whole years"). The triennium 60–63, divided 1+2, at the end of the 2 years, 63. Starts Mar 1.

AD 64

In summer, AD 64, following the great fire of Rome, Nero blamed the Christians and crucified large numbers of them (Tacitus, *Ann.* 15:44). Peter and Paul were both put to death by Nero (Eusebius, *H.E.* 2,25:5–8).

Appendix II

LOCATIONS

The places where the gospel events occurred were as important as the times. Where the surface story appears extraordinarily vague and sometimes unreliable about places, there is in the pesher a full account of every detail of place.

John's gospel gives the starting point by offering exact measurements in stadia in a way that does not relate to the apparent locations. See Chapter 7 for preliminary observations on this subject.

It becomes apparent that a scheme of places was present in the minds of the evangelists, one that was easy to remember. When the mission of ascetics began to expand to the wider world, it became the basis for a world scheme.

The locations of the various centres used by ascetics in the Wilderness of Judea lent themselves to a diagram (Fig. 1) which was very probably conceived as a scribe's pen, its point directed towards Jerusalem. A map of the area shows the actual places on which this pattern was imposed (Fig. 2).

It was possible to draw up such a scheme because a fixed rate of walking was established. The actual times taken to go from one place to the other were adjusted to a mathematical system based on a rate of walking which was, in our distances, about one kilometre an hour. It was a standard

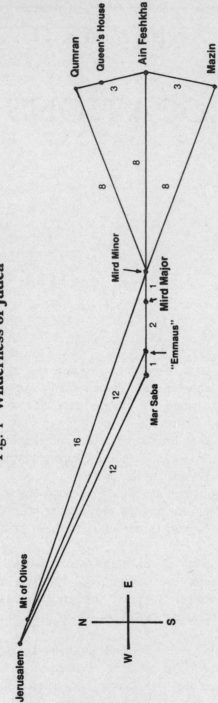

Fig. 1 Wilderness of Judea

Distances in hours between the settlements in the Wilderness of Judea
2000 cubits = 5 stadia = 1 kilometre = 1 hour's walk

Fig. 2 **Wilderness of Judea**

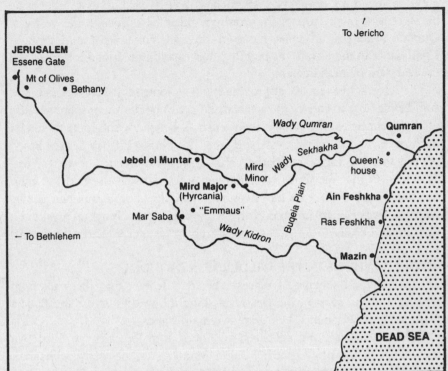

which allowed for the hot, dry conditions and the length of the journeys. Those ascetics who were allowed outside monasteries spent much of their time walking along the wilderness paths.

From the reality, symmetrical mathematics took over, as in the case of the chronology. There was also the assumption—essential in their thinking—that time equals place. Distances were equivalents of hours in their minds, a theory developed from the idea of praying, not only at appointed times, but also in appointed spots. If it were the case that the distance did not exactly match the time allowed, the time formula predominated. The distances, of course, did roughly approximate to the time allowed, and on the smaller scales, closely, even exactly.

Their basic formula was:

2000 cubits = 5 stadia = 1 hour's walking

Two thousand cubits (1000 yards, 3000 feet) were treated as 5 stadia (3035

English feet and 3000 Greek feet). Although cubits can vary, the Qumran cubit is found to have been 18 inches, half a yard. This is the exact measurement of the top of the northern pillar base outside the vestry at Qumran. The pair of pillar bases of dressed stone are found to have significance in the plan of the building, and in addition apparently provided the standard of measurement.

Five stadia equals approximately 1 kilometre (3300 feet); this is sufficiently close to convey the actual distances in modern terms. But because of the symmetries of numbers involved it is better for the modern reader to think in stadia, cubits, yards and feet. The former English system based on the foot (12 inches) and the yard (3 feet) was related to the system of cubits, in that the terms were derived from parts of the body. A cubit was the length from a man's elbow to finger tip; a yard was two cubits, with the arms placed in front of the body, fingers touching. (A royal cubit was longer because a king was considered to be bigger than other men!)

MAIN LOCATIONS IN THE WILDERNESS OF JUDEA

The pen-shaped scheme of places reflected the fact that the walk from Jerusalem to the coast of the Dead Sea along the wadies across the Buqeia plain took just 24 hours. There were two main routes:

a) Taken by priests and celibates; 16 hours from Jerusalem to Mird (via the Mount of Olives, Bethany, Jebel el Muntar and the wady Sekhakha). They arrived at the place here called Mird minor (see further below). Then 8 hours to Qumran via the northern route, further along the wady Sekhakha until it joined the wady Qumran, as it is now called, then down the slope made by the wady at Qumran, along the aqueduct to the buildings.

b) That taken by villagers coming as pilgrims; 12 hours from Jerusalem to Mar Saba via the wady Kidron, which formed a natural route. (Walk 3 a.m. to 3 p.m., then sleep overnight at Mar Saba, their "inn".) Walk 4 hours from Mar Saba to Mird minor, then 8 hours from there to Ain Feshkha, across the middle route.

Some villagers, however, were not permitted to go on to Ain Feshkha because of states of uncleanness, and had to go down the southern route to Mazin, also counted as 8 hours.

Qumran, Ain Feshkha and Mazin on the coast were just 15 stadia from each other, 3 hours apart (the distances indicated in John's gospel, see Chapter 7). The routes from Mird minor thus formed a fan shape, becoming like the tail of a pen when seen with the western, elongated triangle.

As shown in Chapter 7 and the Chronology, page 227, this pattern accounts for the movements of Jesus and the disciples in Mk 6:30–32. They were not making impossible journeys around Lake Galilee, but were taking the two alternative 8-hour routes from Mird minor. One group went on foot across country, starting at 3 a.m., the prescribed time for villagers to set out, and arriving at Ain Feshkha at 11 a.m. The other group, including Jesus, walked down to Mazin, arriving there at 11 a.m., then taking the boat up to Ain Feshkha (1 hour, see boat rates, page 325), arriving in time for the noon meal. Thus the group on foot naturally arrived first, whereas, if they had been going on foot around Lake Galilee, they would have been much later than Jesus going across by boat.

The three main settlements on the coast, Qumran, Ain Feshkha and Mazin, were placed just 15 stadia, 3 hours, apart from each other to indicate degrees of holiness. Ain Feshkha began as the exclusion place for unclean monks, where they washed their clothes according to the rules of the Temple Scroll. This is shown by the remains of frankincense in the shallow pools there, and the cylinders for drying clothes (see Chapter 7). It was thus an outpost of the monastery, and was enclosed with it in a strip of coast terminated by the great headland of Ras Feshkha. South of this celibate strip was Mazin, an equal distance apart but blocked off by the headland. It was associated with those in the married state, less clean by Essene standards.

Unclean Places Attached to the Main Buildings
According to the Temple Scroll, there had to be a place outside every city where the unclean were sent: "those stricken with leprosy, with plagues and scabs, who shall not enter your cities and profane them, and also for those who suffer from a flux; and for menstruating women, and women after childbirth, so that they may not cause defilement in their midst by their impure uncleanness" (11QT 48:14-17). Another rule, in the War Scroll, says that in a military camp latrines were to be placed 2000 cubits away from the camp "so that no indecent nakedness may be seen in the surroundings of their camps" (1QM 7:6-7).

A related fragment, 4Q491, gives the distance as 1000 cubits. It also associates covering the body and sexual purity with readiness for war.

It becomes apparent that places associated with such uncleanness played an important part in the history, because the classes who were treated as similar to the physically unclean, especially Gentiles, were the subject of the reforms brought about by Jesus.

Attached to each of the main buildings were outposts in the form of either buildings or caves, whose usual use was as latrines. Some were at 1000 cubits away, needing a half-hour walk, others 2000 cubits away, needing a one-hour walk.

A feature of the Essenes, for which they were well known among other Jews, was their attention to toilet procedures. Josephus records that as soon as a candidate for membership began his year's probation outside the community, he was given white raiment, a loincloth, and a small hatchet, the latter to be used for digging a trench for defecation (*War* 2:137,148). Josephus also notes that while using the trench they wrap their mantle around them "that they may not offend the rays of the deity". This accords with the implication of 1QM 7:6–7 and 4Q491 that the "holy angels" are offended by such uncleanness. See also 1 Cor 11:10.

It is found from the close detail that there were two categories of unclean annexe:

1) Those for male celibates, theoretically 1000 cubits away, requiring a half-hour's walk. At Qumran, the location was Cave 4, west of the buildings and down the parallel projection. It was used for several kinds of legal uncleanness, including burial of the dead in one of its chambers, according to the rule of 11QT 48:13. (For a detailed description of the cave, which had an upper and lower level, see *DJD* VI, pp. 9–13). It was made the tomb of the Pope and his Second, hence it was called "Abraham's Bosom", and, as their burial place, was also used for their symbolic burials when excommunicated. Luke's parable of the Rich Man and Lazarus enables it to be identified, as seen in Chapter 26. Another of its purposes was to receive a different kind of "filth"; heretical writings. It is probable that the hundreds of scrolls placed in Cave 4 without containers were put there when Qumran was taken over by Peter's party in AD 37 (A 8:1), and left there when Jewish Christians under James moved in a few years later.

At Mird major (the name used here for the buildings on the two hilltops at Mird, or Hyrcania) there was a similar place, as Mird became an alternate sanctuary to Qumran after the earthquake. To the north of the hill, at the wady itself, were the pair of tunnels described in Chapter 7, probably used for an initiation rite of the kind practised by John the Baptist. But as initiation was a form of cleansing from moral uncleanness, the vicinity was also used as the annexe. It is about 1000 cubits from the hill called the "Monument", which will be seen below to have been defined as the "camp".

2) The other kind of unclean annexe kept the rule of the War Scroll for camps, being 2000 cubits or 5 stadia away, one hour's walk. It was for the use of a lower grade of member, classed under the heading "the Beasts" (1QpHab 12:4). Literal beasts were kept in the same buildings, giving them the name the Manger. Those of the grade of Beasts were (i) married men, even those who were temporarily abstinent for periods of prayer; (ii) women,

even celibate women who could attend prayers at the main centres, and (iii) uncircumcised Gentiles, who were of the same legal status as women.

The Manger attached to Qumran, in its second phase, was the queen's house, about a kilometre down from the main building, on the plain (see Chapters 7 and 9). That attached to Mird was the place here called Mird minor, 1 hour from the main building, and nearer to Qumran. Its exact site is at present unclear, but it presumably was on the banks of the wady. It has an important place in the story as a women's centre, and also one for Gentiles. It appears as "the limits of Tyre" and "Sidon" (Mk 7:24,31), as one of the "villages" of Mary and Martha (Lk 10:38, Lk 11:1; it was the place where the Lord's prayer was given); and as the place to which John Mark, the chief proselyte, returned after his journeys (Mk 6:30, Lk 10:17). It may have consisted of wooden huts of the kind used by the Therapeutae (*Contemp. Life* 24–25). It was the original "queen's house", the place to which young girls came to give birth to illegitimate children, and its function was transferred to the Qumran Manger when Mird became a sanctuary after the earthquake.

A similar place was attached to Mar Saba, when it was under the rules of the "camps". (The term "camp" was used by eastern ascetics for the meetings of villagers, CD 14:3.) Its position is also unclear, but it would have been one of the many caves in the vicinity, some of them still used as retreats by the monks of Mar Saba. It features in the detail of the story in Lk 24:13–32, under the name "Emmaus", and, as will be shown below, page 296, it was also "Nazareth" (but not *Nazara*). It was on the opposite side of the wady from Mar Saba, on the route to Qumran.

In Jerusalem itself, once the Essene Gate had been reduced to the status of a village "camp", there was also a Manger, as seen Chapter 9, 5 stadia across from the city on the Mount of Olives (*Ant.* 20:170). It was from here that the Egyptian began his procession to the city, in the style of the David kings, who rode to their coronation on King Solomon's mule (Chapter 34). This place appears as "Ephraim" in Jn 11:54, the place to which Jesus went to renew his marriage. Interestingly, one of the Qumran pesharim (4QpNah 2:2) refers to Jerusalem as "Ephraim".

For annexes at 2000 cubits, a rule was applied treating them as alternative starting points for measurements of distance. There were two points of view about when a day started: at the zero hour, 6 a.m., or the first hour, 7 a.m. While the main building stood for the zero hour, these buildings an hour away stood for the first hour. As Jn 6:19 shows, Mazin was said to be 30 stadia (6 hours) from the main measuring point (Qumran) and 25 stadia (5 hours) from an alternative measuring point (the queen's house). As the two starting points had the same value, the same name could, under certain conditions, be used for both. The phrase "Jerusalem Jerusalem" (Lk 13:34) is not, in the pesher, a rhetorical device, but an indication that there were two places with the same name, the Essene Gate and the Mount of Olives, both of low grade village level.

In Lk 24:13, the "village" (unclean place) called "Emmaus" is said to be 60 stadia from Jerusalem (singular form). This means that it was 12 hours from the Mount of Olives corresponding place. It was 12 hours from the Essene Gate-Jerusalem to Mar Saba, both of the same level (Lk 19:11, p: *engys* means "the same time value"), and 12 hours from the Mount of Olives-Jerusalem to "Emmaus". The two routes from the actual locations gave rise to the shape in the diagram, a sharp point at the western end.

The southernmost route (Essene Gate to Mar Saba) was permanently unclean, for it was only for married villagers. The Herodian version of the communal meal was observed in both places.

Mird minor was also a measuring point. It became the centre of the diagram, as it was common to both main routes. It was 8 hours from Qumran or Ain Feshkha, while the building at Mird major was classed as 9 hours from Qumran or Ain Feshkha.

(A variant text of Lk 24:13 says that "Emmaus" was 160 stadia from Jerusalem. This is not, as is often thought, an attempt to give a more correct distance to the literal Emmaus west of Jerusalem, but another way of speaking about "Emmaus", showing exact knowledge of the pesher. The round trip on the western triangle was 32 hours, 160 stadia. A journey from the ascetic centre took a man to Jerusalem then back via the north road.)

Two further unclean locations are of importance to the history. Both at Qumran, they were additional latrines. One was the cave at the end of the esplanade, described in Chapter 26 as the burial cave used after the crucifixion. Its distance from the main buildings was defined as 250 cubits (see further on measurements at Qumran, page 317). It was the sabbath latrine for celibate laymen, to be used on Friday afternoons, as they were forbidden to walk more than 1000 cubits on the sabbath (CD 10:21); it was more than that distance there and back to Cave 4. After 6 p.m. on Friday it was not to be used at all, as there was a further rule forbidding defecation on the sabbath (*Ant.* 2:147). It was closed until 3 p.m. on Saturday, and after that time Jewish celibates returned to Cave 4. However, those using the Julian sabbath starting at midnight Friday, having missed their 4 a.m. visit, were obliged to visit at 4 p.m. Saturday, and must again use the sabbath latrine. This was the reason why it was possible for the cave to be opened again after the guard had left, so that supporters of Simon Magus could carry him away.

The cave was also used for other kinds of "uncleanness", namely money, "filthy lucre". It became one of the deposits when, at the schism of the Prodigal Son, the funds of half the provinces were transferred to Qumran. The second sentence of the Copper Scroll, the inventory of deposits, names the "tomb of the son of the third Great One" (corrected translation). On Essene values, the David crown prince was the son of the third in the supreme hierarchy, the king (see Hierarchy, page 341). James, the brother of Jesus, held this position in the gospel period. He was the Rich Man who, at an excommunication, was in Cave 8 in Luke's parable of the Rich Man and Lazarus, looking across the chasm to Cave 4 (Lk 16:26). He was also Joseph of Arimathea, the Rich Man in whose cave Jesus was buried (Mt 27:57).

Within the grounds of the Qumran buildings was the row of cubicles which have been suggested to be the priests' latrines, for use in order to ensure continual attendance in the sanctuary (Chapter 24). They defined an area outside the south gate which was defiled.

On the eastern side of the Qumran eastern building the archaeologists found a small urinal (RB 61, 1954, p. 209). Such a place, for minor purposes, is suggested by the timing of Mk 14:26-31, Jn 14:31.

In the Temple Scroll, concerning the plan of the real Jerusalem when the temple was recovered, the latrines were to be placed 3000 cubits away on the north-west. This was to ensure the extra degree of holiness of the holy city. The text also shows that cubicles were used (11QT 46:13-15).

THE BUILDINGS AT AIN FESHKHA, MAZIN, MIRD AND MAR SABA

Most of the events in the gospels took place at Ain Feshkha, Mazin and Mird, rather than at Qumran. This was because of the association of Jesus with excluded grades who were confined to these places.

The role of Ain Feshkha, three hours south of Qumran, was defined by the uncleanness rules, the standard being that of an unclean monk according to the rule of 11QT 45:7-9, 46:17-18.

Ain Feshkha was the place where the high priest lived while he was unclean, that is, by celibate standards, while he was married. Under Essene rules he lived for the most part celibate in a monastic community, but left from time to time in order to continue his dynasty, following the manner of life of the second kind of Essenes (Chapter 8).

A suite of rooms on the western side of the courtyard was suitable for such a purpose. The building had the plan of a Greco-Roman great house, rooms on four sides around a central courtyard, with the entrance doors on the east (de Vaux ADSS pp. 60-87). This building was the "house of Zechariah", where Elizabeth was present, of Lk 1:39-40.

When, in the second phase of occupation of Qumran, the position of the Zadokite high priest was claimed by Simon Magus, he stayed here with Helena in the position of his wife (see Chapter 15). As he was a Samaritan, it became "Samaria" while he was present, on the principle of transposition of place names seen in Chapter 7. Helena was the "Samaritan woman" of Jn 4.

A member of the hierarchy had two grades, the higher one when he was "out of the body", the lower one when he was "in the body". (See more fully on this in Hierarchy, page 342). When he was "in the body"— usually meaning that he was married—he dropped to the status of his own servant, who was three grades below his master. A grade stood for an hour, as each grade prayed at successive hours. A servant not only stood on the third cubit below his master when they were in the same area, but also belonged three hours' distance south of his master, at Ain Feshkha which was three hours south of Qumran. It was for this reason that the high priest went to Ain Feshkha when he was "in the body".

The same principle applied to the king, the heir of David. In the original system, before he too adopted a form of temporary celibacy, he was entirely in the world, and in his highest state could only go as far as Ain Feshkha. A sign of his presence there was "Jacob's Well" of Jn 4:6. His name under the Herods was "Jacob" (Chapter 5) and he acted as a lay bishop, teaching the Law, which was likened to a well (CD 6:4).

When he, in turn, went down "into the body", he had to go three hours further south, to Mazin. His status here was that of an ordinary married man. Such a man, among the Essenes, belonged to the order of Naphtali, meeting at Tiberias or Capernaum on the shores of Lake Galilee. Mazin was "Capernaum" while the men of Naphtali were present.

Jesus spent much of the gospel period at Mazin, because he had entered on the period of 18 months preceding his marriage. The last 18 months of the betrothal period were counted as part of the time when the king was "in the body". But, as he was not yet married, he went between Ain Feshkha and Mazin, making the journeys by boat or on foot.

Ain Feshkha was thus a place to which the high priest came down as unclean, and from which he returned to Qumran as pure. The king (originally) began as unclean, and went down to be more unclean. A man who was unclean sexually was like a "beast". Beasts were also graded; the higher being tame animals such as oxen, the lower wild beasts such as lions. Ain Feshkha acted as the "farm" (*chōra*) to Qumran, and "oxen" belonged there. These grades were expressed in a feature of the building at Ain Feshkha, the narrow and wide doors. At the entrance to the Ain Feshkha enclosure on its east side two doors were made side by side, still to be seen there. One, on the north, was very narrow (1½ cubits, 27 inches, 69 cms) and the other, on the south, unusually wide (3 cubits, 54 inches, 138 cms). Both lead inside the courtyard, and de Vaux, who excavated the building, finds it difficult to explain why these two doors should have been placed so close to one another, only 2½ cubits (45 inches, 115 cms) apart. He conjectures that one was used for humans and the other for animals (*ADSS* p. 61). In this he was not far from the point. Unclean celibates, like a higher kind of beast ("oxen") came in the wide door, until they were thin/pure enough (as asceticism included fasting) to return to the monastery. (While they were at Ain Feshkha, at "Jacob's Well", there might be a case of "an ox falling into a well", Lk 14:5). But the king and lay bishops started at the wide door, and went from there south to "Destruction" (*apōleia*), unrestrained marriage like that of the lowest order of village Essenes at Mazin. Mt 7:13 endorses asceticism, using this symbolism: "Enter by the narrow gate, for the gate is wide and the way is easy that leads to destruction".

The Nazirite Route, Mar Saba to Mird

While Ain Feshkha and Mazin were outposts of the monastery, the locations at Mird and Mar Saba were, originally, for the pilgrims who came to the monastery. These were the men of the Essene order of Zebulun, meeting at Nazareth in Galilee. A grade above Naphtali, they went up from the state of marriage to separate for periods of prayer. At first they simply travelled from the north to Qumran, using the route from Jerusalem via Mar Saba and Mird minor. They brought vital tithe offerings to the exiles at Qumran, and in return were allowed to stay there for a time of prayer and instruction.

If, on reaching Mird minor, a pilgrim was found to be a Sinner, not sufficiently holy to go on to the monastery, he was sent down the 8-hour route to Mazin, where men lived in an ordinary married state. (All those at Mazin were Sinners, compare Lk 5:8, whereas celibates were Saints.)

In the course of the first century BC a Nazirite institution developed, like that of ordinary Jews who took a 30 day Nazirite vow (*Mishnah, Nazir*). But Essenes added abstinence from sex, and also prolonged the periods of time, to 70 or 100 days. For this time they stayed in the wilderness area between Mar Saba and Mird, wearing black clothing and letting their hair and beard grow long, the latter in accordance with Num 6:5. They abstained from drinking wine during the period of the vow (Num 6:3–4).

It happened that letters of the Hebrew alphabet, used to designate their grades, also stood for numerals (see further in Hierarchy, page 336). The letters standing for 70, 80, 90 and 100 (*Ayin, Pe, Sadhe* and *Qof*) were only one apart, standing for grades only one apart (deacon, presbyter, bishop and archbishop). Nazirites earned these grades by spending the required number of days under discipline. So, as it was already established that the difference between one grade and another corresponded to one hour's walking, the places of prayer were spaced one hour apart along the route.

Mar Saba was the starting point, the last building, with attached synagogue, that the Nazirites used. One hour or five stadia to the north-east, on the Qumran side of the wady Kidron, was the next point, at the place described above as "Emmaus", possibly a cave. Here presbyters spent their 80 days. Another hour further on was a cave for the bishops spending 90 days, then, at Mird itself, at the smaller hillock called the "Monument" (G.R.H. Wright, *Biblica* 42, 1961) the archbishop spent the maximum 100 days.

The word "Nazareth" was associated with presbyters and deacons. Variant forms of it in Greek are found: *Nazara*, and *Nazareth* or *Nazaret*. *Nazara*, at which there was a synagogue and a cliff (Lk 4:16, 29), was Mar Saba itself, where a natural platform for a building at the height of the cliff lay beside a slope down which it was easy to climb to the Kidron below. An hour beyond it, "Emmaus" was the same as *Nazaret* or *Nazareth*. This point is shown by Matthew, drawing on the rule for definite articles. Wherever *ta horia* ("the limits") appears, it means an 8-hour walk; e.g. Mird minor was "the limits of Tyre (Mazin)" (Mk 7:24), and also "the limits of Judea" (Qumran) (Mk 10:1) by the south and north 8-hour routes respectively. But, as a word without article was a "servant" to a "master" (3 grades below), *horia* alone meant an 11-hour walk, as the numbers went from smaller (higher grade) to greater. Matthew says that "Capernaum" (Mazin) was in "limits (*horiois*) of Zebulun" (Mt 4:13). On the diagram of the "scribe's pen", the distance between "Emmaus" and Mazin is necessarily 11 hours (not shown, as this was a lesser route).

As an annexe at 2000 cubits, "Nazareth" was a place used by the Beasts, who included also women, even celibate women. So a Virgin began her progress towards marriage from this point, being met on the Qumran side of the wady by the "angel Gabriel", the Abiathar priest who was superior of all celibates (Lk 1:26).

Nazirites were likened to "sheep", as their hair and beard were shorn on becoming married or on resuming marriage. If one of them failed on the pilgrims' route and had to be sent down from Mird minor to Mazin, he was a "lost sheep". The superior, who spent 100 days, was "sheep 100". With him was his bishop, "sheep 90".

For certain offences and in certain states of uncleanness an archbishop could be reduced to the grade of lower novice, whose Hebrew letter was *Mem*, meaning also 40. At these times he went to the unclean place 1000 cubits away from his centre to the wady where the tunnels were built. This was the Wilderness (where John the Baptist gave this early grade to new members). Thus he spent 40 days in the Wilderness. Jesus was in this status 18 months before his marriage, in March AD 29. His 40 days covered the period in the calendar resulting from the intercalation (see Chronology, page 189) (Mk 1:13).

Another way of speaking of a man at *Mem* was to call him a 9, as the grades were numbered consecutively for Greek readers (see Hierarchy Table, page 336). Thus a "9" was in the Wilderness, and a "90" a short distance away, at a time when "sheep 100" became lost. The saying in Lk 15:1-7, concerning the man who left 99 sheep in the Wilderness while he searched for the 100th, is based on the Nazirite system.

The Essene Nazirite order was under the authority of the David crown prince, as it was of lower status than the celibate order, led by the king, whose members spent most of their time in the monastery and only short periods outside. The forms of "Nazareth" are all found in association with Joseph, the name of the crown prince under "Jacob" (Lk 4:22, 2:39, Mt 2:23 referring to Joseph as the last person named).

The crown prince in his highest status, archbishop, acted as guide to pilgrims going from Mird to Ain Feshkha and Qumran. In this role he was called "Cloud", as the Israelites in the wilderness were led by a "cloud by day" (Ex 13:21-22). The name was used when the Nazirites linked with another group using Exodus imagery (below page 298). The Cloud was found in both the west, at Mird, when it was "black" and stood for rain (Lk 12:54), hence was the "cloud overshadowing" (a Nazirite archbishop, Lk 1:35, A 5:15); and also in the east, at Qumran (Mk 9:34, A 1:9).

Ephraim-Manasseh: The "Camps"

Between village Essenes and high monastic Essenes stood the Therapeutae of Egypt and other Diaspora Essenes. They were called the "Joseph" tribes, Ephraim and Manasseh. In many ways they were like monastics, having similar views on purity. They were not enclosed, however, but very much involved in the world and its politics. Their asceticism was for military reasons, as it was believed that abstention from sex helped fighting ability (1QM 7:6).

It was these orders who became the zealots. Writings like 1QM, the War Scroll, give their outlook, showing that it was they who established rules about unclean locations 1000 or 2000 cubits away. The locations are related to their "camps", and rules about latrines are given in the same context as rules about sexual purity and physical perfection (1QM 7:3-7).

Before 31 BC their central meeting place was at Mird, as they were similar in many ways to the Nazirites, including their abstention from wine, which for them was permanent (*Contemp. Life* 73-74). Their higher rank, the order of Manasseh, took over the hillock at Mird used by the 100-day Nazirite archbishops, added a platform, and made it the "camp", from which measurements were taken. It is approximately 1000 cubits from the hillock north to the wady ("the Wilderness").

The exacavators found on the hillock a clear square "of slightly more than 10 metres" (Wright, p. 14). There were no remains of chambers. There was evidence from the sherds of a Herodian date.

The "camp" had a "camp fire". A fire was lit on the hillock, and the head of East Manasseh who was responsible for lighting it became "Fire by night" in association with "Cloud by day", the David crown prince.

One grade below Manasseh was Ephraim; the Therapeutae of Egypt. Their bishops joined the 90-day Nazirite bishop in his retreat an hour before the "camp".

The Sanctuary on the Main Hill

On the main hilltop was the large platform and buildings briefly described in Chapter 7. The rooms in the north wing became a Christian church. There were chambers on the west and east sides, with a large paved courtyard in the centre. It appears that this building contained the rooms where orders like the Therapeutae met every seventh day. (Philo avoids the word "synagogue" for the Therapeutae, calling it a "common sanctuary", *Contemp. Life* 32, but uses "synagogue" for the village Essenes, *Every Good Man* 81.) Luke 13:10 shows a synagogue at Mird major.

The sanctuary, representing places in the Diaspora where Diaspora Essenes met for worship, was staffed by priests and levites of village rank only. The Chief Priest, who was a third in the total hierarchy, was the superior, and under him were the various ranks of levites. Their role is more fully explained in Hierarchy, page 341; they may here be called cardinal, bishop; presbyter and deacon.

Exodus Imagery

The orders of Manasseh and Ephraim based their style of life and worship on imagery of the Exodus. Living in the Diaspora, they thought of themselves as Israelites in the wilderness, saved by their personal discipline from "Egypt", representing sin. As Philo shows, they lived in solitude as hermits most of the time, but met every seven weeks for worship, engaging in a liturgy celebrating their Exodus. Choirs of men and women conducted a sacred dance, the men led by a "Moses", the women by a "Miriam" (*Contemp. Life* 85–87).

It becomes apparent that the series of places established by Nazirites at Mird were set up as the route for a re-enactment of the Exodus (Figure 3).

Members went from an "Egypt" (the 90-day bishops' place to which Ephraim members were attached), through a "Red Sea" (the aqueduct west of the building) to a "camp" (the smaller hillock), to a "Mt Sinai" (the main building) and on into the "Wilderness" (south bank of the wady) (A 7:30-36). The wady became the "Jordan river" (Mk 1:5) and after crossing it they were at the beginning of the "Promised Land". Before the earthquake the "Promised Land" was Qumran.

According to Ex 19:16, Mt Sinai was surrounded by "thunders and lightnings, and a thick cloud". These phenomena were used as names for the ministers of the sanctuary or synagogue at Mird. The Chief Priest was "Thunder"; the cardinal was "Lightning", and the archbishop was "Cloud". Jonathan Annas was the Chief Priest of the gospel period (see Hierarchy, page 339) and was known as Thunder. In Jn 12:29, when Jesus prayed to the Father (Jonathan) "they said it thundered". James and John became "sons of Thunder" when they transferred their allegiance to the Annas priests (Mk 3:17). Simon Magus, the cardinal, was "Lightning", known by that name when he became Pope (Lk 10:18, Mt 28:3). The Nazirite superior, the crown prince at his highest, was already known as Cloud in his role of guide, as seen above. ("Lightning" also could act as a guide from east to west, so "the Lightning comes from the east and shines to the west", Mt 24:27). Earthquakes were also associated with Mt Sinai (Jud 5:5), and the head of Ephraim was called "Earthquake" (Mt 27:54, 28:2, A 16:26).

At the foot of Mt Sinai the Golden Calf had been set up (Ex 32:4). This name was appropriate to the head of West Manasseh, of Samaria, as the Calf was associated with Samaritans. It was later used by the ruling Herod Archelaus, who had the status of archbishop.

"Bethany"

The name "Bethany" (Heb. "house of the Poor", 'ani) was applied to the annexe at the wady, the Wilderness (Jn 1:28). Essene celibates of a certain degree of uncleanness must go either 1000 cubits from a Diaspora "camp", or 3 hours from a holier place, a Palestinian sanctuary. Hence the literal Bethany was 3 hours (15 stadia) east of the Essene Gate in Jerusalem, and Ain Feshkha, another "Bethany" (Jn 11:1), was 3 hours (15 stadia) south of Qumran (Jn 11:18).

The south bank of the wady at Mird was thought of as the place where Israelites were truly in the wilderness, between Mt Sinai and the "Jordan". It stood for the places where the Therapeutae spent the periods between their sabbath and pentecontad gatherings, in isolation, devoted to prayer and study (Contemp. Life 34-36). Living quite alone, they were hermits, a word derived from erēmos, "wilderness". They did not have

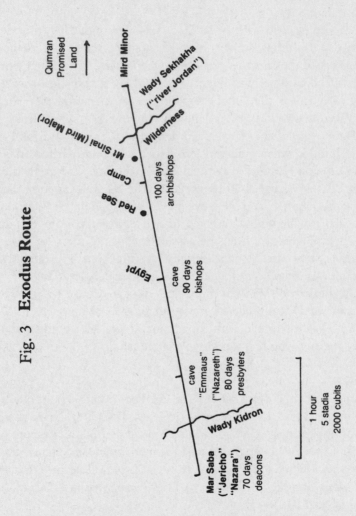

Fig. 3   **Exodus Route**

communal property, but lived very frugally (*Contemp. Life* 24, 38), so were called "Poor" (Gk. *ptōchos*). Their garments were made of animal skin, at least in winter. "Their clothing . . . is the most inexpensive, enough to protect them against extreme cold and heat, a thick coat of shaggy skin in winter and in summer a vest or linen shirt (*othonē*)" (*Contemp. Life* 38). Hence John the Baptist in this place was dressed in camel skin (Mk 1:6). When they met for festivals in the main building, the Therapeutae wore white robes (*Contemp. Life* 66).

Gentiles, of the orders of Asher and Dan, who were attached to Diaspora Essenes, belonged at Mird minor, at the 2000 cubit point. This was the required distance for women, to whom Gentiles were equal.

Herodians at Mird

The public purpose of the building at Mird major was to be a Herodian fortress. It had once belonged to Queen Salome (queen regnant 76 BC), who used it as a treasury (*Ant.* 13:418). Herod the Great had subsequently captured it (*War* 1:364), and he used it for such purposes as entertaining foreign dignitaries (*Ant.* 16:13). The religious activity going on there was conducted by the staff of the synagogue, a kind of royal chapel. Diaspora Essenes, encouraged by Herod (*Ant.* 15:378) had gained control of worship here and in other Herodian establishments, preferred as being more liberal and westernised in their outlook.

It appears that it had also been developed as a school for Herod princes. The Mird locations for Nazirites were originally under the David crown prince. Orders imitating those of the Nazirites were founded by Herod, each under one of his sons. Men of Ephraim–Manasseh, in touch with Greek thought, were appointed tutors. This is seen in the story of Herod the Great as a youth going to his teacher and meeting Menahem the Essene (*Ant* 15:373).

Herodian orders imitated Nazirite ones in some respects, but not in others. The organisation was in sets of 100, following the Essenes, (*War* 2:145). As Diaspora Essenes called their full councils the Many (*hărabbim*, Heb), the Herodian ones used the Greek equivalent, *hoi polloi*. This word, with and without article, refers to the superior Herod in the role of archbishop (Agrippa in the gospel period).

The name the Calf was associated with the "camp", and it was here that the Herodian archbishops observed their 100 days. When a further development used the names of the four living creatures of Ezekiel, one of which was the Calf, this name was used for a ruling Herod. It was especially used for Archelaus (4 BC to 6 AD), who was an ethnarch only (*Ant.* 17:317–321). Archelaus was the "(Golden) Calf" of A 7:41 (in a militant triarchy with the Dragon Joazar, and the Beast Judas the Galilean). When the "fatted Calf was killed", a plot to dismiss Archelaus was formed (Lk 15:23).

Using a related image, the Herodian archbishop was a "lost sheep". This was the preferred image for Agrippa I in the same position. While the true Essene Nazirites were "sheep", the Herods were "lost sheep", being Sinners. They did not practise abstention from sex during their set times for attendance at ascetic centres.

Nor did they practise the associated rules of uncleanness. They did not normally walk distances to the annexes, nor observe a rule forbidding their use on the sabbath. They had no prohibition about going near graves, so the building at Mird contained tomb caves, and at the foot of the hill some ordinary graves (Wright, p. 12, p. 16). As Josephus records, the Herodian prince Antipater was buried at Mird (Hyrcania) (*Ant.* 17:187).

Three hours to the south-west of Mird major was the building at Mar Saba, already *Nazara* for the Essenes. Herods used only buildings, not caves, and it now received an additional name, "Jericho", as it was for Herodian servants who were from the order of Benjamin. Their meeting place was at the literal Jericho, in one of Herod's lesser palaces (*Ant.* 17:161). Mar Saba was visited by Jesus as "Jericho" on his way to Jerusalem in December AD 32 (Mk 10:46).

The "Church"

The word *ekklēsia*, "church" is used sparingly in the gospels, found only in Mt 16:18 and 18:17. It appears in Acts for the first time at 5:11, in the account of the downfall of Simon Magus and Helena (Ananias and Sapphira). This, as the chronology shows, was at the time of the rise of Agrippa to kingship. The word remains associated with Paul and with John of Zebedee (Rev 1-3), both servants of Agrippa. It is plainly a Herodian term. But at the same time it is strongly associated with Peter, who was to be the Rock on which the Church was built (Mt 16:18). Peter was a village Essene, of the level of Sinner (Lk 5:8), that is, of the order of Naphtali. He has been seen to correspond to Simon of Jerusalem, who at first opposed Agrippa then came over to him (Chapter 31). The rise of the term *ekklēsia* (literally "the called out ones") may be traced from a division in the village Essenes, for and against the Herods. Those who were for them had a western orientation, and were willing to relax Essene rules of uncleanness. They had an easy relation with Gentiles, and could take part in "catching" them as the "fish", converts to the Jewish ascetic movement. Gentile men such as James and John of Zebedee, living in the world, became their fellow workers. Whereas celibates when out in the world were "apostles", meaning "sent out", these men felt themselves "called out", belonging in the world rather than in an ascetic community. They looked to the Annas brothers, Sadducees, as priests, rather than to Pharisees.

The first church, on the indications of A 7:38, was at Mird major, at the time of the formation of the peace party under Ananus and Simeon. The phrase "the Church in the Wilderness with the angel" appears. The Wilderness was north of the Mird building, but no "angel" would be found at an unclean annexe (1QM 7:6). The meaning is the alternative place outside the building which was less clean, but not governed by the rules of the "camps". As a later detail shows, this was simply in the courtyard of a Herodian building (Mk 6:39). The congregation was the *ekklēsia*, sitting in the open, while the ministers spoke from "Mt Sinai", the sanctuary-synagogue in one wing of the building.

The *ekklēsia* followed Peter, to Jerusalem (A 11:22) and to Antioch (A 11:26). Paul uses the term also, representing the Herodian side of the combination. Its origin can be seen precisely in the process by which some Essene villagers gave up traditional ways and under Herodian influence adopted a more hellenised way of life.

THE WORLD PLAN
In the time of Herod the Great, a great prospect for Jews opened up. "Myriads" of Jews, as Josephus shows (*Ap.* 1:194) were living in the Diaspora. If they were brought into a New Covenant, a new Israel, paying their half-shekel fees, they would bring in a rich income for the impoverished homeland. But there was a further prospect: the Jewish religion in its hellenised form was of increasing interest to Gentiles, and the numbers of members of the New Covenant, both Jewish and converted Gentiles, had the potential for profoundly influencing Greco-Roman culture. A further step lay ahead: the Roman empire, only just forming, might become so sympathetic to Herodian Judaism that it would be prepared for a Jewish Caesar. The ambition of Herod had no bounds: he hoped that he or one of his descendants would be a world emperor.

A plan for the world was drawn up, to be used for evangelism, and setting the structure of the future empire. (See Chapter 5 for its outline.)

There were to be four world capitals, each associated with a compass point and with one of the four living creatures of Ezek 1:9-10. Ezekiel's description of a chariot heading east used ancient emblems for priests, levites and kings. They in turn were associated with the great festivals, and consequently with the seasons. The seasons had natural associations with colours. The system was:

East	Babylon	Man	Spring	Green
West	Rome	Eagle	Autumn	Red
North	Asia Minor	Calf	Winter	Black
South	Egypt	Lion	Summer	White

The groups meeting at Mird, coming from the Diaspora, were the missionaries. The "hermits" of Manasseh and Ephraim were sent to Babylon and Egypt, places where their orders had actually originated in the first century BC.

King Herod would rule from the east to the west of the world. He himself would be primarily in the centre, in Jerusalem, being represented by his crown prince in Babylon and his next prince in Rome. The world, reflecting the seating arrangements of the supreme men at the table (see Hierarchy, page 347), had uneven values, the east being one grade above the west.

Herod's emblem would be a Man in Babylon, and, appropriately, an Eagle in Rome. Romans were associated with the Eagle, as is shown in 1QpHab 3:10-12. Under this sign Herod would one day be Caesar. The name "Caesar" was used for Herod and his successors; in the gospels it apparently means the Roman emperor, but in the pesher, when "Caesar" alone is used, it means the Herod king (e.g. Mk 12:14, Jn 19:12, A 17:7). When the literal emperor is meant, the specific name is given: "Caesar Augustus", "Tiberius Caesar", or *Sebastos*, "the August One" (Nero) (Lk 2:1, 3:1, A 25:21).

Herod would also rule in Asia Minor, an area with a heavy concentration of population. In another of his roles he would be the black Calf, standing for the north. His main centre in Asia Minor would be Antioch, capital of Syria, due north of Jerusalem. The colour black remained associated with Antioch; a later leader there was called Niger, Latin for "black" (A 13:1).

Herod's adoption of all the major leadership positions was one of the reasons why he was called "the All". Wherever the word *pantes* (plural form) appears, it means the Herod king.

The David, traditionally associated with the Lion, was left the south only, Alexandria and Egypt. Jews of Alexandria were not strong supporters of the Herods (see 11QT 56:16).

The four coloured horses of Rev 6:1-8 (white, red, black, and green) use the colours for seasons, and represent the main cities. The white horse, however, represents Ephesus, for the reason shown below.

The world was conceived as a time circle, the positions for 6 a.m., 6 p.m., midnight and noon being at east, west, north and south respectively. Intermediate hours (9 a.m., 3 p.m., 9 p.m. and 3 a.m.) were also marked, and places at south-east (Arabia, A 2:11, Gal 1:17), south-west (Cyrene,

A 2:10, A 13:1), north-west (Illyricum, Rom 15:19) and north-east (presumably Armenia) were made minor. centres. The conception of the world is seen in Figure 4. This scheme was imposed on the actual positions in the world (see Fig. 5).

Asia Minor

Asia Minor lay on the segment between north and north-west. It was, in actual fact, the most important part of the mission field, as it had a great population of Jews living outside the homeland. Of the expected 60 000 members in any one period (increasing to 600 000 after 40 years), half should come from Asia Minor.

Its five provinces were put under the charge of the Chief Priest and levites who were ministers of the sanctuary at Mird. The Chief Priest, under the name of Thunder, would have oversight, and the bishops, presbyters or deacons would be each assigned to a province. (A province was a taxation unit, 6000 members paying a half-shekel each, as there were 6000 half-shekels in a talent, 4Q159.)

The chief bishop was the levite called Kohath, (see page 343) who was associated with Mt Sinai and the Law. But two other men had been given the same status through promotion. One was the heir of David, who was traditionally associated with the Lion of the south. But the Lion had become a Lamb when the Davids adopted a Nazirite discipline. Revelation 5:5-7 shows that the same man was "the Lion of the tribe of Judah, the Root of David" and also "the Lamb". (The book of Revelation is a major source for the world plan, and especially for the plan for Asia Minor.) The colour white was consequently used for Ephesus also, and a bishop in Alexandria could become a bishop in Ephesus (A 18:24). The other bishop was the Herodian crown prince, who was of the same status as the David; both would be subordinate to Herod. The David as the Lamb was called "Jacob" (Jacob-Heli, the grandfather of Jesus, see Chapter 5), and the Herodian crown prince, to show equality with him, was called "Esau", the twin of Jacob (Gen 25:24-26).

Three of the provinces were assigned to the three bishops: the province of Asia in the west, with its capital in Ephesus, went to Jacob-Heli; Galatia in the centre fell to the levite Kohath, and became the "Mt Sinai" of the Diaspora; and Cappadocia in the east fell to "Esau". The Herod crown prince was thus placed closest to Antioch, where King Herod the Calf was to be found in one of his lesser roles. (There are still to be seen in Cappadocia monasteries and hermit cells carved out of rock by early Christians, R.A. Butler, *Turkey*, p. 64.)

Each of these episcopal provinces could be counted on for 6000

Fig. 4 Herodian World Scheme

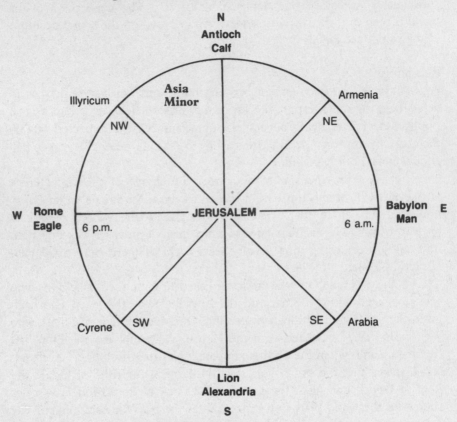

members, one talent each. But Bithynia and Pontus in the north near the Black Sea, and Pamphylia and Cilicia in the south on the Mediterranean, had smaller populations due to remoteness or size. The former were made presbyteral, and expected to produce 4000 members each, and the latter diaconal, 2000 each. Bithynia and Pamphylia together made a single province of 6000, and Pontus and Cilicia another. Each of these combined provinces was called simply by the name of the greater portion. So the five provinces are listed in 1 Pet 1:1 as "Pontus, Galatia, Cappadocia, Asia and Bithynia".

Galatia as standing for the Law, and Bithynia, both rejected the Christian version of the doctrine (Paul's Epistle to Galatians, A 13:14-23, A 16:7)). The names of both are omitted in the list of ministers present in Jerusalem on the Day of Pentecost, A 2:9-10. In the place of Bithynia, Pamphylia, its diaconal portion, is listed. In the place of Galatia, Phrygia, a part of Asia, is treated as a separate province in order to make up the

Fig. 5 Mediterranean World First Centuries BC & AD

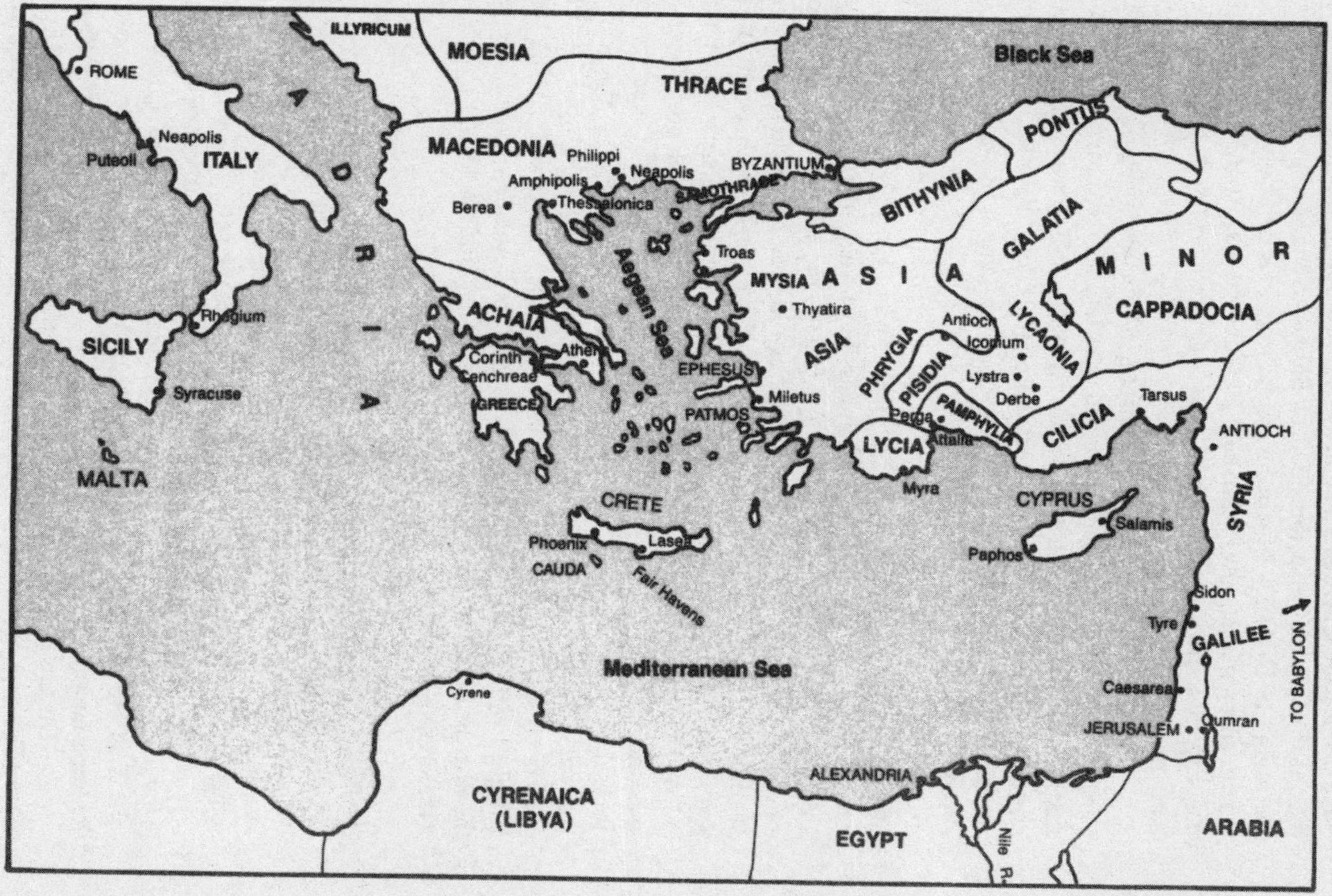

numbers. But the Christians did, in fact, lose 10 000 members in Asia Minor: the 6000 of Galatia and the 4000 of Bithynia. This is the point behind the saying in Lk 14:31–32, concerning a king who had only 10 000 going out to encounter another who had 20 000. The Christians still had the majority in a divided Asia Minor, and were reminding the circumcision party of this fact.

In about AD 1, when the Prodigal Son, Theudas, went to the Father, Simeon, and asked for half of his inheritance, all ten provinces were at that time divided between peace and war. All of Asia Minor was for peace, and the remainder—the two home provinces and Babylon, Rome and Alexandria—were for war. Theudas gained the latter half, while the Elder Brother, Jacob-Heli, held Asia Minor.

Ephesus was also under a "Sarah". Herodians were Hellenists, who allowed ministry to women (A 6:1). Ephesus was a centre of Gentile mission, and "Sarah" was the Mother of Gentiles. It was also the case that pagan Ephesus was devoted to worship of a female; the great temple of Diana, one of the seven wonders of the ancient world, was found there. Herodian methods of evangelism allowed a process of syncretisation between pagan gods and goddesses and Jewish priests and levites, as seen in Chapter 33 (A 19:23–41). The chief Herodian woman, Helena in the gospel period, was the "Sarah". As she was equal to "Isaac" (a son and a wife were of the same rank), she was a cardinal, as was "Isaac". She was "the woman arrayed in purple and scarlet" of Rev 17:4. But, when the split between Simon Magus and the ruling Herods took place, Simon and Helena were attacked with the polemic found in the book of Revelation, claiming Simon as the Beast 666 (see Hierarchy, page 372) and Helena as "Jezebel" (Rev 2:20–29).

Gentile Locations

Gentiles belonged to two orders, Asher and Dan. The former lived as individual ascetics like Ephraim-Manasseh, retreating for periods of private meditation and prayer. The latter lived in celibate communities like monasteries. Their chief was called a "centurion", being first of 100 men (Lk 7:2, A 10:1).

In the Wilderness of Judea, Dan Gentiles had a centre at Mazin, which was of the class of the Beasts. Here the "centurion" (John Mark, the chief proselyte) was found in Lk 7:1–10. He was also linked with Andrew of Capernaum-Naphtali, the lower kind of Essene married men (Jn 1:35–40).

On the scale of the whole country, the men of Dan met at Greater Dan (Caesarea, proselytes), Great Dan (Caesarea Philippi, Shem) and Little Dan (Joppa, Ham), the latter two being in the traditional tribal territory of Dan, which was in two segments. But when these centres turned against

Agrippa I from AD 37, alternative houses were set up by Agrippa supporters. The new centre for Ham was Gaza (A 8:26).

In the gospel period and subsequently, Gentiles were raised in status. The first step was to class them with the intermediate unclean. At Qumran, they went up from Mazin to Ain Feshkha. There they were treated like Nazirite presbyters. John Mark refers to himself as a presbyter in his epistles (2 Jn 1:1, 3 Jn 1:1). Both he and Philip (Shem) are recorded as being at Ain Feshkha as well as Mazin (Mk 11:11, Jn 1:43).

Gentiles had two different attitudes to Jewish priests, according to whether they were proselytes or simply uncircumcised. John Mark, a proselyte, revered Jewish priests. The consequence was that in all buildings in which his order met the architecture was changed. At Joppa (which was under the leadership of "Simon the Tanner", Simon Magus, making it equal to Ain Feshkha, A 9:43), and also at Troas (A 20:7-12), the buildings had three storeys, or rather two storeys and a flat roof. Whereas in other Gentile buildings the congregation sat on the ground floor while the Jewish superior prayed on the roof of the ground floor building, in John Mark's buildings the Jewish priest prayed on the roof of the second storey (called the third storey, A 20:9), an ordinary Jewish minister prayed on the roof of the first storey (called to dōma, A 10:9), and the congregation stayed on the ground floor (see Fig. 6). It was this arrangement that suggested the episode of the "vision" in A 10, in which Jesus, on the highest level, spoke to Peter on "the roof" (to dōma) (see Chapter 31). John Mark as Eutychus was himself on the highest level in A 20:9, and "fell down dead", to be revived to a lower kind of churchmanship by Paul.

Those Gentiles who did not need a Jewish priest were promoted to the level of "Bethsaida", their meeting place being at the city of Bethsaida on Lake Galilee. Philip, of Shem (uncircumcised Gentiles), met here (Jn 1:44, 12:21).

On a world scale, Dan Gentiles had their monasteries or celibate centres at lesser points of the circle. Proselytes met on the north-west division, running through Troas and Macedonia to Illyricum. John Mark, leader of eastern proselytes, was found at Troas, and Luke, who was to replace him, also came there (A 16:8-9). In Macedonia, Luke was the pro-western chief proselyte, appearing as "we" representing Jesus (A 16:11). Shem uncircumcised met on the south-east corner, in Arabia, as the Shem group stood for non-Jewish Semites. Japheth went to the remote south-west corner, Cyrene. Luke, originally head of Japheth, was "Lucius of Cyrene" (A 13:1). Ham met between Shem and Japheth, due south of Alexandria, in Ethiopia. Titus, the head of Ham Gentiles, was the "Ethiopian eunuch" of A 8:27.

The men of Asher, under an individual discipline, met in the same

Fig. 6　Architecture of Proselyte Buildings

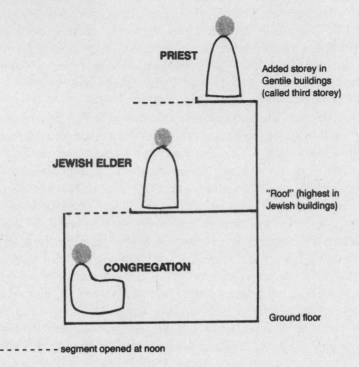

PRIEST

Added storey in
Gentile buildings
(called third storey)

JEWISH ELDER

"Roof" (highest in
Jewish buildings)

CONGREGATION

Ground floor

- - - - - - - - segment opened at noon

places as the women of Asher. As with the Therapeutae, men and women formed part of the same groupings. At Mird, they were found one hour away at the annexe at Mird minor. While they were there it was "the limits of Tyre" (*ta horia Tyrou*) and "Sidon" (Mk 7:31). In Syria itself their graded meeting places were in Tyre (the highest, as it was within the original tribal territory of Asher), then Sarepta (Lk 4:26), then Sidon, the latter also called "Syria". In the Qumran area, the female head of the order, "Sarah", brought "Tyre" to Mazin, as she was also Mother of Dan Gentiles. Consequently Mird minor, 8 hours away from Mazin, was "the limits of Tyre", as *ta horia* meant 8 hours. James of Zebedee, the next below "Sarah", was of the level of Sarepta, and John of Zebedee next below him, of Sidon. James and John, with their "mother" Helena, appear at Mird minor in Mk 10:35, Mt 20:20. They also came to Mazin, working with Peter to catch the "fish", Gentiles of Dan (Mk 1:19).

In the wider world, the women and men of Asher and Dan held their spiritual retreats on the islands of the Mediterranean. Tyre itself was a city built on an island about half a mile from the coast of Phoenicia.

The islands of Cyprus (A 13:4) and Crete (A 2:10, Tit 1:5) were also used. Tyre was of the level of "Sarah", Cyprus of "Rebecca" and Crete of "Rachel" (the three wives of the successive patriarchs) so Cyprus was also of the level of Shem, and Crete of the level of Ham. Consequently Titus of Ham was sent to Crete (Tit 1:5).

Asher Gentiles, like those of Dan, were split on the question of loyalty to Agrippa I. James of Zebedee followed Helena in opposing him (A 12:2,20), but John of Zebedee, like Titus, continued to support him. Pro-Herodians then moved to different islands. John of Zebedee was found on Patmos (Rev 1:9). Mary Magdalene of Dan went to Rhodes, so was called Rhoda (A 12:13).

AFTER THE EARTHQUAKE

The plan of mission was laid down before the earthquake of 31 BC. Different parts of the mission looked to Qumran and its related centres as their home base. Missionaries to Babylon came back to the monastery at Qumran, a base for the east; missionaries to Rome came back to Jerusalem, a base for the west; while those under the Calf and the Lion, Antioch-Asia Minor and Alexandria in Egypt, came to Mird and its outposts.

But the earthquake that struck Qumran defiled it forever. Monastic Essenes went back to Jerusalem, and eventually separated from the mission altogether. Only men of the less clean Diaspora level could frequent Qumran. It was reoccupied after twenty years by the orders of Ephraim and Manasseh.

Qumran was now equivalent to a "camp", such as had been on the hillock at Mird. The "camp fire", the "fire by night" was brought there (see further below, page 322).

An unclean annexe for women, married men and Gentiles must be built 2000 cubits away from a "camp". Now that Qumran was no longer a monastery, it had to add such a place. The "queen's house" was developed from an existing Manger (for real animals), five stadia or one hour away, on the littoral plain south of the plateau. It corresponded to Mird minor, the place where young girls had gone to give birth to illegitimate children. It was this place to which Mary went to give birth to Jesus, whose conception was considered to be extranuptial by the Boethusian high priest in power (Chapter 9).

The intermediate place 1000 cubits away was in Cave 4 (as seen above, page 290).

At Mird there had been an "Egypt", in a cave 2000 cubits from the "camp". Its "Red Sea" had been the aqueduct to the west of the building. At Qumran there was a similar aqueduct, beginning on the west, repaired at the re-occupation, and to its west were the caves in the limestone cliffs.

Some of these were suitable for 90 day retreats, and the caves became "Egypt". When Joseph was told to flee into "Egypt" (Mt 2:13) he was actually hiding from Herod in the caves at Qumran. The whole area, riddled with caves, had been a hiding place for political refugees since the days of King David.

Similarly, when Joseph was "given into Egypt" in A 7:9, he was allying with other nationalists at Qumran.

With the order of East Manasseh, who were bishops of "camps", Qumran became "Sodom", both because it was near the ancient site of Sodom and because of the associations of this order with sodomy (A 17:5, alluding to Gen 19:5). As it also included "Egypt", it became "Sodom and Egypt". Rev 11:8 speaks of it as "the great city which is spiritually called Sodom and Egypt, where their Lord was crucified".

For Diaspora Essenes who still looked to the Holy Land and rejected the literal Jerusalem, Qumran could still maintain its image as a "Jerusalem", although it could not be a sanctuary. So the names "Jerusalem" (plural form) and "Judea" were still used of Qumran after the reoccupation (Mt 2:1).

THE PLAN OF QUMRAN

Archaeologists have discerned the several stages of occupation of the Qumran site (de Vaux, *ADSS*). From the eighth century BC there had been a deep round well, used by much earlier settlers. It was cleared when the site was occupied in the second century BC, and remained in use as a source of drinking water, fed by the aqueduct leading from the wady Qumran.

In the first phase of occupation (1a) two stepped cisterns (A and B, Fig.7) were built close to the well, with several rooms around them. A simple enclosure, retained from early Israelite times, stretched to the east. The position of the cisterns already indicates that the leaders had settled near the well, while workers concerned with the pottery kiln that was installed at this time on the far eastern side were relegated to the east. It was from this phase, as it appears, that the settlement was called "the potters' field", the name used for it in Mt 27:7. It appears from the reconstruction of the chronology that in 140 BC the Essenes had been expelled here, "returning to the land of their desolation" (*TLevi* 17:10). A group of priests took up the space around the well, and their acolytes, celibates of the kind that had long been taken into the solar shrines, became the workers. One of their occupations was the making of pots and dishes of the special shape required for the sacred meals and libations.

In phase 1b, probably not much later, there was a great expansion and development of the buildings. The ground plan was laid, with only minor changes being subsequently made.

Several observations may be made about the plan, following from the well grounded assumption of symmetry in all the activities of Essenes.

Although at first sight there appears only to be a general harmony, a closer study shows that the buildings had an exact plan. The main buildings and installations were governed by a square of 150 × 150 cubits, divided into four squares of 75 × 75 cubits.

The north-east square contained the building that was plainly the monastery, housing the greater number of men, but on the east side as they were subservient to priests. It included the strip containing a great cistern (C) which, before it was damaged by the earthquake, was appropriately placed to be the main initiation cistern. After going through a novitiate of two years, spent in the triangular court east of the building (excluded by the squares), the initiate came to this cistern to undergo an immersion that was part of his final vows. Having now renounced the world, marriage, and property (1QS 6:13–23) he went through the inner door into the main monastery, where he spent the four years of his education. This square included also the cistern on the south of the monastery (D), within the Israelite wall, which is easily interpreted as for the use of visiting villagers when they came as pilgrims. It adjoined the outer hall outside the Israelite wall, in the square below, the position of which makes it plain that it was not for enclosed monks.

This hall, opening on to the southern esplanade, was set up with a system for flushing the floor. A pipe led into it from the water system, and the floor was slightly sloping, so that the water would run through the southern door. De Vaux, who excavated the Qumran site, considered that this supported his view that the hall was the monks' refectory (ADSS p. 11). It is true that meals were taken there, as large numbers of dishes were stacked in the room called the pantry leading off it. But it would be quite unnecessary to use precious water, which flowed from the wady only once a year, simply to clean after meals; a broom would have served as well! However, the location of the hall outside the walls suggests that it was for the meals of visiting village pilgrims. On the view that a man who had recently had sexual intercourse could defile a holy area (11QT 45:11), it would be necessary to use precious water for ritual washings after the visits of such men. In the second phase, this system was abolished, the floor being levelled and the conduit pipe blocked (ADSS p. 26). This accords with the reconstruction of the history given here, that the second phase saw an occupation by the "seekers-after-smooth-things", who engaged in "loose living" by strict Palestinian Essene standards. They no longer held that sex defiled the area.

The south-east square excluded the large south-east cistern (E), the most capacious of all the stepped cisterns. This corresponds to the

Fig. 7 **Plan of Qumran Buildings**

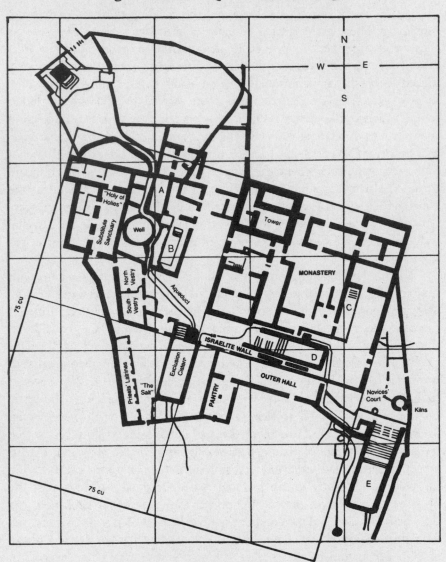

interpretation that it was for novices, receiving the first stage of their membership signified by the "water". They were not yet members and could leave at any time. For two years they had their washings here and their instruction and meals in the triangular court. Their cistern was the largest, as numbers of men might begin but not all went through the whole process.

The north-west square, containing the round well and the two original stepped cisterns (A and B) was thought by de Vaux to contain merely workshops. But this does not allow for the fact that it was occupied first, nor for the dimensions of the long courtyard added in phase 1b. A line of stones placed across it, 10 cubits from the north end, marks off one-third of its length of 30 cubits (when the south wall is included). Its width is 10 cubits. These proportions correspond exactly to those of Solomon's temple, half-size. It was 60 cubits long and 20 cubits wide, and the Holy of Holies, its most sacred area, was its upper third of 20 × 20 cubits, leaving a Holy House of 40 × 20 cubits (1 K 6:2,16,17). The courtyard looks like a substitute sanctuary, with its "Holy of Holies" marked off by the line of stones. On either side of this section windows were placed, as if to allow priests to overlook the Holy of Holies without going into it, as it was used only on the Day of Atonement (Heb 9:1-5). (It has been suggested in the pesher of A 7:55 that Stephen-Annas was looking through such windows when he "gazed into heaven", on a Day of Atonement, Chapter 29.) The proportions are also the same as those of the wilderness tabernacle, which was 30 cubits long and 12 cubits wide, its sides made of curtains on frames (Ex 36:20-30). The stone walls occupy another cubit on each side. This courtyard, running north-south rather than east-west like the true temple and tabernacle, was a sufficient representation of a biblical place of worship to be able to be used by the exiled priests, without itself becoming holy ground. They could hold substitute services there, relying on a platonic doctrine that the true worship of God was conducted in heaven, and they were an earthly reproduction (see Mt 16:18-19). Moreover, their prayers were the true sacrifices, the words, uttered at the appointed times, going up to heaven like smoke. They had rejected animal sacrifices (1QS 9:4-5, *Ant.* 18:19).

On the lower eastern wall of the courtyard was a door, and beside it on the outside a quarter circle of stones, marking a spot where a man could stand. It may have served for the ceremony of the eastern door of Ezek 44:3 and 46:1-3 (the prince stood there, and the people of the land came at the new moons and sabbaths to be allowed to worship outside the gate). The story in A 3:1-11 reflects the practice and places (although in the real Jerusalem; Essene sanctuaries, as reproductions, all had the same pattern).

The southern door of the courtyard communicated, in phase 1b, with the western door of the rooms running south of the round well. The link implies a vestry, to which the priests came from the sanctuary, in order to change their vestments, fulfilling the rule of Ezek 44:19, that when the Zadokites go outside the sanctuary they must put off their holy garments and put on others "lest they communicate holiness to the people with their garments". In the sanctuary, they had been like "gods" and "angels", but when they took off their vestments they "returned to the body". The vestry was associated with the body, and a set of images developed from this concept.

In the bodily state they ate the holy loaves, the "bread of the Presence" which was set out every day before God (1 K 7:48, Lev 24:5-9). A table set up in this room where they sat to eat both ordinary food and the sacred food developed into the holy table of Christian churches. Sacred bread and sacred wine had become the privilege of Essene priests, and through the historical process that is traced here became the Christian communion meal.

The vestry consisted of two long rooms, the southern one divided from the northern by a low dais. As north was established as the superior direction, the Holy of Holies being on the north, the southern chamber was for a lower grade of members. It was associated with the lower laity, who entered through its eastern door. The raised northern room was the "upper room" (*to katalyma*). It was here, according to the indications of the pesher, that the Last Supper was held.

The northwestern square also contained the aqueduct, whose waters fed the main cisterns. The two cisterns in this square (A and B) received its waters first, and were associated with the priests and levites, who occupied this area first.

The remaining square, the southwestern one, contained the unclean installations. The lines of the square isolate the area containing the large unstepped cistern outside the gate (F); and the long row of cubicles that have been thought by the archaeologists to be stables, but are too narrow for such a purpose and are better explained as priests' latrines.

In the Copper Scroll, whose first seventeen sentences refer to deposits in and around the Qumran buildings, there are three sentences (6, 15, 16) which can be seen to refer to this square. They use the word *melach*, "salt" (reading corrected from that of the original editor, *DJD* III). Salt, associated with the sea, alluded to the third kind of washing water, used for unclean grades. (There were three grades of water: first, still water in cisterns; second, running water of rivers; and third, salt water of the sea.) The followers of Jesus were the "salt of the earth" (Mt 5:13) because they belonged to these grades. The unclean square was called the Salt, and because of its associations, was especially used for deposits of money. Sentence 6 reads: "In the cistern in the Salt, under the steps, 42 talents". The unstepped cistern was outside the Israelite wall, but inside it were two small stepped cisterns forming a unit with it.

Sentence 15 reads "In the stand (shith, 'set'; so 'place for setting', such as the base for an urn) which is in the Salt, in its north, an urn of resin . . . under its western corner (pinna)". The word pinna is used for the cornerstone of the temple (1QS 8:7, from Isa 28:16). The description fits the south-west corner of the lower vestry, at the point of entry to the latrine area, where an urn of fragrant resin may have stood to be rubbed on before return to the sanctuary.

Sentence 16 reads: "In the grave (qeber) which is in the Salt, in the north-east, three cubits under the stone, 13 talents". The north-east corner of the unclean square, just outside the gate, in the angle with the exclusion cistern, was the appropriate place for a grave (no longer apparent, as the outer gate has collapsed). Contact with the dead was a defilement for Nazirites (Num 6:6), and a grave would act as a warning that this was a defiled place.

There is good reason, therefore, for identifying a square of 150 × 150 cubits divided evenly into four as the basic plan for the buildings. An additional feature of the plan, a set of concentric squares, is suggested by the Temple Scroll, which offers a design for the real Jerusalem in a series of concentric squares. If an outer square of 200 × 200 cubits is supposed for Qumran, it includes the novice's court and the southeastern cistern, as well as part of the area above the entrance gate on the north. Then a further, larger square of 250 × 250 cubits encloses all installations, including the cistern on the far northwestern corner at the entrance from the neck of land. On the south, a cluster of fixed stones on the esplanade marks off a corresponding boundary.

A measurement in sets of 250 cubits for major divisions is suggested by the unit of 2000 cubits. The whole Qumran "court" would be seen as one-eighth of the distance to the queen's house. Further, the southern esplanade and Caves 7 and 8 below it can be treated as 250 cubits from the cluster of stones. (The end of the esplanade is irregular, but a distance of 170 cubits (255 feet) from the cluster of stones can be measured. Beyond the edge, an extra 80 cubits (120 feet) would cover the extension for the caves (Fig. 8).

Caves 7 and 8 were, then, well within the sabbath limit, requiring a walk of only 500 cubits there and back from the outer square. The term "the holy city" (Mt 27:53) probably refers to this boundary.

Fig. 8   Overview of Qumran Settlement Area

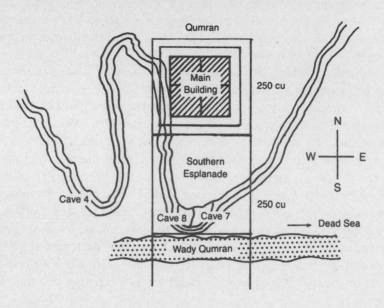

The New Jerusalem
As seen in Chapter 22, the Essenes who had been exiled to Qumran had seen it as a reproduction Jerusalem, a kind of small scale model. The relationship of the main parts was similar: the aqueduct running down the middle was like the Kidron, running north-south between the actual city of Jerusalem on the west and the Mount of Olives on the east. The four squares each contained a district: the northwestern the "city" and "temple"; the northeastern the "Mount of Olives" (Mk 14:26); the southwestern "Siloam" (Jn 9:7, the "blind" man was sent to wash in the "pool of Siloam", that is, the exclusion cistern); and the southeastern "Judea", the beginning of the territory outside the city. "Judea", containing the outer hall, was for visiting villagers (Fig. 9).

Changes within Qumran after the Earthquake
Following the earthquake of 31 BC, the sanctuary could no longer be used as a holy place. The ceremony of atonement and the daily rites were transferred to Mird major. The lower third of the courtyard, called *to hieron* ("the temple/palace") was retained for less sacred observances by visiting villagers, including their giving of money for tithes. Its primary purpose came to be the collection of money; it was here that Jesus "overturned the tables of the moneychangers". Some of the activities of the "city" were retained,

Fig. 9 The "New Jerusalem" at Qumran

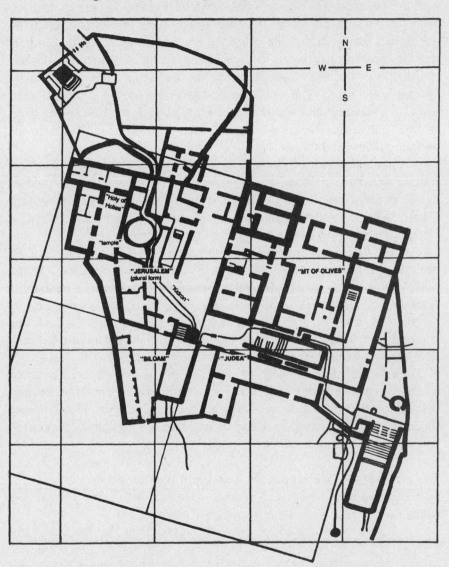

and the square was still called "Jerusalem". Qumran was designated by the northwestern and southeastern squares as "Jerusalem" (plural form) and "Judea" (Mk 3:7–8, Mt 4:25).

In the northwestern corner of the vestry, the door communicating with the sanctuary was blocked up, a substantial vault being put in its place. Of a noticeable heart shape, the vault opens below the quarter circle on which it is supposed that the prince of Ezek 46:2 stood. Acts 3:2 implies that the practice had come to include the giving of money by villagers to their prince-bishop as "alms", that is, the welfare funds for which village Essenes were noted. The vault beside was constructed for their storage. It was the "treasury" and also the "temple" of Jn 8:20, Mk 12:41. The saying "where your treasure is, there let your heart be" (Lk 12:34), alludes to the welfare system and the vault.

Just to the east of the vault a set of seven stone steps was added, leading up to the platform over the north vestry that was now used as the place for the priest to say his prayers, rather than in the sanctuary. (These steps are visible in the first photographs of the excavation, ADSS plate V, but have now been removed, leaving only their support.)

The first sentence of the Copper Scroll, begun at the reoccupation, deals with this vault as the first one built. "At the ruin (choribah) in the valley of Achor (the ancient name for the plain south of Jericho containing Qumran, Josh 15:7, Hos 2:15) under the steps going up on the east, at 40 cubits, a casket of silver, its total weight 17 talents". The "east", in this and other sentences, refers to the east door or wall of the substitute sanctuary, an eastern entrance being used to fulfil the ceremony of Ezek 46:1–3. "At 40 cubits" does not mean "dig 40 cubits"; there is no verb, and it would be an extraordinarily deep hole (60 feet). It is, rather, a way of identifying the south-east corner of the substitute sanctuary, which was 30 cubits long (including the south wall) and had at its north a set of "holy chambers", adding 10 cubits from inside the northern wall.

The places of the Last Supper, the Trials, and the Crucifixion

Some features were now added that make it possible to identify the places where the central events of the gospels took place.

Prayers were uttered in the vestry, rather than the sanctuary, and a series of 12-cubit segments was established, each standing for 12 hours, on the principle that time was equal to space. The dividing lines, each standing for 6 a.m. and 6 p.m., ran due east–west, parallel with the dais.

A prayer was said on each cubit at each hour, by a man of the grade appropriate to the hour. Each segment was also graded and assigned to a minister in the hierarchy. The series began only at the presbyteral

Fig. 10 **Plan of Qumran, Phase Two**

Division in segments. Place of Crucifixion

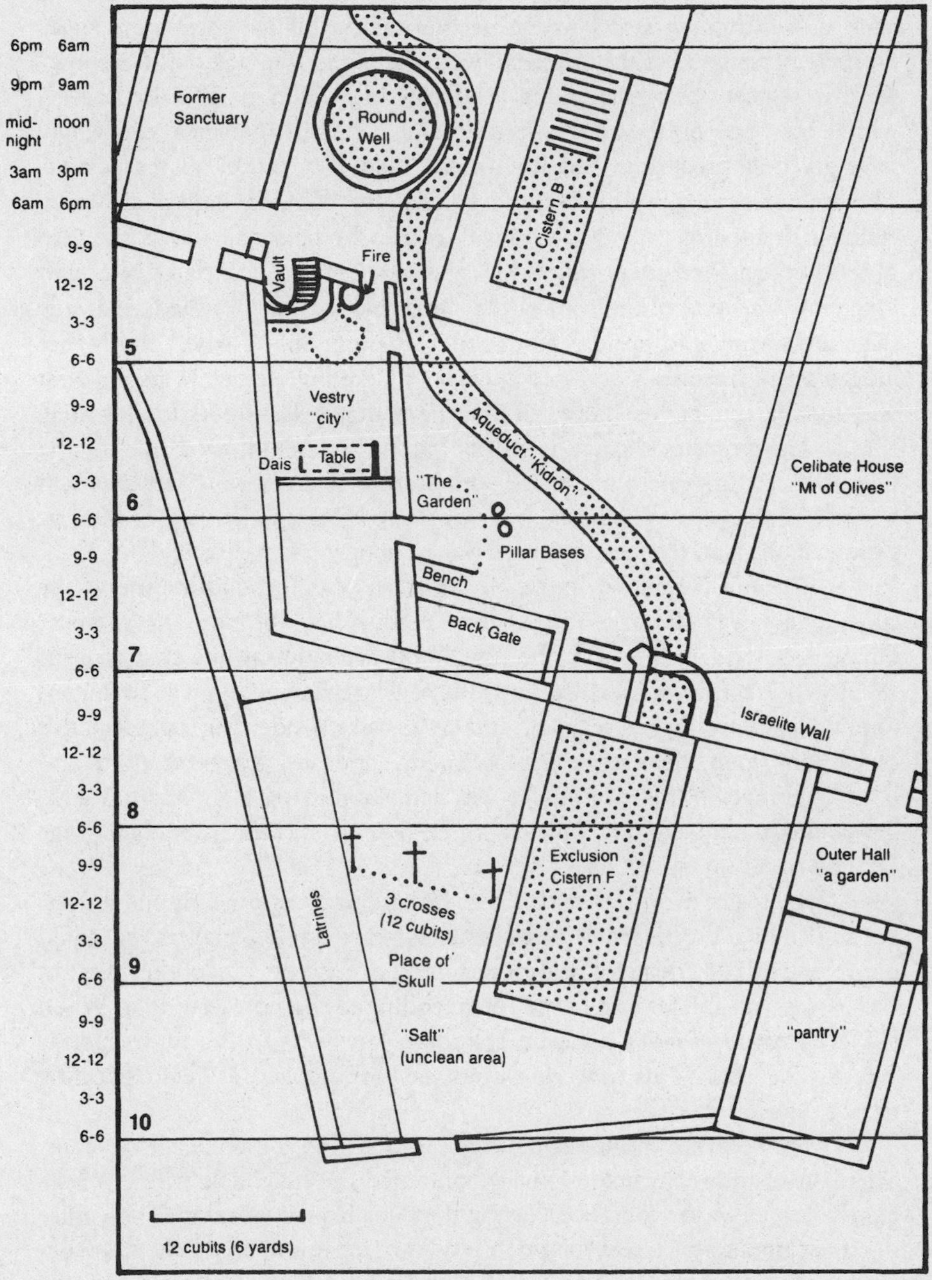

6pm	6am
9pm	9am
mid-night	noon
3am	3pm
6am	6pm
9-9	
12-12	
3-3	
6-6	5
9-9	
12-12	
3-3	
6-6	6
9-9	
12-12	
3-3	
6-6	7
9-9	
12-12	
3-3	
6-6	8
9-9	
12-12	
3-3	
6-6	9
9-9	
12-12	
3-3	
6-6	10

Former Sanctuary

Round Well

Cistern B

Vault

Fire

Vestry "city"

Dais

Table

"The Garden"

Aqueduct "Kidron"

Celibate House "Mt of Olives"

Pillar Bases

Bench

Back Gate

Israelite Wall

Latrines

3 crosses (12 cubits)

Exclusion Cistern F

Outer Hall "a garden"

Place of Skull

"Salt" (unclean area)

"pantry"

12 cubits (6 yards)

level (grade 5, see Hierarchy, page 343), reflecting the lowered status of Qumran following the earthquake.

The northernmost segment included the "treasury", the vault, the back of which now stood in the vestry, cutting off its north-west angle. Presbyters, assigned to this segment, were the grade who acted as treasurers. To this segment also was added a circular fire (*ADSS* p. 28), the base of which has been preserved. It was at least 2 cubits in diameter, and would have given off great heat. The fire was the sign of a "camp", as seen above. The fire had been given further associations also, being thought of as Moses' "unquenchable fire" (A 7:30). God was said to be present in it, as the God of the fiery Last Judgment (Mk 9:43). The segment was associated also with judgment, and one of the uses of the steps that had been added alongside the vault was to lead up to a north-south platform above, where the higher judges sat. A prisoner stood in a specially marked circle below, facing west and looking up at his judges. It was here that Jesus stood for his trial.

The prisoner's space is still apparent, as an unpaved part of the floor, the rest of which was paved with stones. The centre of the area was a circle, 3 cubits in diameter, but the stones that marked its east curve were extended on the west so that it was no longer a simple circle.

The north-south diameter of the circle was the middle line of the room, which was 10 cubits wide. The circle thus had an "east" and a "west". On its east, and in line with the fire, stood Peter during the trial of Jesus (Mt 26:70, *emprosthen*, p-sense, east). As a village Essene, he was permitted to pray in the presbyteral segment, and on its eastern side. The representative of working men, he had to rise at 3 a.m., and say prayers at 4, 5 and 6 a.m. During the trial of Jesus he was actually praying at 1, 2 and 3 a.m., but as the hours were now officially three hours fast (see Chronology, page 181) he stood on the cubits for 4, 5 and 6 a.m.

Jesus stood on the same lines, but facing west towards his judges. Peter, denying the doctrine of Jesus, faced east for his prayers, so could converse with the females and others in the position of doorkeepers, in the passage on the far east of the room leading to the northern door. When the cockcrowing for 3 a.m. again sounded, Jesus was in the same spot as Peter at the end of his trial. He turned east and looked at Peter, standing beside him (Lk 22:61).

The next 12 cubit segment below this was for grade 6, deacons. This part of the room had originally contained the holy table where priests ate the loaves of the Presence, having their main meal at noon. The centre of the segment still stood for noon, and was an especially holy spot. But now the table was for worker deacons, and placed lower. Under the village welfare system, indigent persons could receive "crumbs" from their table.

The common table was now placed on the edge of the dais, and the welfare recipients knelt at the dais to receive their "crumbs". In the body imagery applied to this segment, the edge of the dais was the "bosom", where the poor received comfort.

Under the rules of Ephraim-Manasseh, Diaspora Essenes, a sacred meal was added to the common meal, extending it from two hours to four every evening (1QS 6:7). The Last Supper was held under this rule, and at the table in this room. John Mark occupied the seat at the very edge of the dais, the "bosom" (see Hierarchy, page 361), while Jesus and Jonathan Annas, as Priest and King, were at the holy centre on the north side of the table.

The table was only placed there in the late afternoon, the space being used during the early afternoon for teaching. At noon, the half-roof between the noon line and the 3 p.m. line at the dais was opened, allowing the people to see the priest on the northern half-roof, offering his prayers to heaven above the holy spot. He reached it from the steps and the side platform of the judges. At 3 p.m. he came down to the ground floor in order to receive tithes and petitions from the people (Mk 2:3-12).

The common table which had become a holy table was the first form of the Christian holy table, and the dais at which the poor knelt to receive fragments of the holy loaves became the communion rails in a Christian church.

Outside the eastern door of the lower vestry was an area, 7 cubits wide, containing several striking features which are still to be seen there. Two circular dressed stones, very different in appearance from the rough stones of which the buildings were made, stood outside rows of stones marking a kind of porch to the door. Within the porch was a clear circle of stones to the north of the door, and a well made stone bench to its south, its top covered by smooth plaster.

The line marking off the diaconal area (6) runs between the two circular dressed stones, putting the southern one in segment 7. These two circular stones, if placed on top of one another, would form a pair of millstones. The top of the northern one is exactly one cubit in diameter, its base 1½ cubits, whereas the southern one has a top of 1½ cubits and a base of 1 cubit. Standing separate, they have the appearance of pillar bases. There is a hole in the centre of each.

Detail of the pesher shows that this area was used for Gentile proselytes, who were uncircumcised, lived an ascetic celibate life, but at first were not permitted into the congregation in the vestry. An Eden image was used (see 1QH 8:20). Their minister was called "Adam", and part of the area containing the pillar bases was "the Garden", that is, the "Garden of Eden".

"Adam" was the David in one of his roles (Rom 5:14). "Adam" could also be called the "Gardener". When Mary Magdalene in the tomb thought that Jesus was the Gardener, she had mistaken him for his brother James, who had become the David at that time.

The Place of the Crucifixion

According to Mk 15:25, Jesus was crucified "at the third hour", and according to Jn 19:41 he was crucified in "a garden" (*kēpos*, without article). Both these points enable the pesharist to discover the exact line on which the crosses were placed.

The rule for definite articles meant that if segment 6 was "the garden" ("Eden"), segment 9 was "a garden" (see further in Hierarchy, page 343). Segment 9 also contained the outer hall, called "a garden" (*kēpos*) in Jn 18:18. The crosses were in the 12 cubit segment in line with the outer hall. (Jn 19:41 goes on to say that the burial place was "the garden". On the larger scale of the grounds, the division of the 250 cubit unit beginning at the tomb at the end of the esplanade was of the same value as segment 6. It is called "the Paradise" in Lk 23:43 to distinguish it from "the garden" inside the grounds.)

Although the segment was that of "a garden", the part of it where the crosses were was unclean, for it was marked by a skull (Lk 23:33). As the Copper Scroll shows, there was a grave in the north-east corner of the Salt. Nazirites were not permitted to go near graves (Num 6:6), so a skull reminded the men of the "camp" that in the southwestern square containing a latrine and the cistern for washings after uncleanness they were in a defiled area. It was both "outside the gate" and "outside the camp", phrases used for the place where Jesus was crucified in Heb 13:12–13. The latter phrase means a latrine in Deut 23:12.

Jesus was crucified "at/on the third hour" (Mk 15:25). But, at the same time, it was noon (Jn 19:14). The noon line was in the middle of the segment, but, if the crosses were set up parallel with the line of the Israelite wall, the western end would be 3 cubits north of the eastern end, as the Israelite wall sloped at an angle to the horizontal, 3 cubits further to the north in every 12 cubits (see Fig. 10). At the centre of the segment, the space between the installations was just 12 cubits, measured on the sloping line. Thus the western cross would be on the 9 a.m. line. Jesus was put at the western end, as the arrangement was now that of ministers at the table, Priest (Simon Magus) in the centre, Prophet (Levite, Judas) on the east, and King (Jesus) on the west. He was thus on the 9 a.m. line. This was a further reason, in addition to the fast times, why the crucifixion was at both 9 a.m. and noon.

Under present conditions at Qumran, it is difficult to measure to the exact line of the crosses, because the area containing the gate has collapsed. Part of the back wall of the vestry is standing, however, and, if some of the built up soil beside the exclusion pool were reduced, the line could be found.

It may seem extraordinary that such precision should be possible, but, with the combination of the actual measurements, the assumption of time-based symmetry, and the fact that the text yields to a pesher, such a conclusion may be drawn.

THE SYSTEM FOR BOATS

While proselytes were brought in under an Eden imagery, uncircumcised Gentiles of the order of Dan were "fish", being washed in the third and lowest kind of water, the sea. As it was this class who became Christians, the common symbol of Christians in Rome was the fish. It is well illustrated in the catacombs. (See also Hierarchy, page 373 for an additional reason for the symbol, a play on Hebrew letters.)

The place for their immersions in sea water was at Mazin. The excavations there have shown a great watergate at the eastern end of the enclosure, to which a channel must have led from the Dead Sea. It is now filled in, and the distance to the present edge of the Dead Sea is 314 feet (Stutchbury and Nicholl, p. 97). The several episodes dealing with events at "Capernaum" and the catching of "fish" give the detail of the methods of the mission.

The rate of travelling by boat on the Dead Sea is found to have been set at three times the walking rate. Whereas it took 3 hours to walk the 15 stadia from Ain Feshkha to Mazin, the boat took 1 hour.

Care of the uncircumcised had fallen to village Essenes such as Peter. Peter himself pointed out that he was an *anēr hamartōlos*, "a married man a Sinner" (Lk 5:8), and this meant that he could not come into physical contact with men of higher status. According to Josephus, "a senior [Essene] if but touched by a junior, must take a bath, as after contact with an alien" (*War* 2:150). But a lower grade member could make physical contact with the lowly class of the uncircumcised, performing such ceremonies as washings and laying on of hands.

Gentile mission had been particularly encouraged by the Herods. It is very probable that the superiors of each of the classes were servants in the household of the ruling Herods, where they took part in worship services of a liberalised kind, and to which they brought their own education and outlook. When the Diaspora mission developed, necessitating the use of boats, a Herod took the title of "Noah". He was chief of an "Ark", in which the Beasts, married villagers, were "saved", given a form of full membership. Derived from this kind of mission was the "catching of fish", performed by the married villagers. The chief Essene villager was appointed by "Noah" to this work; in the gospel period this was Peter, with his Second, Andrew.

Essene men like Peter, when living in the cities of the Diaspora, had found that they could persuade Gentiles to adopt the ascetic way of life. Josephus comments on the attraction of Gentiles to Essene ideas (*War* 2:155–158). Such Gentiles did not want to become Jews, but wanted to become part of the celibate system. They retained their own nationality, and were classed in biblical terms in the categories of the three sons of Noah: Shem, Ham and Japheth (Gen 10). (Shem, other Semites than the Jews, their class led by Philip in the gospel period; Ham, including Egyptians and Ethiopians, led by Titus; Japheth, Greeks and Romans, led by Luke.) These were the "fish", the head of Shem being Fish 1, of Ham Fish 2 ("two fishes", but p-sense, "fish 2"), and of Japheth Fish 3.

The classes of Gentiles had been defined from the level of bishop downwards:
a) bishop, grade 4 in the total hierarchy, men who were both circumcised and lived a celibate life;
b) presbyter, grade 5, men who were circumcised but remained married (these were called "Jews", as they lived in all respects like ordinary Jews);
c) deacon, grade 6, proselytes, who were uncircumcised, celibate, and kept some Jewish ritual laws;
d) grade 7, ordinary members, the celibates of Shem;
e) grade 8, lower ordinary members, the celibates of Ham;
f) grade 9, lowest ordinary members, the celibates of Japheth.

The ceremony of washing was performed at the water channel at Mazin, using fishing boats. The channel, leading up to the watergate, was 200 cubits long, as shown in Jn 21:8. This is 100 yards, 300 feet, close to the 314 feet that the distance now measures.

With an extra 50 cubits in the sea itself, it was understood as one of the units of 250 cubits into which longer distances were divided. This was further subdivided into 5 sets of 50 cubits, each of them corresponding to a grade, starting with grade 5, presbyters, nearest to the watergate, and grade 9, Japheth, furthest away.

The grade 5 segment had shallow water only, being nearest to land. Boats could only come into its first 20 or 30 cubits.

On land, a rectangular courtyard ran west from the watergate, ending in a solid building (which has not yet been fully excavated). At its fullest extent the land section covered 100 cubits. It accounted for two more

Fig. 11 **Water Channel at Mazin**

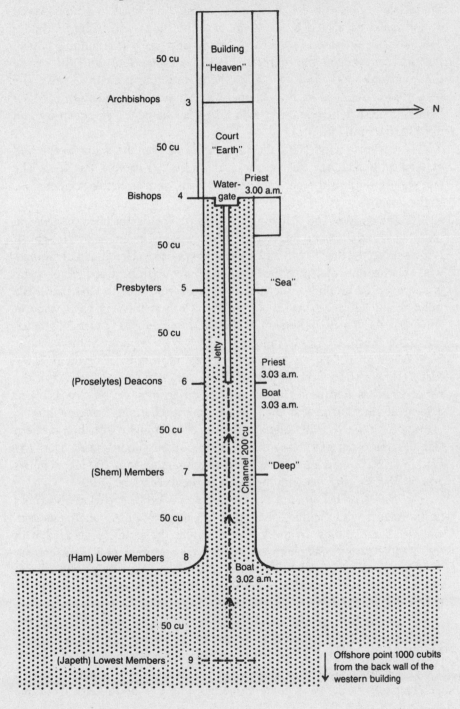

50 cu

Building "Heaven"

Archbishops 3

Court "Earth"

50 cu

Water-gate

Priest 3.00 a.m.

Bishops 4

50 cu

Presbyters 5

"Sea"

50 cu

Jetty

Priest 3.03 a.m.

(Proselytes) Deacons 6

Boat 3.03 a.m.

Channel 200 cu

50 cu

(Shem) Members 7

"Deep"

50 cu

(Ham) Lower Members 8

Boat 3.02 a.m.

50 cu

N

(Japeth) Lowest Members 9

Offshore point 1000 cubits from the back wall of the western building

50 cubit segments, the western one being mostly occupied by the building. These two segments were, it appears, counted as equal to grades 3 and 4, and could be visited by cardinals or archbishops and bishops. Grades 3, 4 and 5 were classed as "heaven", "earth" and "sea". The building (where the priest prayed on the roof, Mk 2:1-12), was "heaven", and the rest of the courtyard was "earth" or "land" (*hē gē* meaning both in Greek). The first, shallow segment of the channel was "the sea" (*hē thalassa*), used for baptising presbyters, grade 5. It was here that the boat was drawn up and used for teaching (Mk 4:1).

A narrow jetty, 100 cubits long, ran out over the water to the end of segment 6. The next segment was "the deep" (*to bathos*), for Shem. The last segment within the channel was for Ham, and Japheth's segment was in the open sea.

The story of the "catching" of Titus, the leader of Ham, is given in Lk 5:1-11, and its later stage, after three years, is given in Jn 21:1-14. It is to be suspected that Titus (Gal 2:1) was Marsyas, a loyal freedman of Agrippa, who was instrumental in borrowing money for Agrippa from Protos (who is suggested to be Philip, the head of Shem) (*Ant.* 18:155, 204, 228). His influence in Agrippa's household would have been of very great value in spreading the Christian version of the doctrine. He was "caught" by Peter, under the direction of Jesus, in June AD 30. For the ceremony of his washing, Peter was told to take his boat down to the beginning of segment 7, the "deep", where there was no jetty (Lk 5:4). He then had to "let down the nets". Titus, washed in sea water, was drawn up into the boat, possibly in a form of sling. The boat then sailed up the channel, bringing him to "salvation". It was a rich "catch", because Titus brought with him western Gentiles, the order of Ham and also Japheth, their subordinates. The "153 fish" of Jn 21:11 meant a Gentile celibate community, with 100 full members and 50 novices, together with the heads of the three racial groups.

With the "fisherman", Peter, there was another superior who could be in contact with Gentiles, a woman (see page 308). As uncircumcised, she was like Gentiles. In the gospel of Philip the point is made that in the original system Gentiles were headed by a Mother only, and had no male priest to touch them, no "Father". "When we were Hebrews we were orphans, and had only our mother, but when we became Christians we had both father and mother" (*GPhil* 52:20-25).

During the gospel period, higher privileges were given to the uncircumcised. They received a "Father" in the person of Jonathan Annas, from the family of priests who particularly encouraged Gentiles.

Jonathan took part in the ceremony at Mazin, when the uncircumcised were baptised in the early hours of the morning by working men. He came to the end of the jetty to line 6, wearing heavy priest's vestments, unlike the working men who did the actual work, either naked from the waist up or wearing a baptismal garment (Jn 21:7). His privileged status aroused some resentment from the missionaries, who said that by using the jetty he was "walking on water".

As seen in Chapter 18, Jesus, in claiming the position of a priest like Annas, adopted this part of his role also. He acted as Father, coming out along the jetty to the boat. He was thus "walking on water", causing controversy, not by a miracle, but by acting as a full priest.

Matthew's gospel shows that Peter tried to walk on water also, but was in danger of "falling into the sea" (Mt 14:30). As he himself was Jesus' "crown prince" he could act as a Second to him, standing with him. But he was impeded by his sympathy for the circumcision requirement, the "millstone" (mylos, a play of words on Hebrew mūl, "to circumcise") which was tied around the neck of Gentiles, causing them to "fall into the sea" (Mt 18:6, using the same verb as in Mt 14:30).

The 3 a.m. ceremony, at the time when village workers arose, would have been carried out with the aid of oil lamps. The parable of the ten virgins in Mt 25:1–13 shows the use of such lamps at midnight by women, who were equal to Gentiles. The lamps remained associated with the Christian "fish", being used in hundreds in the catacombs in Rome to light the underground passages.

It has been shown in the Chronology section that very exact timings were applied to the walk along the jetty and the meeting with the fishing boat. If it came from Ain Feshkha, it arrived at a point 1000 cubits offshore from Mazin at 5 minutes before the hour, (3 a.m.). The boat's rate of travel was 100 cubits per minute, as it covered 6000 cubits (15 stadia) in 60 minutes, three times the walking rate. The 1000 cubits were measured from the western extremity of Mazin, so that the first 100 cubits was on land, then 100 cubits to the end of the jetty on line 6, then 800 cubits more. The 800 cubits to the jetty were covered by the boat in 8 minutes, so that it arrived at 3.03 a.m. At the same moment, the priest, having set out from the watergate at 3 a.m., and covering the 100 cubit jetty at the walking rate of 100 cubits per 3 minutes, arrived at the end of the jetty, and performed the ceremony for the arriving boat without delay. (In Mk 6:48, peri tetartēn phylakēn "about the fourth watch", means 3.03 a.m., as peri "about" has the pesher sense of 3 minutes past the hour, and the fourth watch of the night began at 3 a.m.)

Matthew refines the point by showing that at 3 a.m. the boat was at 400 cubits, 1 stadion, from the watergate (Mt 14:24). This stadion, the last, was the zero, so polloi, a word meaning zero from the system of prayer hours (see pages 335, 351, 359) and it also meant Herod who was the main subject of washings at Mazin.

In the account of the arrival of the ship at Malta in A 27:28, the same pattern is used on a larger scale. The approach began at midnight.

In each hour the depth of the water reduced by 5 fathoms (30 feet, 10 yards, 20 cubits). At midnight the depth was 20 fathoms, at 1 a.m. 15 fathoms (A 27:28), at 2 a.m. 10 fathoms and at 3 a.m., 5 fathoms, the last two stages assumed from symmetry. Thereafter, it was shallow water, and A 27:30–32 deals with the debate on how to proceed, using the different kinds of boats in a double sense.

The numerous episodes in the gospels and Acts dealing with sailing and boats reflect, not simply the necessities of travel, but the set of images used in foreign mission for the lowly class of "fish". When they eventually came to "land", taking over from their Jewish missionaries and becoming ministers in their own right, they would form the Christian Church.

FURTHER DETAIL OF LOCATIONS

Terms for North, South, East and West
Four Greek prepositions, apparently having indefinite meanings, have a precise sense in the pesher, referring to the four compass points. They are:

enōpion	"north"
enantion	"south"
emprosthen	"east"
opisō	"west"

Emprosthen, in its surface sense, means "in front of" and *opisō* means "behind". In Hebrew the directions were taken while facing east, so that the word for "in front of" (*qedem*) also meant the east, and the word for "behind" (*achrith*) also meant the west.

Enōpion and *enantion* have the surface sense "before", "in the sight of".

The words are important indicators. Thus, when Mary Magdalene turned *eis ta opisō* (Jn 20:14, normally meaning "back") the pesher sense is that she turned "to the west". She was in the eastern cave, Cave 7, and now turned and went into the western cave, Cave 8. At the trial of Jesus, Peter stood *emprosthen*, apparently "before", but in the pesher sense on the east side of centre (see above, page 322).

Rates of Travel

Rates of travel are deduced from the locations and the times. They were:

On foot, on a wilderness road	5 stadia per hour
On foot, on a good road	10 stadia per hour
By boat, on the Dead Sea	15 stadia per hour
By donkey	15 stadia per hour
By horse	75 stadia per hour

Appendix III

HIERARCHY

On the surface, the gospels and Acts appear to deal with unlimited numbers of people and many different individuals. Jesus teaches "many", or "crowds", or "a multitude". There are individuals without clear delineation, and individuals called by a feature but not named: a leper, a blind man, a lame man. Leaders appear in groups: "the chief priests", "the scribes". The reader is left with a feeling that the identity of individuals other than Jesus is of little importance to the history, and that curiosity about them cannot be satisfied.

By the application of the pesher technique that has been described, however, a very definite set of individuals emerges, and of a limited number. Jesus was interacting, in the wilderness centres, with individual men who had come to the quarterly councils as representatives of numbers of other people. Some were treated as if the whole group they represented were present. "The chief priests" (*hoi archiereis*) were incorporated in one man, the head of a group of twelve, and he alone is meant when the term is used. Similarly "the scribes" (*hoi grammateis*), and "the Pharisees" (*hoi Pharisaioi*) refer to one man each.

"The Many", and "the crowds" were one man only, an important figure who represented a very large class. When Jesus was teaching "the crowds", he was instructing one person, who would pass on what he had learned to the whole class.

Each "leper" or "blind man" is a nameable individual, once the system is understood that put all lepers, real or metaphorical, into a fixed class under a representative leader who was called after his class.

The figures who were really important in the history, often more influential than Jesus, are called by a number of different pseudonyms. Similarly, in the Dead Sea Scrolls Jesus is called by about five different pseudonyms.

One of the methods of discovering these individuals is to observe repetitions in actions or features.

For example, Simon Magus, the most powerful figure of all, is identified through the series of episodes concerning the woman with the flask of ointment. In John's gospel, she appears in the house of Lazarus of Bethany (Jn 11:2, 12:3-8); in Mark, in the house of Simon, the leper of Bethany (Mk 14:3-9); in Luke, in the house of Simon the Pharisee (Lk 7:36-50). So, using the assumptions of the pesharist, Simon-Lazarus-the leper are all the same man, and he is also Lazarus, the leper of Luke's parable, as all parables concern real people (Lk 16:19-31). He is also the "leper" who was told by Jesus to keep certain laws of washing but who did not, since this feature appears for the leper in Mk 1:40-45 and Simon the Pharisee in Lk 7:44-46. As Lazarus was excommunicated, and both Jesus and Lazarus were threatened with further excommunication by the "chief priests" (Jn 11:1-53, 12:9-11), he was of equal importance with Jesus. A member of the Twelve Apostles was Simon the Zealot (Lk 6:15), and Jesus was crucified with two "thieves", who cannot have been simply thieves, as Roman law did not prescribe the death penalty for theft. Zealotry, however, was a crime against which Pilate would have acted in person. Simon-Lazarus, threatened with Jesus at the season of the crucifixion, was the "Pharisee" crucified with him, the one to whom Jesus spoke with words implying a resurrection (Lk 23:40-43). (Resurrection was a distinctive belief of the Pharisees, held against Sadducees, A 23:6-8. On this question Simon was also a "Pharisee".)

At the crosses stood the woman called Salome in Mk 15:40, Joanna in Lk 24:10, and the Mother of the sons of Zebedee in Mt 27:56. Under the latter name she also appears in Mt 20:20. Zebedee must have been her "husband" in some sense. In Mk 1:19-20 James and John left "their father Zebedee in the boat with the hired servants" and turned to following Jesus. James and John with Jesus showed themselves strongly opposed to Samaritans, wanting to act like Elijah to punish them (Lk 9:52-55). Jesus rebuked them, and allowed an alliance with a Samaritan leper who returned to thank him (Lk 17:11-17).

A Samaritan woman appears in Jn 4:4-42. She is accused of immorality, and of now having a man who is not an *anēr* (married man) (v. 18).

Jesus was crucified with a "Simon-Lazarus the leper", as seen above, and Mary Magdalene was present at the cross to support Jesus. She was the woman with ointment in the house of Simon-Lazarus the leper, and with her was associated Martha (Jn 11:1, 12:2-3, Lk 10:38-42). At the time of the release of Lazarus, Martha took the lead in asking Jesus to help him, while Mary stayed behind (Jn 11:20-27). Jesus and Mary, and Martha and Simon-Lazarus, appear as two pairs.

Martha was therefore "Salome" at the cross, as the third woman was Mary the mother of Jesus (Mk 15:40, Jn 19:25, where "Mary of Cleopas" is introduced but she was the woman betrothed to James-Cleopas, Lk 24:18). She was the Mother of the "sons of Zebedee", who had left their Father and become opposed to Samaritans. "Zebedee" was another name, then, for Simon-Lazarus-the Samaritan "leper".

In Acts 8 appears Simon Magus the Samaritan, offering Peter money in return for the right to "give the holy spirit", that is, to ordain ministers. Peter condemned him vehemently (vv. 21-22). Peter had previously condemned Ananias and Sapphira for financial wrongdoing (A 5:1-11). Simon is said to act as a magician (*mageuōn*, A 8:9).

There is a parallel condemnation by Paul of the magician (*ho magos*) Elymas or Bar-Jesus on Cyprus (A 13:7-12). Both Peter and Paul were leaders of the Christians in Acts, and a man they opposed must have had equal status. Both of them had previously been partly or wholly against Jesus (Peter by denying him at the crucifixion), and Jesus had been associated with the Samaritan Simon-Lazarus-leper.

The picture thus emerges of a powerful leader, Simon, a "magician", who had been an associate of Jesus, whose companion was Martha-Salome-the Samaritan woman-Sapphira, whom Jesus was against on certain matters, as James and John left this pair to follow Jesus, but in sympathy with on other matters, so that Peter and Paul had opposed both Jesus and Simon. The picture is clarified and confirmed by the Clementine books (*Homilies* and *Recognitions*) the subject of which is doctrinal disputations between Peter and Simon Magus, matters of the greatest importance. Simon had a companion, a woman named Helena. He and Helena acted as charismatic figures, attracting followers to their gnostic teachings. Simon acted as a hellenistic thaumaturge, claiming to be able to perform magical actions (*Clem. Hom.* 2:24,26).

Simon had been the teacher of two young Romans named Niceta and Aquila, who had come under the care of the Syro-Phoenician woman. She had asked Simon to instruct them, but they had then left him and turned to Zacchaeus (*Clem. Hom.* 2:19-21). These two become, in the gospels, James and John of Zebedee, and Aquila appears later in Acts under his Roman name (A 18:2).

The foregoing is an illustration of the method by which the personalities and the system of hierarchy are discovered. It runs contrary to modern critical method, which depends on an assumption of the gospels as the deposits of stories arising from the growth of tradition, without control. It is not always logical, but depends on strong and persistent associations, an interlocking set of clues which ultimately give a total and consistent history. The analogy of a jigsaw puzzle lies close. The "proof" is in the final success of the method. A clear and integrated picture emerges, leaving no doubt that the whole process was intended.

The basis and much detail of the hierarchy may now be set out.

DETAILS OF THE HIERARCHY (see Table I)

There was originally a total of 16 positions, numbered 0 to 15. The supreme high priest was the zero. He officiated to perform the atonement only once a year (Heb 9:7, *Mishnah Yoma*).

The first 12 positions were for men, and the lowest 4 for women. Uncircumcised Gentiles had the same status as women.

Each position was known by a letter of the Hebrew alphabet, starting from the last letter, *Taw*. These also stood for the grades of promotion (see further below, page 371). For the benefit of Greeks, numbers were also used. The man in position 7 was known as "the Seven" (*hoi hepta*), in position 10 "the Ten" (*hoi deka*) and so on (Lk 17:17 *hoi ennea*; A 2:14, *hoi endeka*; Jn 6:70, *hoi dōdeka*).

Each of the priestly grades was associated with a day of the week, and also with hours of the day, being responsible for prayers at these appointed times.

The system included the emblems of the four "living creatures" of Ezek 1:5–10, and also Rev 4:6–7. They were associated with the four essential persons in the hierarchy, the three active priests and the king.

The Three Leading Priests

Under King David there had been three main priestly dynasties, those of Zadok, Abiathar, and Levi (2 Sam 20:25-26). One of the main purposes of the Essenes was to preserve these lines and to bring them back to power in the Jerusalem temple. 1QM 17:2-3 shows their loyalty to the old families: "[But Eleazar] and Ithamar (names for the Zadok and Abiathar families, 1 Chron 24:2-3) he confirmed in an everlasting [priestly] Covenant".

Under the growing influence of Iranian thought in the intertestamental period, the heads of the dynasties had come to be called by the names of the archangels, in the belief that they were incarnations of heavenly figures. The book of Enoch gives the original system of archangels (for example, 1 *Enoch* 4:9), and in 1QM 9:15-17 their names and order are

Table I HIERARCHY

Office	Pos-ition	Hebrew Letter and Number	Day	Hours of Prayer	Emblem or Category	Name as Minister	Davids as lay Priests	Herods	Represen-tatives of Herod	
MICHAEL	0	Taw 400	Sat	6–6 12–12				Herod		
GABRIEL	1	Shin 300	Sun	7–7 1–1	MAN			Herod		
SARIEL	2	Resh 200	Mon	8–8 2–2	EAGLE		Son of man	Herod	ABRAHAM (Benjamin)	
RAPHAEL	3	Qof 100	Tue Fri	9–9 3–3	CALF	Cardinal Archbishop	King C.Prince	Herod	ISAAC (W.Manasseh)	
KOHATH	4	Sadhe 90	Wed	10–10 4–4	Dove	Bishop	C.Prince	ESAU C.Prince	Scribe (E.Manasseh)	
GERSHON	5	Pe 80	Thu	11–11 5–5	Raven	Presbyter	Prince	Prince		
MERARI	6	Ayin 70			Cock	Deacon	Prince	Prince		
KING	7	Samekh 60			LION	Member	Prince	Prince		
C.PRINCE	8	Nun 50				Novice				
PRINCE	9	Mem 40				Lower Novice				
PRINCE Guest	10	Lamedh 30			Poor					
GUEST	11	Kaph 20			Crippled					
MOTHER Proselyte	12	Yod 10			Blind					
VIRGIN Shem	13	Tet 9			Lame					
WIDOW Ham	14	Heth 8								
WIFE Japheth	15	Zayin 7								

Abbreviations

C. Prince: Crown Prince   Circ.cel: Circumcised celibate   Circ. mar: Circumcised married

Davids with Herod	Asher Gentiles with Herod	Dan Gentiles with Herod	Asher Gentiles with Jesus	Dan Gentiles with Jesus	Twelve Apostles Lay Members	Twelve Apostles Levitical Members	Twelve Apostles Guest
					JESUS		
					JESUS		
					JESUS	JON.ANNAS	
						S.MAGUS	
JACOB 1 of Ephraim			Circ.cel. 1000		PETER	MATTHEW or JUDAS	THOMAS
JOSEPH 2 C.Prince			Circ.mar 2000			THEUDAS	
Prince 3			"Gentiles" 3000	Proselytes	J.MARK		
Prince 4	Circ.cel. 1000		Uncirc.cel 4000	Shem	ANDREW PHILIP		
	Circ.mar. 2000		Uncirc.mar 5000	Ham	(JAMES Z) JOHN Z		
	"Gentiles" 3000	Proselytes		Japheth			
	Uncirc.cel 4000	Shem					
	Uncirc.mar 5000	Ham					
		Japheth					

given in the form used in the gospel period. "On the first (shield) Michael, [on the second, Gabriel, on the third] Sariel, and on the fourth, Raphael. Michael and Gabriel [shall stand on the right, and Sariel and Raphael on the left]".

Josephus notes that in their vows of initiation Essenes swear to preserve "the names of the angels" (*War* 2:142).

The head of the Zadokite dynasty was called Michael. He appears in Rev 6:7, "Michael and his angels fighting against the dragon", a passage dealing with the conflict between Zechariah, father of John the Baptist, the current Zadokite, with the public high priest Joazar in AD 6. Zechariah is shown by Luke to have been a descendant of Zadok (Lk 1:5, cf. 1 Chron 24:10, 4). John the Baptist was his heir, so, as the Teacher of Righteousness, he was called the Priest (1QpHab 2:8, 4QpPss 2:18).

His Second (*mishneh*), the Abiathar priest, was called Gabriel. The word means "[strong] Man of God"; he was the Man of the four "living creatures". The head of this dynasty in the time of Archelaus was Simon the Essene (*Ant.* 17:346–347), called Simeon in Lk 2:25. He appears as the "angel" Gabriel in Lk 1:11–19, acting as the second to Zechariah on the Day of Atonement, preparing to step into his place when Zechariah left for marriage. He was the most prominent Essene of his time, and initially became involved with the coalition that had reoccupied Qumran, helping to form a peace party with Ananus in AD 5. But in AD 6 he separated, "departing in peace" (Lk 2:29), taking the classical Essenes away from Qumran to continue their separate history. Other men then took the positions of both Michael and Gabriel. Simon was also called "Moses", as the highest priest was an "Aaron" and his Second, the Prophet-levite, a "Moses". He is the subject of the typological history in A 7:20–43.

Sariel was the third, according to the 1QM list, and the leader of a lower group who were placed on the inferior left. The name means "Prince of God", and he was the priest over the class of kings and rulers, which was essentially lay. This man was the Levi priest, acting as the representative of the priestly tribe of Levi who had been dominant in the nomad period of Israelite history but had been reduced in status when the nation turned to agriculture and the solar priests. His dynasty had used a lunar calendar, and in the ascetic coalition adopted the lunisolar form of the solar calendar. They had become the third level of priests, called the "king's priest" (2 Sam 20:26). Their representative under King David had been Ira the Jairite, indicating an Elijah connection (cf. Jud 10:3, 1 K 17:1). The name "Jairus" is used in the gospels for the head of the dynasty (Mk 5:22). He is also called Levi (of Alphaeus) (Mk 2:14).

He went between monastery and villages, coming as the visiting priest to villages on great occasions such as feasts. The emblem Eagle was appropriate; he is called the "flying eagle" in Rev 4:7. His ascetic tradition was an individual one, not coenobitic; he was over the class of hermits who practised varying degrees of discipline in isolation. The Wilderness area around Mird was the place where this kind of life was practised. "Elijah" was its model, the hermits wearing the hair shirt and leather belt of Elijah (2 K 1:8). (When John the Baptist separated from the classical Essenes with their monastic tradition, he adoped the individual eremitical style of life, so was like an "Elijah", Mk 1:6, but at the same time denied that he was "Elijah", Jn 1:21; the title belonged to the village priest.)

In his priestly role he was called the Chief Priest, rather than the high priest (*kohen harosh*, 1QM 2:1, not *kohen gadol*). The term *hoi archiereis*, "the chief priests" refers to him in its pesher sense, as a plural means an individual who was head of a class.

The Chief Priest in the gospel period was Jonathan Annas, one of the sons of the Ananus who had become public high priest under the Romans in AD 6. Living as individuals and using also a lunar calendar, the men of his family could become public high priests over all Jews. One of the main issues among Jews in the first century AD was the question of the high priests, as each was associated with a major political faction. The Annas brothers were supported by those Jews who favoured co-operation with Rome. Five brothers all held the position for a short time (*Ant.* 18:34, 95, 123, 19:316, 20:197, 20:198). They stood for western ways rather than eastern, and were willing to accept Gentiles who were attracted to Judaism but did not want to adopt the ritual law. It was during their reigns, especially that of Matthew Annas (high priest AD 42-43), that the liberalised form of Judaism that became Christianity flourished.

The three leading priests were called Father, Son, and Spirit, and the Annas priest was the Spirit (*to pneuma*, or, in a higher status, the Holy Spirit, *to pneuma to hagion*). The pattern of three was repeated in the village, so that the Chief Priest and the two levites below him were also called Father, Son and Spirit (the last in a different form of the Greek, *to hagion pneuma*). Thus Annas was both Father, and the Holy Spirit (in Lk 10:21, Jesus prays to the Father, rejoicing in the Holy Spirit).

To the villagers, the Chief Priest was "God". The Annas brothers, in tune with Hellenist thought, were prepared to encourage the idea that the priest was an incarnation of God. Prayers were offered to him as standing in the place of God. He stood on the roof of the village buildings, offering prayers to heaven at noon, while the villagers glimpsed him in his glory. When the three hour period was over, he was let down in his palanquin to the ground floor, there to receive the petitions, and the tithes, of villagers.

His use of a palanquin (*krabbaton*, "bed") led to his being called a "paralytic" by critics of his high style (Mk 2:3–12).

He was also called "the Lord" (*ho kyrios*), originally because he, as the Levi priest, was the representative of God under the name Yahweh, the name used by nomads; translated as the Lord in the Greek Old Testament. When Jesus said "I am" (Jn 18:5,8) (Yahweh, Ex 3:14), he was again borrowing one of the titles of Annas, and causing further offence.

Both titles, "Lord" and "God" had been taken by the original Ananus to the highest position when he replaced Zechariah in AD 6 (A 7:32, 33). His taking the place of Michael meant that the monastic form of ascetic discipline was no longer practised in the Mird-Qumran coalition; only varying degrees of individual discipline.

Other names for Jonathan Annas were Nathanael (Jn 1:45), a Hebrew variant of Jonathan ("Yahweh/God gave"); and Dositheus, a Greek form of the word. The latter name is used for him in the Clementine literature, as the man who first succeeded John the Baptist before Simon Magus displaced him (*Clem. Rec.* 2:8). In this source he is said to be a Sadducee (*Clem. Rec.* 1:54). The Annas family were Sadducees, but in the pesher only the last, Ananus the Younger, is called a Sadducee (A 5:17), as by his grade he was fully in the world, where party names were applied.

Priest, Prophet, King. First, Second, Third
The leaders of the hierarchy were always thought of in groups of three, because three priests were essential for the rite of atonement, the central rite in the pre-Christian form of the community.

The position of the Second is well documented. The *Mishnah* (*Yoma* 1:1) describes orthodox Jewish practice on the Day of Atonement: "Seven days before the Day of Atonement the high priest was taken apart from his own house into the counsellors' chamber and another priest was made ready in his stead lest anything should befall him to make him ineligible." In 5 BC the high priest Matthias had become ineligible because on the night preceding the day on which the fast occurred, he had "seemed in a dream to have intercourse with a woman", and another high priest had to be appointed for one day to take his place (*Ant.* 17:165–166).

In Lk 1:11–20, the Zadokite Zechariah was performing the Day of Atonement ceremony before leaving to marry. His subordinate, "Gabriel" (the Second to Michael in 1QM 9:15–16) was standing by in order to take his place. "Gabriel" was standing *ek dexion* (Lk 1:11), a phrase meaning the far right, the place of the Levite (page 423).

The man in the position of "Gabriel" was called the Second (Heb. *mishneh*), a term found in 1QM 2:1 and 11QT 31:4. Another name was the

Levite, the next in rank below Michael, the Priest (1QpHab 2:8).

There was also, it appears, a Third, since, if the Second stepped up to replace the high priest, his own place needed to be taken by another.

In 1QS 8:1, the hierarchy is said to contain "three priests and twelve men". The three priests gave the basic pattern, which was reproduced for the leaders in other hierarchical formations.

The original three were Michael, Gabriel and Sariel. Sariel was the "Prince of God", and, as the king's priest, could take on royal functions. Gabriel could be called "Moses", as seen above (page 338), and Moses was called the Prophet (Deut 18:15). Thus the three leaders could be thought of as the Priest, the Prophet, and the King. This formula became especially appropriate when the David rose to be equal to the village priest (see below, p. 348).

The three priests could also be called "Father, Son and Spirit", as seen above.

The Four Chief Levites

Levites were the class under the priests, the successors of subordinate priests in the Jerusalem temple. Their second position is emphasised in 1QS 1:21–2:10, CD 14:3–4. It was the class of levites who did the more menial work in the temple. In the liturgy described in 1QS 1–2, they uttered the curses on sinners, while the priests uttered blessings on the righteous.

There were four levitical positions in the hierarchy, numbered 3 to 6, making a total of seven priests and levites to correspond to the days of the week.

Their leader was called Raphael, the fourth and lowest of the priests in the list of 1QM. He stood between priests and levites, and in practice was the most powerful person in the village. His title was "son of Levi" as he was the subordinate of Levi, the Chief Priest, and "son of" meant the grade below. In 1QSa 1:22–29 the duties of the "sons of Levi" are described. They are to "hold office under the authority of the sons of Aaron", and "cause all the congregation to come in and go out" (a phrase reflected in A 9:28). They were to direct all religious assemblies, and perform the sanctifications during the three Preparation Days preceding a great council.

One of the important rules of the hierarchy is that the man in a position that was three grades below another was the servant of the other. Number 3 was the servant of number 0, number 4 the servant of number 1, and so on. The reason was that a servant must stand with a yard, 2 cubits, between himself and his master, literally at arm's length. The man standing on cubit 4 had two cubits, 3 and 2, between himself and cubit 1. This was in order to observe the hierarchical rule for which the Essenes were noted: "a senior if but touched by a junior, must take a bath, as if after contact with an alien" (*War* 2:150).

This rule meant that Raphael, number 3, was the servant of Michael, number 0.

Related to the rule was another, that the superior could, on occasions, come down to the level of his servant, being then "in the body" (*sōmatikō*, Lk 3:22). In the sanctuary he was like a divine person, but once he came into the vestry and changed out of his vestments into ordinary clothes, following the rule of Ezek 44:19, he was "in the body". This meant that he wore coloured garments in place of the white linen robes he used in the sanctuary (Ezek 44:17). It had come to be the practice, as 1QM 7:10-11 shows, that the priests' colours, scarlet, purple and blue (Ex 28:5-6) were worn outside the sanctuary. "These (coloured garments) shall be battle raiment; they shall not take them into the sanctuary" (1QM 7:11-12).

It appears that the colours also were hierarchically graded, so that Michael "in the body" was characterised by scarlet, Gabriel by purple, and Sariel by blue. Scarlet was worn by both Michael "in the body" and by Raphael his servant, of the same status. Thus Raphael occupied a position that eventually became that of a Christian cardinal. When certain other men who had not been born priests took the role (called by their opponents "scarlet beasts") the name "cardinal" developed. One of Raphael's many duties was that of directing the times at the four different compass points, north, south, east and west, which are still called the cardinal points. (The word comes from Latin *cardo* "hinge". Villagers, whose superior was Raphael, used imagery connected with a door, for the reason given below, page 373.)

As the servant and executive of Michael, Raphael carried out the actual work of directing prayers at the major divisions of time, 6 a.m., 6 p.m., noon and midnight.

While he directed the 6-6 and 12-12 points of time on behalf of Michael, his own grade, number 3, meant that he must also pray at the third hour, 9 a.m. and 9 p.m., and 3 p.m. and 3 a.m. Thus he was responsible for all eight divisions of the 24 hours.

As a number 3 his day of the week was Tuesday, but, since he also prayed at the sixth hour, he also was associated with Friday, the day when work must be completed before rest on the sabbath. As Tuesdays and Fridays were significant days for solarists, being the days when 31sts fell at the Day and Night positions of the calendar respectively (see Chronology, page 179), Raphael was thus assigned to the two most important days after Saturday.

Raphael was, in fact, the centre of the human clock, and as active executive working for a distant superior, was thought of as "the Power", a name that was later used for the cardinal in his position (A 8:10).

Because he represented the Priest, Michael, Raphael himself was called the Priest. The word *ho hiereus* ("the priest") refers, in the pesher, to the holder of this office, whereas *ho archiereus* or its plural form means the Chief Priest, the Sariel one grade above, who only came to the village as a visiting priest.

As Raphael slept at midnight, his work at that hour was done by another man, one using the ancient emblem of the black Calf. He dressed in black, not scarlet, and his position became that of an archbishop.

The three lower members of the levitical class were the holders of the offices of Kohath, Gershon, and Merari. They were subordinates of the sons of Levi, appointed to do the physical work of the sanctuary. Their names and order of precedence are given in Num 4, and they appear in the Temple Scroll, in positions additional to those of the heads of the twelve tribes (11QT 44:14).

Kohath, number 4, was the servant of Gabriel, number 1, and was associated with the colour purple. He established the position of bishop, which was later taken up by a layman. His position is called that of "a levite" in A 4:36 (*leuitēs*, no article). This was because he was the servant of Gabriel, whose position in the top hierarchy was that of the Levite to the Priest, Michael. (Another important rule is that the word without an article means the position of the servant, three below the master.)

Gershon, number 5, servant of Sariel, was the original presbyter, wearing blue. (The word *presbyteros* was used in Greek to translate the Hebrew *zaqen* "elder", but the office developed into that of Christian priest, whereas the word "elder" means only a layman, so "presbyter" is used here.)

Merari, number 6 in the hierarchy, was too lowly to be associated with a day of the week or an hour, being treated as standing between levites and laity. His position became that of deacon.

Kohath, Gershon and Merari were ruled by Levi, the Chief Priest, according to biblical law. Levi, or Sariel, was also the Eagle, and they were given the emblems of birds to show the relationship. Kohath, as the highest, was the white Dove, Gershon the black Raven, and Merari the domestic Cock. The Dove and the Raven were associated with the Noah-Flood imagery later used in the admissions of Gentiles (Gen 6:6-8). Gershon, the Raven, as a number 5 was the servant of number 2, Sariel, who was also called "Elijah". Ravens acted as the servants of Elijah (1 K 17:4,6).

In the village, Sariel was the Father, Raphael the Son, and Kohath the Spirit (in the form *to hagion pneuma*, Mt 28:19). As Kohath was the Dove, there came to be an association between the Holy Spirit and the Dove.

In the gospel period, the positions of Kohath and Merari were held by two of the Annas brothers under the superior Annas, Jonathan. Matthew Annas was Kohath, the levitical bishop, and the youngest brother, called Ananus the Younger (also Zacchaeus) was Merari. The position of Gershon was held by a layman.

Two of the "birds" were in charge of the lesser watches of the night, 9 p.m. to midnight (Raven) and 3 to 6 a.m. (Cock). Thus 3 a.m. was the "cockcrowing" (Mk 13:35).

Merari was given all the lowliest levitical tasks (Num 4:31-32) and in a celibate community which rated the body as low his work included supervision of physical matters. One of his tasks was to ensure that the sabbath latrine was kept closed from Friday evening to Saturday afternoon, as has been seen. He acted as the Guard, the Jailer, over such matters. By an extension of the meaning, natural to the celibates, he also guarded the "prison": that is, the institution of marriage. Those men who had been bound by the second wedding were in "prison" (*phylakē*). The man who performed weddings was the deacon, or a superior reduced to his position.

The Laity: King and Princes
In the original form of the hierarchy, King David was ranked below all priests and levites, being the representative of the laity. That the laity, "the sons of Israel", ranked third, is shown clearly in CD 14:4, 1QS 2:19-21 and 1QS 6:8-9. The king, long associated with the emblem of the Lion of Judah, was the chief Beast, first among the married classes. His grade was no higher than 7, the grade for full initiation preceding education. The number 7 indicated that he also was associated with the sabbath, like Michael, but he was the man who, if necessary, must break the sabbath. He was the leader in war (one of the primary functions of the king) and must, if necessary, fight on the sabbath. Thus his position already made him an anti-priestly figure. It was later taken by a "Satan" (Judas Iscariot), who was associated with the number 7 (Lk 8:2, Rev 13:1). See also 1 Pet 5:8 "your adversary the devil walks around like a roaring lion".

He was required to have sons, acting according to the rules of the Essene dynastic order. Married (according to Essene celibate rules) at age 36, he theoretically had time to beget at least four sons, even though he waited six years between births; his wife was usually under 20 at the time of her marriage. Two sons, with an optional third, were allowed for in the hierarchy, occupying positions 8, 9 and 10. The crown prince in position 8 was equal to a higher novice, in the year before full initiation. He acted as a Second to his father, and could fill his place when the need arose.

The next prince was equal to a lower novice, and the third, if there was one, was equal to a pre-novice, during his year outside the community.

The Lowest Class: "Sojourners"
According to CD 14:4 there was a fourth ranking of members of the camps, the "sojourners" (gēr). These were persons who were not members of the hierarchy but were associated with them. Position 10 (if there was no third prince) and position 11 were for guests (gēr) who were sometimes invited to Essene village meals in the evening. As Josephus says, "Any guests who may have arrived sit down with them" (War 2:132). They were allowed to stay for the common part of the meal, but, when a sacred two hours were added, were required to leave.

The next four positions were for women, in their ranking. A Mother was considered the highest, then a Virgin, then a Widow, while a mere Wife was the last. They occupied positions 12 to 15.

When Gentiles were added to the membership, they were at first assigned to positions equal to guests or, if uncircumcised, to women. A circumcised celibate Gentile was the highest, position 10; then came a circumcised married Gentile, 11; then an uncircumcised proselyte, equal to a Mother, 12; then the uncircumcised in their nationalities, Shem, Ham and Japheth, 13, 14, 15. It was for this reason that John Mark, the chief proselyte in the gospel period, was called "the Twelve" (hoi dōdeka), and also "the Beloved", as he shared the rank of the Mother, the first woman.

THE HOLY TABLE
It was the duty of priests to eat the twelve loaves of the Presence which were set out every day before God (Lev 24:5-9). The twelve male positions corresponded to the twelve loaves. In the time of King David, the Abiathar priest (Ahimelech, see 1 Chron 24:1-3) had allowed David and his men to eat five of the loaves, on condition that they had "kept themselves from women" (1 Sam 21:1-6; see also Mk 2:25-26). A division of the loaves into a higher seven for the priests and levites and a lower five for the laity was thus established, the division that was maintained in the gospel period. The two "miraculous feedings" used five and seven "loaves" (Mk 6:38, 8:5).

The loaves were eaten in the vestry, where the priests "returned to the body". Two tables were originally established, a higher one for Michael, Gabriel and Sariel, and a lower one, near the edge of the dais (see page 323) for subordinates (Fig. 12). Both tables established a distance of two cubits between those on the north side and those on the south side, the required arm's length between master and servant. Opposite to Michael, Gabriel and Sariel at the higher table sat their servants: Raphael in the middle opposite Michael, Kohath on the east opposite Gabriel (the Man, associated with the superior east) and Gershon on the west opposite Sariel, (the Eagle, in the west).

But at the lower table, standing for the village, servants became masters. Raphael, Kohath and Gershon sat on the north side, and opposite them Merari, the king, and the crown prince.

When Sariel visited the village, carried on his palanquin, he took the place of Raphael, who normally acted as priest in the village. Sariel reclined rather than sat, so that his place had to be extended backwards by another cubit (Fig. 13). Raphael was obliged to go down to his status "in the body", sitting opposite Sariel in the position of deacon. Merari, who normally sat here, had to go outside the room altogether, acting as the doorkeeper outside the door. He took up his position at the northern one of the two pillar bases (see Locations, page 323). Zacchaeus-Merari-Ananus was standing in this position in the story in Lk 19:1-10. As having been "sent out" he was an "apostle" (apostolos, "sent out"). The position of "apostle" was derived from that of Merari.

Guests were admitted to the village table, as seen above, and the lower table in the vestry, as the model for all village tables, could be extended to admit them. A place was added on either side of its north, and corresponding places on the south for the servants of the guests, who had no number. Thus the table came to seat ten men (Fig. 13). The vestry was ten cubits wide, and at first the table may have stretched right across, with a broad allowance of two cubits for each person.

The Sanctification of the King and of the Village Table
Following this earliest form, a process began which led to a new understanding of the village table. It gave the form that was used at the Last Supper.

After the return from exile in the sixth century BC there was a brief period when the Zadokite priest and the David king were restored to office, in the persons of Joshua and Zerubbabel (Ezra 3:2, Zech 3-4). Their Persian overlords, however, imposed on them the condition that the king must give up his primary military role. Kings could become the centres of rebellion, and the Persians soon went further and abolished the kingship altogether. But while Joshua and Zerubbabel were in office, the David accepted that he ruled "not by might, nor by power, but by my Spirit" (Zech 4:6). He became a priestly figure, of the same status as Sariel, taking a position in the sanctuary. This is the meaning of the "apocalyptic" language of Zech 4:1-10, in which Zerubbabel is seen at the Menorah, within the Holy House, the outer chamber of the temple. "Apocalyptic" is here used to speak in a mysterious way about political realities, as also in the book of Revelation.

Fig. 12 **The Holy Tables**

SARIEL 2	MICHAEL 0	GABRIEL 1
HIGHER TABLE Priests		
GERSHON 5	RAPHAEL 3	KOHATH 4

(Presbyter)	(Cardinal)	(Bishop)
GERSHON 5	RAPHAEL 3	KOHATH 4
LOWER TABLE Village		
C. PRINCE 8	MERARI 6	KING 7
(Novice)	(Deacon)	(Member)

The David received "the Spirit", the status of Sariel, in a form of ordination; he was given priesthood by endowment, not by birth. This meant that he acted as a holy person, avoiding war, as priests did (see also 1QM 9:8, 4Q493). Such an attitude was acceptable to the Persians, helping to preserve the kingship for a time.

In his position as equal to a Sariel, the king used the title "Son of Man", as he was in the grade immediately below Gabriel, the Man. The son of Man in Dan 7:13–14 and 1 *Enoch* 46 is a king, acting with a priest who was in the place of God, the "Ancient of Days".

Over the subsequent centuries an institution of lay celibates developed, following the model of the sanctified king. Essenes, protecting the heirs of the great priestly and royal dynasties, and influenced by hellenistic thought, came to value the celibate life while preserving the dynasties through their second order (see Chapter 8). Holy laymen were like David and his men, who could eat the holy loaves while in a state of sexual abstinence.

A new pair of places was made at the village table, allowing the king to recline on a palanquin beside Sariel, with the crown prince, reduced to a deacon like Raphael, sitting opposite. Their former positions, 7 and 8, were taken by ordinary members or lower princes (see Fig. 14). Thus the table came to seat twelve, six on either side. One cubit's width only could be allowed for each person. In the vestry at Qumran, a partition marked off the first two cubits of the dais on the east, indicating that the table occupied six cubits of the width of the room.

Fig. 13 **Village Table with Guests**

		SARIEL 2		
GUEST 11	GERSHON 5	3	KOHATH 4	GUEST 10
SERVANT	C. PRINCE 8	RAPHAEL 6	KING 7	SERVANT

MERARI (Apostle)
9

Fig. 14 The King as Equal to the Priest at the Village Table

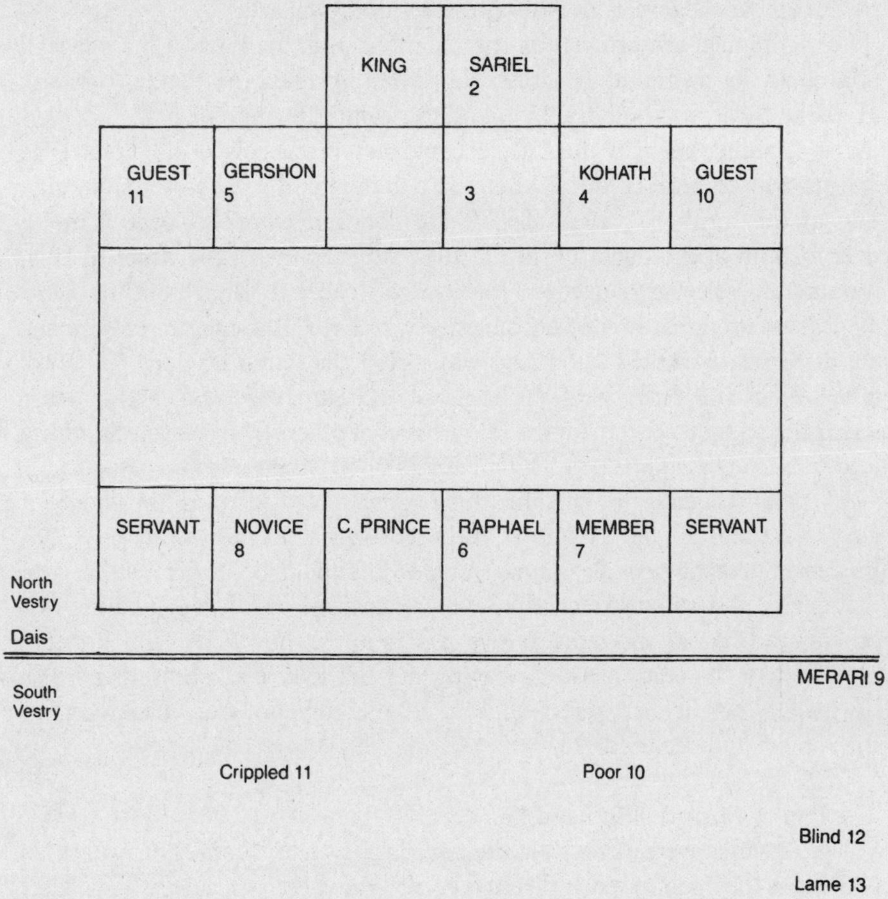

		KING	SARIEL 2		
GUEST 11	GERSHON 5		3	KOHATH 4	GUEST 10

North
Vestry

SERVANT	NOVICE 8	C. PRINCE	RAPHAEL 6	MEMBER 7	SERVANT

Dais

MERARI 9

South
Vestry

Crippled 11   Poor 10

Blind 12

Lame 13

As the institution of lay celibacy grew and diversified, several classes were formed. Vows of varying lengths were taken, indicating different degrees of discipline. Those who took the hardest and highest vows of periodic abstinence from marriage belonged to the Essene order of Judah, under the David, while those who took lesser degrees belonged to the order of Zebulun, whose meeting place was at the literal Nazareth in Galilee. Their superior was the David prince. As has been seen (page 295), they used the route from Mar Saba through the Wilderness, and were given the image of "sheep", as they were "shorn" on resumption of marriage.

Although the prince was the chief Nazirite, the king in his peaceful role could act under the Nazirite rule, so being called the "Lamb" (*arnion*). Thus the David was both the Lion and the Lamb (Rev 5:5-7).

Another man in the village could act in the place of Raphael, as if he were a levitical cardinal. This was a graduate of a celibate community, one of the "orphans", often illegitimate children who had been handed over at birth and brought up to the higher discipline of the order of Levi, renouncing marriage altogether. He also was called a "lamb", but the word *amnos* was used. His immediate superior was Sariel, the superior of Raphael, so, as Sariel was called "God", he was called the "lamb of God" (Jn 1:36). His full celibate order held the ideal of the Suffering Servant, the "lamb led to the slaughter", who atoned for the sins of others by his severe suffering under ascetic discipline (Isa 53:4-9, *amnos* v.7; 1QS 8:1-4).

Consequently, when John the Baptist hailed Jesus as the "lamb of God (*ho amnos tou theou*) who takes away the sins of the world" (Jn 1:29), he meant that he was illegitimate, one who should be under full celibate discipline, and so could act as a levitical cardinal in a village, atoning for others, and having the right to give absolution. When John said the next day "behold the lamb of God", leaving out the following phrase (Jn 1:36), he meant that he had deprived him of the right to give absolution, as the schism had occurred.

The Poor, Crippled, Blind and Lame

Village Essenes were famed for their welfare system. From their wages as craftsmen they supported indigent people who were not able to look after themselves (Philo, *Every Good Man*, 86; CD 14:12-16). The indigent were divided into four categories, under the headings "Poor, Crippled, Blind and Lame" (Lk 14:13, 21).

The indigent were classed as servants of lower members of the table, and placed at arm's length from them, some of them in the south vestry below the dais (see Fig. 14). As the members of the table ate from the holy loaves, the left-over pieces, or "crumbs" were passed down to them.

The Poor and the Crippled (aged) were allowed inside the south vestry, forming a congregation, while the Blind and the Lame had to stay outside with Merari. (Compare the total exclusion of the blind in 11QT 45:12-13.) At a later stage, when the congregation came up in grade, members came forward as far as the dais to receive the broken pieces of bread. This practice was the origin of the Christian communion, with members of the congregation kneeling at the rail of the sanctuary to receive the bread.

At the "miraculous feedings" baskets of crumbs were left over; twelve *kophinoi* in the case of the Five Thousand, and seven *spyrides* in the case of the Four Thousand (two different kinds of basket, Mk 6:43, 8:9). The "baskets" represented two different kinds of ministry for the lower and higher classes of congregation: a more priestly ministry in a structure of seven, for the days of the week, for the "Poor" (celibates), and a more lay ministry in a structure of twelve, for the months, for the married classes.

THE HIERARCHY UNDER HEROD THE GREAT

The established system of the Davids and Zadoks was taken over in the first century BC by Herod the Great, who began the process of its transformation into the Christian ministry.

The essential structure and positions remained the same, but new men were put into the positions, often without regard to traditional dynasties. This was consistent with Herod's policy of appointing any suitable man as public high priest, breaking down long-established priestly traditions.

Herod himself occupied every major leadership office in a nominal capacity, appointing delegates as the active ministers. He was in this way adopting a doctrine of absolute kingship, one that the Davids themselves had practised while in power. King David had acted as a priest (2 Sam 6:12-15) and as the centre of the cult, the temple priests being his representatives.

Herod stepped into the positions of Michael and Gabriel, thus alienating the monastic Palestinian Essenes. The Hebrew letter corresponding to Michael was *Taw*, the last letter of the alphabet, which in its archaic form had been drawn as an X. As early as the time of Ezekiel the letter had been used to distinguish the solarists in Babylon, men who wore linen and practised as scribes (Ezek 9:2-4; the word for "mark" in verse 4 is *"Taw"*). See also CD 19:12, where the words of Ezekiel are applied to members of the Damascus community, who will be saved by "the mark" in the coming destruction. Initiates of the Herodian celibate system were marked with an X on the forehead or right hand (Rev 13:16). The *Taw* (numerical value 400) was part of the "number of the Beast", 666 (see further below, page 372).

Herod was more often than not "in the body", by Essene standards, as he engaged in unrestrained marriage. This made him equal to a Raphael, but the position was taken by his servant. He was also likened to the black Calf, who could substitute for Raphael. The emblem of the Calf was used also by his successor, Archelaus, in the position of ethnarch. Archelaus became the "Calf" of the Exodus theme (see Locations, p. 299).

The servant of M ichael was Raphael, the Power. The executive of Herod, and probably the real founder of the mission, was Menahem the Diaspora Essene, the head of the Magians of West Manasseh. He had been associated with Herod from the latter's youth, as one of his teachers, and had predicted that Herod would become king (*Ant.* 15:373-374). Although the Diaspora Essenes supported the Davids, they could accept another king, with the David in a subordinate role. As a result of Menahem's support, Herod "continued to hold all Essenes in honour" (*Ant.* 15:378).

Menahem, although not a true "son of Levi", took the position of Raphael, as it was possible for "orphans" to act as levitical cardinals. He wore scarlet, and his successor in the gospel period, Simon Magus, was called the "Scarlet Beast" (Rev 17:3).

One grade above him was Hillel, called "the Great" in Jewish tradition. Hillel was associated with Menahem in the earlier part of his career (*Mishnah, Hag.* 2:2). He practised baptisms in Jerusalem, ritual washings for the removal of sin. His doctrine implied that Jewish birth was not sufficient, but that there must be an act of repentance and change of heart. Hillel was the first to teach the Golden Rule, found also in Mt 7:12. Hillel's name means "praising" in Hebrew, and the Greek equivalent is *ainōn*. John's gospel shows the Baptist as baptising at "Ainon near (*engys*) Saleim" (Jn 3:23). This may be understood as the Essene Gate, on the south side of Jerusalem (Saleim), where Essene washing pools have recently been uncovered. Hillel was close to Essene practices on matters such as washing, and the name indicates that he used the site and established it as the first form of what became a baptising mission to Jews of the Diaspora.

Hillel, of the order of Benjamin, was like a Sariel, the visiting priest who came to the village, while Raphael was the resident leader. He was permitted to occupy the position of Sariel, although a layman, on behalf of Herod. As Hillel and Menahem were not true holders of the offices, and as an ideal of a New Israel was developing, they were called "Abraham" (Hillel) and "Isaac" (Menahem). Those who were baptised became "sons of Abraham" (Lk 3:8).

Abraham had been the Father of all Jews, and the new Abraham was also called the Father. The word eventually became "Pope". The offices that became those of Pope and patriarchs in the Christian Church were established in the reign of Herod, in order to create a new Israel.

That there had been an "Abraham" only fifty years before the time of Jesus is shown by Jn 8:57. The "Jews", in attacking Jesus, implied that if he had been fifty years old, he would have seen "Abraham" (or, more exactly, as a variant text shows, "Abraham" would have seen him, as Jesus would have been a baby). The text also shows that Hillel had died in 19 BC, fifty years before AD 32, when the words were spoken.

The name "Isaac" was appropriate for Menahem as a levitical cardinal, as the "lamb of God" could fill the position, and Isaac had been intended as a sacrifice in place of a lamb (Gen 22:7-8).

The Davids with Herod

Herod, in associating with the Essenes, was also associating with the descendants of David, or at least with Heli, a descendant of a junior branch of the Davids. His genealogy is given in Lk 3:23-38. Heli the son of Matthat was descended through forty generations from Nathan, a younger son of David, 2 Sam 5:14. Heli himself was born in 70 BC; see *eteleutēsen* A 7:15, showing that he was 70 in AD 1; so 26 in 44 BC at the birth of Joseph.

In Matthew's gospel, Heli is treated as a descendant of the royal David line, by calling him "Jacob the son of Matthan" (Mt 1:15). A process of grafting a junior branch or new line into a senior branch was well known in priestly and royal dynasties. Matthew allows 25 generations, of 40 years each, to cover the same time span of 1000 years between David and Jacob-Heli, whereas Luke allows 40 generations of 25 years each, and gives the actual genealogy. The royal generations were counted as 40 years, whereas those of a junior line were only 25 years. Thus Jacob-Heli of the junior line was 25 at his marriage, but Joseph, after the grafting process, had to wait till he was 36.

The David could be a leader who appealed to Jewish tradition, but only in the status of a prince, the equal of Herod's own heir. He was reduced to the position of prince, equal to that of a bishop like Kohath.

The title "David" was no longer appropriate, and Heli was called "Jacob" as a patriarch. The triarchy reproducing that of the village Father, Son and Spirit was now called "Abraham, Isaac and Jacob". The two patriarchs, "Isaac" and "Jacob", were assigned to the eastern and western Diaspora respectively.

As the David was now called "Jacob", his son and heir was called "Joseph", the name of the favourite son of the patriarch Jacob. As crown prince, the David heir was always called "Joseph", a title. Joseph the father of Jesus was the crown prince under Jacob-Heli at the time of Jesus' birth. James, the brother of Jesus, was Jesus' heir during the gospel period, and so called Joseph ("of Arimathea"; and Joseph Barsabbas Justus, A 1:23).

As Herod had the head of West Manasseh acting for him, so another

Diaspora Essene, the head of Ephraim, the Egyptian Therapeutae, came in to act for the David.

Although the David had risen above the merely military role of the Lion, the emblem remained, and was now passed over to the head of Ephraim, who as a substitute Lion became the Wild Beast (*to thērion*, plural *ta thēria*, as representing the class). When Paul writes of "fighting with wild beasts at Ephesus" (1 Cor 15:32) he is referring to his conflicts with Apollos, the current head of Ephraim. At the same time he was the Serpent, as the word *thērion* was used to cover both (A 28:4). The serpent was the emblem of healing (Num 21:9) used by the Therapeutae, whose skills included healing, an interest they shared with the monastic Essenes (*War* 2:136). When "Moses lifted up the Serpent in the Wilderness" (Jn 3:14), the meaning is that Simeon ("Moses"), the Father in the story of the Prodigal Son, was receiving back Theudas, the head of Ephraim, who when he "returned to the Father" was joining with Simeon's peace party in AD 4–5.

The role of "Moses" was, in fact, taken over by the head of the Therapeutae, once Palestinian Essenes separated. As seen in the description of Exodus imagery (Locations, page 298) the Therapeutae practised a liturgical dance led by a "Moses".

Another group of Diaspora Essenes, the men of East Manasseh, more eastern in their ways than West Manasseh, were placed at the same grade as Ephraim, that of bishop. A later head was Judas Iscariot, whose position was described as a "bishopric" (*episkopē*, A 1:20). They also were "beasts", with military associations. The heads of Ephraim and East Manasseh, Theudas and Judas the Galilean, had reoccupied Qumran for the nationalists in its second phase. Judas the Galilean was the first Beast of the book of Revelation (Rev 13:1–10).

Each of the heads of Ephraim-Manasseh represented a royal person, and the head of East Manasseh, one grade (4) below West Manasseh (3), became the representative of Herod's heir. The position remained the same, despite the continuous change of heirs. In the gospel period, the man holding the position was Thomas, while the head of East Manasseh was Judas. It is noteworthy that the writer of the gospel of Thomas is called Didymus Judas Thomas, a name not found in the New Testament (*GThom* 1:1).

Herod could also find room for a true Sariel, doing priestly work that Hillel, as a layman, could not perform. The position became that of the public high priest, appointed by Herod and his successors. The first was very probably Ananel, "a rather undistinguished priest from Babylon", whom Herod made high priest at the outset of his reign (*Ant.* 15:22, 39, 56; see also A 7:2 "the God of glory"). Subsequent public high priests who were involved with the movement held the position. They included

Caiaphas, who could be called *archiereus* (Jn 18:13) (but not *hoi archiereis*).

There was also a Kohath, Gershon, and Merari, preserving the original structure of lower levites.

In the village hierarchy, the king sometimes sat beside Raphael, occupying one space only, on the west side (the "left", the term used absolutely, always west). The two together represented "Kingdom" and "Power". In the synagogue used by village Essenes (*Every Good Man* 81) they sat or stood on either side of the Menorah, the seven-branched candlestick, the Light (see 1QH 7:24 for its importance to the Essenes). Each of them had a Second, of the grade of bishop; a lay bishop to the king, and Kohath to Raphael. Either of these was permitted to read from the law of Moses in synagogue services, standing at the centre in front of the Menorah. Both because of the light from the Menorah, and because of the association of Moses with glory (Ex 33:18, 34:29), the position in front of the Menorah was called Glory. Thus a familiar pattern for worshippers was:

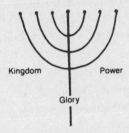

The words found their way into the addition to the Lord's Prayer (Mt 6:13). In their original meaning, they ascribed to the Pope the power to appoint cardinals, archbishops and bishops.

Herodian Numbers

It was in the time of Herod that mathematical systemisation developed, under prevailing Pythagorean influence. New series of numbers were added to make positions more exact, and to give a grade to new kinds of members who now joined.

A Kohath, the levitical bishop, had been a number 4, while the Lion was a number 7. As the head of West Manasseh had become a Raphael, so his subordinate, the head of East Manasseh, became a Kohath. As a man of peace he was a Kohath, but when he went down "into the body" he became a 7, being now a Wild Beast. He could then go to war, being no longer levitical. As the militants were called "demons" by their opponents, he was called "demon 7", a title retained by Judas Iscariot (Lk 8:2).

The David, now "Jacob", in the position of bishop was, however, lay, not levitical. He sat on the west side, not the east. He could not be called a 4, but was now called a 1, and his sons numbered after him. He was linked with hours of the day, but in a Julian, not Jewish method of naming them, calling the seventh hour of the day 1 p.m., and so on. The David and his sons were responsible for prayers at 1, 2, 3 and 4 a.m. and p.m. The sons could be called "man 2" (*andres dyo*), "man 3" (*andres treis*) and "man 4" (*andres tessares*). In A 21:23 "four men" has the p-sense of "man 4", meaning Simon–Silas, the youngest brother of Jesus.

Herod himself was a zero, having taken the place of Michael. He was a zero also when "in the body", as an archbishop. When the word *ouden* "nothing" appears, it means the ruling Herod (Agrippa in the gospel period).

Herod's crown prince had the same rank as the David king, both being bishops. The Herod crown prince was called "Esau", the Twin, to show that he could fill the same position as "Jacob" (Gen 25:24–26). The name was especially appropriate, as Esau had lost his birthright (Gen 27:36), and the heirs of Herod were frequently displaced.

As the Davids were numbered 1, 2, 3, and 4, the corresponding Herods, starting with the crown prince, were called by the ordinal numbers: *prōtos, deuteros, tritos, tetartos*. When their positions were taken by others in the Rome province, they were called by the Latin equivalents. The names Secundus, Tertius and Quartus are found (A 20:4, Rom 16:22–23).

The position of the bishop, at the "Glory", was called "the first seat" (*prōtoklisia*).

The head of East Manasseh, the chief Scribe, represented the Herod crown prince, *ho prōtos*, so he also used "the first seat" (see Mk 12:39: "Beware of the scribes, who want . . . the first seats (*prōtoklisias*) at the suppers"). In Lk 14:8–10, the ministers of Jesus are warned not to try to start as bishops at the *prōtoklisia*, but to begin as deacons in the "last place". They might then be invited to go up higher, and they would then have "Glory".

The Herod princes, however, thought of themselves as not merely lay. King Herod had taken the place of Michael, and at the village table replaced Raphael. His sons were also levitical, taking the positions of Kohath (4), Gershon (5), Merari (6) and the ordinary member (7). They used these numbers, sometimes adding the word "brother". "The (brother) 5" (*hoi pente adephoi*) was the second son, a Gershon; "the (brother) 6" (A 11:12) the man in the position of third, a Merari; "the (brother) 7", the fourth. When the first was "in the body", he went down to be equal to "brother 7" (Mk 12:20, 23, referring to Thomas).

The Herodian System for Gentiles and Women
On Essene assumptions, women, who were periodically unclean, had the lowest places in the hierarchy, positions 12 (Mother), 13 (Virgin), 14 (Widow)

and 15 (Wife). Circumcised Gentiles were above them, and equal to guests in positions 10 (celibate circumcised) and 11 (married circumcised). Uncircumcised Gentiles were the same as women: proselytes (12), Shem (13), Ham (14), Japheth (15).

The equivalences remained, women and Gentiles rising together in a society that was increasingly hellenised and accepting of women. Women were the means through which Pharisees gained their influence in the Herodian court (*Ant.* 17:41), and highly placed Roman women gave patronage to Agrippa, in whose households the Christian version of the doctrine developed.

The first step, taken under Herod, was to bring this class "out of the body". All positions went up 3 grades, becoming 7 to 12. They had now received full membership, being equal to ordinary Jewish members. When, under the Christians, they went up another 3 grades into the different forms of ministry, their transition was complete.

Gentiles belonged to two orders or "tribes", those of Asher and Dan. Anna, the original Mother Sarah, was of "the tribe of Asher" (Lk 2:36). Members of Asher lived in the world as individual ascetics, while members of Dan lived in communities on a monastic model, but still classed as villagers as they were of the unclean grades.

Asher included the circumcised, now 7 and 8, while Dan, less accepting of Jewish ways, began with proselytes, now 9.

The Herodian interest in Pythagorean mathematics led to a plan for 12 000 uncircumcised men of Asher. There would be 3000 of the level of proselytes, 4000 of Shem, and 5000 of Ham, the proportions corresponding to the sides of the right-angled triangle. They were modelled on the 12 000 "men of truth", ascetics who would be Herod's guards according to the plan of the Temple Scroll (11QT 57:5-9). Above them would be 1000 circumcised celibate and 2000 circumcised married. The latter were called "Jews", as they lived in all respects like ordinary Jews.

Over each class would be one of Herod's sons, his heir over the 1000, the next prince over the 2000, and so on. The princes, having a representative role, could be called by the names of the classes, so that the Herod equal to the first prince was a *chiliarch* (translated "tribune", but *chiliarchos*, leader of a 1000, A 21:31, Mk 6:21), and the second identified with the 2000. Antipas was the second in the gospel period, so likened to "2000 pigs" (Mk 5:13). As the class was a position 8, they were not full members, so belonged to the married Beasts.

The men of Dan looked to the Essenes rather than the Herods for leadership. Starting at 9, they were congregation members only. In ordinary life, they were freedmen in the Herodian households, upper servants. Eutychus (John Mark) and Protos (Philip) are both described as *apeleutheros*, "freedman", (*Ant.* 18:167, 168). But at the meetings of their religious society, they entered into the system of promotion for degrees of virtue and knowledge.

Women also had a higher status, but still did not rise above congregation level into grades of ministry.

THE CHRISTIAN REVISION OF THE HIERARCHY

The followers of Jesus were a third stage, revising the Herodian system, which itself was a revision of the Essene.

At the outset, Jesus was in the position of the David king. This meant that at village meetings he was equal with Sariel, sitting beside him at the table, on the west. His title in this position was "Son of Man", as has been seen above, page 348.

But in the Twelve Apostles, the man who was Pope also adopted a position equal to Michael, since he was claiming to be a rival to John the Baptist, as well as to the Herod king, who was the nominal holder of the highest position. He was a *Taw*, with a Second who was a *Shin*, and a Third, who was a *Resh*. Both Jonathan Annas (Pope AD 30–31) and Simon Magus (Pope from AD 31) took the position of *Taw* when in the sanctuary. Moreover, as Hellenists, they held the view that laymen could act in some levitical functions. The David king, as the chief layman, was classed as a *Shin* in the sanctuary, a Second to the Priest. This meant that he was a "Son", as the first three were "Father, Son, and Spirit". When Second to Jonathan Annas, who was "God", the David was the "Son of God". This title was used for him in the Old Testament, in Ps 2:7, where God said to the David at his coronation: "You are my son, today I have begotten you".

Thus, when the "unclean spirits" (*ta pneumata ta akatharta*) said that Jesus was the Son of God (Mk 3:11), the pesher is that the tetrarch Antipas ("unclean spirits", Mk 5:13 p) held the Hellenist view that Jesus, the legitimate David for him, was the Second to Jonathan Annas. What appears to be a supernatural event is, in fact, a statement about politics and history.

The Priest and the David, as First and Second, foreshadowed the positions of Messiah of Aaron and Messiah of Israel. They appear under these names in the description of the future holy meal in 1QSa 2:11–22. It is made plain in that passage that the Messiah of Israel is second to the Messiah of Aaron, as the latter blesses both the wine and bread, while the former, after him, blesses the bread only. The bread was ranked lower than the wine, as seen in the initiation process (1QSa 6:16–23): higher novices could take the bread, but only full initiates, one grade above them, could take the wine.

In the Dead Sea Scrolls, the three anticipated leaders are the Messiah of Aaron, the Messiah of Israel, and the Prophet (1QS 9:11). The names reflect the village grades, in which Kohath (servant of Moses), was the third.

Jesus did not stay in the position of Second, but claimed that of First. This, as has been seen, is a major theme of the history of the gospel period.

The greatest change made by the Christians was the promotion of Gentiles, raising them above the congregation so as to enter the ministry, becoming deacons, bishops, cardinals and, eventually, Popes. As they formed an independent ministry, they were able to separate entirely from their Jewish beginnings, putting aside the two previous stages and keeping the records only in concealed form.

In structural terms, all that had to be done was to take Gentiles up another 3 grades. Positions 7 to 12 became 4 to 9. Circumcised Gentiles became bishops and presbyters, and the uncircumcised deacons (proselytes), members (Shem), novices (Ham) and congregation (Japheth).

John Mark, the chief proselyte, went from 9 to 6, and so became an *Ayin* deacon. Still classed as a villager, his grade brought him under the Herodian Nazirite system, so he was now a "70" (Lk 10:1, 17). The Synoptics, whose writers had party differences from him, continue to call him "the 12" (*hoi dōdeka*), a term he rarely uses in his own gospel.

Philip, head of Shem, went from 10 to 7, and so had his final stage of promotion at the seventh hour (Jn 4:52). But, as seen on page 226, this was a Jewish Christian practice; Jesus changed his rule again to put his final stage at noon, on the same level as celibate proselytes. In AD 30 Philip received the "wine" (the sign of full membership at 7) in the "miracle" of "turning water into wine". Previously, he had been capable of going up one grade by proofs of virtue, but could reach only *Mem*, 9, the highest in the congregation, its sign being the "water", washing in a baptismal cistern. Now he went up to 7, allowing him to sit at the holy table. The following year, AD 31, he went up one grade to be a deacon (Jn 4:46–54).

The celibate "fish" of Shem, Ham and Japheth were also called Fish 1, 2 (Mk 6:41) and 3, preparing for their further elevation to the status of princes.

Japheth, the lowest grade of all, remained congregation members in the gospel period, but by AD 43 had taken their three steps upward to be equal to proselytes (A 10:1–8). Luke (Cornelius) replaced John Mark when he drew away from the western party.

During the gospel period Agrippa was in Judea, as seen in Chapter 13. He appears under a number of different pseudonyms, usually vague sounding terms in the plural. But a plural was a representative of a class. Agrippa was "the Many" (*hoi polloi, polloi*), because he was the head of celibates, who were organised in councils called the Many, (Hebrew *hārabbim*, a term frequently found in the scrolls, for example, 1QS 6:7). He was also "the

All" (*pantes*, because as a Herod he occupied every position, and possibly also as a play on *Kaph–Lamedh*, the Hebrew word for "all", and the letters for the two guest positions where the Herods had started). He is also "the Soldiers" (*hoi stratiōtai*) as head of the army; and "the crowds" (*hoi ochloi*, but not *ho ochlos*, singular; this was a term for Antipas).

He was the head of all grades, and at the village table sat in the position of Raphael. This meant that he could go down to an *Ayin*, deacon (see p. 346). In this position he was "the brother 6" (A 11:12) and also in the class of proselytes of Asher. These were simply called "the Gentiles" (*ta ethnē*), being the grade under "the Jews" (*hoi Joudaioi*), a name used for the circumcised married. Agrippa is also meant when the term *ta ethnē* appears.

The "Jews" were represented by Antipas, the tetrarch. The circumcised married had gone up to a 5, to be equal to Jewish presbyters. Antipas and his successors in office (Herod of Chalcis in the time of Acts) are always meant by "the Jews". Herod of Chalcis was "Brother 5" of Lk 16:28.

The Twelve Apostles and the Last Supper

In AD 29, fourteen men agreed that an opposition government should be formed to oppose the regime of the Baptist. Almost all were Hellenists, with a western orientation. They allowed the promotion of Gentiles, although not necessarily for the sake of peace with Rome. Some Gentiles were prepared to join them in opposing the Roman government.

Theirs was essentially a village formation, with the men of Manasseh and Ephraim representing Diaspora celibate orders. The priestly members, carrying the real authority, were Jonathan Annas (Jacob of Alphaeus, Sariel), Simon Magus (Simon the Zealot, Raphael, now acting in his own right in opposition to Agrippa), Matthew Annas (Kohath), Judas Iscariot (Scribe, a bishop alternating with Kohath), and Theudas of Ephraim (Gershon, see page 366).

On the lay side, Jesus was in the place long claimed by the David king, that of the Son of Man sitting beside Sariel, occupying two places, like Sariel. But, as has been seen, he began to move from this base into positions which even Hellenists could not allow. He challenged the position of Jonathan Annas, several times moving into his place; in this, looking back to the priestly authority of King David. But he did not hold royal power in Jerusalem, and his right to the kingship, if it came, could be challenged. And then he took a step which David had not taken: on the fateful Day of Atonement in September AD 32 he acted as if he *were* a Michael, the supreme high priest.

At the Last Supper, however, Jesus sat for the first two hours in the western position of king. In front of him was his lay bishop, Peter, a *prōtos*, according to Mt 10:2. As has been seen, Peter could not turn round when Jesus spoke behind him, and had to ask John Mark on the opposite side of the table which of the two bishops, himself or Judas, Jesus meant when he spoke of his deputy.

Peter had begun as a deacon (6), one grade above Andrew of Naphtali, and, being lay, had moved up by promotion to be a bishop. He had followed the route of Lk 14:10, beginning in the *eschatos topos*, the place of the last minister, the deacon, then moving into the *prōtoklisia*, in the place of the Glory. Andrew, who had more eastern views, as shown by his association with John Mark (Jn 1:40), remained at position 7.

John Mark (Bartholomew, possibly a play on "servant of Ptolemy", as his order was derived from that of the Egyptian Therapeutae) was a subordinate to Jesus as king, equal to both "queen" and "crown prince". As the crown prince moved to the deacon's place when the king was present (see page 348), he was at the western deacon's place opposite Jesus. When Jesus moved, at 8 p.m., to the eastern position of Sariel, John Mark moved with him, from one side of the "bosom" to the other (*ho kolpos* west, *to stēthos* east (Jn 13:23–25).

One side of the double deacon's seat was vacant because Simon Magus had moved from it. As a Raphael, he had to go down to it when Sariel was present. But he had another role, that of *epitropos* (representative, Lk 8:3) of the tetrarch, who was officially the guest on the western side. The far western seat was that of the presbyter in Rome, where the tetrarch's party met. Antipas was not present at the Last Supper, which only thirteen attended, and Simon, whose power base was also in Rome, took his place.

When Jesus first came in at 6 p.m. he was "with the 12" (*meta tōn dōdeka*, Mk 14:17), meaning that he was at the same level as John Mark, number 12 (*meta* indicates equality). For the first few minutes he was in the vacant eastern deacon's seat, washing the feet of John Mark as a symbolic way of showing care for the indigent (Jn 13:4–12). He then moved up to the king's seat (Jn 13:12), leaving the space vacant for John Mark to move into when he acknowledged that he was now deacon to a priest, not a king.

James of Zebedee of Asher, head of the Four Thousand, had the same rank as Philip of Shem, but this grade were like Virgins, who could go down to the grade of Sister. James could also sit in position 8, leaving the south-east corner to Philip.

Thomas–Esau, although a guest (as a grandson of Boethus, he was a Hebrew, whereas the rest were Hellenists), was allowed to stay at the later part of the meal when guests normally left, to express the higher status of Gentiles. He asked a question at 9 p.m. (Jn 14:4). But at the sacred meal two days later, at Ain Feshkha, he was not present (Jn 20:24).

At the Last Supper, the order of seating at the table for the first two hours was as shown in Fig. 15.

Fig. 15 The Last Supper

6.00 p.m. to 8.00 p.m.

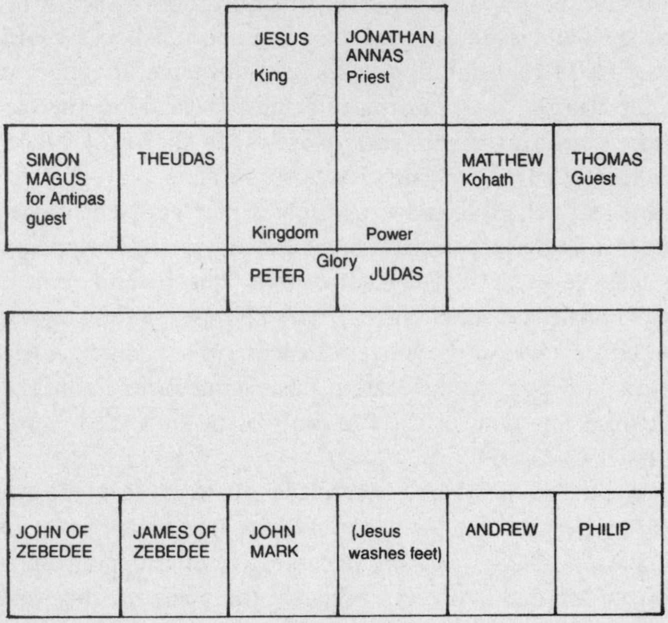

| | JESUS | JONATHAN |
| | King | ANNAS Priest |

| SIMON MAGUS for Antipas guest | THEUDAS | Kingdom | Power | MATTHEW Kohath | THOMAS Guest |

PETER Glory JUDAS

| JOHN OF ZEBEDEE | JAMES OF ZEBEDEE | JOHN MARK | (Jesus washes feet) | ANDREW | PHILIP |

9.00 p.m.

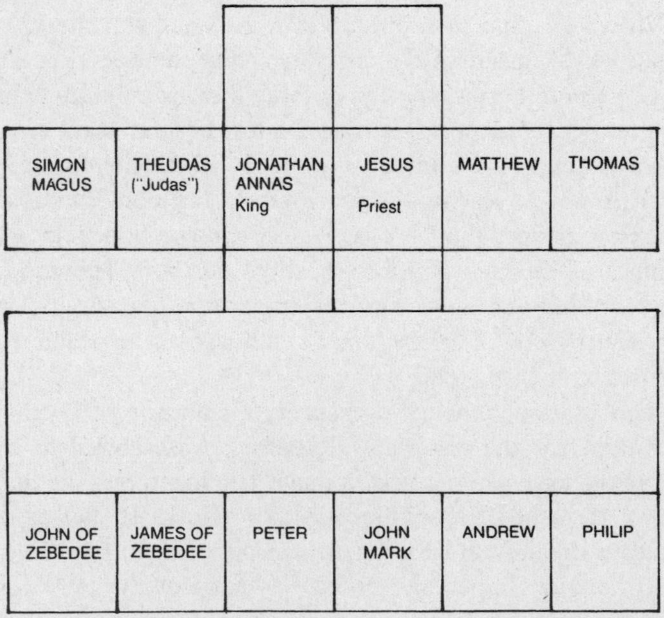

| SIMON MAGUS | THEUDAS ("Judas") | JONATHAN ANNAS King | JESUS Priest | MATTHEW | THOMAS |

| JOHN OF ZEBEDEE | JAMES OF ZEBEDEE | PETER | JOHN MARK | ANDREW | PHILIP |

Shortly after 9 p.m. Judas left (Jn 13:30). The positions of Jesus and Jonathan Annas were now reversed, and both extended their space to include also the two bishops' seats. These were in the Glory, the place of the reader of the law of Moses, so Jesus said: "Now the Son of Man is glorified, and 'God' is glorified in him [in his place]" (Jn 13:31). Peter had moved down to the position of deacon again, beside John Mark on the west, so now was easily able to converse with Jesus across the table (Jn 13:36-38).

During the next hour's discussion, Jesus presided, conducting questions and answers in the manner of 1QS 6:8-13. But those who spoke first were at the eastern extreme of the table, men who would normally have been obliged to leave at the sacred hour: Thomas the guest (Jn 14:4), and Philip the uncircumcised (Jn 14:8). In the later part of the hour, Theudas spoke, under the name of "Judas (not Iscariot)" as he had to take over some of the functions of Judas while Judas was absent (Jn 14:22).

The Brothers of Jesus

The brothers of Jesus were James, Joses, Jude and Simon (Mk 6:3). James appears by name in A 15:13, Gal 1:19 and 2:12, as the leader of Jewish Christians who wanted to impose Jewish ritual requirements on Gentiles, in opposition to the opinions of Paul. He was the author of the epistle of James.

James had a dual role; he was the David ("Jacob", that is, James) to eastern Hebrews, who did not accept Jesus, but the David crown prince ("Joseph") to western Hellenists, who did accept Jesus. James himself accepted the latter position after the decline of the Baptist, so earning, for the Hebrews, the name of a treacherous heir of David, "Absalom" (1QpHab 5:9, the "house of Absalom" should have supported the Teacher but did not when the Man of a Lie "flouted the Law in the midst of the whole congregation" (see 2 Sam 15). (James was also, at times, treacherous *to* Jesus, as Absalom had been to David.)

James was accepted by the westerners in all the roles of a prince (and as prince regent after the birth of an heir to Jesus). As prince he was the chief Nazirite.

The Nazirite "sheep" wore both white and black, but the prince normally wore black. His image was that of a black-robed Nazirite with long hair and beard, a style preserved in eastern orthodox Christian Churches.

Nazirites were villagers, men who were married but abstained from sex for varying lengths of time from 100 days down (see page 295). Their highest rank was equal to an archbishop, the man who could stand in for Raphael, but wearing black. The David prince at this level was an archbishop and judge.

His title in the Exodus imagery was "Cloud". See Lk 12:54, "the Cloud rising in the west". Joseph as prince had "overshadowed" Mary (Lk 1:35), and Prince James appeared as the Cloud, overshadowing in Mk 9:6 on the Day of Atonement, and receiving Jesus on his return to Qumran in A 1:9. When Peter "overshadowed" and healed, he was appointed to the position of Nazirite archbishop (A 5:15).

The prince appeared at all levels of the Nazirites. At the grade below Cloud, he was a lay bishop, and he here used the name "holy spirit" (*pneuma hagion*). It indicated a similarity to Kohath, who was *to hagion pneuma*, but he was not levitical. He was in this position at the time of betrothal before marriage. Prince Joseph was the *pneuma hagion* who "came upon" Mary (Lk 1:35, Mt 1:18). In this role the crown prince was *hē paraklēsis* (A 9:31), as the Chief Priest, *to pneuma to hagion*, was "the Paraclete", *ho paraklētos* (Jn 14:26).

Below this again he was a lay presbyter, like Gershon, and below it again a deacon, like Merari. As a deacon he was called *oudeis* ("no-one", Nemo) as he stood at the centre of a lower line where prayers were also said at noon, the zero hour.

One of his duties as a chief village layman was to act as treasurer, according to the rule of 1QS 5:3, that the laity were to control the property. In this capacity James was called the Rich Man. He was a bishop (Hebrew *mebaqqer*), a lay equivalent of Kohath, and wearing purple like Kohath. As Kohath was one of the "tax-collectors", receiving tithes (Mt 9:9), there was a similar lay position, for a bishop receiving the money of villagers intended to be used for welfare (CD 14:13). He also handled the reserve funds (1QS 6:20), storing them in the outside vault at Qumran. (The funds of full celibates, however, were held by the Herods.) The vaults were the Rich Man's "barns", and when it became necessary to move to Damascus, James "built bigger barns" (Lk 13:13-20). In the parable of the Rich Man in Lk 16:19-31, James sat at the Rich Man's table wearing "purple and white linen", and lived "splendidly" (*lamprōs*). In his own epistle James speaks of the rich man who might come into a synagogue, "wearing a gold ring and in splendid clothes" (*en esthēti lampra*), who might be asked to sit in the bishop's seat as a guest (Jas 2:2-3).

The next brother was called Joses, or Joseph (Mt 13:55). While the crown prince could go as high as archbishop, he could rise only to bishop, and also be a presbyter or deacon. As a presbyter he was a "Joseph" to a "Jacob", in the Herodian form of hierarchy, and as a bishop he was like Kohath, and so could be called a levite (*leuitēs*, without article, A 4:36; the Gabriel, 3 grades above, was *the* Levite to *the* Priest, Michael). Joseph Barnabas, called a "levite" in A 4:36, was a "son of *paraklēsis*", and *hē paraklēsis* ("exhortation") is a title of James in A 9:31, so Joseph Barnabas was his subordinate, a younger brother. He stepped into the position of a Kohath-like bishop because he was a celibate (Mk 8:26). The man called Barnabas, important in the history of Acts, was, then, a younger brother of Jesus. He was more in sympathy with the outlook of Jesus than was James, but he also valued celibate traditions, so continued in association with John Mark rather than Paul (A 15:36-37). The Epistle of Barnabas represented his outlook; it was not included in the New Testament but valued in some parts of the early Church.

Another name for him was Matthias. He was the man who replaced Judas in the list of apostles (A 1:23, 26). This is known from *Clem. Rec.* 1:60, where it is said that Barnabas, who was also called Matthias, was put in the place of Judas. The Kohath in the Twelve Apostles was Matthew Annas, and Barnabas was another Matthew as a Kohath like bishop. His responsibility for money is seen in A 4:37.

The third brother was Jude, whose opinions were similar to those of James, as seen in the New Testament epistle under his name. He appears only infrequently in the gospels and Acts. In A 15:22 he appears as "Judas called Barsabbas", the latter word a title used by James also (A 1:23). In A 23:13 he is the "40" who led an attack on Paul. A Nazirite "40" was also a number 9, the position of a 6 (Jude) when "in the body".

The fourth brother was Simon, at the level of the "lame" who were below the "blind" in the congregation. He was the "lame man who had never walked" of A 14:8. Born in AD 22 (as shown by A 21:23; he was to marry at the age of 36 in June AD 58) he came to maturity in the period of Acts, and replaced Barnabas as the David prince who travelled with Paul, using the name Silas (A 16:40).

The brothers of Jesus were called the "princes of Judah" in CD 8:3. They were condemned in that passage because they had left the Damascus party and had returned to Qumran as Jewish Christians.

The Head of the Therapeutae

The head of the Ephraim Therapeutae had a special relation to the David princes. He had been appointed by Herod as the representative of David, and continued in the position in all grades that the David king took, including that of Son of Man equal to Sariel (2). In this position he was called "Prince [nāsî'] of all the Congregation", as "Sariel" meant "Prince of God". (But the David king was the "Prince of the Congregation" without "all"; see page 413.) The head of Ephraim was also called the Sceptre, as he was holding an office equal to a king (CD 7:20). As the David prince was a grade below his father, so he was also a grade below the Sceptre. The David prince could also be called the Star (of David), and the two together, when politically allied, used the names the Sceptre and the Star, from Num 24:17 (CD 7:18–21). Theudas and Joseph had formed such an alliance in about AD 1, as shown in Chapter 10. The relationship was continued between Theudas and James, as the former had a greater political sympathy with James than with Jesus. They moved together to Damascus, and were still together at the time of writing CD 7, one of the earliest parts of the Damascus Document.

Being like a Sariel, the head of Ephraim was called "our fathers" (*hoi pateres hēmōn*, A 7:39), reflecting the name "Father" for Sariel.

In the Twelve Apostles, there were three men of grade 2: Jonathan Annas, Jesus, and Theudas. As only two could preside at the centre of table, Theudas went down "in the body" to a (5), becoming the Gershon, whose seat he occupied at the Last Supper. His name in this position was "Barabbas", meaning "servant (*bar*, Aramaic, used for "servant", not "son") of *Abba*, the Father" (Mk 14:36).

Women in the Christian Revision

Following the pattern of "Abraham", "Isaac" and "Jacob", women of the order of Asher were called "Sarah", "Rebecca" and "Rachel". A woman's grade was always one below that of her "husband".

Sarah the Mother, equal to proselytes, became a deacon under the Christian revision. Helena, who filled the position in the gospel period, "served" (*diakonein*, Jn 12:2, Lk 10:40). This meant that she was still lay, so, like a villager, her main religious occasions were at the new moons (Ezek 46:3). As communal prayers were "sacrifices", it was as if she "shed blood" once a month; an image of menstruation was naturally used. But when proselytes went up higher, Helena wanted to keep pace. John Mark, the chief proselyte, acted both as a Nazirite, his positions modelled on those of the David prince, and also as a lay cardinal. Having four years of monastic education, he acted within his own community as a *Qof*, position 3.

Helena, a woman who had received a Greek education (she is the Syro-Phoenician woman of *Clem. Hom.* 2:19–20, Mk 7:26), claimed equality with a graduate, and consequently the position of cardinal. She is "the woman arrayed in . . . scarlet" of Rev 17:4. She was consequently equal to the Many, *hoi polloi*, and her ministry is described as *pollē diakonia* (Lk 10:40). She was no longer a "Sarah", but a "Martha". This meant that she must offer "sacrifices" of prayer every day, suggesting the image of a woman with a menstrual disorder (Mk 5:24–34). In a more positive view of her education she was called Wisdom, *hē sophia* (see Prov 1:20, and the frequent image of Wisdom as a woman in contemporary Wisdom literature), and, as levitical, the "Wisdom of God" (Lk 11:49).

Helena lived in the world and held property of her own (Sapphira, another name for her, owned property in A 5:8). But the Essene women of Dan lived in community without private property, more like nuns in the traditional sense of the word. However, one of the purposes of their order was to prepare brides for the men of the great dynasties. They were to live separately from their husbands for most of the time, and needed to be taught the dedication necessary to such a life.

They had the same grades of Mother, Virgin, Widow and Wife, but treated them a little differently. A woman at her marriage was a Virgin, and kept the same grade at her second wedding, when she was again a bride. At the second wedding, she was three months pregnant. At the time of conception after her first wedding, she was said to "receive" the seed, the heir to the dynasty, and the formula was repeated at the second wedding. The heir to the dynasty was of the same grade as herself, as the son was one below the father and the wife was one below the husband.

When she was six months pregnant, she was promoted to the first stage of being a Mother. Her position was then the same as that of the prince in a higher status. As a Virgin, or between weddings, she was in the part of the order called Great Dan, meeting in the tribal territory of North Dan. By a play on Greek *megas* "great" with "Dan", the word became Magadan, then Magdala (see Mt 15:39, and variant texts of Mk 8:10). When she moved up to Mother, she was in Greater Dan (meeting at Caesarea).

She also moved down one grade, at times of separation during the marriage. She then lived like a sister to her husband, so was called a Sister. (See 1 Cor 9:5, where Paul speaks of being accompanied by a "sister as wife"; Paul's wife is called his "sister" in A 23:16.) A Sister was of the same grade as a Widow, so was said to "weep" at the times of separation (Lk 7:38, Jn 20:11). In this status, the Sister was part of Little Dan. The Widows of Little Dan lived at South Dan, meeting at Joppa (A 9:36–42).

Women such as these, associated with the Essene "prophets" and their solar calendar, were a kind of prophetess, and the title used for them was Miriam, the prophetess sister of Moses (Ex 15:21). In Greek it became Maria, Mary. The title was used of all women in the order who were the brides of the David kings, as seen in *GPhil* 59:5, where the three women associated with Jesus were all called Mary. For women who were the brides of the high priests, the title was Elizabeth (Lk 1:5). But "Elizabeth", when she became a Mother at her sixth month of pregnancy, could not be levitical; no woman of the order of Dan could be a priest in the Jewish sense. She became like the prince in his higher status, and so was said to be "filled with a prince" (Lk 1:41).

The women of Dan were likened to lay Nazirites, usually wearing black after marriage. Their progress under the Christians followed that of John Mark, also of the order of Dan, when he followed the David prince. Mothers and Virgins, already brought to be deacons (6) and full members (7), were given further education, taking them three grades up. This meant that a Mother was a (black) archbishop (3) and a Virgin a bishop (4). A Nazirite bishop, as seen above, could be either fully lay (*pneuma hagion*) or like Kohath, wearing white and purple. Lydia of A 16:14 was a Virgin who was like a levitical bishop; she was a "seller of purple" (giving promotions to women, the fee paying system still being in operation).

The Virgin, or bride, or wife between weddings, now "received the prince" in his grade of bishop (*pneuma hagion*), she being also a lay bishop. When she was six months pregnant she was "filled with the prince" (*pneuma hagion*) (Lk 1:41, of Elizabeth). The same expressions were used of the men of the order of Dan, because of their equivalence with women. When John Mark became a lay bishop equal to Jewish bishops, he "received the holy spirit" (*pneuma hagion*), the formula used for the female bishop at her first and second wedding (Jn 20:22). Three months later, on the Day of Pentecost, Agrippa was "filled with the holy spirit" (*pneuma hagion*, A 2:4). The expression came to be used of all bishops and archbishops working with Gentiles. Paul was "full of the holy spirit", and changed his name, in September AD 44 (A 13:9).

The women of Dan holding more eastern views, those of the Jewish Christians, stayed at the level of members rather than going on to be bishops. Mary the mother of Jesus is presented in the Synoptics as holding such opinions. Her status is the subject of Lk 13:10–17. She had become a widow at the death of Joseph in AD 23, "year 18" of the dating starting from AD 5 and 6 (see Chronology, page 176) (Lk 13:11, 16). As a widow, she was of the grade of the aged, or "crippled", so she is presented as stooped (v. 11). She was now preparing for a stage of ministry described in 1 Tim 5:9: "let a widow be enrolled if she is not less than 60 years of age, having been the wife of one husband".

Mary was now beginning a repetition of the three-year process leading to full initiation. Thus her age is being given: she was 57 in December 32. Born in 26 BC, she was 17½ in June 8 BC at the time of the conception of Jesus, and had her last child, Simon–Silas, in June AD 22 at the age of 46½ (A 21:23, Simon–Silas was 36 in June AD 58).

A woman was said to "come to an end" (*teleutao*) at 60, whereas the same was said of a man at 70 (Mt 2:15), meaning that sexual activity had ceased. Matthew plays on words by saying that Mary Magdalene had "come to an end" when she was in the status of Sister, the same as that of a Widow. (Mt 9:18).

The history of Sarah, however, suggested to the order of Asher that childbearing, at least metaphorically, did not cease until the age of 91 (Gen 17:17, 21). Anna, the original Sarah, had reached this age in 2 BC (Lk 2:36, see Chronology, page 214). She had then become a Virgin again, like the "aged virgins" who joined the Therapeutae (*Contemp. Life* 68). Luke's note on Anna indicates that the chief woman could be called the Virgin at any age. While Mary the mother of Jesus was always a Widow to Jewish Christians (see Lk 7:12), in western opinion she could be called the Virgin.

The detail of the two weddings of Mary Magdalene includes figures about numbers of denarii. At the first, a comparison was made between Mary, who owed Jesus 500 denarii, and another woman who only owed him 50 (no coin is named) (Lk 7:41-43). At the second, the vase of ointment which Mary broke was worth 300 denarii (Mk 14:5). As with all exact figures, important information is being given.

As Virgins and Widows were classed with indigent people (CD 14:15), the orders of Dan and Asher were among those who were fed with "crumbs" from the king's table. A 12:20 shows that Asher ("those of Tyre and Sidon") were fed by Herod.

But the women of Dan also brought their own money into the order, surrendering it to the common stock. It had to be held as the property of a man, as even the chief woman of this order did not own property. It was handed over to the heir of David as the king to whom they looked, and he paid it back to them for their support. Wedding imagery was commonly used for village initiations, the priest or king being the "bridegroom". When the chief woman handed over the money, it was considered as the "dowry" of the "brides of Christ". Mary Magdalene was the chief laywoman of Dan, and should have handed it over at her wedding. But Jesus was changing the financial system for female orders, as it was based on the Jewish tithing rule (CD 14:12-20). He therefore forgave her the amount.

The exact sum she owed at the first wedding was 500 denarii, and this gives information on the female structure and calendar. There were 500 women and 500 men in Dan, on the model of the order of Manasseh in two half-tribes. The women were sub-divided into tens, the basic number used by men at a village table (1QS 6:6). In their celibate communities they followed the pentecontads, divisions of the year into sets of 49 (50) days, as they were the "Miriams" of the Therapeutae, who met for their liturgical dances at the pentecontads (*Contemp. Life* 65). (See Chronology, page 196). On each day of the 50 (the 49 were counted as 50 by numbering the last one twice) the king paid 10 denarii for the support of the chief table of 10, standing for the rest, so he owned and paid 500 denarii on their behalf. A denarius was the amount needed for one day's support for a labourer (Mt 20:2).

But when the woman left the order to marry, she changed to follow a monthly calendar, with a division of the year into sets of 30 days. On every day of the month, the ten women received 10 denarii, so 300 for the month. The chief woman brought this money, in the form of a vase of ointment, to her second wedding, after she had been in the married state (Mk 14:3-5). Judas' objection at the time of the second wedding, that the money ought to have been given to the Poor, indicated that he thought it was not a legal wedding, and Mary ought to join a fully celibate order (Mk 14:4-5, Jn 12:4-5). As has been seen in Chapter 17, it appears that this was because Mary had been married previously. Her age can be discovered from information given in Luke's account of Anna (Lk 2:37 and see Chronology, page 215), who had begun her life as a dedicated woman under Queen Salome in 79 BC. As she was a "Sarah", aged 91, in 2 BC, she was born in 93 BC, and initiated at 14 in 79 BC. An initiation age for girls at 14 shows that Mary Magdalene, "born" in AD 17 ("year 12" Mk 5:42), was literally born in AD 3, and so was 27 at the time of her wedding in AD 30.

The head of Dan women who owed 500 denarii is compared with the head of Asher, who owed 50, with no coin specified. Helena was a rich Widow, of the kind mentioned in 1 Tim 5:16, a "believing woman who has Widows". She kept a table for 10 at which she supported other women. They normally worked for a living, doing work such as sweeping (Lk 15:8), but for five days a month withdrew into the places set apart for menstruating women (11QT 48:16). The head of Asher then supported them. The money, 50 coins for 10 women for five days, was technically owned by the king and was given to her, so she had 10 coins for the 10 women on one day. Her women were of a higher social class and were worth a drachma each, considerably more than a denarius (Lk 15:8). When the woman who had the 10 drachma "lost" one, it was because one of her women had ceased to support herself and had married. When the "lost coin" was found, it was because the woman had returned, either because she was widowed, or because she was divorced. The Herodian order of Asher followed Pharisee opinions and permitted divorce (Mk 10:4). Divorced women were "not real widows" (1 Tim 5:16), and Paul rules that a "believing Widow" could assist them, but that the Church should not be burdened with them.

In Matthew's parable of the Ten Virgins (Mt 25:1-13), two groups are described, each led by a Number 5 (*pente*), a female presbyter. One was foolish and did not have oil for her lamp, the other was wise and did have oil for her lamp. The meaning is that the wise female presbyter thought of herself as lay, more an elder than a presbyter; while the foolish one thought of herself as a priest. "Oil" stood for a lay status, as it was rejected by priestly Essenes, who, according to Josephus (*War* 2:123) never used oil on their skins.

Further Details of Grades

The system of grades underlay all aspects of the hierarchy. When higher education was introduced into the monasteries and later celibate communities, each year's progress brought the student to be equal to one of the positions in the hierarchy, and was called by the corresponding letter. At graduation, a student was considered equal to Raphael or to a Nazirite archbishop (3), so was awarded a *Qof*. As *Qof* also meant "eye of a needle", he "went through the eye of a needle" when he graduated. The saying in Mk 10:25 about a "camel going through the eye of a needle" is referring to the graduation of a celibate, as there were four main classes denoted by the first four letters of the alphabet (priests *Aleph*; levites *Beth*, celibates *Gimel*; married *Daleth*) and "*Gimel*" also meant "camel".

A man who progressed normally through the grades took them at fixed ages. His real education began at 20, the age when he was eligible for marriage according to 1QSa 1:8. At this point, he decided for or against a celibate vocation, and if he decided for it, he began the three years described in 1QS 6:3-23, the detail of which is amplified by Josephus (*War* 2:137-142). After a year outside the community, he came to the celibate building (originally the Qumran monastery) and received his first washing in the water of a stepped cistern, the highest kind of water (Josephus describes it as "the purer kind of holy water" *War* 2:138). The location and size of the southeast cistern at Qumran suggests that this was the cistern used for giving the "water", the privilege by which this stage, grade *Mem*, was known.

Two years of novitiate instruction followed, probably spent in the triangular court north of the cistern, excluded from the main building by the Israelite wall. At the end of the first of these years, he received the bread of the sacred meal, as its lower element, and put his property into reserve; it could be returned to him if he changed his mind (1QS 6:16-21).

At the age of 23 he took the decisive step, entering grade *Samekh*, the grade of full initiation. He now handed over all his property, and it no longer was legally his; he had become one of the Poor ('*ebionim*). The privilege of this stage was the wine, the Drink, given only to full members (1QS 6:20). Only those in an enclosed celibate discipline took part in the sacred meal of bread and wine, for it had begun as the meal of the priests eating tithe offerings, and was extended only to the purest laymen (Chapter 7).

Four years of education followed, taking him to *Qof*, graduation, at the age of 27. Then three more years brought the most privileged to the highest grade. Of these three years, the first year was again spent outside, and only on reaching *Resh* did the graduate enter the sanctuary. He then progressed within it for two further years, through *Shin* until at 30 he finally reached *Taw*, being given the sign X.

Thus the steps that brought a marked change in his condition were *Samekh*, for full initiation, *Resh*, when he entered the sanctuary; and *Taw*, when he reached the top. The numerical values of these letters in Hebrew were 60 (*Samekh*), 200 (*Resh*) and 400 (*Taw*), totalling 660. When the letters were put together and a *Waw* added, as the usual letter attached to a Hebrew letter to make it a word, then, since *Waw* was 6, the combination gave 666. The number of the Beast, of Rev 13:18, refers to the original Jewish monastic system in a way that could be understood only by those who had been through it. Revelation 13, written by John of Zebedee, is attacking the whole system and its current head, Simon Magus, the second Beast.

A three-year period leading to full initiation (*Samekh*) was used for Jews in the homeland, but when the Herodian mission began, an extra year was needed for the missionaries to find suitable candidates and persuade them to enter the process. A four-year period was allowed for each batch of members, as has been seen in Chapter 6. Over forty years there were ten such periods, leading to the original minah of the missionary increasing to 10 minahs (100 members per period, each paying a half-shekel initiation fee; 100 half-shekels is 1 minah; see 4Q159). Four years was the period for ordinary initiates, but some would go on to the higher education up to *Qof* graduation. The seven years for this process in the homeland became eight years in the Diaspora, giving five periods in forty years (Lk 19:18).

The parable in Lk 16:1–8 records a change in the original system, so as to give longer periods of education to Gentiles. A steward (*oikonomos*) had a "debtor" who owed 100 measures of oil, and another who owed 100 measures of wheat. He revised the figures for "oil" to 50, and for "wheat" to 80. This meant that members of the "oil" grade had periods of eight years instead of four, being given four years of monastic education. These were the proselytes, men like John Mark, who in their own communities adopted celibate structures. An association with oil meant that they were excluded by Palestinian Essenes, who considered oil defiling. (The name Bethsaida means "house of the olive" (*zaith*) and was linked with Dan Gentiles; see Jn 1:44, 12:21.) The other class, "wheat", were Gentiles like James and John of Zebedee, who could be made full members in the village, and now could go on another year to be deacons, so had five-year periods, giving eight in the forty years. (Each figure for periods was multiplied by 10, for the ten provinces.)

A similar set of figures is found in Mk 4:8, in the parable of the Sower. The "good soil" (the revision of Jesus) was to multiply thirtyfold, sixtyfold, and a hundredfold. The figures fit only into a period of thirty years, that between 3970, in the gospel period, and 4000 (see Table B, page 182). Periods of instruction of ten years, five years, and three years were to be given to different kinds of members, leaving out the year for recruitment, as this was a revision for existing members.

As noted above, the four broad classes were called by the first four letters of the Hebrew alphabet. Priests belonged to *Aleph* (1) (giving the name Alphaeus, Mk 3:18); levites to *Beth* (2); celibates to *Gimel* (3); and villagers to *Daleth* (4). Daleth means "Door", giving an association of villagers with imagery associated with a door (Mk 1:33), including the cardinal as a "hinge" (page 342). (See 1QSa 1:23). Gentile celibates of Dan were a special case, as they were of the class of villagers, *Daleth*, and yet were celibates, *Gimel*. When the two letters were put together they gave *Daleth–Gimel* (Hebrew *dag*, "fish"), a further reason why Gentiles were called "fish".

"TRIBES"

A list of the "tribes", or orders, follows, briefly showing their origin and type of discipline. They had obviously grown spontaneously, then been artificially systematised in the time of Herod the Great. Each met at a centre in the ancient tribal territories (see Fig. 16). Each contained a thousand members, the number of an Israelite tribe, further subdivided into hundreds (celibates from *Samekh* to *Qof* in four classes of 25 each), fifties (novices from *Mem* to *Samekh*, in two classes of 25 each) and tens (groups of individual ascetics) (1QS 2:21-22, 11QT 57:4, Mk 6:40).

Palestinian Essenes

Levi	Full celibate monks, permanently renouncing marriage. "Orphans".
Judah	The second Essene order (*War* 2:160-161) for men of the great dynasties, living celibate for most of the time but leaving at times for marriage. The order of the priests and the Davids. David princes were called "the princes of Judah". This was the order of Jesus.
Zebulun	Villagers following a discipline of short periods of abstinence for the sake of prayer. Meeting at Nazareth in Galilee. Men of Judah while in the world for marriage belonged to its higher ranks.
Naphtali	Essene villagers leading an ordinary married life, meeting at Tiberias or Capernaum on the shores of Lake Galilee. Peter and Andrew belonged to this order.

As there were four Essene orders of 1000 each, the Essenes were counted

Fig. 16 The Twelve Tribal Territories and the Community Centres in the New Testament Period

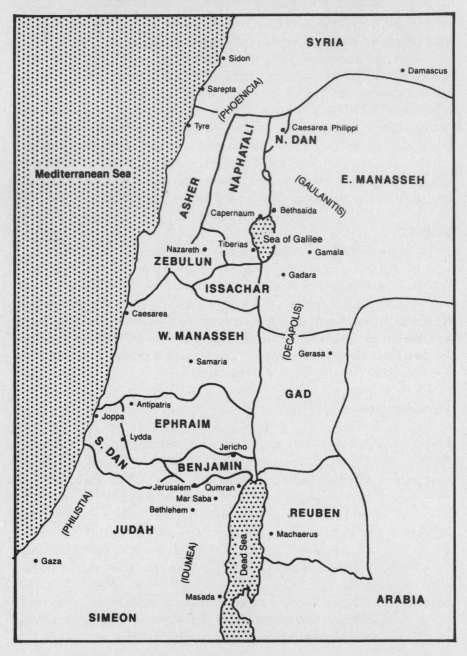

as numbering about 4000 (Philo, *Every Good Man*, 75).

The Gentile order of Dan, for women and Gentile celibates, was counted with Essene villagers but followed a way of life like the higher orders. (The book of Revelation, being anti-monastic, omits it in its list of tribes, Rev 7:5-8.)

Diaspora Essenes

Manasseh	Celibates, living like the order of Judah. Divided into two half-tribes, West (Magians, Samaritans, using the Julian calendar) and East (anti-western nationalists like Judas the Galilean, requiring circumcision for Gentiles. The whole order was dedicated to the recruitment of Gentiles, and the cultural differences between them were basic to the history. Josephus deals with them in describing the conversion of the eastern Gentile Izates: Ananias the merchant did not require him to be circumcised, but Eleazar of Galilee did (*Ant.* 20:34-43).
	Simon Magus when acting as a deacon could be called a Pharisee (Lk 7:39). Those in this lowest position were in the world, and among ordinary Jews there were only two main schools of thought, those of Pharisees and those of Sadducees. They differed on such questions as resurrection, the Pharisees affirming it. At the time of the nationalist uprising Judas the Galilean had joined with "Saddok, a Pharisee" (*Ant.* 18:3). The name, and the structure of West and East Manasseh, suggests that this was the current head of West Manasseh, the successor of Menahem. As a solarist he was a follower of Zadok, and claimed the position of Zadok's servant. As a celibate, he was a Diaspora Essene, but while in civil life chose the Pharisee point of view.
Ephraim	The Therapeutae of Egypt, fully described by Philo.
Benjamin	These were not Essenes, being lunisolarists, but were linked with them in the ascetic institution. The order of Hillel, regarded as Pharisees, but the "sect of the Pharisees" (A 15:5). Paul's order.

Herodian Orders

Herod added five "tribes" on the model of the Essene ones, headed by himself or his sons.

Simeon	Meeting in Idumea, Herod the Great's original home, with its ascetic centre on Masada (*Ant.* 14:10).
Reuben	Order of the Herod crown prince, meeting at Machaerus (*War* 7:171).

Gad   Order of the next Herod prince (Antipas in the gospel period) meeting at Gerasa (Mk 5:1, Mt 8:28).
Issachar   Order of the next Herod prince, meeting in Galilee.
Asher   Herodian women and Gentiles, meeting at Tyre, Sarepta, and Sidon (Lk 2:36, 4:26, Mk 7:31, A 12:20) (see page 310).

The original order and value of the "tribes" is indicated by the Temple Scroll (columns 39, 40), which plans a four-square court with three gates on each side for the heads of tribes to enter. On the eastern side were the gates for the most important, Levi in the centre, Herodian Simeon to its north, David's Judah to its south. On the south side were Reuben and the Diaspora orders Manasseh-Ephraim (counted as one, tribe of Joseph) and Benjamin. Lesser ranks were on the west (Issachar, Zebulun, Gad) and women, Gentiles, and married villagers on the north (Dan, Napthtali, Asher).

The same plan is found in the book of Revelation (21:10-21), with a list of tribes in 7:4-8. It is striking that if the Rev 7 list is placed at the twelve gates, but starting at the south-west corner, then six of the names (Gad, Naphtali, Simeon, Levi, Joseph and Benjamin) are at the same gate as in the Temple Scroll; and four more are directly exchanged (Judah and Issachar; Zebulun and Reuben). This is a clear sign of the dependence of Revelation on the plan of the Temple Scroll.

PARTIES
From the start, the ascetic orders had different backgrounds and purposes, and the history from Herod's time is one of tension and schism, until the Christians finally emerged and separated.

There were essentially two categories, best described as eastern and western. The name "Hebrews" was used for the former, "Hellenists" for the latter (A 6:1, Ep Heb). Hebrews used the Hebrew language in worship, and followed Jewish social customs such as the ritual law and the refusal of ministry to women (which implied also Gentiles). Hellenists, based in the Diaspora, used the Greek language in worship, the Old Testament in Greek (Septuagint), and followed hellenised ways in such matters as the treatment of women and Gentiles.

To the Hebrews belonged those Palestinian Essenes who were in the ascetic coalition of the second phase at Qumran, John the Baptist and James the brother of Jesus. They included also the Pharisee order of Benjamin, and also Pharisee high priests such as Caiaphas, whose line was linked with the Boethus family.

The moral views of the Hebrews, under Boethusian influence, were such as to deny the legitimacy of Jesus. If any of them changed his views on this question, it was a significant change.

Agrippa I, while in Judea in the gospel period, came under the influence of John the Baptist and was with the Hebrews. So also was Thomas, whom the Baptist supported in regard to the question of Herodias. After the Baptist's decline Agrippa changed to accept Jesus ("Many believed in him", Jn 2:23). Jesus, however, asserted his independence of Agrippa and all Herods.

The Hellenists, although all westernised, had two views about Rome: Manasseh-Ephraim zealots wanted to take over empire by force of arms, their leader being Simon the Zealot; while those under the alternative Hellenist Pope, Jonathan Annas, wanted peace with Rome. The former, who were supported by the tetrarch Antipas, were called the Figtree, the latter the Vineyard. When the Vineyard lost its priestly leadership and vested all leadership offices in Jesus, it had become the Christians. They in turn divided into western and eastern, the latter being called Jewish Christians. The party history is presented diagrammatically below.

Fig. 17 **History of the Parties**

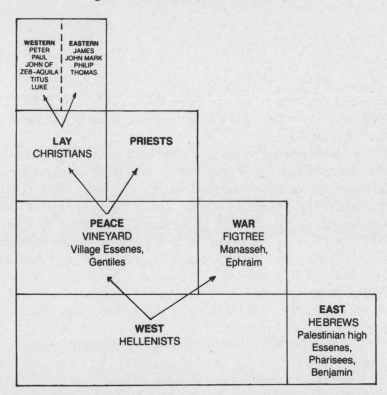

The development of the parties lends itself to depiction as a set of steps with a progressive narrowing resulting from divisions in the parties until only the Christians survived in western and eastern form.

Appendix IV

RULES FOR THE PESHARIST

The modern reader working out the pesher of the gospels and Acts has to learn some new habits. In a way, he or she has to become legalist, even naively literalist, in order to learn something that is not for the naive. The expectation is for exactitude.

The word *akribōs*, "accurately", when used in the gospels and Acts, refers to the technique that is intended to be applied. Luke prefaces his gospel by saying that he has followed matters accurately, *akribōs* (Lk 1:3), and the same word is used in a patristic source for the method of writing Mark's gospel (*Eccl. Hist.* 3:39, 15). In the Acts account of the re-education of Apollos (A 18:24–28), he is said to have previously taught about Jesus accurately (*akribōs*), but under the instruction of Priscilla and Aquila was taught more accurately (*akribesteron*); meaning that the Christian pesher was an advance on previous ones.

The expectation of exactitude gave rise to some rules which would not be those of the modern reader.

Basic Rules

1) One of the main principles is that *no words are to be assumed.*

Only the words that are in the text are to be relied on. This sometimes makes a considerable difference to the meaning. An example is in A 5:29, *apokritheis de Petros kai hoi apostoloi eipan*, usually translated "Peter and the apostles answered . . . ". The literal translation is: "Peter having answered and the apostles said . . .". For the pesharist, Peter answered (with words that are not quoted), then only the apostles said the words that are quoted. As "the apostles" mean John Mark (a plural stands for a single person representing a group), and as Peter and John Mark had different political opinions, the interpretation of the quoted words is affected.

In Lk 24:40, Jesus after the crucifixion "showed them the hands and the feet" (cf. also v. 39). There are no words indicating that they were injured. John 20:25 shows that there were nail holes in the hands, but there is no mention of feet. The rule that no words are to be assumed means that Jesus' feet were not injured, so that he was able to walk after the crucifixion.

The same rule applies in many places where the surface meaning seems to indicate a question, but no Greek words for a question are used. The words themselves are in the form of a statement, and punctuation has to be added to show a question. The words must therefore be read as a statement, not a question. For example, Lk 24:18, *ouk egnōs ta genomena*, apparently "did you not know the things that have happened?" in its p-sense means: "You did not know (acknowledge) the things that have happened".

A direct question must have an indicating word, usually *ei*. It normally means "if" or an interrogative particle, but in its p-sense is an interrogative particle only. In Mk 15:44, *ho de Pilatos ethaumasen ei ēdē tethnēken*, "Pilate wondered if he was already dead", in its p-sense is: Pilate asked: "Is he dead already?". The fact that Pilate's actual words are quoted means that he could use the verb "to die" in its ordinary sense, not in its p-sense, "to excommunicate". Pilate did not know the special language. (But the words do have a p-sense, unknown to Pilate, "Did he become defiled at 3 p.m.?").

2) Conversely, all words must be accounted for; nothing may be omitted. One effect of this is that a double negative is a positive. When Jesus said at the Last Supper "I will not not eat" (*ou mē phagō*, Lk 22:16), he meant "I will eat and not fast".

When Thomas said in Jn 20:26 *ou mē pisteusō*, apparently "I will not believe", the p-sense is "I will believe", as the words mean "I will not not believe". Thomas' saying meant: "If I do not see the physical signs of suffering . . . I will believe", a gnostic viewpoint.

3) Another rule is that *all events in narrative are consecutive*. There are no "flashbacks", going back to a previous event.

For example, in Jn 4:3 Jesus "left Judea and went . . . into Galilee".

The next verse says "he had to pass through Samaria". This means, using the rule, that he came first to Galilee, then had to pass through Samaria. It does not make sense for the literal places, as Galilee is north of Samaria, but it makes sense when it is understood that both "Galilee" and "Samaria" were parts of the building at Ain Feshkha.

Mt 2:15 appears to speak of the death of Herod, then in a following verse, Mt 2:16, Herod acts again. This means that the word for "death" in v. 15 does not mean death, but has a metaphorical meaning.

In Mk 6:14-17 the order of events is: i) Herod heard about Jesus (v. 14a); ii) Some people said "John the Baptist is risen from the dead" (v. 14b); iii) Herod said that he had removed John from the headship (*apekephalisa*, v. 16) and that he was risen iv) Herod seized John and bound him (followed by the account of the banquet at which the Baptist was condemned). This makes sense when it is understood that "to rise from the dead" means "to return to the celibate state after marriage". The events were: i) Herod heard about Jesus; ii) the Baptist's return to the celibate life was announced (at the equinox); iii) Herod said that the Baptist was no longer Pope, but he had returned to the celibate life, so was under authority; iv) Herod acted to punish John (and at the banquet agreed to give the papacy to Simon Magus, as Helena requested. John was subsequently executed).

The rule of consecutive events in narrative does not apply to speech, where there may be references to past or future events.

Narrative may contain a time phrase and related words referring back to the past, when it indicates the grade or status of a person. For example, the "daughter of Jairus" (Mary Magdalene) was "of year 12" (*ēn etōn dōdeka*, Mk 5:42), meaning that she had been given initiation in year 12, AD 17 (see Chronology, page 176). This shows that she was one of the female order encouraged by Eleazar Annas' Hellenist reforms in AD 17.

4) An assumption does have to be made, however, one not normally made in our own day. Because of the Pythagorean background of his thought (said to be characteristic of the Essenes in *Ant.* 15:371) the pesharist is intended to *assume a system*. If one or two items appear that would naturally form part of a larger system, then the larger system is to be assumed to be in operation.

If, for example, the numbers "the 7", "the 10", "the 12" appear, they must be part of an active system in which all numbers are used (see Hierarchy, page 335).

If the numbers 1000, 2000, 3000, 4000 and 5000 all appear, and some of them relate to people (4000 and 5000 in Mk 8:9, 6:44), then there is a numerical system using all the numbers for people, and a reason for naming people in this way.

If a term is clearly a symbol, then all terms in the same class are also symbols. If people are "sheep" (Jn 10:2, 21:16), then all animals are symbols of people: pigs, oxen, asses, foxes, wolves, lions, wild beasts. All refer to classes of persons. So, the "2000 pigs" into whom Legion's unclean spirits went (Mk 5:12-13) were a class of men, and the story means a change of allegiance. Legion gave up a certain loyalty under the influence of Jesus, but other men took up that loyalty, and it destroyed them.

The parable of the Sower says that members of the Church are "seed" (Mk 4:1-20). Another verse gives a hierarchy for wheat seed: "first the blade (*chortos*), then the ear, then the full grain in the ear" (Mk 4:28). Lk 12:28 says that the blade (*chortos*) "today is, and tomorrow is cast into the oven". This means that a cooked loaf is at the end of this sequence, so "loaves" are men of a high status. When this point is associated with the practice of setting out the twelve loaves of the Presence (Lev 25:5-9, referred to in Mk 2:26), then the twelve loaves of the "feedings of the multitude" are seen as men representing the holy loaves, that is, levites.

Other kinds of plants also act as symbols. A vineyard clearly stands for Israel in Mk 12:1-9, and a figtree was planted in a vineyard (Lk 13:6), so a "figtree" is also a group of people, and when the "figtree" was cursed by Jesus, (Mk 11:13-14) the meaning is that he expelled these people, not that he destroyed a tree. Nathanael, who had been seen by Jesus "under a figtree" (Jn 1:48) had belonged to this group (the following of the tetrarch Antipas); this tells more of his history.

There are other sequences of natural phenomena. "Thunder" was a man, as James and John were "sons of Thunder" (Mk 3:17), so "Lightning", "Earthquake", "Cloud", "Fire", "Wind", "Sun", "Moon" and "Star" are also men.

Birds also stand for people: the Eagle, the Dove, the Raven (Lk 12:24), the Cock, the Hen, are all titles of levitical ministers.

The principle of sequences of symbols is familiar from elsewhere in the New Testament. In 1 Cor 3:12 Paul speaks of members of the Church as "gold, silver, precious stones, wood, hay, straw". "Silver" is second, so a man associated with silver is a Second in a hierarchy. Judas, who received "thirty pieces of silver" occupied the position of Second at the Last Supper (see Hierarchy, page 362). "Alexander the coppersmith" of 2 Tim 4:14 must be part of such a system also. "Sapphira", or "sapphire" (A 5:1) is one of the "precious stones".

5) The pesharist must not be selective; nothing can be overlooked or set

aside. One of the most important indications that there is a puzzle to be solved is in Mk 8:14-21. Under the form of a riddle, Jesus sets out the figures for the two feedings of the multitude (5 loaves for 5000, with 12 baskets (*kophinoi*) of crumbs left over; 7 loaves for 4000, with 7 baskets (*spyrides*) left over. He then says that there is something to be understood, and the question is left open. As Austin Farrer said a generation ago, before the scrolls were known, the "riddle of the loaves" is not to be overlooked. It is pointing to something, and if the modern reader disregards it, he is losing something of value.

6) The pesharist's main task is to look for the special meanings of words. Words in the gospels and Acts often seem generalised, vague, not giving as much information as the inquiring mind would like. The pesharist is to expect them to have precise meanings, with a great deal of important information to convey.

The special meanings come from many different sources: plays on words, pseudonyms, nicknames, names of classes, common words with an institutional meaning, associations, titles derived from incarnational theory, universals with a particular meaning, slogans, loose terms made precise, Old Testament allusions, hierarchical terms, items in a chain of symbols. All of them come from special experience, that of a man who has been a member of the ascetic community for long enough to have learned its distinctive terminology and practices.

Human institutions tend to develop a private language in order to give identity. The more exclusive the institution, the more it develops a language that acts as a set of passwords, giving admission to those who are "in the know", keeping out those who are not. The institutional language may be so rarefied that it looks like nonsense to the outsider. To take some examples:

If someone remarked: "I saw the bench talking to a silk", apparently making no sense, it would, in fact, convey to a member of the legal profession that a judge had been talking to a queen's counsel.

Similarly, "the White House spoke to the Kremlin" would make sense to anyone who followed politics. "The Sharks play the Dragons" would be quite natural to an Australian football fan. A "foundation chair" in a university means the position of a first professor. An actor "treads the boards"; and "the House rises" means that parliament adjourns.

The purpose of this book has been to show that the secondary meaning is objectively there in the gospels and Acts. It has set out the story that emerges, and the elements of the basic systems that lie behind the gospel history: chronology, locations, and hierarchy. A great many lesser systems remain to be set out, with their associated vocabulary. But enough has been done to show that a quite new chapter in our understanding of the New Testament and of Christian origins has been opened up by the discovery of the Dead Sea Scrolls.

A GUIDE TO PEOPLE & EVENTS

WHO'S WHO IN THE HISTORY

"Abraham" Hillel the Great, whose teaching that Judaism was entered spiritually through baptism became the foundation of a mission to Diaspora Jews in the time of Herod the Great. Jews in a "new Israel" were baptised as "sons of Abraham". As "Abraham" was the "Father" of Jews, he established the position of Pope (Father).

Agabus A name for Matthew Annas used during his exile in Antioch, after his deposition as high priest in AD 43.

Agrippa I Grandson of Herod the Great. Born 11 BC. During his education in Rome he gained influence in the Roman court through Antonia, the mother and grandmother of emperors. He aimed to restore the Herodian dynasty to power in Judea. Profligate with money, he was expelled from Rome for debt. He was in Judea during the gospel period, and after attempting suicide came under the influence of John the Baptist. After the Baptist's death, Agrippa began to favour Jesus as the potential David, but his ambitions were opposed by Simon Magus and John Mark. On his return to Rome shortly before the death of Tiberius, Agrippa was put under arrest for plotting against Tiberius, then released on the accession of Gaius Caligula, who gave him the title of king of the Jews. He returned to Judea, at first supported by parts of the ascetic movement, but after deposing Matthew Annas and claiming to be god-emperor, he was assassinated in AD 44 by Simon Magus, with the approval of most of the ascetics.

Agrippa II Son of Agrippa I and Cypros. Born AD 27. On his father's death, Agrippa II was not named successor because of his youth. He became king in AD 49, and remained unmarried. He came under the influence of Paul, whose order acted as tutors to the Herods. Agrippa II encouraged the Pauline form of the ascetic doctrine, and opposed Samaritans, who had been responsible for his father's death, thus leading to the separation of Christians and Samaritans. When given Galilee by Nero in AD 54, he received a separate Christian baptism from Paul, replacing that of the Baptist. Agrippa II remained with eastern ascetics in the position that had been held by Thomas, accepting Jesus as the Lord, Priest and Pope, but not as the David.

Alexander Title of the head of the Egyptian Therapeutae, whose main centre was in Alexandria. The title was held by Theudas and his successor, Apollos. "'Alexander the Coppersmith" was Apollos, who brought about Paul's arrest in Rome.

All (Greek *pantes*) A pseudonym for the Herod king, as he held all leading positions. It refers to Agrippa I in the gospel period.

Ananias The name for Simon Magus as the servant of the Samaritan high priest Ananias (taking the name of his master). Probably indicating that Simon was the same as the merchant Ananias who did not require eastern Gentile converts to be circumcised.

Ananus, son of Seth High priest of the Jews, AD 6 to 15. He was appointed by the Romans, as he was in favour of peace with Rome. Ananus was allied with Simon the Essene in the peace faction of AD 5 to 6. He was a Sadducee, allowing high priests to be called "God" and treated as exalted persons. His five sons became high priests after him at times when peace with Rome was a desirable policy.

Ananus the Younger Youngest son of the first Ananus. A Sadducee, he was high priest of the Jews for a short period in AD 62, and again subsequently. A young man during the gospel period, he came under the influence of Jesus, and as guard at the burial cave helped Jesus to recover and escape. He remained loyal to Agrippa I, and was associated with Paul during the reign of Agrippa II. Other names: Zacchaeus, Sosthenes, the (Philippian) Jailer.

Antipas, the tetrarch Son of Herod the Great by Malthace the Samaritan, full brother of Archelaus. Antipas had been promised the succession by Herod about a year before his death, and was disappointed when Archelaus was given the position. He led a campaign against Archelaus in Rome, establishing an alternate Herodian party there, known as the Figtree. In the gospel period Antipas was allied with the war faction of Hellenists led by Simon Magus and conspired with the Parthians against Rome. He was married first to the daughter of Aretas, the Arab king, then divorced her to marry Herodias, who left her first husband Herod (Thomas), half-brother of Antipas. Aretas took revenge on Antipas by declaring war in AD 37. Herodias tried to persuade her husband to claim the Herodian kingship against Agrippa I, as Antipas had a better right, and he, although unwilling, finally agreed. But in Rome he was outwitted by Agrippa, and he and Herodias were exiled to Gaul in AD 39.

Apollos The successor of Theudas as head of the Egyptian Therapeutae, from AD 44. Apollos brought Alexandrians to more westernised views in the final years of Claudius. Under Nero, he joined with western Christians, as all factions were driven together in opposition to Nero. Although he had previously had the views of the Baptists and Hebrews about Jesus, he accepted, for the sake of union, that Jesus was the legitimate David. His change of doctrine came about at a council at Philippi in AD 50, and was presented symbolically as an "earthquake". Apollos continued in the western mission, but in tension with Paul, as he held eastern views on the admission of Gentiles. He followed the Exodus imagery of the Therapeutae, acting as a "Joshua" and dem nding that the walls of Jerusalem fall down. He was later arrested, sent to Caesarea, then to Rome. In Rome, Apollos accused Paul of complicity in Felix's murder of Jonathan Annas, leading to Paul's arrest and trials.

"Apostles" A name for John Mark as the chief proselyte, in the position of a levitical deacon, a Merari, one who was "sent out" from the meal chamber when the village priest came. The plural form of the name is used as John Mark represented a class. He did not use the name in his gospel, but it was used for him by the Synoptics.

Archelaus Son of Herod the Great by Malthace the Samaritan. The only survivor after most of Herod's heirs were executed or disinherited, Archelaus ruled 4 BC to AD 6, but was challenged for the title of king by his brother Antipas, and received only the title of ethnarch. Archelaus was dismissed through the influence of a coalition of public figures in AD 6, apparently ending the Herodian era.

Aristarchus the Macedonian A name for Peter after he entered a Nazirite celibate order as a widower. His centre was then in Macedonia, as Christian Nazirites established centres there after their expulsion from Rome in AD 49. He returned to Rome with Paul's party in AD 60, using this name.

Barabbas A name for Theudas as the servant (Aramaic *bar*) of Jonathan Annas, who could be called Abba, the Father.

Barnabas A name for Joses, a younger brother of Jesus, next after James. Called Joses, or Joseph, as he was the successor of James when James was the "Jacob", (the David king under the Herods). Barnabas had more western views than James, and was appointed to the Twelve Apostles as a bishop, equal to a Kohath, or levitical bishop, so called Matthias, as another Matthew. In this position he was a "servant of the Prophet", hence called *Bar* (servant) *nabas* (prophet). Barnabas worked with Paul for a time, but separated from him on celibacy and the question of Jewish identity for Gentiles, preferring the intermediate requirements for proselytes. Barnabas remained associated with the chief proselyte John Mark. He was author of the non-canonical Epistle of Barnabas, teaching a mystical form of Judaism.

Bartholomew The name used for John Mark in the Twelve Apostles. Possibly a play on "servant of (*bar*) Ptolemy (Tholomaeus)", as he was attached to the Egyptian Therapeutae.

Beloved Disciple John Mark, in his role of "wife" to Jesus, a man standing in for the wife of a dynastic celibate after his return to the celibate house.

"Caesar" A name for the ruling Herod, when used without a further name such as Tiberius. The name reflected the ambitions of the Herod family to have a Jewish Caesar at the head of a Jewish empire.

Caiaphas High priest of the Jews AD 18 to 36. Caiaphas was a Pharisee, related to the Boethus family of priests. He supported the eastern doctrine of the Hebrews, with strict views on morality, and so held that Jesus was not the legitimate David, but his brother James was. Caiaphas supported John the Baptist on this question. In the latter part of his reign the Twelve Apostles, Hellenists, were working to have him replaced as high priest. He was dismissed in AD 36.

"Chief Priests" (Greek *hoi archiereis*). In the plural form, a title of Jonathan Annas as representative of the village priests. In the singular form (*ho archiereus*), used for a non-representative chief priest, Caiaphas (not in the ascetic system) or Annas when out of power.

Claudius Roman emperor, AD 41 to 54. Claudius gained the goodwill of westernised Jews. The Christian version of the doctrine flourished during his reign, but demonstrations taken to be supporting Jewish nationalism were punished.

Claudius Lysias A name for Agrippa II, used because Agrippa was appointed king by Claudius in AD 49, and used his name as a servant used the name of his master.

"Cloud" A name for the David crown prince who, as head of the Nazirites, led them on their pilgrimages to Qumran, so was the "Cloud by day" in Exodus imagery. In the west, he was "Cloud overshadowing". The name was used of James in the gospel period.

Cornelius A name for Luke as the head of Japheth uncircumcised Gentiles, "the Italian band".

"Crowds" (Greek *hoi ochloi*). Agrippa I, in his role of representative of ordinary

Jews who flocked to hear John the Baptist. He was instructed by the Baptist and subsequently by Jesus. But singular *ho ochlos* ("the crowd") means the tetrarch Antipas, who lived like an ordinary Jew but, not being their ruler, was not representative.

Demetrius the Silversmith Simon Magus, when acting as a bishop in Ephesus, supporting the cult of Helena as an incarnation of Diana of the Ephesians.

"Disciples" Proselytes, in the status of lower novice, were called "disciples", or "learners". Their chief was called by the plural term. "The disciples of John (the Baptist)" means Agrippa I. "The disciples of Jesus" means John Mark.

Dositheus A version of Jonathan Annas' name ("gift of God"). This name was used in the Clementine literature for Jonathan as successor of the Baptist, acting Pope AD 30–31.

"Earthquake" A title of the head of the Egyptian Therapeutae, used as part of their Exodus symbolism, and also because their leaders were in power at the time of the earthquake of 31BC. The title was used for both Theudas and Apollos.

"Elders" (Greek *hoi presbyteroi*). Refers to James in his role of Third, the position given to the David king by Hebrews. (Jacob–Heli was the "Elder Brother" in the story of the Prodigal Son, under a Boethusian high priest.)

"Elijah" Title of the chief hermit, practising a discipline like that of Elijah. The title was used by John the Baptist, then by Jonathan Annas as his successor.

Eutychus The given name of John Mark, used in his position as a freedman of Agrippa I, and his chariot driver. The name was used at the time of John Mark's reconciliation with western Christians in AD 58, when he was re-admitted, stripped of his titles.

"Fear" (Greek *ho phobos*). Title of the Herod kings as rulers of celibates, to be obeyed (feared) by them. "The fear of the Jews" was Agrippa I in the gospel period, in the position of deacon.

Gabriel Title of the heir of the Abiathar priesthood, as the second "archangel" under "Michael". It meant Simon the Essene in the time of Herod the Great.

Gaius Caligula ("Little Boots"). Roman emperor AD 37–41. Friend of Agrippa I, to whom he gave the title of king of the Jews. After two years' reign he showed symptoms of dementia, and was assassinated by a general conspiracy in January AD 41.

Helena The mistress of Simon Magus. She was a Gentile who joined the Jewish religion in its Herodian form at the time of her divorce. She was a member of the female order of Asher, women who practised an individual discipline of prayer and good works while living in the world and holding private property. Her order, based in Tyre, could adopt the practice of sacred prostitution continuing from Canaanite times, and were then called "harlots". Helena was associated with Simon Magus as "a whore from a brothel in Tyre". As female cardinal in Ephesus, Helena was the "Sarah" to Gentiles; and her order had a centre in Thyatira, where she was called "the prophetess Jezebel". She and Simon acted as Mother and Father to their followers, and were believed to be incarnations of deities. She was called Helena as the servant and spiritual adviser of Queen Helena of Adiabene who was converted by Simon-Ananias to Judaism in the forties AD.

Herod the Great Son of Antipater, an Idumean, who gained favour with the Roman general Pompey, who occupied Jerusalem in 63 BC. At the decline of the Hasmoneans Herod gained popular support and received the endorsement of the Romans to become king of the Jews in 40 BC, being crowned in 37 BC. Herod undertook vast building projects, and became the stimulus for a mission in the Diaspora, to bring Jews into a world-wide society that would have significant political power. Their membership fees were used to finance his building projects. In his declining years Herod suffered increasing anguish of mind, leading to the execution or disinheriting of most of his heirs borne to him by his nine wives. He died in 4 BC.

Herod of Chalcis Grandson of Herod the Great, brother of Agrippa I. Herod of Chalcis supported Samaritans, and was probably involved with Simon Magus in the plot against his brother. After Agrippa's death Herod of Chalcis was named regent, with the power to appoint high priests. He appointed Ananias the Samaritan high priest. After the banishment of Antipas Herod of Chalcis took over his duty as head of circumcised married Gentiles, the "Jews". He died in AD 48.

Herodias Granddaughter of Herod the Great, sister of Agrippa I. Herodias was promised as a child to Herod (Thomas), and during her marriage with him bore a daughter, Salome. She then left him to marry the tetrarch Antipas. She incited Antipas to contest Agrippa I's right to the throne, and was banished with her husband to Gaul in AD 39.

Isaac Title of Menahem as cardinal and patriarch of the east in the Herodian triarchy of "Abraham, Isaac and Jacob".

Jacob of Alphaeus Title of Jonathan Annas in the Twelve Apostles, treated as a king, "Jacob", rather than a priest.

Jacob-Heli The grandfather of Jesus. Jacob-Heli was a descendant of King David through Nathan, a younger son. Allied with Herod the Great, he accepted a third position in the triarchy of "Abraham, Isaac, and Jacob" as patriarch of the west. He was born in 70 BC, and died in AD 17. As the "Elder Brother" in the story of the Prodigal Son, he held out for peace in Asia Minor at the time of the zealot uprising, causing a schism and splitting of the funds with Theudas, the "Prodigal Son".

James, the brother of Jesus The younger brother of Jesus, born AD 1. James was conceived in wedlock, so for the Hebrews he was the legitimate David. When Hellenists were in power, James was prepared to act as successor to Jesus, so was called "Joseph". But under the Hebrews he would be the David, so was called "Jacob" (James), the name for the David king when with the Herods. For Jewish Christians, who finally accepted Jesus as the Lord (Priest and Pope), James was the David, so was called "Jacob" by them. James was also called "Absalom" by his critics, who regarded him as the treacherous heir of David. James held that Gentiles should become proselytes; they should not be circumcised but should keep aspects of the ritual law and obey Jewish priests. On this point he was opposed by Paul, who allowed Gentiles to abandon Jewish identity. James was stoned to death in AD 62 on the orders of the high priest Ananus the Younger.

Jesus Son of Joseph, a descendant of King David through the Nathan line, and of Mary. Jesus was conceived during his parents' betrothal period before their legal marriage, so was regarded by the party of Hebrews as an extranuptial son of Joseph. He was born in March, 7 BC. For Hellenists in the ascetic movement, he was the legitimate David, and would rule when the Kingdom came, either as an independent king, or as a subordinate of the Herods. In AD 29 he joined with the Twelve Apostles, Hellenists, to oppose John the Baptist, who held the doctrine of Hebrews. But Jesus introduced entirely new doctrines, claiming to be able himself to fill the position of high priest, as well as king. Thus he taught the priesthood of all believers, and also the free admission of all members, including Gentiles, without hierarchical grading on the grounds of birth, race, sex or physical condition. He was opposed by all parties working for Jewish supremacy, and was called by them the "Wicked (Anti-)Priest" and "Man of a Lie". Jesus was crucified through a political stratagem, on the grounds that he was technically an associate of zealots. He was given poison on the cross to end his sufferings, but merely lost consciousness, and was helped to revive by his friends. He remained with the pro-Gentile party in its successive forms, guiding its leaders, John Mark, then Peter, then Paul. In AD 61 Jesus led his party to Rome, where they established a separate mission to Gentiles, no longer attempting to make them Jews. He was still alive in AD 64, and his death is not recorded.

"Jews" Name for the head of circumcised Gentiles, living as married men in the world like ordinary Jews. It meant the tetrarch Antipas during the gospel period. He was succeeded by Herod of Chalcis, then by his son Aristobulus. John's gospel prefers this term for Antipas.

John the Baptist Son of Zechariah, the heir of the Zadokite dynasty. At the split between classical Essenes and those Essenes who remained politically involved with zealots, John chose political activity, but only as one who worked to earn heaven's intervention at the time appointed by prophecy. He lived as a hermit, enduring self-imposed hardship as a way of gaining merit. John the Baptist was called the Teacher of Righteousness by ascetics at Mird and Qumran, as he was the successor of the original Teacher and Pope, Hillel. He was opposed by the Twelve Apostles on the grounds of his priestliness and eastern views. He wrote or influenced some of the Dead Sea Scrolls, in which Hellenists were called "seekers-after-smooth-things". John attacked the tetrarch Antipas, who was associated with the Twelve Apostles, for his marriage with Herodias, and was put to death by Antipas. Some followers of John claimed that Jesus, the "Wicked Priest" and "Man of a Lie", was involved in his death, as Jesus was a member of the Hellenist party. After the Baptist's death many of his followers, including Agrippa I, turned towards Jesus. Others remained with the east, their traditions preserved in the Dead Sea Scrolls.

John Mark Chief Gentile proselyte in the gospel period. Proselytes were not circumcised, but accepted some Jewish ritual laws while rejecting others. John Mark obeyed Jewish priests, causing places of worship for his order to have three storeys, so the priest could stand at the highest level above a Jewish elder. His given name was Eutychus. In Rome in about AD 36 with Agrippa I, he betrayed his master to Tiberius when he overheard Agrippa plotting with Gaius Caligula. He was allied with Simon Magus against Agrippa. During the gospel period he had been close to Jesus, both as a friend and as a representative of proselytes. He became the sponsor of John's gospel, which represented his outlook. At the rise of Agrippa I in AD 37 he lost his influence. Under Agrippa II John Mark was allied with James. As Eutychus, he became reconciled with Paul in AD 58 on the eve of Paul's visit to Jerusalem.

John of Zebedee A Gentile, a Roman of high standing with links with the Roman court, whose Roman name was Aquila. With his brother Niceta (James of Zebedee) he joined the new Jewish religion, and at first was instructed by Simon Magus ("Zebedee"), whose doctrine included opposition to Agrippa I. Subsequently John–Aquila changed his political views to support Agrippa I, and so came under the instruction of "Zacchaeus" (Ananus the Younger), the servant of Agrippa. He and James then became "sons of Thunder", as subordinates of the Annas priests. He worked with Peter in the mission to Gentiles. He was a married man, with a similar discipline to that of Peter, and his wife, Priscilla, worked with him as a minister. He was head of the Five Thousand, that is, married uncircumcised Gentiles of the order of Asher. He worked with Paul during the period of Paul's ascendancy under Agrippa II, travelling between Ephesus and Rome. He wrote the book of Revelation. With the Christians, he occupied the position of Eagle (Sariel, the Spirit); his name, Aquila, meant "eagle".

Jonathan Annas Son of Ananus the high priest of AD 6. Johnathan Annas was himself high priest for six months in AD 37. He was a Hellenist, at first with John the Baptist as the Good Samaritan, opposing militant zealotry. Then he joined the Twelve Apostles, who worked to bring Hellenist high priests into power. Like all the Annas brothers, he supported Gentile members and taught peace with Rome, but insisted on priestly superiority, and the treatment of village priests in the Diaspora as divine persons. Jesus supported him on the Gentile question, but opposed him on the priestly question, often claiming his position. Jonathan Annas thus had a personal animosity to Jesus, despite their political agreement. When it was clear that Jesus would be crucified, he ordered Jesus to take poison, and himself supplied the poison. He was subsequently opposed by Paul, who took part in the process of his deposition in September AD 37. Jonathan Annas was put to death in AD 57 by the Roman governor Felix, for the reason that he was constantly interfering in Felix's management of the state.

Joseph Son of Jacob-Heli, born 44 BC. He was given the title "Joseph" as crown prince to "Jacob". In 8 BC he was 36, and due to marry in September of that year. His son, Jesus, was conceived in June, after the final betrothal ceremony but before the wedding. Having a liberal outlook, he chose to continue with the marriage, but when he was under a high priest holding the doctrine of the Hebrews he had to accept that James, his next son, was the heir. At the political crisis brought about by the Roman domination, he joined with moderate nationalists, allying with Theudas. He was the "Star" (of David) to Theudas' "Sceptre". Joseph became the potential David on the death of Jacob-Heli in AD 17. He died in AD 23.

Joseph of Arimathea Name for James, the brother of Jesus, as the successor to Jesus under Hellenist rule. "Arimathea" may refer to his alliance with Agrippa I, who said "*ari' meth*" ("the lion is dead") at the news of the death of Tiberius.

Joses, or Joseph Name of the next brother of Jesus after James. When James was the "Jacob", as the David king with the Herods, this brother would be the "Joseph". See "Barnabas."

Judas Iscariot The successor of Judas the Galilean, the nationalist leader of AD 6. Judas Iscariot was head of East Manasseh, fervent militant nationalists. He required all Gentiles to be circumcised and to become fully Jewish. In AD 29 and 30 Judas was the dominant head of Manasseh, and, as "Satan", proposed an alliance with Jesus. He would be Priest and Pope, and Jesus King. But Jesus rejected him, allying with the peace faction in the Twelve Apostles, thus causing him to lose power. At the time of the crucifixion Judas attempted revenge, notifying Pilate of the whereabouts of three wanted zealots, and working with Agrippa I to offer a bribe to Pilate for his own release. But Pilate then accepted a bribe from the tetrarch Antipas for the release of Theudas, and Judas was crucified in the place of Theudas. When the method of execution was changed to burial alive, his legs were broken and he was placed in the cave, becoming one of the two "angels" seen there. When Simon Magus was rescued, Judas was punished for his betrayal of his comrades by being thrown down the cliff from the window of the cave.

Jude Name of the third brother of Jesus. Author of the epistle of Jude. He had pro-eastern views, and although allied with James and Jewish Christians, he condemned the extreme western form of the doctrine taught by Paul. In AD 58 he attempted to have Paul excommunicated.

Lazarus A name for Simon Magus when under expulsion, used in John's gospel and in Luke's parable of Lazarus and the Rich Man.

"Leper" Name for Simon Magus when expelled from the celibate community, as he was sent down to the level of lepers, who were not permitted on holy premises.

"Lightning" Name for Simon Magus as Pope, succeeding "Thunder", Jonathan Annas. The name was drawn from Exodus imagery.

Luke (Lucius) Alternate name for Cornelius, head of Japheth. Luke took the place of John Mark as the physician and close personal friend of Jesus, using the term "we" to speak of himself when representing and accompanied by Jesus. Luke was author of Luke–Acts.

Malchus From the Hebrew for "king". This was the title of James when he became the David at the arrest of Jesus.

"Many" (Greek *hoi polloi*). The name for the head of celibates in their meetings of 100 full members. The term is found frequently in the Dead Sea Scrolls (Hebrew *harabbim*). In the gospels it is used for Agrippa I, who as the Herod was the nominal head of celibates.

Mary, mother of Jesus Born 26 BC. Mary was aged 17½ at the conception of Jesus in June, 8 BC. She was a member of the order of Dan, in which women were called Virgins, or nuns, until their legal marriage. She was widowed in AD 23. In December AD 32, Mary began three years' preparation to become a Widow, an order of ministry given to women at the age of 60. She was chosen by the Christian party to be the chief woman, Mother of Gentiles. John Mark, as chief Gentile, was made her "son", so she was also "Mary the Mother of John Mark". "Mary" (Miriam) was a title used for the chief woman of the Therapeutae, acting as Miriam, the sister of Moses.

Mary Magdalene A member of the order of Dan, using the title "Miriam", but in a branch of the order under Herodian influence, allowing divorce and remarriage. Her marriage to Jesus in AD 30 may have been her second. Mary Magdalene was born in AD 3, and was aged 14 in AD 17 at the time she was "born" (the first initiation, at age 14 for girls, 12 for boys). Older than usual at the time of her marriage, Mary Magdalene conceived in December AD 32, during the trial marriage. She had a daughter (Tamar) born in September AD 33, a son (Jesus Justus) born June AD 37, and a second son in March AD 44. She subsequently separated from Jesus, leading to a crisis which was resolved by the ruling that she was not a Christian believer, as the Christians had adopted a separate identity and name in AD 44.

Mary of Cleopas Named in John's gospel as the fourth woman at the cross. She was the betrothed of James (Cleopas), whom she married in AD 37 when he was 36. She was presumably about 14 in AD 33, so did not take part in the visits to the cave by the older women.

Matthew Annas One of the Annas brothers. He was a Hellenist, a member of the Twelve Apostles, and the Annas who was most in sympathy with the Christian version of the doctrine. Matthew Annas was high priest in AD 42–43. When he was deposed by Agrippa I, the Christians separated and went to Antioch, where Matthew was also present, as Agabus, and "the Holy Spirit" (in the form *to hagion pneuma*). He was levitical bishop (Kohath) of the five provinces of Asia Minor, and he was sponsor of Matthew's gospel, the most Jewish of the gospels.

Matthias Name for Barnabas when he was appointed to the Twelve Apostles. As a celibate, he was made not simply a bishop, but a levitical bishop, a "levite", so was another Kohath like Matthew.

Menahem A Diaspora Essene who, in 44 BC, founded the Magians of West Manasseh. Menahem was associated with Hillel, as the "Isaac" to his "Abraham". In the position of cardinal, he was the effective founder of the mission to Jews and Gentiles of the Diaspora.

"Moses" Pseudonym of the Prophet, Second in the hierarchy of priests, a term used in AD 5 for Simeon, whose new constitution for ascetics was called "the laws of Moses". The name was also used by his "servant", the head of the Ephraim Therapeutae in a role equal to Kohath, third in the village hierarchy, acting as the "Moses" in the liturgical dances. Theudas in the gospel period was the "Moses" who was with Jesus at the "Transfiguration".

Nathanael Name for Jonathan Annas, an alternate form of "Jonathan", both meaning "God/the Lord gave".

Nero Roman emperor, AD 54 to AD 68. A capricious tyrant, whose regime brought about a degree of reunion between eastern and western members of the mission, brought together in opposing him. The Christian and Jewish members in Rome intensified their hope of an eschatological crisis leading to the destruction of all pagans. Their demonstrations in the years AD 60 to AD 64, for the year Anno Mundi 4000 brought about their arrest. Nero used them as scapegoats at the time of the great fire of Rome.

Paul Member of the order of Benjamin founded by Hillel, an order consisting of Pharisees who adopted an ascetic discipline while remaining in public life. They were philosophers, teachers of the Herod princes. Paul, as Saul, was instructed by Gamaliel, a descendant of Hillel. He was born in AD 17. As a young man he was a fervent nationalist, holding the eastern views of the Hebrews, and bitterly opposed to Jesus. But in AD 40, at the time of Jesus' visit to the Damascus centre, Saul met him, and was converted to a western viewpoint. He went to the opposite extreme, holding that Gentiles had no need to adopt Jewish identity. He remained loyal to Agrippa I, having no part in his death, so was trusted by Agrippa II, to whom he was tutor. From AD 44 to 58 he campaigned for his doctrine in Asia Minor. In AD 58 he led his party ín a last visit to Jerusalem, then went with them to Rome, where they would have their own base and organisation. He was author of the majority of the epistles in the New Testament.

Peter See Simon Peter.

"Pharisees, the" (Greek *hoi Pharisaioi*). Term used in the gospels for Caiaphas as head of the Pharisee party.

Philip Chief uncircumcised Gentile in the gospel period, head of the order of Shem (as uncircumcised Gentiles were left in their ethnic groupings of Shem, Ham and Japheth). Philip was associated with Samaritans, both Jonathan Annas–Nathanael and Simon Magus. He is to be identified with Protos, a freedman of Agrippa's mother Bernice, who lent Agrippa money, then was defrauded by him. Philip was hostile to Agrippa I, and so was politically close to John Mark and Simon. He was promoted by Jesus as the "centurion's servant", and at the "miracle of changing water to wine", being given full membership, even though uncircumcised.

Salome Name for Helena as the servant and spiritual adviser of Salome, the daughter of Herodias.

"Satan" Pseudonym of Judas Iscariot as the chief zealot in AD 29 and 30. He "tempted" or "tested" Jesus, as a bishop tested candidates for initiation. His doctrine, however, was rejected by Jesus.

Simon Magus The main character apart from Jesus. Simon Magus was a gnostic, self-styled miracle worker, head of West Manasseh Magians in the gospel period, and a Hellenist, in the war faction of the Twelve Apostles. He became Pope in AD 31. Jesus was associated with him, as Hellenists accepted Jesus as the David. Simon was a bitter enemy of Agrippa I, and at Agrippa's rise in AD 37 a schism took place. Those who supported the Agrippas began a formation which became Christian, while Simon, despite his western ideas, was driven back to ally with the eastern Hebrews, conducting a rival mission to that of the Christians. He became the anti-Pope to the party of Peter and Paul. Presented in the gospels under many different pseudonyms, as Jesus has many pseudonyms in the Dead Sea Scrolls, Simon is a well documented figure in literature outside the New Testament.

Simon Peter A village Essene, married, leading the sober family life of the Essene order of Naphtali. Jesus associated with Simon Peter's class, despite their differences in grade. A Hellenist, accepting Jesus as the David, he became a Second to Jesus in his position as King, and believed that Jesus should claim only to be King ("the Christ") and not the Priest. He is to be identified with Simon, the scrupulous citizen of Jerusalem who was won over to Agrippa I. Under Agrippa II he was not dominant, as he had joined with those who finally turned against Agrippa I. But on becoming a widower he joined the higher order of Nazirites, and at the transfer of the Christian party to Rome became the representative of Jesus in his capacity as King.

Simon Youngest brother of Jesus, also called Silas. He and Joses-Barnabas were the two brothers of Jesus who had a western viewpoint, and both worked with Paul. Simon-Silas remained with Paul after Barnabas separated from him.

Simon the Essene, or Simeon Head of the Abiathar dynasty of priests, Second to the Zadokite head. He was known as "Gabriel" to the Zadokite's "Michael". Simon was a dominant figure of the high Essenes in the reign of Archelaus, and was asked by Archelaus to prophesy the length of his reign. He allied with the peace faction under Ananus to bring about the deposition of Archelaus. But in AD 6 he separated, taking the classical Essenes into a separate, non-political way of life. Those Essenes who remained with the political activists were classed with the "fourth philosophy", the zealots.

Thaddeus Name for Theudas as a member of the Twelve Apostles.

Theophilus One of the Annas brothers, high priest AD 37 to AD 41. Theophilus co-operated with Rome, leading the people to take the oath of loyalty to Caesar. Luke dedicated Luke-Acts to him.

Theudas The head of the Egyptian Therapeutae from about 9 BC to AD 44. Theudas was leader of moderate nationalists who reoccupied Qumran in its second phase, making it "Egypt". Allied with Joseph, the father of Jesus, he was displaced when Judas the Galilean, with more extreme views, took over Qumran in AD 4 to AD 6. Theudas then returned to the peace faction as the Prodigal Son. He joined the Twelve Apostles as Thaddeus and took part in the uprising against Pilate of December AD 32. He held the position of King in the Hellenist zealot triarchy of Priest, Prophet and King, and was wanted by Pilate. Theudas was arrested in March AD 33 with Simon

Magus and Jesus. He would have been crucified but for the intervention of the tetrarch Antipas, who offered a bribe to Pilate to have him released, partly on the ground of his age. Instructed by the tetrarch to look after Simon Magus in the cave, he helped to bring about the resuscitation of Jesus by supplying the medicines and helping to have them administered. In AD 44 he led an imagined "entry to the Promised Land" by commanding the waters of Jordan to part, and was executed.

Thomas (Didymus, the Twin) Guest of the Twelve Apostles, to be identified with the son of Herod the Great by Mariamme II the daughter of the high priest Simon Boethus (23 to 5 BC). Thomas was disinherited in 5 BC when his grandfather and mother were discovered to be involved in a poisoning plot against Herod. He was called "Esau", the Twin (of "Jacob", as the crown prince of Herod in a village formation was equal to the David, called "Jacob"). The name was appropriate as Esau had lost his birthright. He represented the One Thousand, circumcised Gentiles who lived as celibates. His wife, Herodias, left him to marry his half-brother the tetrarch Antipas. Thomas had the views of the Hebrews, and was supported by the Baptist in the dispute about Antipas' marriage. He became the representative of Jesus in the east, holding him to be Pope and Priest ("my Lord and my God") but not the David (Christ).

"Thunder" Pseudonym of Jonathan Annas as Pope, using Exodus imagery.

Tiberius Roman emperor, AD 14 to AD 37. Tiberius usually held the goodwill of the Jews, but cared little for the eastern provinces, and was prepared to appoint Pontius Pilate to Judea, accepting that he would receive bribes. Opposed by Agrippa I, whom he had befriended, Tiberius died on the island of Capri in March AD 37.

Timothy Probably the son of Aristobulus, son of Herod of Chalcis, a possible heir to Agrippa II while Agrippa had no son. Timothy was instructed by Paul, who was tutor to the Herod princes, and was influenced by him to the Christian version of the doctrine.

Titus Head of the uncircumcised Gentiles of Ham. Titus was the "Ethiopian eunuch", and probably Marsyas, the loyal freedman of Agrippa I. Titus refused the invitation of Philip, his superior, to join in a conspiracy against Agrippa I. He worked with Paul, who was also loyal to Agrippa I, and was tutor in Corinth to Jesus Justus, who was called Titius Justus as a disciple using the name of the master. When he was sent by Paul to Crete, to a centre for Gentiles of his order, the epistle to Titus was written to him.

Zacchaeus Name for Ananus the Younger as the Merari, who was sent out from the vestry equivalent at Mar Saba ("Jericho") to stand at the northern pillar base, the "sycamore tree" (as the Herods were associated with figtrees). Zacchaeus was the loyal servant of the Agrippas.

Zebedee Name for Simon Magus, meaning "my gift", to contrast him with the other Samaritan, Jonathan Annas, whose name meant "Gift of God". Zebedee was also the "Father" of James and John, as he had instructed Niceta and Aquila before they turned to Zacchaeus.

OUTLINE OF EVENTS 168 BC to AD 74

168 BC   "Abomination of desolation". The Seleucid king Antiochus Epiphanes placed a statue of Zeus in the Holy of Holies of the Jerusalem temple. Signal for the Maccabean revolt. War of liberation, resulting in the overthrow of the Seleucids. The Maccabees as national heroes were made high priests and kings (the Hasmonean dynasty), although they were not from the traditional families.

The Essenes at first co-operated with them, but then tried to use the opportunity to get back the temple for themselves. They wrote the book of Daniel in support. Failing in their attempt, they were exiled to Qumran.

88 BC   Essene calculations had shown that this was the year 4000 from creation, when a catastrophic event should occur. Nothing happened. They then found an error in their records; when they had a truer date for the fall of Jerusalem, the year 4000 would fall in AD 60. Eighty years before this date, in 3920 (21 BC) the Essenes should, according to a prophecy in the book of Enoch, regain the temple, the high priesthood, and the kingship.

45 BC   Introduction of the Julian calendar (the one we now use) by Julius Caesar.

44 BC   Formation of the order of Magians, liberal Essenes of the Diaspora, who used the Julian as well as the solar calendar.

41–   37 BC   Herod the Great, a strong, ambitious personality, became king of the Jews. Under his impetus, the concept of the kingdom of God was formed: a world empire of Jews to rival the Roman empire.

Hillel the Great (a famous Jewish sage who taught the Golden Rule and practised baptisms) was one of the spiritual influences. The active leaders were Menahem the Magian Essene, and Heli, the grandfather of Jesus. These three would be the "Abraham", "Isaac" and "Jacob" respectively, of the New Israel and New Covenant.

The years 41 and 37 BC were the year 3900 (falling twice due to a calendar complication). As the whole span of world history was to be 4900 years according to the Enoch prophecy, Herod had inaugurated the final millennium of world history, a thousand year empire of Jews. Its first forty years, 41 to 1 BC, a generation, were to be used for evangelism.

31 BC The earthquake at Qumran. The site was abandoned, but the Essenes were now welcomed back to Jerusalem by Herod as they were part of a vast money-making scheme.

21 BC Herod announced his plan to rebuild the temple. The Essenes, foreseeing the fulfilment of their prophecy for 3920, offered the Temple Scroll, containing their plan for the temple. But Herod turned their plan down.

An anti-Herodian party was now formed. Joseph, the father of Jesus, was a member of it, so also was Theudas, the Prodigal Son.

11 BC Reoccupation of Qumran by a coalition of ascetic Pharisees, Sadducees, and Diaspora Essenes. This was the group responsible for most of the sectarian scrolls. They were nationalists, brought together when the Pharisees at Herod's court refused to take the oath of loyalty to Caesar.

Diaspora Essenes included the Therapeutae of Egypt. Qumran, defiled by the earthquake and no longer a holy place, became "Egypt" when their leaders were there, and also "Sodom", when the leaders of a celibate order allowing sodomy were present. So Qumran was later called "Sodom and Egypt, the place where their Lord was crucified" (Rev 11:8).

9 BC
Sep Zechariah, a descendant of the high priest Zadok, was told by Simon the Essene, the "angel Gabriel" to leave the priesthood after the Day of Atonement to marry and have an heir. He became "dumb", that is, forbidden to preach.

9 BC
Dec Elizabeth his wife conceived John the Baptist. (She was not elderly, but "advanced in her days", a reference to her use of a solar calendar that intercalated later.)

8 BC
Jun Joseph would be 36 in September 8 BC, and due to marry. According to the rules, there should be a wedding in September, sex would be permitted in December, and a son was hoped for the following September. But Mary and Joseph broke the rules by conceiving a child in June 8 BC, at the time of their final betrothal. By strict Essene rules the child, Jesus, was conceived out of wedlock, so could not inherit the throne of David; by the looser rules of the Magians, he was considered legitimate.

8 BC
Sep Birth of John the Baptist.

7 BC
Mar

Birth of Jesus in the "queen's house" (named in the Copper Scroll), about a kilometre south of the Qumran plateau.

4 BC
Mar

Death of Herod. Five days before his death Herod ordered his heir Antipater to be executed, appointing Archelaus as the successor.

1 BC

The anti-Herodian party at Qumran now began the millennium again, declaring the Herodian generation 41 to 1 BC a zero generation. The year 1 BC (3940) became 0, AD 1 was 1. This is the dating that we still use.

　　　　The anti-Herodian party would appoint an heir of David as the king in the world empire, not a Herod. Joseph (the father of Jesus) called the Star, would have the position. With him was Theudas, the Prodigal Son, called the Sceptre.

AD 1
Sep

Birth of James, the brother of Jesus, the legitimate heir of Joseph by the stricter rule.

AD 5
Sep

John the Baptist twelve years old.

AD 6
Mar

Jesus, twelve years old, was given his first form of initiation, so was "born". He was "brought forth" by his mother and dressed in a ceremonial garment.

　　　　More fervent nationalists under Judas the Galilean took control at Qumran. Their leaders were called the Calf (Archelaus), the Beast (Judas) and the Dragon (the high priest Joazar). When Archelaus was dismissed and the census of Quirinius imposed, they staged a revolt. The zealots continued to harass the Romans, using Qumran and fortresses down the coast, until they brought about the destruction of Jerusalem in AD 70.

AD 17
Mar

The initiation ceremony of Jesus, aged 23. He took a political stance in favour of his "father", the Annas high priest, who taught peace with Rome and the promotion of Gentiles.

AD 18

Caiaphas became high priest.

AD 23

Joseph died. As Caiaphas held the stricter eastern views on morality, James was declared his legitimate successor.

AD 26

John the Baptist, who had left the high Essenes to adopt the life and discipline of a hermit, became Pope. The doctrine was revised in order to reform militarism and financial exploitation.

AD 29
Mar

Jesus was rebaptised by John the Baptist. He then became involved in a schism from the Baptist, together with the party called the Twelve Apostles. They were united against Essene priestliness but divided on politics: some, including Jesus, were for peace with Rome; others, including Judas Iscariot and Simon Magus, were zealots.

AD 30
Jun

The "miracle" of turning water into wine, that is, Gentiles, formerly given baptism only, were allowed to take the sacred meal of bread and wine.

Sep

First wedding of Jesus and Mary Magdalene. A trial marriage began, but conception did not take place until December AD 32.

AD 31

The Baptist's chronological prediction for the year was not fulfilled, and he was arrested and executed as a false prophet.

AD 32
Mar

The "feeding of the Five Thousand", that is, ordinary laymen were permitted to act like levites, giving out the bread at the communal meal. The first ordination of ministers, soon to become Christian.

Sep

The Day of Atonement, when a fulfilment of prophecy was again expected. As no sign came, Jesus used the occasion to challenge the doctrine. Although he was expected to take part in the rites in a lesser role only, he put on the vestments of the high priest and claimed to be the Zadokite high priest. This was a total break with tradition and alienated all parties.

Dec

An uprising of Jews against a tactless action by Pontius Pilate took place. Jesus and the peace party were not present, but after the event he broke his neutrality, went down to Qumran, and released Simon Magus ("Lazarus"), who had been excommunicated because of the failure of the uprising. Jesus was technically a member of the same party, and now showed complicity with zealots; he was thus legally an accomplice.

AD 33
Mar

All parties met together at Qumran for their seasonal council. The zealots were in danger only if someone broke ranks and informed Pilate of their whereabouts.

The meeting began early in March, and at a time when some members expected a fulfilment of prophecy. Jesus was given a mock coronation, riding on an ass (the equivalent of King Solomon's mule) from the queen's house, the Manger, up the chasm to Qumran. When there was no fulfilment, he attacked the financial practices of the movement, overturning the tables of the moneychangers.

The hoped-for fulfilment was more likely to come at the equinox, and, for the doctrine held by Jesus and Simon Magus, on the Thursday night, the night of the Last Supper. When no heavenly intervention came, Judas Iscariot, who coveted Simon Magus' position and who was hostile to Jesus, sent a message to Pilate informing him of the whereabouts of the men wanted for the previous December's riot. Judas himself had been involved, but planned to buy his freedom with a bribe to Pilate.

Simon Magus and Jesus were tried as false prophets before the Jewish priests. Pilate arrived, and began the trial of zealots. The tetrarch Antipas then offered Pilate a higher bribe to release Theudas, who was an old man. Judas was put in his place. Pilate tried to release Jesus as well as Theudas, but no one in authority would offer a bribe for him.

Simon Magus, Judas, and Jesus were crucified, in the unclean area at Qumran. Simon, as the leader, was on the middle cross, and Jesus on the western one. At 3 p.m. Jesus was offered poison to end his suffering. He drank it, but lost consciousness only. His friends knew that he was still alive.

The tetrarch Antipas then persuaded Pilate to allow the matter to be completed under Jewish law. This meant that the method of execution would be changed to burial alive. The three men were placed in a cave at the end of the esplanade. The legs of Simon Magus and Judas were broken. A large quantity of aloes, a purgative, was left in the cave. During the night Simon Magus was carried to the side of Jesus, and he administered the medicines and brought about a resuscitation. Jesus was helped to escape from the cave by friends. The guards allowed the escape, as their duty was to guard Simon Magus. Simon deliberately began the story that he had brought about a resurrection.

During the next few days Jesus "appeared" at the various centres in the Wilderness of Judea and Jerusalem; that is, he came to the meals and worship services, showing remarkable fortitude. On the Tuesday he returned to the Qumran monastery, "ascended into heaven", as "heaven" was the place where priests and levites, called "gods" and "angels", conducted worship.

AD 36
Sep
Jesus returned from a three year seclusion in accordance with the rule for dynastic Essenes after the birth of a daughter. He came back into public life at the same time as Agrippa I was beginning his rise to the Herodian kingship.

AD 37
The emperor Tiberius died and Gaius Caligula became emperor. He appointed his friend Agrippa I as king of the Jews. In Judea there were consequent changes. The pro-Roman Annas high priests gained power, and Jesus was again declared legitimate. The pro-Agrippa party, led by Simon Peter, displaced the anti-Agrippa party, led by Simon Magus and John Mark. In June, a son, Jesus Justus, was born to Jesus and Mary Magdalene.

AD 40
Conversion of Paul, in the year when the Herodian chronological

scheme finally came to nothing. Paul, under the influence of Jesus, whom he met in Damascus, changed from eastern, nationalist views to western, pro-Roman views.

AD 41   Assassination of Gaius Caligula, who was suffering from a form of dementia. Claudius became emperor.

AD 44   Assassination by snake poison of Agrippa I, who was claiming to be a god-emperor. The western parties of both Peter and Simon Magus had joined forces against him, and after his death went into exile to Antioch and Cyprus. Peter's party in Antioch declared independence, and began to use the name "Christian".

AD 50   Under Agrippa II Paul rose to dominance, as his order had remained loyal to the Agrippas. The Samaritans, opposed by Agrippa II because of their involvement in the murder of his father, were driven into alliance with the eastern factions. They continued as the remains of the Qumran community, now based in Damascus. Their leader, Simon Magus, became the anti-Pope to the Christians. Paul and his party crossed to Europe and established bases there.

AD 54   Nero became emperor.

AD 57   The conflict between the two missions, Magian and Christian, came to a head in Ephesus, the limit of the east. The Christians were driven out.

AD 58   Paul and his party, including Jesus, returned to Jerusalem for a final visit, and for a possible fulfilment of prophecy. Paul was giving instruction to the Roman governor Felix, who had married Agrippa II's sister and was preparing for full membership.

AD 60   When Felix was replaced and sent to Rome for trial, Paul and his party went with him on the boat. On the sea journey to Rome, a crisis occurred when the expectation for the year 4000 was not fulfilled. Those on board the boat landed at Malta, where they spent January and February at a monastery belonging to the community. Paul was attacked on the grounds of possible complicity in the murder of Jonathan Annas by Felix.

AD 61
Mar   The whole party, including Jesus, arrived in Rome. Paul was kept in custody, pending hearings connected with the trials of Felix.

AD 64   The Christians were arrested for their part in demonstrations in Rome connected with the later occurrence of the year 4000, and were made scapegoats by Nero for the great fire of Rome. Peter and Paul were executed. Shortly before his death, Paul had sent a code message, saying that Jesus was "not fettered". Jesus was at this time seventy years old. His family, including two sons, may be presumed to have travelled north, to the Herodian estates in southern France.

AD 70   Destruction of Jerusalem by the Romans, in reprisal for the zealot uprisings.

AD 74   Mass suicide of remaining zealots on Masada.

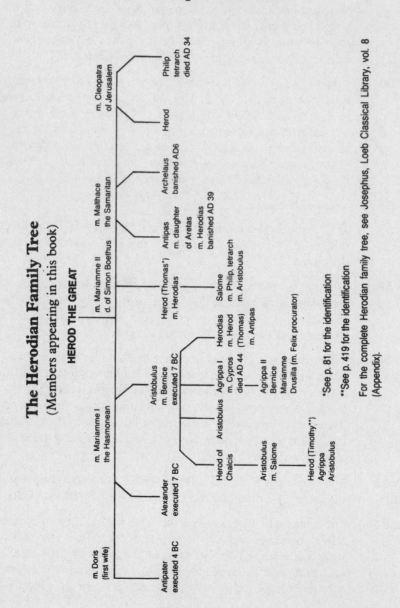

The Herodian Family Tree
(Members appearing in this book)

HEROD THE GREAT

m. Doris (first wife)

Antipater executed 4 BC

m. Mariamme the Hasmonean

Alexander executed 7 BC

Aristobulus m. Bernice executed 7 BC

Herod of Chalcis

Aristobulus

Aristobulus m. Salome

Herod (Timothy**) Agrippa Aristobulus

Agrippa I m. Cypros died AD 44

Agrippa II Bernice Mariamme Drusilla (m. Felix procurator)

m. Mariamme II d. of Simon Boethus

Herod (Thomas*) m. Herodias

Herodias m. Herod (Thomas) m. Antipas

Salome m. Philip, tetrarch m. Aristobulus

m. Malthace the Samaritan

Antipas m. daughter of Aretas m. Herodias banished AD 39

Archelaus banished AD6

m. Cleopatra of Jerusalem

Herod

Philip tetrarch died AD 34

*See p. 81 for the identification

**See p. 419 for the identification

For the complete Herodian family tree, see Josephus, Loeb Classical Library, vol. 8 (Appendix).

TEXT NOTES AND REFERENCES

Full details of books and articles will be found in the Bibliography.

Note on Text
The Greek text used is that of Codex Vaticanus (B), regarded by textual critics as of a high degree of reliability. See B.M. Metzger, *The Text of the New Testament* (1964), p. 47. No choice has been made between texts.

Where there are striking variant readings, they show an understanding of the pesher, and the intention to supplement or change for ecclesiastical reasons. Many of these have been noted in the detailed treatment of Chronology (Appendix I), Locations (Appendix II) and Hierarchy (Appendix III).

One: Qumran—Home of the Scrolls

1 Pliny, *Nat. Hist.* 5:73.
2 Josephus, *War* 4:476, 486.
3 *DJD* I, pp. 5–7.
4 Milik, *Ten Years of Discovery in the Wilderness of Judea*, Ch. 1.
5 Vermes, *DSSE*.
6 Yadin, *The Temple Scroll, The Hidden Law of the Dead Sea Sect*.

7 Yadin, *Megillat-hammiqdaṣ* (1977); *The Temple Scroll* (1983).
8 de Vaux, *ADSS*, Ch. 1.

Two: Christian Connections

1 1QS 6:2-7, 1QSa 2:11-22; A 2:42-46.
2 1QS 1:12, 1QS 6:22; A 2:45, 4:34-35 (community of property); 11QT 45:11-12; Rev 14:3-4, 1 Cor 7:8-9; Mt 19:10-12 (celibacy); 1QS 3:4-5, 1QS 5:13; Jn 4:1-2, A 2:41 (baptism); 1QM, 1QH 3:19-36; Mk 13 (apocalyptic crisis).
3 1QS 5:24, 8:10, 13, 9:18 ("Way" capitalised by Vermes) 9:21, and frequently; (the Way. See also Fitzmyer, *Semitic Background*, p. 282, "The same absolute use of 'the Way' (as in Acts) occurs in the Qumran writings to designate the mode of life of the Essenes"). CD 6:19, 8:21; 19:33, 20:12; Lk 22:20, 1 Cor 11:25 (New Covenant). 1QS 1:9, 1QM 1:1, and frequently; Jn 12:36 (Sons of Light).
4 CD 1:13, A 9:1-2.
5 1QS 6:12, 20, CD 9:18 and frequently; 1 Tim 3:2, 1 Pet 2:25. Thiering, "*Mebaqqēr* and *Episkopos* in the Light of the Temple Scroll"
6 11QT 39, 44; Rev 21:10-13, 7:5-8. Thiering, "Date of Composition of the Temple Scroll".
7 See also 1QS 3:18-26 with *Ep. Barn.* 18 (the two Ways of Light and Darkness). 2 Cor 6:14-7:1 has been recognised as "Qumranian in both thought and style; a meteor fallen from the heaven of Qumran into Paul's epistle" (Benoit in Murphy-O'Connor, *Paul and Qumran*, p. 5).
8 Josephus, *War* 2:119-161; Philo, *Every Good Man*; Pliny, *Nat. Hist.* 5:73.
9 Renan, *Histoire du peuple d'Israel*, vol. 5, pp. 70ff.
10 E. Wilson, *The Dead Sea Scrolls*, p. 107.
11 J.M. Allegro, *The Dead Sea Scrolls* (1947), *The Sacred Mushroom and the Cross* (1971), *The Dead Sea Scrolls and the Christian Myth* (Westbridge Books, 1979).
12 11QT 45:7-14.
13 Mk 1:40-45, Mk 8:22-26, Lk 13:10-17, Lk 5:8, Mk 5:24-34.
14 1QpHab 8:1-2.
15 1QpHab 2:1-4.
16 1QpHab 5:11-12.
17 4QpPss 2:17-19.
18 CD 4:19, 1:14-17. See G. Jeremias, *Der Lehrer der Gerechtigkeit* Ch. 3.
19 1QpHab 8:16-9:2.
20 1QpHab 9:9-12.

21 4Q *Serekh Milḥamah*. Translated by Robert Eisenmann UCLA Long Beach, California, USA, and Michael Wise, University of Chicago, USA. See Ch. 33 for a possible context for the fragment.

Three: A Question of Dates

1 Vermes, *DSSE* pp. 30–33.
2 Cross, "The Development of Jewish Scripts", pp. 146, 182.
3 Milik, *Ten Years of Discovery in the Wilderness of Judea*, p. 58.
4 Milik, "Fragment d'une source du Psautier". Milik states in a footnote in this article (note 4, p. 103), that the piece was formerly called 4QD[b], but the siglum was subsequently altered to 4QD[a].
5 P.R. Davies, "How Not to Do Archaeology. The Story of Qumran", *BA* Dec. 1988, pp. 206–207.
6 E.g. 1QS 1:11, 15, 2:24, 3:24, 1QpHab 7:12, 11QT 57:8.
7 1QpHab 8:9.
8 1QpHab 7:10, 1QS 4:5, 17.
9 See B. Thiering, *Redating the Teacher of Righteousness*, Ch. 2.
10 CD 1:5–11.
11 1 Pet 5:13.
12 Rev 18:2, 10. See also Rev 17:9, "the seven mountains" (the seven hills of Rome).
13 Ezek 4:5.
14 Josephus, *Ant.* 18:1–10.
15 Lk 3:1.
16 Josephus, *Life* 10–11. E. Bréhier, *Les Idées Philosophiques et religieuses de Philon d'Alexandrie* (on Philo).
17 1QpHab 2:10–15.
18 4QpPss 2:18.
19 J. Carmignac, *Textes de Qumran Traduits et Annotés* Vol. II, p. 50.
20 For a full discussion, see Thiering, *Redating the Teacher* . . . pp. 207–212. *Moreh haṣṣedeq*, "Teacher of Righteousness", is a play on words, meaning both "he who teaches righteousness" and "he who rains down (baptises with) righteousness".
21 Jn 1:1–8 opposes John to Jesus in Jesus' role as the Light, implying that there was support in some quarters for John in these exalted roles. John is said to be "not the Light" (Jn 1:8), while Jesus *was* the Light (Jn 8:12). A general Jewish background, and now 1QH 7:23–25, in which the Teacher likens himself to the Menorah, shows that the Light means the Menorah, the seven branched candlestick as the central symbol of Judaism. A man who was "the Light" was a claimant to the high

priesthood.The passage in the Prologue to John's gospel therefore implies considerable party tension.

Further, the message from John to Jesus in Lk 7:19: "Are you the Coming One (the Messiah), or shall we look for another?" also implies great tension, and a threat to find another Messiah.

In A 19:1-7 Paul rebaptised twelve disciples of the Baptist. This not only implies that John had an organisation, but that there was rivalry between the two groups.

22 In a recent book, *The Dead Sea Scrolls Deception*, M. Baigent and R. Leigh have written of the "scandal of the scrolls". They have argued that there has been a suppression of the scrolls, led by the Church, out of fear that their contents might be damaging to Christianity.

The general theme of the book deserves consideration, but there is, unfortunately, a tendency to confuse the issues. It is not the case that whole scrolls of any significance have been suppressed. Everything of a reasonable size has been published and is fully available both to scholars and the general public; for the latter in Vermes' book *The Dead Sea Scrolls in English*, which has gone through many editions, from 1962 to 1987.

A very large number of fragments have remained unpublished, but the primary reason has been that they were small, and thought to be of little interest.

It may still be that whole scrolls come to light, but they are not at present in the hands of scholars.

The point at which this book converges with Baigent and Leigh is that the contents of the already published scrolls, which offer themselves as the most important material relevant to early Christianity that has come to light in recent centuries, have not been given the scholarly attention that they call for. But it appears doubtful whether it is a conspiracy, or the result of a conscious intention. Rather, a series of errors was made at the outset, due to haste and inexperience, which led subsequent scholars astray.

What is needed now is simply the refinement of our scientific methods, unimpeded by any fear that exposing the truth can be damaging to true religion.

Four: The Pesher Technique

1 1QpHab 3:2-6, 11:2-8.
2 Gen 40:5 (in the form *pitron*, 40:8 (*poter*); Dan 2:36 (Aramaic); Ecc 8:1.
3 4QpPss 2:12-15, 4:7-10.

4 Philo, *Works*. Philo's life work was to go through the books of the Law, finding in them, in allegorical form, the insights of Greek philosophy and science. In the pagan world, writers such as Plutarch were treating the myths of the gods and goddesses in the same way. Cf. Plutarch, *Isis and Osiris*.

5 Mk 4:9-12. Clement of Alexandria wrote: "For neither prophecy nor the saviour himself declared the divine mysteries in a simple manner, so as to be easily comprehended by ordinary people, but rather he spoke in parables". (*Miscellanies* 6.15.124.5-6).

6 Mk 12:1-9.

7 Jn 11:1-44, Mk 5:35-43, Lk 7:11-17, A 9:36-42, A 20:7-12.

8 Mk 11:12-14, 20-25.

9 Mk 5:2-20.

10 Mk 6:30-44.

11 Mk 8:1-10, 14-21.

12 Mk 6:45-52, Mk 5:35-41.

13 Phil 2:5-11.

14 Jn 2:1-10.

15 Jn 4:46-54, Jn 5:2-9, Jn 6:1-14, Jn 6:16-21, Jn 9:1-12, Jn 11:1-44.

16 1QS 6:13-23, *War* 2:137-142. See Thiering, "Inner and Outer Cleansing at Qumran as a Background to New Testament Baptism" and "Qumran Initiation and New Testament Baptism". See further Hierarchy, p. 371.

17 CD 15:15-17: "No madman, or lunatic, or simpleton, or fool, no blind man, or maimed, or lame, or deaf man, and no minor, shall enter into the Community, for the Angels of Holiness are with them". Cf. also 1QSa 2:5-10. 1QpHab 12:1-5 suggests that the "Simple" (*peti'im*) are the category of all excluded persons, rather than the simple-minded. This point would make better sense of CD 13:6 "if the leper (not the priest) is a *peti'*, the priest will guard him (as he is a lower community member)".

18 11QT 45:7-14.

19 Jn 6:1-14, Mk 6:30-44, Lk 9:10-17, Mt 14:13-21.

20 Lev 24:5-9. The table for the loaves was in the Holy House (Ex 26:35), associated with levites and Israel, not the Holy of Holies, associated with priests (1QS 8:4-6). Twelve levites, 11QT 57:12-13, 1QM 2:2. See further in Hierarchy, p. 381.

Five: The Empire of the Jews

1 Josephus, *War* 1:19, 181, *Ant.* 14:10.

2 *Ant.* 20:173.

3 *Ant.* 15:97–103.
4 *Ant.* 15:194–195.
5 *Ant.* 15:318, 323–325, 331–341, 380–425; 16:136–145 Yadin, *Masada.*
6 See art. "Hillel" in *Jewish Encyclopedia.*
7 CD 15:9–10, 16:1–2.
8 *Ant.* 15:373–378.
9 See Chronology, p. 176
10 *Ant.* 15:374, 378.
11 See Chronology, p. 168
12 See Hierarchy, p. 353
13 See World Plan, p. 303

Six: "The Ransom for One's Soul"

1 Rev 2:17.
2 4Q159 (*Ordinances*, Vermes p. 297) 6–13 contains the calculations on the financial system. They do not concern the ordinary temple tax (Ex 30:13), as Essenes did not attend the temple, and the number to be taxed, 600 000, was artificial. See Weinert, "4Q159: Legislation for an Essene Community Outside of Qumran?".
3 Initiates of hellenistic mystery cults were buried with gold plates containing precepts for the dead to use in the afterlife. They were bought in the present life as a passport to salvation. (Guthrie, *Orpheus and Greek Religion* pp. 171–180).
4 4Q159 6–7: "[Con]cerning [the ransom], the money of assessments that one gives as a ransom for himself, half [a shekel by the shekel of the Sanctuary as an offering to God]: only one time shall he give it all his days". Cf. Ex 30:12–16, Ex 38:25–26; the phrase "only one time shall he give it all his days" has been added to the biblical text.
5 Weinert completes line 10: ". . . the minah . . . [Their] pea[ce offer]ing, according to [their registered groupings: a thousand m]en per ten minahs; [a hundred men per minah; fifty men per half of the minah]".
6 A hoard of eighteen bronze coins, stuck together by oxidisation, was found lying on top of a wall at Ain Feshkha, and the imprint of the bag in which they had been kept was preserved in the encrustation of the oxide (de Vaux, *ADSS* p. 67, plate XXXVc).
7 *DJD* III (2 vols, text and plates). See further Locations, p. 320. The last sentence, sentence 64, refers to another copy of the same work.
8 Lk 19:11–27, Mt 25:14–30.
9 Josephus, *War* 2:145.
10 Lk 19:11–27.

11 Mt 25:14–30.
12 11QT 44–45, Rev 7:4–8.
13 Jn 2:14–16.

Seven: Exiles in the Wilderness

1 2 Sam 6–24, 2 Sam 20:25, 1 K 1:38–40, Ezek 44:15.
2 Josephus, *War* 2:129.
3 de Vaux, *ADSS*, pp. 8–10.
4 11QT 20:12–21:10.
5 1QS 5:13, 6:16, 7:3, 16, 19, 8:17; CD 9:21, 23.
6 1QS 6:24–7:25.
7 1QS 6:4–6, 1QSa 2:17–21.
8 de Vaux, *ADSS* p.3.
9 de Vaux, *ADSS* p. 11. See Locations, p. 313.
10 See Locations, pp. 287–288.
11 de Vaux, *ADSS* pp. 58–59.
12 de Vaux, *ADSS* pp. 60–83.
13 Stutchbury and Nicholl, "Khirbet Mazin".
14 Jn 6:19.
15 11QT 45:7–10, 15–16, 49:16–20.
16 de Vaux, *ADSS* pp. 75–83.
17 CD 11:4 *lebonah*, "frankincense". "Frankincense burns with a bright white flame, leaving an ash consisting mainly of calcium carbonate, the remainder being calcium phosphate and the sulphate, chloride and carbonate of potassium" *Encyclopedia Britannica*, art. "Frankincense".
18 Milik, *Ten Years of Discovery* . . ., pp. 15–16. G.R.H. Wright, "The Archaeological Remains at El Mird in the Wilderness of Judea".
19 Quoted by de Vaux, *ADSS*, p. 75, from John Moschus, *Pratum Spirituale*, PG lxxxvii, 3026.
20 Josephus, *Ant.* 13:417, *War* 1:364. See Locations, p. 301.
21 3Q15 (Copper Scroll), Ss 22, 23, 24, 26.
22 Milik, *Ten Years* . . ., 97, 152. G.R.H. Wright, "The Archaeological Remains . . . ", Appendix by J.T. Milik, p. 21.
23 Lk 4:16–30.
24 A 11:27–30, 12:25.
25 Mk 5:1–2.
26 J.W. Crowfoot, *Early Churches in Palestine* (Schweich lectures, 1937, London, OUP 1941, p. 43).
27 Mk 6:31–33.
28 See Locations, pp. 285–289.

29 See Locations, p. 311.

30 Josephus, *Ant.* 15:121–122.

31 de Vaux, *ADSS* pp. 20–21.

32 *Ant.* 15:380–387.

33 See Chronology, p. 168.

34 11QT 56:12–58:21.

35 A 13:22. See Chronology, pp. 172–173.

36 Philo, *Every Good Man*, 76.

Eight: The Virgin Birth

1 Lk 1:26–55, Mt 1:18–25.

2 Lk 3:23–38, Mt 1:1–17. Both are presented as the genealogy of *Jesus*, not Joseph. The modifying phrase *hōs enomizeto* "as was supposed" in Lk 3:23, has a pesher: "according to common law" (the ordinary law of Moses used by Jews, but not the higher celibate law).

3 Rom 1:3.

4 Josephus, *War* 2:120.

5 11QT 45:11–12.

6 CD 12:1–2.

7 Josephus, *War* 2:120.

8 Ezek 16:1–22.

9 Josephus, *War* 2:160–161 briefly describes their rule:

"There is yet another order of Essenes, which, while at one with the rest in its mode of life, customs and regulations, differs from them in its views on marriage. They think that those who decline to marry cut off the chief function of life, the propagation of the race, and, what is more, that, were all to adopt the same view, the whole race would very quickly die out. They give their wives, however, a three years' probation, and only marry them after they have by being three times pure given proof of being able to bear [i.e. the woman is three months pregnant, having missed three periods, so been 'pure' on Essene and general Jewish assumptions, cf. 11QT 48:16]. They have no intercourse with them during pregnancy, thus showing that their motive in marrying is not self-indulgence but the procreation of children".

10 Cf. the passage quoted above: "(the order is) at one with the rest in its mode of life, customs, and regulations".

11 CD 4:21, 11QT 57:17–19.

12 1 Cor 7:36.

13 Hegesippus, 5, quoted Eusebius, *Eccl. Hist.* 2:23. Josephus *War* 2:123.

14 The Ebionites were Jewish Christians, who were called the Poor in Rom

15:26, Gal 2:10. See Fitzmyer, *Semitic Background*, Ch. 16. "The Qumran Scrolls, the Ebionites and their Literature".

15 1QpHab 12:3,6,10; 1QM 11:13; 1QH 3:25; 4QpPss 1:9, 2:10, CD 6:21, 14:14.

16 Mt 1:19.

17 Mt 1:20.

18 4QSir Sabb, Jn 10:34–36.

19 Mt 1:25.

20 Lk 1:35.

21 1QpHab 2:2, 5:11, 10:9, 1QH 2:31, CD 1:15, 8:13, 19:26, 20:1.

22 The equivalent ceremony, for his own betrothal in June AD 30, is called a "wedding", *gamos* (Jn 2:1).

23 Philo, *Every Good Man*, 86–87.

24 Lk 2:1–7.

Nine: Born to be King?

1 See Locations, p. 289.

2 *Ant.* 20:169–172, A 21:38.

3 1 K 1:38.

4 Ps 2:7.

5 See Locations, p. 318.

6 *Ant.* 15:320.

7 *Ant.* 16:394.

8 Mt 2:5.

9 Mt 2:8. Note that Lk 2:15 means the symbolic Bethlehem, as it is used in speech, so "called Bethlehem".

10 *Ant.* 19:342, the high priest Elionaeus son of Cantheras, of the Boethus family (cf. *Ant.* 19:297, Simon son of Boethus, surnamed Cantheras) is also called the son of Caiaphas in *Mishnah Parah* 3:5.

Ten: Joseph in "Egypt"

1 *Ant.* 17:185–187.

2 *Ant.* 17:188–189, 224–227.

3 *Ant.* 17:269–298.

4 *Ant.* 17: 41–46.

5 Mt 2:14, A 7:9. See Locations, pp. 311–312.

6 *Contemp. Life* 89.

7 CD 7:19–21. (The title "Prince of *all* the Congregation", *nesi' kol ha 'edah*, is used of the Sceptre, cf. also 1QM 5:1. But "the Prince of the Congregation" without "all" is a title for the Messiah in 1QSb 5:20, and

apparently also in the newly announced fragment of Eisenmann and Wise (see Ch. 2, note 21). It is shown here (see Hierarchy, p. 365) that the head of the order of Ephraim was the representative of the David in the Herodian system. Theudas in AD 1-4 acted for the elderly Jacob-Heli, and is the subject of 1QM 5:1. He remained associated with the David crown prince. See further this book Ch. 33 on the new messianic piece.

8 Mt 2:13.

9 See Locations, pp. 311-312.

10 Joseph came out of hiding while Herod was still alive. *Eōs tēs teleutēs tēs Hērōdou* (Mt 2:15) has the p-sense "until Herod turned 70" (see p. 368). During 5 BC Matthias became high priest (*Ant.* 17:78); his ascetic tendencies are shown in *Ant.* 117:165-166. He was the Sadducee "God" of A 7:7, so accepting Jesus as legitimate. Mt 2:20 p: "those who seek the kingship (soul) of the Child (Jesus) are excommunicated (dead)" means that Simon Boethus was no longer high priest. So in September, 5 BC, when Herod turned 70 (Mt 2:19) Joseph was pardoned and Jesus accepted.

11 A 7:17 *ho laos ēuxēsen* "the people increased" p-sense "the prince (Joseph, representative of the laity) had a son".

12 *Ant.* 17:164.

13 See Hierarchy, pp. 344, 352. Judas succeeded Theudas, who was a "wild beast" as the representative of the Lion (Hierarchy, p. 354).

14 Rev 12:1-5. This passage bears a resemblance, in terminology and structure, to 1QH 3:1-18. Both deal with the birth of a Messiah, designated by an OT text (Rev 12:5 the "rod of iron", cf. Ps 2:9; 1QH 3:9-10 "wondrous counsellor", cf. Isa 9:6), and opposed by an anti-Messiah.

15 A 7:18.

16 *Ant.* 18:26, A 7:30-34.

17 See Chronology, p. 172. The expectation was still for a this-worldly kingdom, a Jewish world empire under a new David. Rev 20-22 conveys its character: the "new Jerusalem" would come down out of heaven to earth.

The same form of expectation was held by some Christians after the gospel period. Papias, a second generation Christian, believed "that there will be a millennium after the resurrection of the dead, when the kingdom of Christ will be set up in material form on this earth". (*Eccl. Hist.* 3:39, 12).

Eleven: The Prodigal Son

1 Lk 15:11-13.

2 Luke gives twelve historical parables (in the form of a narrative in the past). The first four (the Sower 8:4-8, the Good Samaritan, 10:30-37, the Rich Fool, 12:16-21, the Figtree, 13:6-9) deal with Essene history, in chronological order starting from the millennium of the Davids, AD 1. The next six (the Great Banquet, 14:15-24, the Prodigal Son, 15:11-32), the Dishonest Steward, 16:1-8, the Rich Man and Lazarus, 16:19-31, the Widow and the Judge, 18:1-8, the Pharisee and the Tax Collector, 18:9-14) deal with Herodian history, in chronological order, starting with the Herodian millennium, 41-40 BC. The final two (the Ten Pounds, 19:11-27, the Vineyard, 20:9-16), deal with the whole first generation of the millennium of the Davids.

3 *Ant.* 17:346-347.

4 Lk 2:25.

5 Lk 1:26. See Hierarchy, p. 338, on Simeon as the descendant of the Abiathar line.

6 Lk 2:29-32.

7 See World Plan in Locations, pp. 305-308.

8 A 5:36. Theudas was not killed, but "lifted up" *anērethē*, that is entered the eremitical life.

9 Rev 2:20-23.

10 Lk 15:13.

11 See Hierarchy, p. 357.

12 Ant. 17:224-227. After the death of Herod the Great, Antipas sailed to Rome to claim the throne from Archelaus, and received some support among family members there. The two Herodian parties founded in Rome at this time were the basis of the subsequent history, Antipas' party continuing as the "Jews", and Archelaus' party, coming later under the Agrippas, developing a Christian wing under Paul and Peter.

13 *Ant.* 18:3-10, 23-25. Cf. the speech of Eleazar, leader of the Sicarii on Masada, persuading the zealots to commit suicide, as they would rise from the dead (*War* 7:341-388.

14 See Hierarchy, p. 354, on the Beast. Judas succeeded Theudas, the head of Ephraim and the "wild beast".

15 See Hierarchy, p. 372.

16 *Ant.* 17:342-344.

17 *Ant.* 18:1-4.

18 Ananus (senior) AD 6-15 (*Ant.* 18:26, 34); Eleazar Annas, AD 16-17 (*Ant.* 18:34); Jonathan Annas, March to September AD 37 (*Ant.* 18, 95, 123); Theophilus, AD 37-41 (*Ant.* 18:123, 19:297) Matthew Annas, AD 42-43 (*Ant.* 19:316, 342), Ananus the Younger, AD 62 (*Ant.* 20:197, 203).

19 Lk 3:22 Jonathan Annas as *to pneuma to hagion* was symbolised by a

dove when "in the body" (*sōmatikō*). Matthew Annas was called "Peace" (A 9:31).

20 Lk 2:7, cf. Mk 14:14.

21 Lk 2:8–14.

Twelve: Jesus the Young Man

1 See Chronology, p. 176

2 See Hierarchy, pp. 371–372.

3 *Ant.* 18:36.

4 *Ant.* 18:34.

5 *Ant.* 18:34, 35.

6 Lk 2:41–52.

7 The baths at the Essene Gate, on the south of Jerusalem, have been uncovered. (Pixner, *Revue de Qumran* 43, 1983, p. 333).

8 A 7:45, "the days of David". As he found "grace north of God" (A 7:46 p) it was AD 17, the year when proselytes (led by "grace", John Mark, "John" meaning "grace") were promoted to *Qof*, the grade of "Calf", the north (see Hierarchy, p. 371).

9 A 7:47.

10 Lk 13:10–17. See Chronology, p. 233 and Hierarchy, p. 368.

Thirteen: John the Baptist

1 Lk 10:30.

2 See Ch. 3.

3 *Ant.* 18:35.

4 Lk 1:59–63. A priest and a levite were "Grace, Grace" (Zech 4:7) as they could pronounce the absolution, giving forgiveness of sins. *Ho Iōannēs*, the Greek form of the name Jehochanan ("the Lord has grace") was used in Hellenist village meetings, where Greek was spoken. The Baptist had renounced monastic status and become like a village priest. But the scrolls, coming from Hebrews, never use this name, as it reflects Hellenist interests. Instead, they call the Baptist the Teacher, another name for the village priest, probably used by Hillel. "Of Righteousness" (*haṣṣedeq*) adds the Zadokite element.

4 1QS 3:13–4:26 reflects the doctrine of the Teacher.

5 G. Jeremias, (*Der Lehrer der Gerechtigkeit* Ch. 6) has established, on the basis of vocabulary, style and ideas, that certain of the Hymns of Thanksgiving (*DSSE* p. 165) are by the Teacher of Righteousness. They are: 2:1–19, 2:31–39; 3:1–18; 4:5–5:4, 5:5–19, 5:20–7:5, 7:6–25, 8:4–40.

6 1QH 2:8–14.

7 Lk 3:16–17; *Ant.* 18:116–119; 4QpPss 4:27.

8 See Chronology, pp. 170–171.

9 1QH 3:31–36.

10 *Ant.* 18:142–204.

11 *Ant.* 19:350.

12 *Ant.* 18:144.

13 *War 1:552, 557, Ant.* 17:78.

14 *Ant.* 18:110–111, 136.

15 *Ant.* 18:109–115.

16 Mk 6:17. Herod (Thomas) the first husband of Herodias, is here called Philip. The tetrarch Philip, a son of one of Herod's lesser wives (*War* 1:562) was nominal head of Dan celibates of Shem, whose meeting place was in Caesarea Philippi in his tetrarchy. Their active head was Philip of the Twelve Apostles, whose status was that of servant to the tetrarch Philip, so he was called by his name. The tetrarch Philip was himself servant to Herod (Thomas), as he was three grades below him (see Hierarchy, pp. 341–342, p. 362). Master and servant could take each other's names, as a master was sometimes "in the body", three grades down, and a servant was sometimes "out of the body", three grades up. So Herod (Thomas) could be called "Philip" when he was "in the body", in the married state.

17 *Ant.* 18:82–83.

18 A 8:18–19.

19 4QpNah 1:6–7. See Thiering, *Redating the Teacher* . . . Ch. 3. The Young Lion of Wrath cannot be Alexander Jannaeus, as has been thought, as the text implies that all the "lions" are Gentiles, and Alexander was a Jewish king.

20 A 6:1. See further in Hierarchy, pp. 366–371.

21 Mk 10:46, the blind man of "Jericho". Jericho was in the traditional tribal territory of Benjamin. Saul, later Paul, had been the student of Gamaliel (A 22:3) and was of the "tribe" (order) of Benjamin (Rom 11:1).

22 Phil 3:5.

23 4QpPss 2:17.

24 Mic 4:4.

25 See Locations, p. 302.

26 Mk 1:4.

Fourteen: Jesus the Man

1 A. Schweitzer, *The Quest of the Historical Jesus*, 1906, p. 397.

2 Jn 20:15.

3 A 14:12.

4 Lk 2:44–45, Mk 6:47–50, A 7:8–10.

5 Jn 2:4.

6 A 8:18–24; A 13:6–11.

7 A 11:26.

8 Simon Magus is still treated positively, his "raising" as Lazarus being the climax of the seven signs. In AD 37, when Agrippa I was given the rule of Judea on the accession of Gaius, Simon Magus, John Mark, and Philip all lost their authority, as they were enemies of Agrippa. Leadership then passed to Peter and Paul, supporters of the Agrippas.

9 Acts concludes in AD 63, leaving the story unfinished.

Fifteen: The Twelve Apostles

1 See Chronology, p. 217 for detail.

2 Lk 15:22, the Prodigal Son on returning was given the "first stolē". He was permitted by Simeon to act as a lay priest, wearing a priestly robe (*stolē* Ezek 44:17 LXX). The Scribes wore such robes (Mk 12:38). To dress like a priest meant that they claimed also to be able to receive the tithes of priests, so becoming "hired servants" (Lk 15:19).

3 Mk 3:14–19. The p-sense of "the twelve" and "the apostles" is John Mark, as he was a number Twelve, and also a deacon, "sent out" (see Hierarchy, pp. 345, 346). But the name the Twelve Apostles may be used for convenience, for the whole council.

4 See Hierarchy, pp. 360–361.

5 *Clementine Recognitions* and *Homilies*. See Bibliography. See also Jonas, *The Gnostic Religion*, Ch. 4.

6 See Fitzmyer, *Semitic Background*, pp. 447–460.

7 Jonas, *Gnostic Religion*, pp. 110–111.

8 Mk 3:16–19, Lk 6:12–16, Mt 10:1–4.

9 See Hierarchy, pp. 333–334.

10 See Hierarchy, pp. 333–334.

11 Jonas, *Gnostic Religion*, p. 111.

12 Jn 11:5.

13 See Hierarchy, p. 299.

14 *Ant.* 20:162–164.

15 A 6:5.

16 Jn 1:45, *Clem. Rec.* 1:54, 2:8, *Clem. Hom.* 2:24.

17 Lk 4:5–8.

18 See Hierarchy, pp. 305, 356.

19 See Hierarchy, p. 302.

20 *Ant.* 18:183–186.
21 Mk 8:29.
22 *Ant.* 19:332–334.
23 1 Cor 9:5, Gal 1:18.

Sixteen: "He Has Beelzebul"

1 The Light, as the high priest standing at the Menorah Jn 1:6–8. Cf. 1QH 7:23–25, the words of the Teacher: "I shine forth in a sevenfold light . . . for thou art an everlasting heavenly light to me". He was also "the Sun" as the Zadokite responsible for the solar calendar.
2 1QH 4:5–9.
3 4QpPss 2:17–18.
4 Mk 6:21–29.
5 Herodias had a daughter named Salome by Herod (Thomas)—"Philip" (*Ant.* 18:136). In the story in Mk 6:21–29, the "daughter" of Herodias is not named. Helena was a deacon, so a grade below Herodias, a presbyter, hence her "daughter". Helena is called Salome in Mk 15:40, 16:1, as she and the real Salome were in the relation of teacher and student or disciple, the same as the relation between master and servant, hence the same name could be used.

It is suggested that Herodias and (the real) Salome were "your grandmother Lois and your mother Eunice" of 2 Tim 1:5. Salome married Aristobulus, a nephew of Agrippa I, after AD 34, and had by him three sons (*Ant.* 18:137). As Agrippa II was childless the eldest of these three sons, called Herod, was a possible heir. The young man called Timothy (12 years old in AD 48, A 16:1–3 p) was a student of Paul, whose order were tutors to the Herodian princes. As a Herodian heir who became fully Christian, Timothy was of the greatest importance to the advancement of the Christian party.
6 CD 20:13–15.
7 Mk 9:7, cf. Jn 1:23, A 4:6 "John", Mk 3:22.
8 *Ant.* 18:55–59, 62.

Seventeen: Mary Magdalene

1 Mk 14:3–9.
2 Cant 1:12.
3 Jn 12:3.
4 *GPhil* 63:30–64:10.
5 Lk 7:37–50, Jn 12:3–8, Mk 14:3–9.
6 See Chronology, p. 251.

7 Lk 8:2.

8 *Contemp. Life* 87.

9 Mk 5:21-24, 35-43. "Jairus" was a name for the Chief Priest (see Hierarchy, p. 338). Single women were ruled by the monastic Second, Gabriel or the Scribe (Demon 7), while women elders, including married women, were ruled by the village priest.

10 See p. 370.

11 Mk 14:4-9, Jn 12:2-8.

12 Jn 20:15, A 12:13-15 (see Locations, p. 311 on her name as Rhoda), Lk 7:39, Mk 14:4-5.

Eighteen: Miraculous Feedings and Walking on Water

1 Jn 6:1-14, Mk 6:30-44, Lk 9:10-17, Mt 14:13-21.

2 See Hierarchy, p. 337.

3 See Ch. 4.

4 See Ch. 4, and Hierarchy, p. 345.

5 See Hierarchy, p. 325.

6 See System for Boats in Locations, pp. 325-330.

7 He was also breaking the sabbath. See Chronology, pp. 227-228.

Nineteen: The Day of Atonement

1 Heb 9:7.

2 *Mishnah, Yoma* 1:1.

3 See Locations, p. 320.

4 1QpHab 11:6-8.

5 Mk 9:2.

6 Jn 7:37-38. Cf. 1QH 8:16-27.

7 See Chronology, p. 231.

8 Heb 3:1, 5:1-10, 7:1-22.

9 11QMelch, Gen 14:18-24, Ps 110:4.

Twenty: Raising Lazarus

1 Lk 10:17-42.

2 Lk 13:1. *Ant.* 18:55-59, 62.

3 Mk 15:7.

4 Lk 10:18.

5 Lk 10:21.

6 *Ant.* 18:150-154.

7 Cf. *War* 2:143-144, 1QS 7:22-25.

8 Lk 16:19–31.
9 See Locations, p. 290. For a full description of the cave, see *DJD* VI pp. 9–13.
10 Jn 11:2.
11 *Ant.* 18:151–154.
12 Jn 11:39.

Twenty-One: Thirty Pieces of Silver

1. See Chronology, p. 173 on the 3½ years. Expectations were for either March AD 29 and September AD 32; or September AD 29 and March AD 33, both 3½ years apart.
2 Mk 8:31, 9:31, 10:32 use double meanings. They are both the formula used to speak of departure from the community in order to resume marriage, a temporary "death", and at the same time an expected real death.
3 The emperor Tiberius said that it was "a law of nature that governors are prone to engage in extortion" (*Ant.* 18:172).
4 Mk 11:8–10.
5 Mk 11:15–19.
6 Mk 14:3–9.
7 Mk 14:10–11.

Twenty-Two: The Last Supper

1 See Locations, p. 322.
2 Rev 11:8.
3 Jn 19:20.
4 See Locations, p. 324.
5 See Hierarchy, p. 342.
6 See Locations, pp. 345, 323.
7 See Hierarchy, pp. 360–363.
8 Jn 13:21.
9 Jn 13:23–25 (*kolpos* v. 23, *stēthos* v. 25).
10 Mk 14:26, Jn 14:31.

Twenty-Three: Arrest and Trial

1 See Locations, p. 313.
2 Mk 14:32 (*hoi mathētai autou* "his (Jesus') disciples") always means John Mark.
3 Mk 14:35–39.

4 Jn 18:5-6.

5 Jn 18:10. See Locations, pp. 360-363 on the seating at the table. The vestry was the "body", and the imagery was extended to its different parts. The priest and king at the centre were the "head", Kohath on the right (east) was the "right ear", and Gershon on the left (west) the "left ear". The deacon on the lower side of the table was on the "bosom", and the congregation in the south vestry at the "loins". Names for the parts of the body of persons using the vestry are also literal, as they resumed a real body while "in the body".

6 Mk 14:51-52.

7 Mk 14:30.

8 Mt 27:24.

9 Mt 27:3-5.

Twenty-Four: The Crucifixion

1 See Locations, p. 324.

2 Heb 13:13.

3 See Locations, p. 293.

4 11QT 45:7-10.

5 Jn 19:20. Copies of the OT in Greek have been found among the scrolls.

6 See Locations, p. 324.

7 Jn 19:18, Mk 15:27.

Jn 19:18 p: "They crucified him (Jesus) on the west" (*hopou*, "where" p: west, as the direction of the village to which the king went away as lay; causing celibates in the east to ask "where is he?". In Jn 20:12 *hopou* means the western chamber, Cave 8).

"And with him a celibate acting as priest" (Simon Magus; *allous dyo* "other two", a Sariel was a number Two—see Hierarchy, p. 336, *allos*: celibate substitute for priest or levite. Simon, as Priest, was in the centre).

"East and east" (*enteuthen kai enteuthen. Enteuthen kai ekeithen* means "east and west", Rev 22:2). The three positions were:

King	Priest	Levite (= Kohath)
West	East	far east
Left	Right	far right
(*ekeithen*)	*enteuthen*	*enteuthen*
hopou		
mesos		
(layman)		
Jesus	Simon Magus	Judas

Mk 15:27 p: "And with him they crucify Thief 2" (Simon Magus as a "thief", a zealot, and a number Two as in the place of a priest).

"(Judas) one space east of the priest (the right) and (Simon) one space east of the king (the left)". (*Ek*: "out of", means "one space east" on the E–W timeline.)

8 *Treat. Seth* 55:30–56:15.

9 4QpNah 1:6–8.

10 Josephus records that some prisoners had been crucified, implying that it was before he went on a journey to Tekoa. When he returned from his journey, they were still alive. He ordered some of them, who were his acquaintances, to be cut down and given medical treatment. "Two of them died in the physicians' hands; the third survived" (*Life* 420–421).

11 Mt 27:34 *cholē* "poison".

12 *War* 7:389–401.

13 Mk 15:34, Ps 22:1.

14 *GPet* 5, in the context of a plan to put him to death while he was on the cross: "One of them said, 'Give him to drink gall with vinegar'. And they mixed it and gave him to drink". *Ep. Barn*. 7:3 "But moreover when crucified he had vinegar and gall (*cholē*) given him to drink".

15 Mk 15:37 *exepneusen*.

Twenty-Five: A Death that Failed

1 *GPhil* 56:15–20.

2 *Treat. Seth* 55–56, *Apoc Pet* 81–82.

3 CD 10:20–21.

4 Deut 21:22–23, 11QT 64:6–13.

5 Mt 27:64. See Locations, p. 292.

6 3Q15, S2 *benephesh ben rabbah hashelishi* "in the 'soul' (burial place) of the son of the great one, the third". Milik, *DJD* III p. 285, assumes that the whole phrase is a proper name.

7 "Joseph" as the David crown prince, see Hierarchy, p. 353.

8 Mk 15:44 p Pilate asked: "Is he dead already?" (*ei* in p-sense introduces a direct question). See p. 379.

9 Jn 19:34. *Black's Medical Dictionary* (London: A. & C. Black, 1955) p. 235: "An important sign (of death) is that if a cut be made in the skin or a vessel be opened no bleeding takes place after death".

10 Jn 19:39. *Litra*, a Roman pound, 12 ounces, 327 grams.
11 *Black's Medical Dictionary*, p. 34.

Twenty-Six: Inside the Cave

1 *DJD* III, pp. 27-31.
2 Lk 16:19-31.
3 See Hierarchy, pp. 344, 385.
4 The point of the discussion in Mt 27:63-65 was that John Mark, who was also a disciple of Simon Magus, "the Deceiver" (*ho planos*, v. 63) was legally entitled to come to the cave at 1 a.m. on Saturday, and might remove Simon then. As a proselyte, he kept some ritual laws but not others. He kept the law about walking less than 1000 cubits on the sabbath, so used the sabbath latrine. But he did not keep the law forbidding defecation on the sabbath, so could visit it at 4 a.m. on Saturday, the normal time (4 p.m. and 4 a.m. were set times as they were 10 hours after meals at 6 a.m. and 6 p.m.). On this particular Saturday he could come at 1 a.m., as he was still using the fast times; he would not adjust by 3 hours until Saturday afternoon (see Chronology p. 199). At 1 a.m., he would still be able to enlist the aid of those keeping the Julian sabbath to lift up the stone, as 1 a.m. was the sabbath extension.
5 Ananus appears as Zacchaeus in Lk 19:2-10, an episode in December AD 32.
6 Jn 20:1.
7 Jn 20:7.
8 Jn 20:11-12. *Hopou* "where", means the western chamber, see Ch. 24, note 7.
9 Jn 20:14. *Ta opisō* means "the west".
10 Jn 20:17.
11 Mt 28:2-3.
12 Mk 16:6.
13 The church historian Eusebius received from Papias (a disciple of c. AD 130 who passed on many early traditions) something told him by the "daughters of Philip" (i.e. Christian nuns, cf. A 21:8): "Papias . . . received a wonderful story from the daughters of Philip; for he relates the resurrection of a corpse in his time and in another place another miracle connected with Justus surnamed Barsabbas, for he drank poison but by the Lord's grace suffered no harm" (*Eccl. Hist.* 3:39, 9). "Justus" was a title of the Davids as "the Righteous One" (Lat. *iustus*, Gk *dikaios*, Heb. *saddiq*). It was used by James, who was Joseph Barsabbas

Justus of A 1:23. James was normally known by this title (Hegesippus, quoted *Eccl. Hist* 2:23). Jesus is called "the Righteous One" (*ho dikaios*) in A 22:14. (The name *Saw* for the rival teacher in CD 4:19 is probably the initial *Sadhe*, with *Waw* indicating an initial, standing for *saddiq*). Consequently, Jesus Justus of Col 4:11 is the son of Jesus. "Barsabbas" is a title of the sons of Joseph; James in A 1:23, Jude in A 15:22.

14 A 1:18.

Twenty-Seven: The Appearances

1 Jn 20:19-23.
2 Jn 20:28.
3 Lk 24:13-33. "Cleopas" (v.18) was James, cf. "Mary of Cleopas" as one of the four women at the cross in Jn 19:25 ("his mother's sister", Helena, and three Marys: queen mother, queen and princess.) Hegesippus (quoted *Eccl. Hist.* 3:32, see also 3:11) shows that Cleopas was a family name, being that of an uncle of Jesus, the brother of Joseph. The unnamed companion was Theudas, as the pair were the Star and the Sceptre.
4 Lk 24:36-43.
5 Lk 24:51, A 1:10.
6 A 4:6, Simon is "John".
7 See Chronology, p. 251.

Twenty-Eight: Kings and Governors

1 *Ant.* 18:224-225.
2 *Ant.* 19:2-16; Cary and Scullard, *History of Rome*, pp. 354-355; *Smaller Classical Dictionary*, "Caligula".
3 *Ant.* 18:261-262.
4 *Ant.* 19:78-83.
5 *Ant.* 18:168-204.
6 *Ant.* 18:228. '*ari meth* in Hebrew. This phrase may have been used as a nickname for Agrippa, giving "Arimathea". James, or "Joseph of Arimathea", was a servant of Agrippa at the time of the crucifixion.
7 *Ant.* 18:237, 240-252.
8 A 20:7-12.
9 Jn 1:35-39.
10 *Ant* 19:332-334.
11 A 5:1-11.
12 *Ant.* 18:88-89, *Ant.* 18:95.
13 Lk 12:13-21.
14 CD 7:15-21.

Twenty-Nine: At the Right Hand of God

1 A 6:7. See Chronology, p. 254.
2 See Ch. 26, note 13.
3 A 6:2–6.
4 *Ant.* 18:123. A 6:8–8:1.
5 Ant. 18:123, 124.
6 A 7:55–56.
7 *Ant.* 18:240–255.
8 *Ant.*18, 137, 19:277, 353, 20:103, 145.
9 *Ant.* 20:97–98.

Thirty: Saul the Indignant Student

1 In A 19:22, at a date shown by the chronology to be September AD 57, Paul *epeschen chronon*, "had a generation (of 40 years)". This suggests a birth date of September AD 17. In September AD 53 he was married (cut his hair, A 18:18; see Chronology, p. 269), and, as he now followed the Way, with its celibate rule, he was aged thirty-six. Thus, in September AD 37, he was twenty.
2 *Ant.* 18:115, 120–126.
3 1QpHab Vermes, *DSSE* p. 283.
4 1QpHab 2:10–6:11.
5 1QpHab 8:3–12:14.
6 1QpHab 8:1–3, cf. Rom 1:17; 1QpHab 2:1–10, cf. A 13:40–41.
7 *Ant.* 19:297.
8 *Ant.* 18:297–309.
9 A 9:1–19.
10 A 13:9.
11 A 9:23–25. See Chronology, p. 258.

Thirty-One: Assassination and Change

1 *Ant.* 17:78. "Peace" (*eirēnē*) in A 9:31 means Matthew.
2 A 11:26. See Locations, p. 302 on "church".
3 CD 8:3–13.
4 A 12:24.
5 *Ant.* 18:143, 19:328.
6 A 9:36–43.
7 A 10:9.
8 A 10.
9 A 12:1–17.

10 A 12:7.
11 *Ant.* 19:343, A 12:20-23.
12 A 13:1-3.
13 A 13:6-12, cf. v. 7 "hear the Word of God". "Sergius Paulus" on the island of Cyprus, the "proconsul", was the seventeen-year-old Agrippa II. His name, Paulus, indicates that he was a "servant" of Paul, that is, a pupil, as the master-pupil relation was the same as that of master and servant. Paul of the order of Benjamin acted as a tutor to the young Herods, teaching such subjects as Greek philosophy (cf. A 24:25, the platonic content of Paul's instruction to Felix, a relative by marriage of the Herods). Cf. also Paul's relation with Timothy, and the argument in Ch. 16, note 5, that Timothy was a Herod. The Herod princes would have been apprenticed to proconsuls as part of their education.

Thirty-Two: A Family Problem

1 *Ant.* 19:360, 362.
2 *Ant.* 20:135.
3 A 26:28.
4 *Ant.* 13:4-12.
5 A 12:13. See Locations, p. 311 on the name Rhoda.
6 A 12:15.
7 A 16:14.
8 1 Cor 7:10-16.
9 Mk 10:11-12.
10 A 16:9.
11 A 16:11-15, Rev 2:20-23.
12 CD 4:19-5:6.
13 1 Tim 3:2.
14 Heb 2:18.

Thirty-Three: Away From the East

1 From the Clementine source it can be seen that James and John of Zebedee were the same as Niceta and Aquila, two brothers from a noble Roman family. Having arrived in Judea, they became members of the Jewish religion under the Mother (Sarah-Helena, the Syrophoenician woman) and were at first instructed by Simon Magus, then changed their doctrine to follow Zacchaeus (Ananus the Younger; that is, they changed from hostility to Agrippa I to supporting him). John of Zebedee-Aquila, a married man, worked with Peter then with Paul. This history is derived from *Clem. Hom.* 2:19-21, together with the pesher

of the gospels and Acts.
2 Gal 2:9.
3 Suetonius, *Vita Claudii* 25:4.
4 Rev 1:9-16.
5 A 18:2.
6 A 18:9-10.
7 A 18:18.
8 Rom 16:1.
9 A 17:34.
10 2 Sam 13:1.
11 A 19:23-41.
12 A 14:11-13.
13 A 19:11-19.
14 *Ant.* 20:162-164.
15 *Ant.*20:142-143.
16 *Ant.* 20:200.
17 *Eccl. Hist.* 2:23, 10-16.
18 See Ch. 2, and Ch. 2, note 21.

Thirty-Four: The Great Pentecost

1 See Chronology, pp. 168-169.
2 Mk 13:26.
3 See Chronology, p. 170.
4 Paul's anxiety about the arrival of Titus in 2 Cor 2:12-13, 7:5-7, was partly because Titus was expected from Corinth. He was bringing an answer from Jesus, to whom Paul had sent a message in 1 Cor 16:22 "Our Lord, come!" (Maranatha). Paul wanted Jesus to join him for the journey back to Jerusalem, but was not sure if Jesus would be willing to come.
5 A 20:7-12.
6 *Ant.* 20:169-172.
7 A 21:27-36.
8 A 23:11.

Thirty-Five: The Final Journey

1 A 27:1.
2 A 27:12.
3 A 27:20, cf. Mk 13:24-25.
4 A 27:27-32. See System of Boats in Locations, p. 330.
5 A 28:4-6.

6 A 28:11-15. See Chronology, p. 283.

7 2 Tim 2:9.

8 *Eccl. Hist.* 2:25, 5–8: "It is related that in his [Nero's] time Paul was beheaded in Rome itself, and that Peter likewise was crucified, and the title of 'Peter and Paul', which is still given to the cemeteries there, confirms the story . . . " Another writer, Caius, is quoted: "But I can point out the trophies of the Apostles, for if you will go to the Vatican or to the Ostian Way you will find the trophies of those who founded this Church". A further writer, Dionysius, is cited to show that Peter and Paul were martyred at the same time.

9 Tacitus, *Ann.* 15:44.

ABBREVIATIONS

Biblical

Gen	Genesis
Exod	Exodus
Lev	Leviticus
Num	Numbers
Deut	Deuteronomy
1 Sam	1 Samuel
2 Sam	2 Samuel
1 K	1 Kings
2 K	2 Kings
1 Chron	1 Chronicles
Ps	Psalms
Prov	Proverbs
Cant	Song of Solomon
Isa	Isaiah
Jer	Jeremiah
Ezek	Ezekiel
Dan	Daniel
Mic	Micah
Nah	Nahum

Hab	Habakkuk
Zech	Zechariah
1 Macc	1 Maccabees
Mt	Matthew
Mk	Mark
Lk	Luke
Jn	John
A	Acts
Rom	Romans
1 Cor	1 Corinthians
2 Cor	2 Corinthians
Gal	Galatians
Eph	Ephesians
Phil	Philippians
Col	Colossians
1 Thess	1 Thessalonians
2 Thess	2 Thessalonians
1 Tim	1 Timothy
2 Tim	2 Timothy
Tit	Titus
Phlm	Philemon
Heb	Hebrews
Jas	James
1 Pet	1 Peter
2 Pet	2 Peter
1 Jn	1 John
2 Jn	2 John
3 Jn	3 John
Jud	Jude
Rev	Revelation
1 Enoch	1 Enoch
Jub.	Jubilees
TLevi	Testament of Levi
GPhil	Gospel of Philip
GThom	Gospel of Thomas
Apoc. Pet.	Apocalypse of Peter
Treat. Seth	Second Treatise of the Great Seth
GPet.	Gospel of Peter

Ep. Barn	Epistle of Barnabas

Dead Sea Scrolls

1QS	Manual of Discipline, Community Rule
1QSa	Rule of the Congregation, Messianic Rule
1QSb	Blessings
11QT	The Temple Scroll
1QH	Thanksgiving Hymns
1QM	War Scroll
CD	Damascus Document, Damascus Rule
1QpHab	Pesher on Habakkuk
4QpPss	Pesher on Psalms
4QpNah	Pesher on Nahum
11QMelch	Melchizedek fragment
4Q159	Ordinances
3Q15	The Copper Scroll
4QSir Sabb	The Angelic Liturgy

Ancient Writers

Ant.	Flavius Josephus, *Jewish Antiquities*
War	Flavius Josephus, *The Jewish War*
Life	Flavius Josephus, *The Life*
Every Good Man	Philo, *Every Good Man is Free*
Contemp. Life	Philo, *The Contemplative Life*
Eccl. Hist.	Eusebius, *The Ecclesiastical History*
Nat. Hist.	Pliny, *Natural History*
Ann.	Tacitus, *The Annals*
Clem. Rec.	*Clementine Recognitions*
Clem. Hom.	*Clementine Homilies*

Modern Writers

DSSE	Vermes, *The Dead Sea Scrolls in English*
ADSS	de Vaux, *Archaeology of the Dead Sea Scrolls*
DJD I, II, etc.	*Discoveries in the Judean Desert*, vols. I, II etc.
BA	*Biblical Archaeologist*
JBL	*Journal of Biblical Literature*
JSJ	*Journal for the Study of Judaism*
NTS	*New Testament Studies*
RB	*Revue Biblique*

General

cf.	compare
p:	pesher
p-sense	pesher sense
Sam.	Samaritan
Reg.	regular

BIBLIOGRAPHY

Sources

The Bible
    English, *Revised Standard Version*
    Greek, *The Greek New Testament*, ed.
    K. Aland, M. Black, C.M. Martini,
    B.M. Metzger and A. Wikgren, (United
    Bible Societies) (published also by
    Deutsche Bibelstiftung, Stuttgart, as *Novum
    Testamentum Graece*)

Dead Sea Scrolls
    G. Vermes, *The Dead Sea Scrolls in English*
    (3rd ed. containing the Temple Scroll)
    (London: Penguin, 1987)
    E. Lohse, *Die Texte aus Qumran, Hebräisch und
    Deutsch* (Munich: Kösel-Verlag, 1971)
    Discoveries in the Judean Desert, vols I–VIII,
    (Oxford: Clarendon Press, 1955–1990)
    Y. Yadin, *Megillat-hammiqdas* (the Temple
    Scroll) (Jerusalem: Israel Exploration
    Society, 1977) (English ed. 1983)
    J. Maier, *Die Tempelrolle vom Toten Meer*,
    (E. Reinhardt Verlag, Munich, 1978)

1 Enoch, Jub., TLevi
    J. H. Charlesworth (ed.) *The Old Testament
    Pseudepigrapha*, vols I & II (London:
    Darton, Longman & Todd, 1983)
    R. H. Charles, *The Apocrypha and Pseud-
    Epigrapha of the Old Testament in English*
    (Oxford: Clarendon Press, 1913)

GPhil, Apoc.Pet., Treat. Seth
    J.M. Robinson (ed.) *The Nag Hammadi Library
    in English* (San Francisco: Harper & Row,
    1988)

GPet
    E. Hennecke, *New Testament Apocrypha*, vols I

& II (London: SCM, 1963)

Ep. Barn.   Staniforth, *Early Christian Writings* (London:
                      Penguin, 1968)

Josephus   *Josephus* (The Loeb Classical Library, 9 vols)
                      (London: Heinemann)

Philo   *Philo* (The Loeb Classical Library, 10 vols)
                      (London: Heinemann)

Eusebius   *Eusebius* (The Loeb Classical Library, 2 vols)
                      (London: Heinemann)

Pliny   *Pliny* (The Loeb Classical Library, 10 vols)
                      (London: Heinemann)

Tacitus   *Tacitus* (The Loeb Classical Library, 4 vols)
                      (London: Heinemann)

Clem. Rec.,   Roberts and Donaldson, *The Ante-Nicene*
Clem. Hom.   *Fathers*, vol. VIII (American Reprint, rev.
                      edn. A. Cleveland Coxe, Grand Rapids:
                      Eerdmans, 1951)

Modern Works

Baigent, M. and Leigh, R., *The Dead Sea Scrolls Deception* (London: Jonathan
    Cape, 1991)

Bréhier, E., *Les idées philosophiques et religieuses de Philon d'Alexandrie* (Paris,
    1925)

Brooke, G., *Temple Scroll Studies, Journal for the Study of the Pseudepigrapha*,
    Supplement Series 7 (Sheffield Academic Press, 1989)

Butler, R.A., *Where to Go in Turkey*, (New York: Hippocrene Books, 1988)

Carmignac, J., *Les Textes de Qumran Traduits et Annotés* (vols I and II) (Paris:
    Gabalda, 1961 and 1963)

Cary, M. and Scullard, H.H., *A History of Rome* (London: Macmillan, 1975)

Cross, F.M., "The Development of the Jewish Scripts", in G.E. Wright (ed.)
    The Bible and the Ancient Near East (London: Routledge & Kegan Paul,
    1961)

Crowfoot, J.W., *Early Churches in Palestine* (OUP, 1941)

Danby, H., *The Mishnah* (OUP, 1933)

Davies, P.R., "How Not to Do Archaeology. The Story of Qumran" *BA* Dec.
    1988, pp. 204–211

De Vaux, R., *Archaeology and the Dead Sea Scrolls* (OUP, 1959)

Farrer, A., *A Study in St Mark* (London: Dacre Press, 1951)
    St Matthew and St Mark (London: Dacre Press, 1954)

Finegan, J., *Handbook of Biblical Chronology* (Princeton University Press, 1964)

Fitzmyer, J.A., *Essays on the Semitic Background of the New Testament* (London:

Chapman, 1971)

Guthrie, W.K.C., *Orpheus and Greek Religion* (New York: Norton, 1966)

Jeremias, G., *Der Lehrer der Gerechtigkeit* (Göttingen: Vandenhoeck & Ruprecht, 1963)

Jonas, H., *The Gnostic Religion* (Boston: Beacon Press, 1958)

Kuhn, K.G., *Konkordanz zu den Qumrantexten* (Göttingen: Vandenhoeck & Ruprecht, 1960)

Metzger, B.M., *The Text of the New Testament* (Oxford: Clarendon Press, 1964)

Milik, J.T., *Ten Years of Discovery in the Wilderness of Judea* (London: SCM, 1959)

Milik, J.T., "Fragment d'une Source du Psautier (4Q Ps 89) et Fragments des Jubilés, du Document de Damas, d'un Phylactère dans la Grotte 4 de Qumran", *RB* 73 (1966) pp. 94–107

Murphy-O'Connor, J., *Paul and Qumran* (London: Chapman, 1966)
>   *The Holy Land. An Archaeological Guide from Earliest Times to 1700* (Steimatzky Ltd, 1985)

Schürer, E., *The History of the Jewish People in the Age of Jesus Christ*, rev. edn. ed. G. Vermes, F. Millar and M. Black, vols I–III (Edinburgh, T&T. Clark, 1973)

Smaller Classical Dictionary (London: Dent, 1937)

Star, L., *The Dead Sea Scrolls. The Riddle Debated* (ABC Enterprises, 1991)

Stendahl, K., *The Scrolls and the New Testament* (London: SCM 1957)

Stevenson, J., *A New Eusebius* (London: SPCK, 1957)

Stutchbury, H.E. and Nicholl, G.R., "Khirbet Mazin", *Annual of the Department of Antiquities of Jordan*, 1962, pp. 96–103

Thiering, B.E., *Redating the Teacher of Righteousness* (Sydney: Theological Explorations, 1979)
>   *The Gospels and Qumran* (Sydney: Theological Explorations, 1981)
>   *The Qumran Origins of the Christian Church* (Sydney: Theological Explorations, 1983)
>   "*Mebaqqer* and *Episkopos* in the Light of the Temple Scroll" *JBL* 100, 1, 1981, pp. 59–74
>   "The Date of Composition of the Temple Scroll" in G. Brooke (ed.) *Temple Scroll Studies* (Sheffield Academic Press, 1989)
>   "Inner and Outer Cleansing at Qumran as a Background to New Testament Baptism", *NTS* 26, 2, 1980, pp. 266–277
>   "Qumran Initiation and New Testament Baptism" *NTS* 27, 5, 1981, pp. 615–631

Weinert, F.D., "4Q159: Legislation for an Essene Community Outside of Qumran?", *JSJ*, 1974, pp. 179–207

Wilson, E., *The Dead Sea Scrolls* (Collins, 1971)

Wright, G.R.H., "The Archaeological Remains at El Mird in the Wilderness of Judea", *Biblica* 42, 1961, pp. 1–27

Yadin, Y., *The Temple Scroll. The Hidden Law of the Dead Sea Sect* (London: Weidenfeld & Nicholson, 1985)

 Masada (London: Weidenfeld & Nicholson, 1966)

INDEX